Ambrose of Milan's
Method of Mystagogical Preaching

Craig Alan Satterlee

Ambrose of Milan's Method of Mystagogical Preaching

A PUEBLO BOOK

The Liturgical Press   Collegeville, Minnesota

www.litpress.org

A Pueblo Book published by The Liturgical Press

Design by Frank Kacmarcik, Obl.S.B.

Scripture quotations unless otherwise noted are taken from the New Revised Standard Version Bible, Catholic Edition, © 1989 by the Division of Christian Education of the National Council of Churches of Christ in the United States of America. Used by permission. All rights reserved.

© 2002 by The Order of St. Benedict, Inc., Collegeville, Minnesota. All rights reserved. No part of this work may be reproduced in any form or by any means, electronic or mechanical, including photocopying, recording, taping or any retrieval system, without the written permission of The Liturgical Press, Collegeville, MN 56321.

Library of Congress Cataloging-in-Publication Data

Satterlee, Craig Alan, 1959–
    Ambrose of Milan's method of mystagogical preaching / Craig Alan Satterlee.
        p.   cm.
"A Pueblo book."
Includes bibliographical references and index.
ISBN 0-8146-6185-8 (alk. paper)
    1. Ambrose, Saint, Bishop of Milan, d. 397. 2. Mystagogy—Catholic Church. 3. Preaching. I. Title.

BR1720.A5 S27 2001
251—dc21
                                        2001038236

*To Cathy, who made it all possible,
with gratitude and love*

O God, who gave to your servant Ambrose grace eloquently to declare your righteousness in the great congregation, and fearlessly to bear reproach for the honor of your Name:

   Mercifully grant to all bishops and pastors such excellence in preaching, and faithfulness in ministering your Word; that your people may be partakers with them of the glory that shall be revealed; through Jesus Christ our Lord, who lives and reigns with you and the Holy Spirit, one God, in glory everlasting.

Lesser Feasts and Fasts, Book of Common Prayer

Contents

List of Figures   xv

Preface   xvii

Introduction   xxiii

Chapter 1
"You saw what is seen, but not what is done":
The Need for Mystagogy   1

    The Need for Mystagogy   4
    Hypothesis   8
    The Investigation   10
        Why Study Ambrose?   10
        Method   14
    Excursus: The Critical Problem of *De sacramentis*   20

Chapter 2
"Having been renewed by baptism,
hold fast to the style of life
that befits those who have been washed clean":
Setting the Stage   31

    Birth, Family, and Faith Formation   33
    Education   36
    The Governor and His City   38
    Election as Bishop   44
    The Bishop and the Empire   51
    Ambrose the Pastor   67
    The Moral Leader   72
    Ambrose's Private Side   78

Ambrose the Theologian 83
Ambrose the Saint 84

Chapter 3
"I yield to my desire to teach":
Ambrose: The Preacher 87

Ambrose the Preacher 89
Ambrose on Preaching 93
What Made Ambrose an Effective Preacher? 106
Reflection: The Pneumatic Dimension of the Preacher 108
Appraising Our Portrait 110

Chapter 4
"This family clothed in white":
The Newly Baptized of Milan: The Listeners 111

Listening to the Listeners 112
The Newly Baptized of Milan 116
    The Church of Milan 116
    The Decision to Be Baptized 120
    Mystagogy in Context 122
    Summary 123
The Newly Baptized as Participants in Mystagogy 124
    Think, Feel, Decide, and Do 125
    The Neophytes' Ability to Listen 126
    Involving the Neophytes in Mystagogy 127
        Catechetical Style 127
        Recreating the Neophytes' Experience 136
        Speaking for the Neophytes 141
Reflection: The Pneumatic Dimension of the Listeners 142

Chapter 5
"I shall begin now to speak of the
sacraments which you have received":
Initiation in Milan: The Text 145

Initiation in Milan 148
    Stage One: Enrollment 148
    Stage Two: Lenten Formation 149
        Lenten Instruction 149

Fasting 151
Scrutinies 152
Creed 153
Disciplina Arcani 155

Stage Three: The Rites of Initiation 156
    Ephphatha 157
    Entrance into the Baptistry 158
    Prebaptismal Anointing 161
    Renunciation 163
    Exorcism and Consecration of the Water 165
    Baptism: Descent into the Font, Baptismal Profession and Immersion, Coming Out of the Pool 166
    Postbaptismal Anointing 170
    Washing of the Feet of the Neophytes 172
    Vesting with White Robes 174
    Spiritual Seal 176
    Procession to the Altar 179

Stage Four: Easter Eucharist 180

Liturgy and Mystagogy 185
    The Rites Are Inseparable from Scripture 185
    Explanation Follows Experience 186
    The Rites Are God's Means of Giving Faith 188
    The Rites Are Specific and Authentic 190
    The Rites Are Means and Not Ends 191
    The Rites Are the Continuing Drama of Salvation 195
    The Rites Speak Symbolically 197
    The Rites Are a Mystery 197
    Interpretation of the Rites Is in Keeping with Their History, Structure, and Theology 198
    A Variety of Methods Is Used to Incorporate and Interpret the Liturgical "Text" 200
        Direct and Uncritical Transfer of the Text to the Listener 200
        Allegorical Interpretation of the Text 200
        Typological Interpretation of the Text 201
        Interpretation of the Intent of the Text 201
        Thematic Interpretation 202
        Interpretation by Translation of the Text 203

Reflection: The Pneumatic Dimension of the Rites 204

Chapter 6
"Gather from the holy scriptures":
Interpreting the Rites   207

    The Importance of Scripture   209
    Selecting the Text   211
    Scripture and Mystagogy   219
        The Mystery of Scripture   220
        Methods of Interpretation   225
            Typology   225
            Allegory   230
            Construction of Intricate Chains of Reasoning   234
            Interpretation by Translation   238
            Direct and Uncritical Transfer of the Text   241
        Means of Incorporation   242
            Quotation   242
            Narration   243
            Summary   244
            Allusion   245
            Speaking the Bible   245
    Reflection: The Pneumatic Dimension of Scripture as Interpreter of the Rites   246

Chapter 7
"Milky speech":
The Shape of Mystagogy   249

    The Shape of *De sacramentis*   250
        Overall Structure   250
        The Structure of the Sermons   252
            Using Inductive Reasoning   253
            Providing Definition   254
            Moving From Problem to Solution   256
            Progressing from the Lesser to the Greater   257
            Flashback   258
        Enriching the Structure   260
            Language   261
            Description   263
            Illustration   266
            Tone   269
        Summary   270

Structure and Mystagogy   271
    Unity   272
    Ecclesial Consciousness   273
    Recognition   274
    Identification   276
    Anticipation   277
    Intimacy   278
Reflection: The Pneumatic Dimension of the Shape of Mystagogy   278

Chapter 8
"But now my voice grows weak and time is running out":
Mystagogy as Proclamation Event: Delivery   281

    Why Delivery Is Essential to Effective Preaching   282
    Essential Components of Effective Sermon Delivery   284
        The Preacher   284
            Attitude   284
            Character of the Preacher   285
            Habits   287
            Style and Method of Delivery   288
            Voice   293
            Nonverbal Communication   294
        The Liturgical Context   295
        The Architectural Setting   299
    Reflection: The Pneumatic Dimension of Sermon Delivery   304

Chapter 9
"We too are not without discernment":
Discerning a Method of Mystagogical Preaching   309

    Question Ambrose's Assumptions   311
        God's Presence and Activity in the Rites   311
        Church and Culture   312
        Explanation and Participation   317
        The Preacher: Steward of the Mysteries and Spiritual Guide   320
        The Patristic Approach to Scripture   322
        Summary   327
    Arrive at the Message   327
        Establish the "Text"   327

        Evaluate the Rites   328
        Interpret the Rites   329
            Begin with the Rites Themselves   329
            Turn to Scripture   331
            Use Several Tools of Interpretation   332
            Typology   332
            Allegory   334
            Chains of Reasoning   335
            Intent of the Text   336
            Translation   336
            Direct and Uncritical Transfer of the Text   336
            Pile Up Meanings   336
            Rely on the Church's Tradition   337
        Spell Out the Implications of Participating in the Rites   338
        Summary   340
    Craft the Homily   340
        The Structure of Mystagogy   341
        Enriching the Structure   344
            Language   344
            Description   345
            Illustration   346
            Incorporate the Texts of Liturgy and Scripture   346
            Tone   347
        Summary   350
    Retrace the Journey   350
        The Preacher   351
        The Liturgical Context   352
        The Architectural Setting   353
    Applying Our Method   354
        Question Ambrose's Assumptions   355
        Arrive at the Message   356
        Craft the Homily   358
        Retrace the Journey   362
    Reflection: The Pneumatic Dimension of a Method of
      Mystagogical Preaching   362
    Conclusion   364

Bibliography   367

Index   387

List of Figures

Figure 1   Mosaic of Ambrose, Milan, Church of Sant'Ambrogio, Chapel of San Vittore in Ciel d'Oro.   79

Figure 2   Ambrose preaching, inspired by an angel. Milan, Panel of the altar frontal of the Church of Sant' Ambrogio. Photograph by Cathy Satterlee.   88

Figure 3   Reconstruction of the Battistero di San Giovanni alle Fonti, Milan. Adapted from Mirabella, *Il Battistero Ambrosiano di San Giovanni alle Fonti*. Reprinted with permission.   159

Figure 4   The large octagonal baptismal font. Photograph by Chelsey Grace Satterlee.   160

Figure 5   Reconstruction of the Basilica di Santa Tecla and baptistry, Milan. Plan adapted from Richard Krautheimer, *Early Christian and Byzantine Architecture* (New Haven, Conn.: Yale University Press, 84). Reprinted with permission.   301

Preface

Although written in the context of Notre Dame's doctoral program in liturgical history and homiletics, this study grows out of more than a dozen years of parish ministry. Confronted by a culture that increasingly cannot be counted on to reinforce the Christian faith or participate in the formation of Christians, the Church today questions the nature of the connection between Word and Sacrament on the one hand and liturgy and mission on the other. Today the Church is struggling to make worship relevant to people's lives and to articulate how baptism and the Eucharist are formative and reflective of the everyday life of faith, and not merely an eschatological sacrament and a memorial of Christ.

As I sought to answer these questions and address these concerns in the course of pastoral ministry, I looked to the history of the liturgy, particularly to the period of the early Church. I was intrigued by the catechumenate, which uses liturgy to form Christians and takes seriously that they live in a culture at odds with the faith. I was particularly fascinated by the period of mystagogy or postbaptismal catechesis, which is characterized by sermons that probe the mysteries, the rites of initiation, for their biblical resonances and importance for Christian life. I found that while this type of preaching holds great potential for the Church today, it remains largely undefined. While we know what the Fathers did in the period of mystagogy or postbaptismal catechesis, we do not know how they did it.

The goal of this volume is to develop a method of mystagogical preaching for today's Church by looking at the sermons of Ambrose of Milan and asking, What did Ambrose do and how did he do it? The hypothesis of this study is that our best way to learn how to preach *mystagogically* is by using one of the fourth-century mystagogues as our guide. In this regard this work is a case study, one way of doing mystagogy. In very broad terms, it is modeled after William Harmless's

Augustine and the Catechumenate[1] and is rightly understood as a companion volume to that work. In order to address every stage of the process of sermon preparation, from the influence of the preacher and the listeners to the text and its interpretation to crafting and delivering the sermon, I present topics beyond preaching and liturgy. Still, this study is neither an exhaustive biography of Saint Ambrose nor a complete history of the Church of Milan nor a detailed analysis of patristic exegesis. While this volume is primarily intended for preachers, pastors, catechists, and all who are interested in exploring the depth of the meaning of the Christian sacraments and their implications for daily life, it will also be of interest to those who study early liturgy, early Church history, and the history of preaching, especially since the subject of Ambrose as a preacher remains largely unexplored.

Inasmuch as the task I am undertaking is to develop a method of mystagogical preaching, I have structured this study using headings, points, and stages. My intention is to provide the reader with a clear path through the process of sermon preparation and delivery and clear markers along the way. The risk is that the structure of this study may strike some readers as a bit schematic, make the process seem mechanical, and make Ambrose's preaching seem flat. My hope is that this criticism is balanced by the ease with which readers can return to this work in order to review a particular topic or answer a specific question. As for Ambrose's preaching, this study is in many ways a commentary on *De sacramentis* and *De mysteriis*. Consequently, it is best to read this volume with Ambrose's mystagogical works close at hand.

If we understand mystagogy as reflection on the rites of initiation, then these prefatory remarks are mystagogical in that they are my reflection on the rite of initiation that is writing a dissertation. The images that hold the meaning of this rite of passage are all found in my "holy of holies," not a large octagonal baptistry but carrel 1210 in Hesburgh Library. The contents of my carrel evoke the truth of writing this dissertation; although it has in large part been a solitary process, I have never been alone. A nun from Nigeria was once brought to my carrel for the view of the Dome from my window. Looking at the stuff on the walls, she smiled and said, "Your work must surely be holy, for you are blessed to be surrounded by a wonderful cloud of witnesses."

[1] William Harmless, *Augustine and the Catechumenate* (New York: Pueblo Publishing Co., 1995).

Whether this work is holy, I cannot say. I can, however, gratefully acknowledge the wonderful cloud of witnesses that surrounds me and give thanks for the ways I have been blessed by the company that keeps me.

Looking out on the Notre Dame campus reminds me of the many ways I have been blessed by the University of Notre Dame, chief among which are the opportunity to be a part of an extraordinary Theology Department, the University Presidential Fellowship and John S. Marten Teaching Fellowship that made it possible to spend two years writing this dissertation, and a grant from the Notre Dame Zahm Research Travel Fund and other financial support that enabled me to study in Milan. The Hesburgh Library staff, particularly Trish Kelley and Judy Kendall, cheerfully and creatively made materials accessible to me. Carolyn Gamble steered this dissertation safely through the often treacherous seas of bureaucratic process.

To the right of the window hangs the crucifix that has hallowed my study throughout the years of my ministry, reminding me that this dissertation was written for and not apart from the Church. I am grateful to the Evangelical Lutheran Church in America for providing ongoing financial support in the form of Grants for Advanced Theological Education and to the ELCA's Upstate New York Synod for repeatedly awarding me their Samuel Trexler Fellowship. I am especially grateful to the people of St. Timothy Lutheran Church in Sturgis, Michigan, where I served as pastor, while writing this book, for supporting my research with both their prayers and their generosity and for inviting me to test my scholarship in pastoral practice.

Next to the cross hangs an icon of the mosaic of Saint Ambrose found in the Chapel of San Vittore in Ciel d'Oro in the Church of Sant'Ambrogio in Milan. In June 1999 my writing shifted from the Notre Dame campus to Milan. While there, I was given extraordinary access to what the Milanese lovingly call "the archeological and artistic places related to our holy father Ambrose." I am grateful to Elena Bartoli of the Jesuit Guest Bureau in Rome for helping to plan the trip, to Dr. Paul and Callie Perry of Chiesa Evangelica Metodista for hosting my family and me, and to Don Alberto Rocca of the Ecumenical Commission of the Archdiocese of Milan for being an extraordinary guide.

My shelves are filled with books from The Liturgical Press, outstanding scholarship essential for the study of liturgy. I am, therefore, humbled that this volume is included in this collection under the

Pueblo imprint. I would like to thank Rev. Michael Naughton, O.S.B., and Mark Twomey for their willingness to bring this work to publication and John Schneider for his gracious collaboration in shaping a dissertation into a book.

The coffee cups and drafts of chapters that clutter my carrel speak of the superb community of which I am a part. This community includes many friends, special people like Kent Burreson, Walter Ray, David Rylaarsdam, and Diane Steele, who took it upon themselves to read my work and, more importantly, to see me through the ebbs and flows of writing. This community includes faculty members whose quiet counsel helped me to maintain perspective, especially Robert A. Krieg and Kern R. Trembath. Most important, this community includes my dissertation committee, which is stellar. Brian E. Daley, S.J., who served as co-director of this dissertation, generously provided his expertise while encouraging me to claim my own. Maxwell E. Johnson helped me to question the claims and assumptions of others as he helpfully questioned the claims I assumed. James F. White was an unfailing source of knowledge, inspiration, affirmation, and support. Michael S. Driscoll was my conversation partner when the idea for this dissertation took shape and has been the source of unfailing humor along the way. John Allyn Melloh, who directed this dissertation, is a treasured mentor and friend whose sense of grace and commitment to helping me become my best leads him to share the best that he has, which is very, very good. My years in the Notre Dame community have been a rare time in life when I knew that I was doing what I was supposed to be doing with the people I was supposed to be with. For this I am most grateful.

To the left of the window hang assorted family portraits drawn by my daughter Chelsey. Chelsey was my special helper throughout the writing of this dissertation. Pulling books from the shelves and pages from the printer, she learned to love Ambrose and always loved her dad. She was patient with my work and seemed to know instinctively when I needed to stop. Chelsey's smile warmed many hearts and opened many doors in Italy, and her attempts at photography produced some of the best pictures of the archeological sites that I have.

Finally, my wife Cathy has always seen in me something better than I see in myself. Cathy's vision for and belief in me led me to undertake doctoral work; throughout the journey she has tirelessly and lovingly sacrificed to make this undertaking possible. As Ambrose tells the newly baptized to look into the rites and behold God's invisible activity, so I look into the pages of this dissertation and behold my wife's unseen efforts, which, as Ambrose says, are greater than what is seen. For all that she is to me and has done for me, this volume is dedicated to Cathy, with gratitude and love.

Introduction

This volume proposes a method of mystagogy for today's Church based on the preaching of Ambrose of Milan. Mystagogy *(mystagogia)* is sustained reflection on the Church's rites of initiation, preaching on the "mysteries" of the Christian faith. Mystagogy is scripturally based, takes place within a liturgical setting, is addressed exclusively to the Christian community, and has as its goal the formation *of* Christians rather than providing religious information *to* Christians. Mystagogy draws the hearers into the mysteries, moving them to enter spiritually and intellectually into the rites in which they have previously participated but may have understood only in terms of sense-perception. Thus, the ultimate goal of this sustained reflection is to have a persuasive, enlightening, deepening effect on the hearers' understanding of the Church's rites of initiation so that their experience of the mysteries leads them to live the Christian life.

The hypothesis of this study is that our best way to learn to preach mystagogically is by using a fourth-century mystagogue as our guide. This hypothesis rests on three realities: we need a method of mystagogy based on actual practice; we have no such contemporary models; and the works of the early Church were used to create contemporary ministries of Christian formation such as the R.C.I.A.

Chapter 1 establishes the need for mystagogy: to provide both a better understanding of the period of postbaptismal catechesis in ministries of Christian formation such as the R.C.I.A. and effective sacramental catechesis generally. Chapter 2 lays out the historical context of Ambrose and his Church. Chapters 3 through 8 are a series of six historical studies: on Ambrose as preacher, on the neophytes of Milan as audience, on the rites of initiation as the "text" on which mystagogy is based, on Ambrose's use of Scripture to interpret that text, on the way he crafts these sermons, and on the characteristics of his delivery. Then, in the last chapter, we do as Ambrose reports to have done and discern from the practice of others what it is well for us to maintain by proposing a method of mystagogy for the contemporary Church.

Chapter 1

"You saw what is seen, but not what is done": The Need for Mystagogy

Addressing his *neophytes*, or "newly baptized," during the week after their baptism at the Easter Vigil, Ambrose of Milan raised an issue that was of concern to the Church of his day and continues to concern the Church today—the need for effective sacramental catechesis. Ambrose summarized the problem as follows:

"You came into the baptistry, you saw the water, you saw the bishop, you saw the levite.[1] And if anyone should perhaps be thinking of asking: 'Is that all?' I say, indeed, it is all. There truly is all, where there is all innocence, all devotion, all grace, all sanctification. You saw all you could see with the eyes of the body, all that is open to human sight. You saw what is seen, but not what is done."[2]

---

[1] "Priest" is Ambrose's normal term for the bishop; "presbyter" refers to the modern term "priest." The "levite" is the deacon. See Edward Yarnold, S.J., *The Awe-Inspiring Rites of Initiation: The Origins of the R.C.I.A.*, 2nd ed. (Collegeville, Minn.: The Liturgical Press, 1994) 101, n. 7.

[2] *De sacramentis*, 1.3.10 (SC 25bis.64). Numbers following the title of the work refer to sections in the English translation. Numbers following *Corpus Christianorum*, Series Latina (hereafter CCSL), *Corpus Scriptorum Ecclesiasticorum Latinorum* (hereafter CSEL), and *Sources chrétiennes* (hereafter SC) indicate volume and page. Numbers following *Patrologia cursus completus, series Latina* (hereafter PL) and *Patrologia cursus completus, series Graeca* (hereafter PG) indicate volume and column. Numbers following Cazzaniga (see Bibliography, 367) and Navoni (see Paulinus of Milan in the Bibliography, 369). English translations are indebted to the available sources listed in the Bibliography, but modifications for accuracy and felicity are made without notice.

The early Church responded to the newly baptized's seeing but not comprehending the meaning of the Christian sacraments with a type of preaching known as *mystagogy*. Stated simply, mystagogical preaching is sustained reflection on the Church's rites of initiation. It is *mystagogia*, preaching on the "mysteries" of the Christian faith. It is *preaching* in that it is scripturally based, takes place within a liturgical setting, is addressed exclusively to the Christian community—the baptized and the newly baptized, called "neophytes," and has as its goal the formation of Christians rather than providing religious information to Christians. Mystagogical preaching is distinct from other types of preaching in that it draws the hearers into the mysteries, moving them to enter spiritually and intellectually into the rites in which they have previously participated but may have understood only in terms of sense-perception. Thus the ultimate goal of this sustained reflection is to have a persuasive, enlightening, deepening effect on the hearers' understanding of the Church's rites of initiation that leads them to live in the different, new dimension that is the Christian life.

Mystagogical preaching developed most fully in the fourth century in response to the increasing number of catechumens brought about by the Peace of Constantine,[3] the Trinitarian and christological contro-

---

[3] After the Peace of Constantine (312), the catechumenate, or process of Christian initiation, underwent a significant change. Originally a time of continuous personal conversion toward a Christian way of living, it became a compulsory step for anyone who wanted to count in society. As a catechumen a person was officially a member of the Church while at the same time remaining free from the burdens borne by baptized Christians. Thus it became possible for people "whose motives were often politics and fashion rather than faith" to become catechumens without experiencing an authentic conversion. See Aidan Kavanagh, *The Shape of Baptism: The Rite of Christian Initiation* (New York: Pueblo Publishing Co., 1978) 117. In this context the catechumenate became more defined, as evidenced in the sharp differentiation between the Liturgy of the Word and the celebration of the Eucharist or, as Yarnold describes them, "the Mass of the Catechumens and the Mass of the Faithful." See Yarnold, *The Awe-Inspiring Rites of Initiation*, 56. Instruction on the meaning of the *mysteria* was reserved for those who had undergone baptism, creating the need for mystagogical preaching after baptism and introduction into the eucharistic assembly.

versies of the age,[4] the evolving role of the bishop as official preacher,[5] and the development of the liturgy and liturgical calendar.[6] The chief representatives of this genre of homily are the mystagogical catecheses of Ambrose of Milan, Cyril of Jerusalem, John Chrysostom, and Theodore of Mopsuestia. In *The Awe-Inspiring Rites of Christian Initiation*, Edward Yarnold, S.J., writes that these "mystagogues," who preached to the newly baptized during the week following their initiation at the Easter Vigil, "thought of themselves as guiding the neophytes into knowledge of the Christian mysteries,"[7] both in terms of their sacramental life and experience and the new kind of behavior that they should now manifest. The mystagogues accomplished their task by

---

[4] The fourth century witnessed a series of bitter controversies over doctrine, as evidenced by the succession of synods and councils that punctuated the century. Councils and synods include Nicaea and Constantinople, which are accepted today, and Sirmium and Seleucia, which were later repudiated. Yet, theological controversy was not confined to bishops and councils, "but became part of the routine banter one heard in bazaars and bathhouses." William Harmless, *Augustine and the Catechumenate* (New York: Pueblo Publishing Co., 1995) 54. See especially the quote from Gregory of Nyssa, *De Deitate Filii et Spiritus sancti*. In this climate bishops addressed doctrinal issues from the pulpit generally and in their catechetical instruction in particular. This is especially true of the Arian controversy, because the neophytes had been baptized in the Trinitarian faith and would be called upon to defend it in the public arena.

[5] In the later ancient Church, prophecy—speaking to the present with divine authority in order to transform the historical revelation into a contemporary, living reality—was replaced by teaching. The task of preaching therefore became the bishop's prerogative, as the possessor of the teaching office, though the presbyter could be given the responsibility of preaching. With the election of bishops who did not possess charismatic gifts of preaching, the Church had to pay greater attention to the outward forms of sermons. See Yngve Brilioth, *A Brief History of Preaching*, trans. Karl E. Mattson (Philadelphia: Fortress Press, 1965) 19.

[6] As this liturgical development took place, the sermon was fitted into the developed order of service more than had previously been the case. It followed the readings and attempted to establish a connection with the texts that had been read. The great festivals and the more sharply differentiated seasons of the liturgical year determined the choice of subject. By the fourth century, Easter was accepted as the normal time for administering baptism and Easter week as the occasion for instruction on the mysteries.

[7] Yarnold, *The Awe-Inspiring Rites of Initiation*, ix.

preaching "spiritual commentaries on the rites of initiation based on biblical themes . . . which were intended to encourage neophytes to persevere in their new life."[8] Thus, the purpose of mystagogical preaching was to "explain"[9] to the neophytes or newly baptized "the meaning and nature of the liturgical actions in which they have participated: baptism and the Eucharist."[10]

THE NEED FOR MYSTAGOGY

With the implementation of the Rite of Christian Initiation of Adults (R.C.I.A.) within Roman Catholicism,[11] as well as a growing catechumenal movement within the Lutheran, Anglican, and other traditions,[12]

---

[8] Michel Dujarier, *The Rites of Christian Initiation: Historical and Pastoral Reflections*, trans. and ed. Kevin Hart (New York: William H. Sadlier, 1979) 215.

[9] By "explain" we mean probing, deepening, intensifying, and illuminating rather than defining and making plain.

[10] Enrico Mazza, *Mystagogy: A Theology of Liturgy in the Patristic Age*, trans. Matthew J. O'Connell (New York: Pueblo Publishing Co., 1989) x.

[11] The revision of Christian initiation brought about by the Second Vatican Council was published in three stages: the rite for the baptism of children in 1969, the rite of confirmation in 1971, and the rite of Christian initiation of adults (R.C.I.A.) in 1972, although the interim English translation of the latter did not appear until 1974 and the final version until 1985, being made mandatory in the United States from 1988. Between the sixteenth and the twentieth centuries, an authentic movement to recover the catechumenate developed in mission countries—first Latin America, then Asia, and then Africa—before finally returning to Europe. See J. Beckmann, "L'Initiation et la célébration baptismale dans les missions, du XVI siècle à nos jours," *La Maison-Dieu* 58 (1959) 48–70; Michel Dujarier, *The History of the Catechumenate: The First Six Centuries*, trans. Edward J. Hassl (New York: William H. Sadlier, 1979) 136–139. For an excellent discussion of the radical ramifications of the R.C.I.A. for the life of the Church, see Ralph Keifer, "Christian Initiation: The State of the Question," *Worship* 48, no. 7 (August–September 1974) 392–404, in which Keifer calls the R.C.I.A. "either suicide or prophecy of a very high order" (p. 402). On the power of the catechumenate to restore parish life, see Raymond Kemp, "The Rite of Christian Initiation of Adults at Ten Years," *Worship* 56, no. 4 (July 1982) 309–326.

[12] See, for example, the series of resources of the Evangelical Lutheran Church in Canada entitled *Living Witnesses: The Adult Catechumenate* (Canada: ELCIC, 1992) and that of the Evangelical Lutheran Church in America entitled *Welcome to Christ* (Minneapolis: Augsburg Fortress, 1997). Both series include rites for the catechumenate and guides for the stages of the catechumenal process.

mystagogical preaching has found renewed importance within the life of the Church. Like ancient practice, the fourth and final period of the modern catechumenate is the time of mystagogy.[13] However, this period within the catechumenal process remains largely undeveloped in the contemporary Church. In *Augustine and the Catechumenate*, William Harmless asserts that while the R.C.I.A. "provides fairly detailed directions for executing its complex of rites . . . its directions and goals for catechesis, while provocative and innovative, [seem] rather sketchy."[14] Harmless asserts that while each period has its own

---

[13] The R.C.I.A. is not so much a rite as a process consisting of four periods of time that are linked to one another by three liturgical steps. It begins with a period of evangelization and precatechumenate of no fixed duration or structure, during which there is a dialogue between the local church and the inquirer. Candidates are accepted into the catechumenate itself only when they are judged to have attained a basic grounding in Christian teaching, the beginnings of faith, and a commitment to a changed way of life, and a liturgical rite is provided for this step.

This second period may last for several years and consists of formation and maturation through teaching, the support of others in the Christian life, regular participation in the Church's worship, and active involvement in the Church's mission. Several liturgical rites are provided for use during this time. Particularly noteworthy is the expectation that the catechumens will generally be dismissed during worship before the celebration of the Eucharist begins as a public sign of their status as not yet fully initiated into eucharistic fellowship.

When those responsible for the catechumens' formation determine that they are ready, the catechumens may proceed to the third stage, known as the period of purification and enlightenment. This period usually coincides with Lent and is intended as a time of spiritual recollection. The entire local church is involved in the rite of election or enrollment of names on the first Sunday in Lent, which constitutes the liturgical step in this period and is presided over by the bishop. Other rites assigned to this period include public scrutiny and exorcism on the third, fourth, and fifth Sundays and celebrations in which the candidates are formally presented with the Creed and Lord's Prayer and subsequently expected to recite them back.

The third liturgical step, the sacraments of initiation themselves—baptism, confirmation, and the Eucharist—will then normally take place during the Easter Vigil, though some preparatory rites may be done at an earlier assembly of the elect on Holy Saturday. The final stage in the process is the period of *mystagogia*, or postbaptismal catechesis, which extends throughout the Easter season.

[14] Harmless, *Augustine and the Catechumenate*, 18.

particular goal, that of mystagogy being immersion into mystery, the R.C.I.A. gives few specifics on what is to be taught, how it is to be taught, how conversion is to be fostered and discerned, and how the interplay of culture and faith is to be incorporated.[15]

Writing specifically of postbaptismal catechesis in the R.C.I.A., Michel Dujarier observes that "in contrast to its rather lengthy development of the first three catechumenal periods, the R.C.I.A. speaks only briefly of the fourth period—*mystagogia*, or postbaptismal catechesis."[16] The period of mystagogy remains undeveloped because, while we know *what* the Fathers did during this period—preached a series of sermons probing the rites of initiation, their gestures, symbols, and words in terms of their biblical foundation and essential role in Christian living—we know very little of the method by which the Fathers did it. Thus, the R.C.I.A. gives a descriptive rather than prescriptive definition of the period:

"This is a time for the community and the neophytes together to grow in deepening their grasp of the paschal mystery and in making it part of their lives through meditation on the Gospel, sharing in the eucharist, and doing the works of charity."[17]

This text indicates that the goal of mystagogy within the R.C.I.A. is to enable the newly baptized to acquire a more profound experience of the paschal mystery, not only on an intellectual level but also on the level of lived personal experience, and that the means for attaining this goal are meditation on the Gospel, participation in the Eucharist, and practicing charity and doing good works.[18] True to the model of the ancient catechumenate, the R.C.I.A. also states that the context of

---

[15] Ibid., 18–20.

[16] Dujarier, *The Rites of Christian Initiation*, 203.

[17] International Commission on English in the Liturgy, *The Rite of Christian Initiation of Adults*, rev. ed. (Collegeville, Minn.: The Liturgical Press, 1988) 244.

[18] See *Apostolic Tradition*, 21, where the instructions on the sacraments conclude: "When these things [baptism and Eucharist] have been done, each one shall hasten to do good works and to please God and to conduct themselves rightly, being zealous for the Church, doing what they have learned and advancing in piety." As cited in Geoffrey J. Cuming, *Hippolytus: A Text for Students* (Bramcote, Notts.: Grove Books, 1976). Cf. Bernard Botte, *Hippolytus, La tradition apostolique de Saint Hippolyte*, Liturgiewissenschaftliche Quellen und Forschungen 39 (Münster, Westfalen: Aschendorff, 1963) 58.

mystagogy is essentially the Sunday celebration of the Eucharist during the Easter season.[19] Yet, the method of mystagogy is left undefined, with the result that both the period and the practice of mystagogy remain largely an undiscovered treasure in today's Church.

Of even greater significance for today's Church is the potential that mystagogical preaching holds for helping all the baptized to deepen and expand their experience and understanding of both the rites of initiation and the Christian identity and mission that God bestows on both the Christian and the Church through these sacraments. My own tradition illustrates the seriousness of this need. Reporting on the Evangelical Lutheran Church in America, Dr. Paul Nelson, Director of Worship, said that respondents to the initial draft of the ELCA's 1997 statement on sacramental practices commented that this was the first opportunity they had experienced as adults to learn about and comment on the Church's sacramental life.[20] Assuming that liturgical and sacramental catechesis was occurring within the congregations of the ELCA prior to this study, we cannot but conclude from these responses that it was not happening effectively.

In response to the needs of the R.C.I.A., Harmless concludes his study of Augustine's catechumenate by calling for giving modern catechesis an oral rather than a written character, cultivating the art of persuasion, reconnecting liturgy and catechesis, and employing a mystagogical rather than a solely cognitive approach to teaching.[21] These suggestions are equally appropriate for sacramental catechesis generally. Our attempt to discover a method of mystagogical preaching can be seen as implementing these suggestions. Rather than teaching about the rites, mystagogical preaching has as its goal conveying a vision of the sacraments to the Church that both shapes and enlivens it. This vision is grounded in the actual experience of the faithful and articulated within the context of worship. Thus, even where the catechumenate has not yet become a part of a congregation's ministry, mystagogical preaching offers great promise for enlivening and enlarging the faith community's liturgical and sacramental life and the identity and mission that flow from it. In sum, the obvious need for

---

[19] International Commission on English in the Liturgy, *The Rite of Christian Initiation of Adults*, 245.

[20] Paul R. Nelson, unpublished presentation given to the Lutheran caucus of the North American Academy of Liturgy, January 4, 1997, Chicago, Illinois.

[21] Harmless, *Augustine and the Catechumenate*, 350, 345, 350, 362.

developing the period of mystagogical catechesis within the catechumenal movement and the potential of this type of preaching as a means of sacramental instruction of the baptized make the development of resources for equipping pastors to preach mystagogically essential to the life of the Church.

HYPOTHESIS

The hypothesis of this study is that our best way to learn how to preach mystagogically is by using one of the fourth-century mystagogues as our guide. This hypothesis rests on three realities: (1) the need for a method of mystagogy based on actual practice, (2) the lack of contemporary models, and (3) the wisdom of the Fathers. First, any actual method of mystagogical preaching must be individual and unique because its goal is to help specific neophytes discover the meaning of the specific rites of Christian initiation in which they have participated. The real-life circumstances of the neophytes and the particular celebration of the rites in which they participated must be considered. This study therefore demands particularity—a specific, concrete mystagogical work—in order to avoid creating a theoretical model rather than discovering an actual method. Furthermore, recognizing that the preaching event cannot be reduced to a sermon text but is in fact the complex interaction of preacher, listeners, message, and setting, we must account for each of these factors when describing any method of mystagogical preaching. It is also important for us to be able to compare our preacher's mystagogical homilies with examples of his other types of sermons in order to detect any distinctive characteristics of mystagogical preaching.

Second, we lack contemporary models from which we can derive a method of mystagogical preaching. Current scholarly literature on the ancient catechumenate pays little attention to the specific questions and concerns of preachers. While we have excellent studies on the course and structure of the ancient rites as they are described in the mystagogical catecheses and the sacramental theology on which the mystagogical homilies are based, attempts to determine a method of mystagogical preaching are limited to examples of homilies, short articles, and brief passages in books on the history of preaching.[22]

[22] Current resources on mystagogy include E. Ancilli, *Mistagogia e direzione spirituale* (Milan, 1985); Balthasar Fischer, *Signs, Words and Gestures: Short Homilies on the Liturgy* (New York: Pueblo Publishing Co., 1981); Mary C. Grey,

The closest we come to any sort of method is provided by Harmless, though even he confines his explicit discussion of how to preach mystagogically to four pages.[23] Harmless is correct that this state of affairs is ironic in that "the primary fourth- and fifth-century documents that liturgists study are not liturgical documents per se (Church orders, *ordines*, sacramentaries) but are transcripts of actual catecheses."[24] And these catecheses are, in fact, sermons.

Third, in light of the absence of contemporary models to draw from or point to, it follows that if we want to discover how the preacher evokes, clarifies, and enlarges the meaning of the sacraments in such a way that the neophytes in particular but also all the baptized experience a more profound conversion to the grace of Christ symbolized in the liturgy, we are best served by the mystagogical catecheses that constitute the model for this kind of preaching. Harmless reminds us

---

The Candles Are Still Burning: Directions in Sacrament and Spirituality (Collegeville, Minn.: The Liturgical Press, 1995); Romano Guardini, *Sacred Signs* (St. Louis: Pio Decimo Press, 1956); idem, "La prédication mystagogique," *La Maison Dieu* 158 (1984) 137–147; Gabe Huck, *Preaching About the Mass* (Chicago: Liturgy Training Publications, 1992); Kathleen Hughes, *Saying Amen: A Mystagogy of the Sacraments* (Chicago: Liturgy Training Publications, 1998); Pamela E. J. Jackson, *Journeybread for the Shadowlands: The Readings for the Rites of the Catechumenate, RCIA* (Collegeville, Minn.: The Liturgical Press, 1993); Maxwell E. Johnson, *The Rites of Christian Initiation: Their Evolution and Interpretation* (Collegeville, Minn.: The Liturgical Press, Pueblo, 1999); Jan Michael Joncas, *Preaching the Rites of Christian Initiation* (Chicago: Liturgy Training Publications in cooperation with the North American Forum on the Catechumenate, 1994); Mazza, *Mystagogy: A Theology of Liturgy in the Patristic Age*; William McDonald, "Paideia and Gnosis: Foundations of the Catechumenate in Five Church Fathers" (Ph.D. diss., Vanderbilt University, 1998); David Philippart, *Saving Signs, Wondrous Words* (Chicago: Liturgy Training Publications, 1996); David Regan, *Experience the Mystery: Pastoral Possibilities for Christian Mystagogy* (Collegeville, Minn.: The Liturgical Press, 1994); Hugh M. Riley, *Christian Initiation: A Comparative Study of the Interpretation of the Baptismal Liturgy in the Mystagogical Writings of Cyril of Jerusalem, John Chrysostom, Theodore of Mopsuestia, and Ambrose of Milan* (Washington: Catholic University of America Press, 1974); D. Satore, "La mistogogia, modello e sorgente di spiritualita cristiana," *Rivista Liturgica* 73 (1986) 508–521; James A. Wilde, *Before and After Baptism: The Work of Teachers and Catechists* (Chicago: Liturgy Training Publications, 1988); Yarnold, *The Awe-Inspiring Rites of Initiation*.

[23] Harmless, *Augustine and the Catechumenate*, 364–367.
[24] Ibid., 27.

that this is precisely what the liturgists who created the R.C.I.A. did and what contemporary commentators on the rite do.[25] Yet, it is not enough to supply contemporary preachers with copies of these patristic documents and exhort them to "go and do likewise."[26] As we have said, in order for mystagogical preaching to take its rightful place within the catechumenate and to reach its potential as a means of sacramental catechesis, contemporary preachers need a *method* of mystagogical preaching: a process that leads preachers from their initial reflections on the rites of initiation through crafting their message to delivering the mystagogical homily.

THE INVESTIGATION

The design of this investigation is *historical*. We will *describe* a single instance of a method of mystagogical preaching, that of Ambrose of Milan. In other words, this is a case study. It addition to exploring in detail what Ambrose said to the neophytes about their experience of Christian initiation and how he said it, the study will include the impact of the personalities of the preacher and the listeners and the setting in which these sermons were preached. Thus, our approach to Ambrose's mystagogical homilies will be from the perspective of the study of a preacher, looking for the ways that Ambrose employs Scripture and the rites of initiation, makes his message applicable to his audience, shapes his sermons and selects his language, and, finally, delivers his mystagogical homilies.

We will also study the life of Saint Ambrose and the history and culture of his church and city in order to deduce the impact that the mystagogue and the neophytes have on the preaching event. We will endeavor to compare Ambrose's mystagogical homilies with his other sermons in order to discover distinctive characteristics of Ambrose's mystagogical preaching and explore metatextual elements such as assessments of Ambrose's preaching from those who heard him and archaeological research on Ambrose's basilica in order to get a sense of his delivery.

Why Study Ambrose?

Before turning to questions of scope and method, we will review the process that led to the selection of Ambrose of Milan as the focus of

[25] Ibid., 24.
[26] Cf. Luke 10:37.

this study. An examination of the classical mystagogical catecheses of Ambrose of Milan, Cyril of Jerusalem, John Chrysostom, and Theodore of Mopsuestia leads to the conclusion that three of the mystagogues are less appropriate for this study because their method of mystagogy may be more difficult to transfer to the modern Church. The homilies of John Chrysostom are not mystagogical in the strict sense of "explaining" the mysteries but are generally moral in nature, devoted to outlining the essential rules of the spiritual life. Only fragments of the Greek text of Theodore of Mopsuestia's mystagogical works are extant; although many were translated into Syriac and these texts were recovered in the early part of the last century,[27] we have lost the sermons that Theodore preached. While we possess Cyril of Jerusalem's catechetical preaching, we have none of his other sermons, making it impossible to uncover any distinctive characteristics of his mystagogical preaching.

Finally, we come to the mystagogical catecheses of the bishop of Milan —*De sacramentis* and *De mysteriis*. In addition to the Latin texts found in *Patrologia Latina* and *Corpus Scriptorum Ecclesiasticorum Latinorum*, *De sacramentis* and *De mysteriis* are available to us in two critical editions, Bernard Botte's Latin-French edition and a Latin-German edition by Josef Schmitz.[28] English translations of *De sacramentis* and *De mysteriis* include those of T. Thompson and Roy J. Deferrari.[29] Additionally, Yarnold provides an English translation of *De sacramentis*, 1-5, and both H. DeRomestin and Boniface Ramsey provide one of *De mysteriis*.[30] While the Scriptures play an essential role in Ambrose's preaching, his treatment of the text is often characterized by striking

---

[27] Thomas M. Finn, *Early Christian Baptism and the Catechumenate*, Vol. 1: *East and West Syria*, Message of the Fathers of the Church 5 (Collegeville, Minn.: The Liturgical Press, 1992) 81.

[28] PL 16.405–426, 435–482; CSEL 73.13–116; Bernard Botte, *Ambroise de Milan: Des Sacrements; Des Mystères; Explication du Symbole*, SC 25bis (Paris: Éditions du Cerf, 1980); Josef Schmitz, *Ambrosius: De Sacramentis = Über Die Sakramente. De Mysteriis = Über Die Mysterien*, Fontes Christiani (Freiburg im Breisgau: Herder, 1990).

[29] T. Thompson, *On the Sacraments and On the Mysteries*, rev. ed. (London: S.P.C.K., 1950); Roy J. Deferrari, *Saint Ambrose: Theological and Dogmatic Works* (Washington: Catholic University of America Press, 1963) 3–30, 265–328.

[30] Yarnold, *The Awe-Inspiring Rites of Initiation*, 98–150; H. DeRomestin, *Saint Ambrose: Select Works and Letters*, A Select Library of Nicene and Post-Nicene Fathers of the Christian Church, 2nd series 10 (Grand Rapids: Eerdmans

simplicity rather than extreme allegory. His preaching is set within the context of worship, as is evident from his references to the readings,[31] and he directs his attention to the relationship between the spoken word and its liturgical context. Finally, Ambrose's other writings consist largely of sermons or the expansions of sermons into treatises.[32] This fact both indicates the priority that Ambrose placed on preaching and provides us homiletic works with which to compare his mystagogical preaching.

Yet, before we can select *De sacramentis* and *De mysteriis* as the subject of our study, we must first determine whether they are in fact mystagogical sermons preached by Saint Ambrose. Both *De mysteriis* and *De sacramentis* are now generally recognized as genuine works of Saint Ambrose. In fact, Neil McLynn notes that much work on the relationship between Ambrose's treatises and their homiletical core is undertaken by using *De mysteriis* and *De sacramentis* as a control.[33] *De sacramentis* is a stenographic record of the addresses given by

---

Publishing Co., 1978) 315–326; Boniface Ramsey, *Ambrose* (New York: Routledge, 1997) 145–160.

[31] See *De sacramentis*, 2.2.3; 2.7.23; 3.2.8; 6.2.9 (SC 25bis.77; 86; 96; 140).

[32] In this study we will make use of those works considered genuinely Ambrosian. These works are traditionally grouped as exegetical, moral/ascetic, dogmatic, sermons, and letters. Of Ambrose's exegetical writings, *De Ioseph* is a sermon and *Hexaemeron*, the first book of *De Abraham*, *De bono mortis*, *De fuga saeculi*, *De Iacob et vita beata*, *De patriarchis*, *De Helia et ieiunio*, *De Nabuthae*, *De Tobia*, *De interpellatione Iob et David*, *Enarrationes in xii psalmos davidicos*, and *Expositio evangelii secundum Lucam* are based on sermons. Of Ambrose's moral/ascetic writings, *De institutione virginis* and *Exhortatio virginitatis* are sermons and *De virginibus* and *De virginitate* are constructed from sermons. Turning to Ambrose's dogmatic works, *Explanatio symboli ad initiandos* and *De sacramentis* are sermons, and *De mysteriis* is an edited form of *De sacramentis*. Works traditionally classified as sermons include *De excessu fratris*, *De obitu Valentiniani*, *De obitu Theodosii*, and *Contra Auxentium de basilicis tradendis*. Finally, in *Epistola extra coll.* 1 (Maur. 41), Ambrose tells his sister Marcellina of the sermon he preached before Emperor Theodosius in reaction to the emperor's response to the burning of the Jewish synagogue at Callinicum. Of this sermon material, *De Abraham* and *Explanatio symboli ad initiandos* are sermons delivered to catechumens and *De sacramentis* is a sermon series delivered to the newly baptized.

[33] Neil B. McLynn, *Ambrose of Milan: Church and Court in a Christian Capital* (Berkeley and Los Angeles: University of California Press, 1994) 238, n. 67.

Ambrose to the neophytes during Easter Week, which treat the rites and meaning of the sacraments of initiation. *De mysteriis* is a version of *De sacramentis* polished and edited for publication (doubtless by Ambrose himself), which maintains only the literary appearance of a sermon and omits certain details, perhaps out of respect for the *disciplina arcani*.[34]

The rites described in these two works are substantially the same, and the explanations of those rites are often given in almost identical terms. Nevertheless, there are differences in content. At two points *De mysteriis* brings in a mystical commentary on certain passages of the Song of Songs.[35] *De sacramentis* contains the oldest extant Latin text of portions of the Roman Canon of the Mass, the oldest text of the Latin liturgy for baptism, as well as a very interesting exposition of the Lord's Prayer and a discussion of how and where Christians ought to pray.[36] In this discourse Ambrose notes with regret that the people of Milan did not receive the Eucharist as frequently as they should, and he speaks of the advantages to be derived from the washing of feet during the liturgy, a custom that he recognizes was not observed at Rome.[37]

Both works are believed to have been written between 380 and 390.[38] Inasmuch as *De sacramentis*, as a stenographic record of the addresses given by Ambrose to the neophytes during Easter Week, brings us the closest to Ambrose's actual mystagogical preaching, it

---

[34] The *disciplina arcani*, or "discipline of secrecy," the practice of preserving the central elements of the faith as a secret from outsiders, will be discussed in Chapter 5. See below, 155–156.

[35] *De mysteriis*, 7.35–41; 9.55–58 (SC 25bis.174–178; 188–190).

[36] *De sacramentis*, 4.5.21–25, 4.6.27; 2.7.20; 5.4.18–30: 6.3.4.11–5.25 (SC 25bis.114–116; 84; 128–136; 142–150).

[37] Ibid., 5.4.25; 3.1.5–7 (SC 25bis.132; 94–96).

[38] Finn declares that both works were most likely written during the middle of the decade 380 to 390. See Thomas M. Finn, *Early Christian Baptism and the Catechumenate*, Vol. 2: *Italy, North Africa, and Egypt*, Message of the Fathers of the Church 6 (Collegeville, Minn.: The Liturgical Press, 1992) 58. Yarnold asserts that the sermons contained in *De sacramentis* were probably preached in the week after Easter about 391. Cf. Yarnold, *The Awe-Inspiring Rites of Initiation*, 98. Deferrari argues that both works were written before the year 392, that is, before the composition of *De institutione virginis*, in which (5.39) is contained a certain imitation of a passage (7.36) of the *De mysteriis*. Cf. Deferrari, *Saint Ambrose: Theological and Dogmatic Works*, 267.

will be the primary focus of our investigation. Since our purpose is to study *De sacramentis* as the mystagogical sermons of Saint Ambrose, it is necessary to acknowledge and respond to the questions of authorship and document type that have historically surrounded *De sacramentis*. These questions were answered decisively by Otto Faller and R. H. Connolly and later confirmed by Bernard Botte and Christine Mohrmann, who summarized and expanded upon Faller's and Connolly's work.[39] Most recently, the debate over the authorship of *De sacramentis* has been taken up by Klaus Gamber and Josef Schmitz, with the former attributing the work to Nicetas of Remesiana and the latter successfully refuting this claim.[40]

Method

With Ambrose's mystagogical homilies before us, our task now is to determine how we will go about uncovering his method of mystagogical preaching. Two factors must be considered in determining our strategy. First, we define a *method of mystagogical preaching* as a process that leads preachers from their initial reflections on the rites of initiation and those who have participated in them through discerning and crafting their message to delivering the mystagogical homily. Whatever strategy we adopt must, therefore, address all these stages of this process.

Second, inasmuch as our goal is to uncover a method that contemporary preachers can use to learn to preach mystagogically and not to study Ambrose's mystagogy *in se*, our strategy will need to be so accessible to today's preachers that it is something they are willing to

---

[39] Otto Faller, "Ambrosius, der Verfasser von *De sacramentis*. Die innere Echtheitsgrunde," in *Zeitschrift für katholische Theologie* 64 (1940) 1–14, 81–101; R. H. Connolly, *The De Sacramentis a Work of Ambrose, Two Papers* (Oxford: Downside Abbey, 1942); Bernard Botte, *Ambroise de Milan: Des Sacrements; Des Mystères*, 7–25; Christine Mohrmann, "Le style oral du *De sacramentis* de Saint Ambrose," in *Vigiliae Christianae* 6 (1952) 168–177. Both the historical background of these critical issues and the work of Faller, Connolly, Botte, and Mohrmann are summarized in the excursus that concludes this chapter. Below, 20–29.

[40] Below, 29. Klaus Gamber, *Die Autorschaft von De Sacramentis* (Regensburg: Pustet, 1967) and "Nochmals zur Frage der Autorschaft von De Sacramentis," *Zeitschrift für katholische Theologie* 91 (1969) 587–589; Josef Schmitz, "Zum Autor der Schrift 'De Sacramentis,'" *Zeitschrift für katholische Theologie* 91 (1969) 58–69.

learn. Thus, while using Aristotle's *Rhetoric* and *Poetics*, Cicero's *On Oratory*, Quintilian's *Institutio Oratoria*, or Augustine's instructions on preaching as our model might be the best choice from the perspective of the historian,[41] these models are not being taught in seminary preaching classes, and so they are not generally familiar to today's preachers. We would, therefore, need to teach preachers the model before we could teach them Ambrose's method, and then we would need to transfer that method into a contemporary frame of reference in order to apply it to our own preaching. In light of these considerations, the strategy that we will employ in uncovering Ambrose's method of mystagogical preaching is to use contemporary methods of preaching in order to create the template for our study.[42]

Drawing upon contemporary methods of preaching in order to create our template raises the legitimate questions of whether we are forcing Ambrose's preaching into categories that are not appropriate or judging it by standards that are not applicable to fourth-century Milan. For example, looking ahead to our review of assessments of Ambrose's preaching, we will find that his scriptural *suavitas*, his ability "to sound like the Bible,"[43] is a characteristic of his preaching that captivated his hearers but would be lost on us today.[44] Thus, Yngve Brilioth is correct when he warns of "the danger that in the modern evaluation of style and taste we depend upon the yardstick of a later time and treat the rhetorical production of the bygone era unfairly."[45] We will guard against this danger by concentrating more

---

[41] Aristotle's *Rhetoric* and *Poetics*, Cicero's *On Oratory*, and Quintilian's *Institutio oratoria* are models that Ambrose himself studied, and Augustine's *On Christine Doctrine* is a christianization of these models from the same time period. See W. Rhys Roberts, *Aristotle: Rhetoric*; Ingram Bywater, *Poetics* (New York: Modern Library, 1984): Marcus Tullius Cicero, *De oratore* (Cambridge, Mass.: Harvard University Press, 1988); Jean Cousin, *Quintilian: Institution oratoire* (Paris: Société d'édition les Belles lettres, 1975–1980); R.P.H. Green, *Augustine: On Christian Teaching* (New York: Oxford University Press, 1997).

[42] Texts consulted are listed in the Bibliography under the heading "Works on Preaching and Rhetoric." Below, 376–378.

[43] Gerard Nauroy, "L'Ecriture dans la Pastorale d'Ambroise de Milan, *Le Monde Latin Antique et La Bible*, ed. J. Fontaine and C. Pietri (Paris: Beauchesne, 1985) 404; McLynn, *Ambrose of Milan: Church and Court in a Christian Capital*, 240.

[44] Below, 98–99.

[45] Brilioth, *A Brief History of Preaching*, 45.

on the structure than on the content of contemporary methods and by describing rather than evaluating Ambrose's preaching. Still, this major concern is outweighed by the benefit that employing contemporary models to organize our study will help to ensure that our investigation remains relevant to today's Church and world and "user-friendly" to today's preachers.

While we will draw upon several contemporary methods of preaching, our template is especially influenced by that of Fred Craddock as it is developed in his book *Preaching*.[46] Craddock's intended audience, like ours, is "the men and women for whom preaching is or will be a regular responsibility in ministry."[47] His pedagogical approach is based on recognition rather than recall. "Learning by recognition is simply being enabled to see how much we already know about a subject about which we had no clear terms or categories."[48] Our underlying assumption is that in studying Ambrose's mystagogy we will recognize a method that we can appropriate for ourselves. Craddock also reminds us not to abandon the models that historians might prefer—those of Aristotle, Cicero, Quintilian, and Augustine. He argues that a weakness of contemporary preaching is its failure to listen carefully to its own tradition, declaring that "there are fundamentals to good writing and speaking and preaching that abide, and it is the burden of a textbook to offer these, *especially* in a time of fascination with experimentation."[49] We find articulated in *Preaching* those abiding fundamentals to good preaching that Ambrose studied and Augustine christianized. Yet, the chief insight that Craddock's model provides is its format, which "provides the reader with both a clear walk through the entire process of sermon preparation and delivery and clear markers along the way for the benefit of those who might wish to review or refresh themselves on one particular phase of the process."[50]

---

[46] Fred B. Craddock, *Preaching* (Nashville: Abingdon Press, 1985). Craddock is arguably one of the most influential homileticians in the United States today. Although *Preaching* was published almost fifteen years ago, it is still widely used as a textbook in seminary preaching classes across denominational lines and, therefore, familiar to countless preachers.

[47] Ibid., 14.
[48] Ibid., 15.
[49] Ibid., 14.
[50] Ibid., 15.

We will begin each chapter of this dissertation by summarizing the pertinent phase of the process of sermon preparation as a way of framing the discussion to follow. Here we provide a synopsis of our template in order to explain the way that our study will unfold.

We have previously asserted that in order to preach mystagogically, the person of the preacher and real-life circumstances of the neophytes must be considered. In the next chapter, Chapter 2, we will therefore provide a historical narrative of Ambrose, his life, and the church of Milan.

In Chapter 3 we will create a portrait of Ambrose the preacher by assessing Ambrose as a preacher, by drawing from Ambrose's works his views on preaching, and by attempting to determine the influences that shaped him as a preacher.

In Chapter 4 we will determine who heard Ambrose's sermons by exploring the characteristics and traits of the neophytes and baptized that comprised Ambrose's congregation. Next, we will outline how this congregation influenced the content of Ambrose's mystagogy. We will then explore Ambrose's hearers' *ability to listen* and the influences that shaped this ability. Finally, we will discuss the methods that Ambrose used to lead his hearers to participate in mystagogy and enter more deeply into the sacraments.

In Chapter 5 we will present the rites of initiation that Ambrose is describing as the "text" on which the sermons in *De sacramentis* are based. We will first reconstruct the rites of initiation that Ambrose explains in his mystagogical sermons and then discuss his theology of these rites. We will then explore how the rites function as the "text" on which *De sacramentis* is based.

In Chapter 6 we will explore Ambrose's use of Scripture in his mystagogical preaching as the means of interpreting the rites of initiation to his people. First, we will analyze how Ambrose selected his Scripture texts. Next, we will discuss Ambrose's exegetical method. Finally, we will determine how Ambrose interprets Scripture for his congregation.

In Chapter 7 we will examine the form of Ambrose's mystagogical sermons, first by reconstructing the form of these sermons, and second in terms of the qualities that make a sermon congenial to the Gospel, the listeners, the context and sound principles of communication.[51]

---

[51] Ibid., 58.

In Chapter 8 we will attempt to move from text to delivery by exploring whether there was anything distinct about Ambrose's delivery of mystagogical preaching compared with his delivery of other sermons.

We conclude in Chapter 9 by drawing from our study of Ambrose's mystagogical preaching a method that we can use ourselves. In addition to providing principles for every stage of the process of mystagogical preaching, we will also discuss the implications of this method, both positive and negative, for contemporary mystagogy.

Finally, we must acknowledge two limitations inherent in our study. First, while we can analyze the texts of Ambrose's mystagogical sermons, we cannot experience his mystagogical preaching. As our methodology suggests, mystagogy, like all preaching, is an event that involves the complex interaction of preacher, listeners, Scripture, message, setting, and world. Consequently, while our work is primarily textual, this is in fact only one dimension of the actual process employed by Ambrose. Unfortunately, and obviously, we can neither experience firsthand the preaching of the bishop of Milan nor interview either Ambrose concerning his method or his hearers concerning their experience of his preaching. While we will attempt to compensate for this limitation through metatextual evidence,[52] we must acknowledge that we cannot push open the door to Ambrose's study and surprise him as he prepares his sermons or stand in the doorway of his basilica and overhear him as he preaches.

Second, we must acknowledge the impossibility of documenting the presence and activity of the Holy Spirit, which is vital to sermon preparation and gives life to the preaching event. The role of the Holy Spirit in preaching has been acknowledged throughout the history of the Church, from Jesus preaching in the synagogue at Nazareth to contemporary theories of preaching.[53] My experience as one privileged both to preach to God's people week in and week out and to have a

---

[52] Under the heading of "metatextual" evidence we include records of the responses of Ambrose's hearers to his preaching, the history of the Church and city of Milan, and architectural studies of the baptistry in which the rites of Christian initiation were celebrated and the church building in which Ambrose preached.

[53] See Luke 4:16-24; National Conference of Catholic Bishops, *Fulfilled in Your Hearing: The Homily in the Sunday Assembly* (Washington: Office of Publishing Services, United States Catholic Conference, 1982) 31, 41–42; Rudolf Bohren, *Predigtlehre* (Munich: Chr. Kaiser Verlag, 1971) 82–88; David Buttrick, *Homiletic: Moves and Structures* (Philadelphia: Fortress Press, 1987) 452, 454,

small role in shaping the Church's preachers convinces me that it is through a method, a step-by-step process, that the Holy Spirit speaks to preachers. There is profound truth in the old preacher's joke:

"There was a preacher who determined not to prepare a sermon but to trust that when the time came to preach, the Spirit would speak to him. And when the time came and the preacher was standing in the pulpit, facing the congregation, the Spirit did in fact speak. The Spirit said to the preacher, 'You really should have prepared a sermon.'"

As profound as the truth that the Spirit is active in preaching is the truth that "the wind blows where it chooses, and you hear the sound of it, but you do not know where it comes from or where it goes."[54] The Spirit is of God and not contingent upon our willing or doing. Christians do not agree how to ascertain the Spirit's presence in preaching, let alone have the technology for documenting it. We do possess Christ's promise to be with us in preaching.[55] We can actively listen and wait for the Spirit to speak and act and be open to what the Spirit says and does. We can also trust that the participation of the Holy Spirit was as vital to Ambrose's preaching as it is to our own. Thus, while we cannot document the pneumatic dimension of preaching, we can watch and listen for and then reflect upon how and where the Spirit might be blowing through the various components of Ambrose's process of mystagogical preaching.

While not recognized as a scholarly discipline, this kind of reflection will help us to undertake our analysis of Ambrose's method of mystagogical preaching with the conviction that it will not result in something ancient, rote, mechanical, and one-dimensional, but that we will come away with a vessel through which the Spirit will breathe new life into the Church's rites of initiation and our appreciation of them, so that they will shape us as God's people as we live in the world. And so, trusting that the Holy Spirit will be our conversation partner every step of the way, brief reflections on the pneumatic dimension of Ambrose's mystagogical preaching will bring to a close each of the following chapters.

457; Craddock, *Preaching*, 29–31; Mary Catherine Hilkert, *Naming Grace: Preaching and the Sacramental Imagination* (New York: Continuum, 1997) 85–88.

[54] John 3:8. The Greek word πνεῦμα means both "wind" and "spirit."

[55] Cf. Matthew 28:19; Mark 16:20.

EXCURSUS:
THE CRITICAL PROBLEM OF *DE SACRAMENTIS*

Inasmuch as *De sacramentis* is generally thought today to be a stenographic record of the addresses given by Ambrose to the neophytes during Easter Week, it brings us the closest to Ambrose's actual mystagogical preaching and is thus the primary focus of our investigation. We have already noted that the authorship and genre of *De sacramentis* have been and continue to be contested on theological grounds, on account of its apparent difference of style from *De mysteriis* and other writings of Ambrose, and also because its treatment of the sacraments is less orderly than that found in the more sober and literary manner of the undisputed *De mysteriis*.[56] It is, therefore, appropriate to provide a summary of the scholarship on which our conclusions about the authorship and genre of *De sacramentis* are based.[57]

The authenticity of *De sacramentis* was not in doubt prior to the sixteenth century. It passed into the manuscript tradition of Ambrose and, beginning in the eleventh century, is quoted as an authentic work of Ambrose by Paschasius Radbertus and Ratramnus of Corbie.[58] In the period of the Reformation, however, its authenticity was assailed by Protestants and Catholics alike on the assumption that its eucharistic teaching and practice could not have come from Ambrose. The summary of sixteenth-century criticism of *De sacramentis* that we find in the preface of the eighteenth-century Maurist edition, which is included in Migne's *Patrologia Latina*, illustrates how blunt this criticism was: one finds in *De sacramentis* many false and ridiculous things; it is full of bad Latin, and its author "apes" Ambrose.[59] The Lutheran scholar Casimir Oudin (1638–1717) went so far as to attribute it to

---

[56] Objections raised to the authenticity of Ambrose in the case of *De mysteriis* have not generally won acceptance from modern scholars. The many parallels and points of contact between *De mysteriis* and well-established works of Saint Ambrose, as well as strong manuscript evidence, leave no doubt as to its Ambrosian authorship.

[57] In the following discussion I am indebted especially to Bernard Botte's treatment of these issues in the Introduction to his critical edition. See Botte, *Des Sacrements; Des Mystères*, 7–25.

[58] Cf. Otto Faller, "Was sagen die Handschriften sur Echtheit der sechs Predigten S. Ambrosii de Sacramentis?" in *Zeitschrift für katholische Theologie* 53 (1929) 49–52.

[59] Cf. PL 16.427.

Ambrose of Cahors, who lived in the eighth century.[60] Cardinal Bona declared that in reading *De sacramentis*, he had the impression of hearing a different language from that of Ambrose, that the biblical citations found in *De sacramentis* are from a different version than the one Ambrose cites in his authentic works, and that there are several places in *De sacramentis* where the Latin would be judged inappropriate by the standards of Ambrose's day.[61]

Remi Ceillier estimated that *De sacramentis* had to be dated after the time of John Chrysostom because of the criticism of the Greeks for receiving Communion only once a year.[62] He also judged the style to be "low, rambling, filled with cold questions, improper expression, and mixed up and badly constructed sentences."[63] Lenain de Tillemont also declined to grant *De sacramentis* Ambrosian authenticity, partially on the ground that another treatise of Saint Ambrose bears the same title, and it was unheard of that the same author would publish two works on different subjects under the same title.[64]

If theologians continued to defend the authenticity of *De sacramentis*, those with some critical sense rejected attributing the work to Saint Ambrose. Though the Maurists defended the author against the undeserved criticism of the Reformers,[65] they finally judged the text in the same way. They put forth four arguments against Ambrosian

---

[60] Cf. Remi Ceillier, *Histoire générale des auteurs sacrés et ecclésiastiques* (Paris: L. Vivès, 1858–1863) 5:464. The *Commentarivs de scriptoribvs ecclesiae antiqvis* (Lipsiae: M.G. Wiedmanni, 1722) dates from the period of Oudin.

[61] Bona states that he leaves it to those more learned than himself to illustrate his suspicions. *Rerum liturgicarum libri II* (Augustae Taurinorum, 1757) 1:111. The first edition was published in Rome in 1671.

[62] *De sacramentis*, 5.4.25 (SC 25bis.132).

[63] Cf. Ceillier, *Histoire générale des auteurs sacrés et ecclésiastiques*, 5:461.

[64] Tillemont is speaking of *De sacramentis* and *De sacramento regenerationis sive de philosophia* (CSEL 11.131). The former is the work that we are considering, and the latter is a lost work, except for some fragments preserved in Augustine, *Contra Jul.*, 2.6.15 and *Retract.*, 2.4. Lenain de Tillemont, *Memoires pour servir à l'histoire ecclésiastique des six premiers siècles* (Paris, 1705) 10:766.

[65] In particular Heinrich Bullinger, Edme Aubertin (who labeled the author of *De sacramentis* "the ape of Ambrose"), and Jean Daillé. Aubertin assigned *De sacramentis* to the seventh century and Daillé to the eighth. T. Thompson and J. H. Srawley, *St. Ambrose: "On the Mysteries," and the Treatise "On the Sacraments," by an Unknown Author* (New York: The Macmillan Company, 1919) xvii.

authorship: (1) the differences in style between *De sacramentis* and *De mysteriis*, (2) the improbability of Ambrose's copying himself with such sloppiness, (3) the fact that nowhere else does Ambrose criticize the people of Milan for communing so rarely, and (4) the author's criticism of the Church of Rome concerning the washing of feet.[66] Only at the end of the nineteenth century did this opinion change.

In 1893, F. Probst first proposed seeing in *De sacramentis* a stenographic redaction of sermons preached by Ambrose.[67] However, he was refuted by T. Schermann.[68] Meanwhile, G. Morin, having first proposed Nicetas of Remesiana as the author of *De sacramentis*,[69] later defended the authorial unity of *De sacramentis* and *Explanatio symboli ad initiandos* and proposed that these works are sermons preached by Saint Ambrose and noted down in haste by a listener.[70] These first attempts had no immediate follow-up. However, Morin took up the subject of the authenticity of *De sacramentis* again more than thirty years later,[71] and his case for Ambrosian authorship was supported by O. Faller. Still, Faller's first article was far from convincing.[72] His examination of the manuscripts led him to conclude that there were two strands in the manuscript tradition: the first strand, certainly of Italian origin, gave no author's name; the second strand, represented by the overwhelming majority of manuscripts, put *De sacramentis* within authentic works of Saint Ambrose. This second strand, which consists of a good number of ninth-century manuscripts, seems to allow us to

---

[66] PL 16.434.

[67] *Die Liturgie des vierten Jahrhunderts* (Münster, 1893) 232–239.

[68] Schermann argues that the theory that *De sacramentis* was compiled from notes taken by those who had heard the sermons of Ambrose fails to explain the peculiar characteristics that distinguish it from the genuine works of Ambrose. Schermann, who points out that in the oldest MS *De sacramentis* follows immediately after the *Homilies* of Maximus, suggests Maximus of Turin as the author. T. Schermann, "Die pseudo ambrosianische Schrift *De sacramentis*," in *Römische Quartalschrift* 17 (1903) 36–53.

[69] G. Morin, "Nouvelles recherches sur l'auteur of the Te Deum," in *Revue bénédictine* 11 (1894) 76.

[70] Idem, "Notes additionelles," ibid. 12 (1895) 343, and "Essai d'autocritique," ibid., 386.

[71] Idem, "Pour l'authenticité du *De sacramentis*," in *Jahrbuch fur Liturgiewissenschaft* 8 (1928) 86–106.

[72] Faller, "Was sagen die Handschriften sur Echtheit der sechs Predigten S. Ambrosii de Sacramentis?" 41–65.

date *De sacramentis* earlier than the ninth century. However, even if we suppose that this manuscript tradition brings us to a seventh-century archetype, we are still three centuries removed from Saint Ambrose. Thus, Botte, finding the reflections of Morin subjective and Faller's article unconvincing, originally attributed *De sacramentis* to Pseudo-Ambrose.[73]

Around the same time that Faller's article appeared, C. Atchley, repeating the now generally accepted view that *De sacramentis* could not be a genuine work of Saint Ambrose, attempted to demonstrate that *De sacramentis* could not have been written earlier than 476. Atchley argued that the year 476, the date of the fall of the empire in the West, is reflected in the reference to several kings found in *De sacramentis*.[74] His only basis for this theory is that in the Mass one prayed *pro regibus*;[75] one argument does not provide a solid foundation. The argument is further weakened by the fact that the term *pro regibus* is found in 1 Timothy 2:2, where the verses indicate those for whom Christians should pray. Rather than a reference to the several kings of the fallen empire, *pro regibus* is probably an allusion to this scriptural text. Thus, the issue remained far from settled.

In 1940 two studies were published independently of each other by Faller and R. H. Connolly, which are decisive.[76] Botte reports that their examination of the style, biblical citations, and thinking of *De sacramentis* leads back, after a four-century detour, to Saint Ambrose himself in a decisive way.[77] Inspired by these works, Botte undertook a personal examination of these issues for his critical edition, which confirmed the conviction that *De sacramentis* is the work of Saint Ambrose. What follows is a summary of Botte's findings.

Botte first deals with the dating of *De sacramentis*. Ceillier had already mentioned the indices of its antiquity.[78] First, Ceillier notes that the only polemic against heresy is against the Arians.[79] There is no

---

[73] Bernard Botte, *Le canon de la messe romaine* (Louvain: Abbaye du Mont César, 1935) 37, 39, 41.

[74] C. Atchley, "The Date of *De sacramentis*," *Journal of Theological Studies* 30 (1929) 281–286.

[75] *De sacramentis*, 4.4.14 (SC 25bis.108).

[76] See above, 14, n. 39.

[77] Botte, Des Sacrements; Des Mystères, 11.

[78] Ceillier, *Histoire générale des auteurs sacrés et ecclésiastiques*, 5:464.

[79] *De sacramentis*, 6.1.10 (SC 25bis.142).

allusion to either christological battles or to the controversies about grace.[80] Moreover, Ceillier argues that the fact that Ambrose spent the week after Easter preaching on the sacraments suggests a large number of baptized adults. By the fifth century, when the churches were fighting Pelagianism, the baptism of infants prevailed and mystagogical catecheses were rendered unnecessary.[81] Botte contends that these two converging indices are enough to discredit the thesis of Atchley, who wants to place *De sacramentis* in the sixth century. The outer limit would be the middle of the fifth century.[82]

Second, these sermons could only have been preached in Milan or in a church with a liturgy identical to that of Milan. If a bishop wanted to adapt the work of Ambrose in order to use it with his own neophytes, that bishop would need to modify the liturgical formulas cited by Ambrose, if Ambrose's formulas are not identical to those used by the bishop's church. *De mysteriis*, 2.5 says: "*Renuntiasti diabolo et operibus eius, mundo et luxuriae eius ac uoluptatibus.*"[83] In *De sacramentis*, 1.2.5 the same text is expressed as a liturgical formula: "*Quando te interrogauit: Abrenuntias diabolo et operibus eius, quid respondisti? Abrenuntio. Abrenuntias saeculo et uoluptatibus eius, quid respondisti? Abrenuntio.*"[84]

Obviously, the preacher would refer to this liturgical formula only because it was the liturgical formula used in his church. This formula, however, is rare. In addition to the Ambrosian rite, one finds *diabolo*

---

[80] If *De sacramentis* was written in the fifth century, the author would probably have addressed Nestorianism, the belief that there were two "sons" in Christ, one human and one divine, which was condemned at Ephesus in 431; Monophysitism, the belief that Christ's human nature was absorbed into Christ's divine nature, which was condemned at Chalcedon in 451; and Pelagianism, which denied original sin and held that all human beings have the power not to sin and, therefore, to achieve salvation apart from the grace of God. Pelagianism was condemned at Ephesus in 431. For a complete discussion of the history of early Christology, see Alois Grillmeier, *Christ in Christian Tradition*, 2nd rev. ed., trans. John Bowden (Atlanta: John Knox Press, 1975).

[81] See Kavanagh, *The Shape of Baptism*, 90, 91.

[82] Botte, *Des Sacrements; Des Mystères*, 12.

[83] SC 25bis.158. "You renounced the devil and his works, the world and its wantonness and pleasures."

[84] Ibid., 62. "When he asked you, 'Do you renounce the devil and his works?' what did you reply? 'I renounce them.' 'Do you renounce the world and its pleasures?' what did you reply? 'I renounce them.'"

only in the Mozarabic rite.[85] All the other Western rites we know of have *satanae*. Moreover, the rest of the Mozarabic formula is quite different. In fact, the precise formula of *De sacramentis* is found only in Ambrose and at Milan. Again, *De mysteriis*, 5.28 alludes to the cross in the baptismal interrogation: *"Hoc solo excepto quod in crucem solius domini fateris esse credendum."*[86] In *De sacramentis*, 2.7.20 this is once again expressed as a liturgical formula: *"Credis in dominum nostrum et in crucem eius?"*[87] Botte contends that a bishop adopting Ambrose's formula for his own use would not include the four words *et in crucem eius* unless his own liturgical formula was identical to Ambrose's. Botte argues that, once again, this additional formulaic expression is found only in Ambrose. One must therefore suppose a liturgy identical to that of Milan at the time of Saint Ambrose.[88]

Third, Connolly and Faller show that the scriptural citations found in *De sacramentis* are from the same version as the scriptural citations found in the authentic works of Saint Ambrose, even in those places that have no parallel in *De mysteriis*. The fact that Cardinal Bona believed that the biblical citations in *De sacramentis* reveal an altogether different version of the Bible than that cited in the genuine works of Ambrose can be explained by the fact that Cardinal Bona probably read the famous Roman edition of *De sacramentis*.[89] In this edition the monk Felix de Montalto,[90] who edited the work, decided to "correct" the biblical citations that he found in *De sacramentis* and, in so doing, made them different from the version found in the genuine works of Ambrose.

Furthermore, there was such a diversity of Latin biblical texts, particularly at the end of the fourth century, that it would be surprising

---

[85] M. Férotin, *Liber ordinum en usage dans l'église wisigothique et mozarabe d'Espagne du V au XI siècle*, Monumenta Ecclesiae Liturgica 5 (Paris, 1904) 32. For the other formulas, see, for the Gelasian, H. Wilson, *A Classified Index to the Leonine, Gelasian, and Gregorian Sacramentaries* (Cambridge, 1892) 79; the Gregorian, ibid., 54; the Bobbio Missal, E. A. Lowe, *Inquisitio de lege ad missam celebrare*, Henry Bradshaw Society 58 (London, 1920) 74.

[86] SC 25bis.170. "The sole difference consists in this—that you say that one must believe in the cross of Jesus, our only Lord."

[87] Ibid., 84. "Do you believe in our Lord Jesus Christ, and in his cross?"

[88] Botte, *Des Sacrements; Des Mystères*, 13.

[89] On this edition, see ibid., 40–41; Thompson, *On the Sacraments and On the Mysteries*, 45.

[90] Felix de Montalto, surnamed Peretti, afterward became Pope Sixtus V.

that someone copying from *De mysteriis* would reproduce the quotes found therein, not only without adapting them systematically to his own text but without making mistakes. The copyists of Ambrose did not always succeed in copying exactly and, in more than one place, they made corrections, probably automatically, according to the Vulgate. The only explanation for the fact that the biblical quotations found in *De sacramentis* are from the same version as those found in Ambrose's genuine works is that whoever wrote the text had the same translation that Ambrose had. When one remembers how rapidly the biblical text evolved at the end of the fourth century, one must conclude that if it was not Ambrose himself who wrote *De sacramentis*, it was at least someone very close to him geographically and chronologically.

Fourth, when we compare different works of the same author, we must take into account the distinctive character of different literary genres. When comparing *De sacramentis* with other works of Saint Ambrose, we must recognize that different genres have different styles. We cannot expect the same level of style in a series of sermons preached by an overworked bishop during the week after Easter that we find in a literary work composed by a rested mind, intended for publication, and edited at leisure. Taking this into consideration, Faller shows that although the stylistic quality of *De sacramentis* is different from the authentic works of Saint Ambrose, it was still written by the same person. In particular, the famous questions[91] once judged to be childish, cold, and ridiculous are perfectly Ambrosian.[92] Phrases such as *quare, qua ratione, uis, scire quia,* and *quomodo* abound in Ambrose's authentic works, not to mention the other familiar transitions such as *hoc ergo absoluamus, hoc igitur adstruamus, nunc ergo considerem audi quia, considera, didicisti ergo, habes, uide quia*.[93] The only difference is that these expressions are still more numerous in *De sacramentis* than in the

---

[91] The rhetorical questions found in *De sacramentis* convey an impression only in their totality. Here we can provide only a few examples of these questions: What did we do? *(quid egimus sabbato?) De sacramentis,* 1.1.2 (SC 25bis.60); Why . . . ? *(Quare . . . ?* ibid., 1.1.3; cf. 2.2.4; 5.2.8 (SC 25bis.60, 74, 124); What does it mean? *(Quid . . . significat?)* ibid., 1.5.15; cf. 2.4.13; 3.1.3; 6.3.15 (SC 25bis.68, 78, 92, 144); What is . . . ? *(Quid est . . . ?)* ibid., 3.1.2; cf. 5.1.2 (SC 25bis.90, 124).

[92] Faller, "Ambrosius, der Verfasser von *De sacramentis*. Die innere Echtheitsgrunde," 83–85.

[93] Botte, *Des Sacrements; Des Mystères,* 15.

other works, undoubtedly because Ambrose, rereading his sermons and editing them into treatises, suppressed those too frequent transitions. For example, a preacher who repeats a phrase such as "isn't it" dozens of times in a preached sermon would not do so in a written text, especially one intended for circulation or publication. Thus, these "fillers," once judged unworthy of the great orator are, in fact, perfectly authentic.

Fifth, the views found in *De sacramentis* are consistent with Ambrose's authentic works. Consider, for example, that *De sacramentis*, 3.1.7 gives a different explanation of the washing of feet than that found in *De mysteriis*, 6.32.[94] One might conclude that either the works come from two different authors or the copyist was not satisfied with the original Ambrosian explanation. Yet, the explanation in *De sacramentis* is found in Ambrose's commentary on Psalm 48, an authentic work.[95] This is but one example; however, Botte's "Notes Critiques"[96] of *De sacramentis* shows that the entire work is dotted with Ambrosian thoughts and expressions that do not come from *De mysteriis*.

Sixth, Probst completely resolves Tillemont's objection that *De sacramentis* could not be authentic because Ambrose composed another work entitled *De sacramentis* on a different subject, and it was unheard of that the same author would publish two works on different subjects with the same title.[97] Probst concludes that Ambrose never published *De sacramentis*. These were sermons that were written by a *tachygraphos*, or stenographer. Furthermore, *De sacramentis* is not a title, properly speaking, but the first two words of the first sermon. Christine Mohrmann summarizes the characteristics of oral style found in *De sacramentis* and confirms the hypothesis that it consists of sermons taken down by a *tachygraphos*.[98] Mohrmann demonstrates that several characteristics of *De sacramentis* all point to the spontaneous character of the improvisational discourses of the bishop of Milan.[99] These

---

[94] SC 25bis.94, 172.

[95] Ibid., 96, n. 1.

[96] Botte, *Des Sacrements; Des Mystères*, 200–213.

[97] Above, 22, n. 67.

[98] Christine Mohrmann, "Le style oral du *De sacramentis* de Saint Ambrose," *Vigiliae Christianae* 6 (1952) 168–177; idem, "Observations sur le De Sacramentis et le De Mysteriis de Saint Ambroise," *Ambrosius Episcopus* (Milan: Università Cattolica del Sacro Cuore, 1978) 107–123.

[99] We will discuss Mohrmann's findings in detail in Chapter 8 when we explore Ambrose's delivery. See below, 288–293.

characteristics include the high frequency of rhetorical questions, the less literate and more conversational structure of sentences, and the presence of techniques that reflect the author's direct address of his audience.[100] As an edited version of *De sacramentis*, *De mysteriis* eliminates the mannerisms of the preacher and creates a systematic liturgical commentary.

Seventh, Botte dismisses Ceillier's conclusion that the criticism of the Greeks for communing only once a year found in *De sacramentis*[101] dates the work after the time of Chrysostom. Ceillier argued that in Chrysostom's time the Greeks did not commune that infrequently. Botte responds that we cannot know how infrequently the Greeks in Chrysostom's time communed because Chrysostom neither informs us of the extent of his congregation's infrequency nor gives us the impression that his criticism is addressed at only a few people.[102] Thus, Botte concludes that, while Ambrose may be exaggerating the situation among the Greeks, infrequency of communing was nevertheless real.

Finally, turning to the Maurists' argument that *De sacramentis* cannot be authentic because Ambrose would have never criticized the Church of Rome for not practicing footwashing, Botte argues that *De sacramentis*, 3.1.5–6 does not criticize what is done in Rome but defends what is done in Milan. "This I say not to find fault with others but to recommend my own practice."[103]

Only two scholars have objected to the Ambrosian authorship of *De sacramentis* since Atchley (1929). F.R.M. Hitchcock, attributes it to Venerius, bishop of Milan from 401 to 408.[104] Hitchcock bases this attribution on the version of the Bible cited in *De sacramentis*. Botte finds inconsistency in Hitchcock's arguments.[105] Furthermore, Hitchcock concedes that *De mysteriis* is dependent upon *De sacramentis* and consequently not more authentic. Finally, Hitchcock attributes *De sacra-*

---

[100] These techniques include recitation, placing the present verb in the prominent position, and the use of the nominal element.

[101] *De sacramentis*, 5.4.25 (SC 25bis.132).

[102] Cf. Chrysostom, *In Tim.*, hom. 5.3 (PG 62.529).

[103] SC 25bis.94. "*Hoc dico non quo alios reprehendam, sed mea officia ipse commendem.*"

[104] F.R.M. Hitchcock, "Venerius, Bishop of Milan, Probably Author of the *De sacramentis*," *Hermathena* 70 (1947) 22–38; ibid., 71 (1948) 19–35.

[105] Bernard Botte, *Bulletin de théologies ancienne et médiévale* 6 (1950) 110, n. 373.

mentis to Venerius, whom we know primarily through his epitaph but who did not leave one line written by his hand.

Most recently, the debate over the authorship of *De sacramentis* has been taken up by Klaus Gamber and Josef Schmitz.[106] Gamber points to differences between the baptismal rite and the shape of the eucharistic prayer found in *De sacramentis* and those described in the genuine writings of Saint Ambrose, particularly in *De mysteriis*. Gamber argues that the baptismal rite and eucharistic prayer found in *De sacramentis* are not those of Milan but are Roman-African in nature. Furthermore, he finds in *De sacramentis* indications that the author used as sources the "Commentary on the Symbol" of Rufinus and the "Mystagogical Catecheses" of John of Jerusalem. These works imply that *De sacramentis* was written after the time of Ambrose. According to Gamber, the undeniable resemblances to *De mysteriis* are accounted for by Nicetas of Remesiana, whom he considers to be the author, using this treatise as one of his sources. Finally, Gamber compares *De sacramentis* with the works of Nicetas and finds a similarity in style. Schmitz has convincingly shown that Gamber's conclusions rest upon a contestable methodology, particularly Gamber's reconstruction of the works of Nicetas.[107]

Thus, current scholarship overwhelmingly concludes that *De sacramentis* is an authentic work of Ambrose that must be placed before *De mysteriis*. We have already noted that other works of Ambrose are edited versions of his sermons and bear traces of their origin. The difference is that while for these works we no longer possess the preached sermons on which they were based, in the case of *De mysteriis* the preached sermons have been preserved for us in *De sacramentis*.

---

[106] See above, 14, n. 40. Gamber, *Die Autorschaft von De Sacramentis* and "Nochmals zur Frage der Autorschaft von De Sacramentis"; Schmitz, "Zum Autor der Schrift 'De Sacramentis.'"

[107] Schmitz, "Zum Autor der Schrift 'De Sacramentis,'" 59.

Chapter 2

"Having been renewed by baptism, hold fast to the style of life that befits those who have been washed clean": Setting the Stage

"Having been renewed by baptism, hold fast to the style of life that befits those who have been washed clean."[1] Perhaps these words from *De mysteriis* strike us as pious, theological, and generic. Yet, for Ambrose they are realistic, concrete, and specific. These words constitute the exhortation of a particular preacher addressing specific *neophytes* in order to help them discover the meaning of the unique rites of initiation in which they have participated. The point we are making is that in order to fully understand and appreciate these words in particular and mystagogical preaching generally, we must understand the influences that formed the preacher, the real-life circumstances of the listeners, and the particular celebration of the rites of initiation being explained.

In our next chapter, Chapter 3, we will explore the influences that shaped Ambrose as a preacher and the influence that Ambrose as preacher brought to his preaching on the sacraments. In Chapter 4 we will discuss how the *neophytes* of Milan as listeners both impacted and were impacted by Ambrose's mystagogical preaching. In Chapter 5 we will present the rites of initiation as the text on which the sermons contained in *De sacramentis* are based. In order to set the stage for these discussions, we include this chapter, a historical narrative on Ambrose and the church of Milan, in our study.

This chapter is not intended to provide a detailed biography of Ambrose's life or a complete history of the church of Milan in the

---

[1] *De mysteriis*, 1.2 (SC 25bis.156).

fourth century. Many biographers of Saint Ambrose have successfully undertaken these tasks.[2] Rather, we will draw upon their work in order to present the backdrop to Ambrose's mystagogy. Thus, whereas the purpose of Angelo Paredi's biography of Ambrose is to "spread the fame of one who strove strenuously for the good, especially through the example of his own life, and who lived in an age no less tragic than our own,"[3] and the goal of Neil McLynn's biography is "to relate the form and convention of Ambrose's 'portraiture' to the vicissitudes of his career,"[4] our purpose in this chapter is to review the major events of Ambrose's life and ministry with an eye to how they inform his preaching on the sacraments. In this way our historical narrative will provide the frame of reference from which to understand *De sacramentis* and *De mysteriis*. By reading this chapter in its entirety, the reader will be prepared to explore how Ambrose as a preacher impacted his preaching on the sacraments and how the *neophytes* of Milan as listeners both shaped and were shaped by their mystagogical instruction. Alternatively, the reader might use this narrative as a reference tool when reading subsequent chapters in order to learn more about subjects of interest, to clarify points made, or to answer questions that arise. In order to facilitate using this chapter as a reference tool, our narrative, while chronological, is subdivided according to subject headings.

---

[2] For biographical material on Ambrose see Hans Freiherr von Campenhausen, "Ambrosius," in *Latienische Kirchenväter*, 2nd rev. ed. (Stuttgart: W. Kohlhammer, 1965) 77–108; idem, *Ambrosius von Miland als Kirchenpolitker* (Berlin and Leipzig: W. de Gruyter, 1929); Frederick Homes Dudden, *The Life and Times of St. Ambrose*, 2 vols. (Oxford: Clarendon Press, 1935); Maria Grazia Mara, "Ambrose of Milan," *Patrology* 4, ed. Angelo di Bernardino, English translation by Placid Solari (Westminster, Md.: Christian Classics, 1994) 144–179; Neil B. McLynn, *Ambrose of Milan: Church and Court in a Christian Capital* (Berkeley and Los Angeles: University of California Press, 1994); Jean Rémy Palanque, *Saint Ambroise et l'Empire romain* (Paris: E. de Boccard, 1933); John Moorhead, *Ambrose: Church and Society in the Late Roman World* (London and New York: Longman, 1999); Angelo Paredi, *Saint Ambrose: His Life and Times*, trans. M. Joseph Costelloe (Notre Dame: University of Notre Dame Press, 1964); Boniface Ramsey, *Ambrose* (New York: Routledge, 1997); Daniel H. Williams, *Ambrose of Milan and the End of the Nicene-Arian Conflicts* (Oxford: Clarendon Press, 1995).

[3] Paredi, *Saint Ambrose: His Life and Times*, vi.

[4] McLynn, *Ambrose of Milan: Church and Court in a Christian Capital*, xviii.

BIRTH, FAMILY, AND FAITH FORMATION

Ambrose was born in Trier, in present-day Germany, probably in 339.[5] According to Paulinus,[6] Ambrose's father, who was also named Ambrose, was the praetorian prefect, or governor, of Gaul and therefore responsible for a vast territory, which he administered from Trier, a city famous for its size and beauty and as the residence of emperors and the political capital of the empire north and west of the Alps.[7] Ambrose's family was both Roman and distinguished, providing the empire with consuls and prefects and the Church with at least one martyr, a virgin named Soteris.[8] We know nothing of Ambrose's father except the office that he is said to have held and that he died while Ambrose was relatively young,[9] leaving behind a wife, who is

---

[5] The date, which is disputed, is suggested by a reference in *Epistola* 49 (Maur. 59).4 (CSEL 82/2.55), in which Ambrose speaks of being fifty-three years old at the time of some barbarian unrest that several scholars claim can be situated in 392. See Homes Dudden, *The Life and Times of Saint Ambrose*, 1:2, n. 2 (Note that scholarly works on Ambrose refer to this author equally as "Dudden" and "Homes Dudden." We are following the example of Harmless and McLynn). For different dates for Ambrose's birth see Emilien Lamirande, *Paulin de Milan et la "Vita Ambrosii"* (Paris and Montreal: Desclée/Bellarmin, 1983) 45, n. 2. Ambrose's letters are cited according to the CSEL edition. The enumeration of the Maurist edition is provided in parentheses.

[6] The only extant source for Ambrose's early years is the *Vita Ambrosii* composed by his secretary Paulinus in 422. For discussion of the literary genre and historical context of this work, see Homes Dudden, *The Life and Times of Saint Ambrose*, 1:715; Paulinus of Milan, *Vita di Sant'Ambrogio*, ed. Marco Navoni (Milan: Edizioni San Paolo, 1996) 15–48 (hereafter Navoni); Palanque, *Saint Ambroise et l'Empire romain*, 409–416; M. Pellegrino, in *La Scuola Cattolica* 79 (1951) 151–162; Williams, *Ambrose of Milan and the End of the Nicene-Arian Conflicts*, 105–109.

[7] Ambrose's father's actual position has been questioned on the ground that there is no evidence of his prefecture apart from Paulinus. See Lamirande, *Paulin de Milan et la "Vita Ambrosii,"* 45, n. 2. For a description of Trier at the time of Ambrose, see Moorhead, *Ambrose: Church and Society in the Late Roman World*, 20–21.

[8] *Exhortatio virginitatis*, 12.82 (PL 16.360); *De virginibus*, 3.7.38 (Cazzaniga, 75). On Ambrose's family, see also Homes Dudden, *The Life and Times of Saint Ambrose*, 1:2, n. 3.

[9] McLynn argues that the timing of the elder Ambrose's death suggests a connection with Constantine II's disastrous invasion of the Italian territory of his brother Constans in 340. See McLynn, *Ambrose of Milan: Church and Court in a Christian Capital*, 32.

unnamed, and three children—an older daughter named Marcellina, an older son named Satyrus, and Ambrose.

At some point in Ambrose's youth, perhaps as the result of his father's death, the family moved to Rome.[10] Ambrose remained in Rome from 340 to about 365, that is, for all of his childhood.[11] During these years Ambrose's sister Marcellina formally embraced the ascetic life. Ambrose indicates that Marcellina made public profession of her virginity "on the birthday of the Savior" in the Basilica of Saint Peter, in the presence of Bishop Liberius.[12] Ambrose calls Soteris, the virgin martyr who had died at the beginning of the century in the Great Persecution of Diocletian and whom his family claimed as a member, the inspiration for his sister's profession of virginity and his personal example.[13] After taking the veil, Marcellina remained at home and, joined by her mother and another consecrated virgin, lived a routine of strenuous asceticism, which consisted of seclusion, study, devotional exercises, good works, and visits from the clergy.[14] Paulinus tells of young Ambrose mimicking these guests by presenting his hand to be kissed by the women of the house.[15]

Marcellina's profession of virginity throws into relief the piety of the household in which Ambrose was raised. To practice the Christian faith publicly would risk Ambrose's future career in public life. In Italy pagan worship remained an active part of public life until the last

---

[10] Paulinus, *Vita Ambrosii*, 3 (Navoni, 52).

[11] Ibid., 4 (Navoni, 56).

[12] *De virginibus*, 3.1.1 (Cazzaniga, 57). Ramsey dates this event in the period from 352 to 354, since Liberius was elected bishop in May 352 and was forcibly removed from Rome by the Arian emperor Constantius II not long before Christmas 355. Liberius did not return to his see until 358, when Ambrose would have been nineteen according to most calculations, and too old for his mother and his sister, by then already a virgin, to declare, as Paulinus says, that he was "'a young man who did not know what he was talking about,' when he would joke with them that he was going to become a bishop (cf. 4)." Ramsey, *Ambrose*, 17. Homes Dudden and Paredi state that the year was 353. Cf. Homes Dudden, *The Life and Times of Saint Ambrose*, 1:3; Paredi, *Saint Ambrose: His Life and Times*, 22.

[13] *De virginibus*, 3.7.38 (Cazzaniga, 75); *Exhortatio virginitatis*, 12.82 (PL 16.360). McLynn questions whether Soteris was, in fact, related to Ambrose's family. See McLynn, *Ambrose of Milan: Church and Court in a Christian Capital*, 34–35.

[14] Homes Dudden, *The Life and Times of Saint Ambrose*, 1:4.

[15] Paulinus, *Vita Ambrosii*, 4 (Navoni, 56).

decades of the fourth century. A public career included both sacrifice and attendance at the gladiatorial games. As long as they wished to remain in public life, Christian noblemen were unwilling to commit themselves to the interests and controls of the Church. They were content to become catechumens and to appear irregularly, if at all, in church.

Thus, for Ambrose, the *cubiculum*, the inner bedroom of the house, rendered sacred by the presence of Marcellina and her companion, was the wilderness in which he found holiness as he grew to adulthood.[16] That Marcellina had a major influence on Ambrose is revealed by the fact that we know of some of his most heroic confrontations with the emperors in Milan only because he wrote about them in great detail to Marcellina, whom he called "my lady, my sister, dearer to me than life and my very eyes."[17] Ambrose's relationship with Marcellina explains his own fascination with the virginal life, consistently holding celibacy up as a higher form of life, particularly suited to the Christian ideal. Ambrose himself never married when he was elected bishop in his mid-thirties; for him to have remained unmarried was an uncommon occurrence in Roman society. After his ordination he wrote no fewer than four treatises on the topic of virginity, frequently referring to it elsewhere. Ambrose's brother Satyrus also remained unmarried, and in his funeral sermon for him, Ambrose praises his brother's chastity.[18] It is certainly noteworthy that all three offspring of a widowed mother would elect to live as celibates.

From the evidence available to us, we can conclude that Ambrose's family was Catholic[19] as well as ascetic. The sermon preached by Bishop Liberius when Marcellina professed virginity was punctuated with Trinitarian doctrine that was unmistakably Nicene. The involvement of the bishop of Rome in the life of Ambrose's family indicates

---

[16] In *De institutione virginis*, 1.7 (PL 16.307) Ambrose explains that the bedroom stands for the inner life.

[17] *Epistola* 77 (Maur. 22) (CSEL 82/3.126–140).

[18] *De excessu fratris*, 1.52 (CSEL 73.237).

[19] The patristic use of both "Arian" and "Catholic" is propagandist. The terms *homoean* and *Nicene* are more accurate. Nicene refers to adherence to the doctrine of one substance shared by Father and Son, as embodied in the Creed of Nicaea. Homoeans rejected this doctrine in favor of the belief that the two Persons are similar, *homoioi*. Neither term designates a united and organized movement.

that it belonged to Liberius's inner circle and was therefore Nicene. From Rome Ambrose witnessed the disruptions in the Church that resulted from the Arian conflict—the Council of Milan (355), the exile of Bishop Dionysius, and the imperial campaign against and eventual kidnaping and exile of Bishop Liberius.[20] Ambrose's intervention in the episcopal election that resulted in his becoming bishop,[21] as well as his firmness in matters of faith when he as bishop assumed the role of a high-level defender of orthodoxy,[22] may reflect this earlier experience. This experience may also explain why Ambrose's brother Satyrus was baptized with the stipulation that the rites be performed by a bishop who was in agreement with the Catholic bishops[23] and why Ambrose "asked to be baptized by no one but a Catholic bishop, for he was wary of the treachery of the Arians."[24]

EDUCATION

In Rome Ambrose was "educated in the liberal studies"[25] and trained in law. His education included extensive training in rhetoric, because in the fourth century rhetoric was the key to wealth and power. "Rhetoric remained the 'Queen of subjects' because it dealt with what mattered in the public life of late antiquity—with the manner in which notables related, face to face through the spoken word, with their official superiors, with their peers, and with those subject to their power and protection."[26] Those who passed through the school of a rhetor were considered to have developed a more active intelligence, a more refined speech, and a more harmonious and impressive bearing than anyone else, characteristics that would cause them to stand out for the rest of their lives.[27] Those trained in rhetoric "were expected to carry into the public world an uncanny ability to 'charm,' even to 'overawe' through speech."[28]

---

[20] McLynn, *Ambrose of Milan: Church and Court in a Christian Capital*, 36–37; Williams, *Ambrose of Milan and the End of the Nicene-Arian Conflicts*, 52–59.

[21] See below, 44–47.

[22] See below, 51–57.

[23] *De excessu fratris*, 1.47 (CSEL 73.235).

[24] Paulinus, *Vita Ambrosii*, 9 (Navoni, 62).

[25] Ibid., 5 (Navoni, 56).

[26] Peter Brown, *Power and Persuasion in Late Antiquity: Toward a Christian Empire* (Madison, Wis.: University of Wisconsin Press, 1992) 42.

[27] Ibid., 41.

[28] Ibid., 44.

In the grammar school in Rome (the equivalent of our high school), Ambrose took up the liberal arts, which were the regular course of studies for a youth at that time. They consisted primarily, if not exclusively, in the development of oratorical skills and in the appreciation of a limited number of classics written by the great Greek and Latin authors.[29] Ambrose not only learned diction and grammatical construction but was also trained in pronunciation and spelling, with the teacher concentrating on explaining types of error. In studying the poets, lessons consisted not only in reading aloud but also in the detailed exposition of the master. In the rhetorical school, the poets, like the historians and orators, were perused with the objective of eliciting and imitating those features of style and treatment that were likely to be useful to the future orator.[30]

After completing grammar school, Ambrose entered a school of rhetoric until he was at least twenty years old. In the rhetorical school the theory of eloquence and oratory composition were taught. The instructors lectured on the textbooks, especially those of Cicero and Quintilian, and on the best models of oratory. For their part, students first practiced writing on given themes, paying particular attention to arrangement and style. They would then work on delivering speeches, first of legendary or historical figures in critical situations and then of legal arguments in supposed civil or criminal trials. They recited their speeches before their teacher and the class, who criticized their performance.[31] In Rome students in the school of rhetoric also translated texts from Greek into Latin.[32]

Ambrose's rhetorical training was further refined when he devoted the next four to five years to the unremitting study of Roman law.[33]

---

[29] Homer and Virgil were chief among the authors that Ambrose studied. In many of his later works Ambrose shows that he was very familiar with Virgil, Cicero, Sallust, and Seneca, and, among the Greeks, Homer, Plato, and Xenophon. His quotations from Sophocles and Euripides, however, were taken from Plato. For Ambrose's quotations and imitations of the classical Greek and Latin authors, see the indices to his works in the CSEL. Paredi reports that Ambrose was particularly familiar with Virgil, quoting him only three times but constantly imitating him. Paredi, *Saint Ambrose: His Life and Times*, 382, n. 14.

[30] Stanley Bonner, *Education in Ancient Rome* (Berkeley: University of California Press, 1977) 189, 212–213.

[31] Ibid., 250.

[32] Ibid., 251.

[33] C. Pharr, "Roman Legal Education," *The Classical Journal* 34 (1939) 265.

The *juris prudens* was one who knew all the laws, the customs, the rules of procedure, the whole system of precedents that could be referred to in order to support a case by analogies from the past or by tradition. The *juris prudens* could cite the law, applying "all this vast knowledge, all the material furnished by his erudition and memory, to any individual case. [The *juris prudens*] could discern at once what category it belonged to, and suggest the perfect solution, that pierced through the difficulties of the case and the ambiguity of the law."[34] The rhetoric of the lawyer was further enhanced by the belief that his wisdom was based on an elevated sense of justice, goodness, and order.

THE GOVERNOR AND HIS CITY

In about 365, having completed their education, Ambrose and Satyrus left Rome to begin legal careers at Sirmium. There they practiced in the court of the praetorian prefect of Italy, Valcatius Rufinus, and quickly gained attention because of the brilliance of their oratory.[35] In 368 Rufinus died and Sextus Anicius Petronius Probus, a monumental figure in the life of the Western empire in the second half of the fourth century, was appointed praetorian prefect. Probus was impressed with Ambrose and appointed him his counsel or legal advisor. Sometime after that Probus was instrumental in having Ambrose, now not much older than thirty, raised to the rank of consular and made governor of Aemelia-Liguria, with Milan as his place of residence.[36]

Until the last decade of the third century, Milan was a respectable county seat, a commercial and administrative center similar to towns all over the empire.[37] "Situated on the crossroads of the great east-west and north-south highways from the Balkans to Gaul and from Africa and Rome to the Alpine passes and the Rhineland, it was strategically

---

[34] Henri-Irénée Marrou, *A History of Education in Antiquity*, trans. George Lamb (Madison, Wis.: University of Wisconsin Press, 1982) 289.

[35] Paulinus, *Vita Ambrosii*, 5 (Navoni, 56); Ambrose, *De excessu fratris*, 1.49 (CSEL 72.235).

[36] Paulinus, *Vita Ambrosii*, 5 (Navoni, 56). For a discussion of Ambrose's reflections on his service as governor, see Andrew Lenox-Conyngham, "The Judgement of Ambrose the Bishop on Ambrose the Roman Governor," *Studia Patristica* 17, Part 1, ed. E. Livingstone (Oxford: Pergamon Press, 1983) 62–65.

[37] On Milan at the time of Saint Ambrose, see Marta Sordi, "Milano al Tempo di Agostino," *Agostino a Milano: Il Battesimo: Agostino nelle Terre di Ambrogio*, ed. M. Sordi (Palermo: Edizioni Augustinus, 1988) 13–23, particularly 13–16.

located both to encounter the increasing threats from the barbarians across the Rhine and the Tweed and to maintain communications between the eastern and western halves of the Empire."[38] Thus, around A.D. 300 the town was architecturally transformed into an imperial city.[39] Milan was enlarged toward the northeast and provided with new walls, a large bath—the thermae Herculianae, a circus located at the southern edge of town, and a palace presumably nearby. The road out of town toward Rome was flanked for a mile's length by colonnaded porticoes similar to those of Thessalonica and other imperial capitals in the East. Outside town, as custom required, and inside a fortified precinct, Maximiam built his mausoleum.

The most complete description of imperial Milan comes from the Roman poet Ausonius (c. 310–c. 395), who passed through Milan in 379 upon his return from Rome to Bordeaux. In his *Ordo urbium nobilium* Ausonius ranks Milan as the seventh city of the Roman world, describing it in poetic terms:

"At Milan there are all sorts of wonderful things—an abundance of goods, innumerable elegant homes, men of marvelous eloquence and pleasing manners. Moreover, the beauty of the place is accentuated by a double wall. And there are a circus, which is the people's delight, the wedge-shaped bulk of the theater, the temples,[40] the bulwarks of the

---

[38] Richard Krautheimer, *Three Christian Capitals* (Berkeley: University of California Press, 1983) 69.

[39] Ibid., 69–70.

[40] Though Ausonius was nominally a Christian, his works are almost completely pagan in character, as is evident particularly in the obscene nuptial canto that he made up from lines drawn from Virgil. His reference to temples in his description of Milan should therefore be understood as referring to pagan rather than Christian structures. In the Archeological Museum there are some thirty marble statues of pagan deities. More than a third of the extant votive inscriptions are dedicated to Jupiter. There are six dedicated to the *Matronae*, divinities of Celtic origin worshiped in Northern Italy before the advent of the Romans.[1] Of the remaining inscriptions, three are dedicated to Hercules, two to Mercury, and one to Minerva. Among the Milanese inscriptions referring to priestly offices, there is one of a pontiff who was at the same time an employee of the city, another of a pontiff who was also a decurion, another of a flamen of Titus, another of a flamen of Trajan, another of a priest for the worship of Augustus and Rome, another of a priest for the youth of Milan, and still others of the same kind. Six inscriptions refer to the cult of Cybele, the Great Idaean

palace, the splendid mint, the district that is celebrated because of the Baths of Hercules, all the colonnades adorned with marble statues, the encircling defenses that are banked up at the city's edge. All these things, which rival each other, so to speak, by their massive workmanship, are of surpassing excellence, and the proximity of Rome does not detract from them."[41]

In his description of Milan, Ausonius fails to mention an amphitheater, one of the most popular places of amusement in a typical Roman town.[42] Yet we know that such a structure must have existed from

---

Mother. Albucia Magiana left a sum of money to thedendrophori, the cannophori, and the Martenses. The first two of these three sacred colleges took part in the processions in honor of Cybele on March 15 and 22. There was at least one Mithraeurn in imperial Milan, as there was in all of the cities of the Late Empire where troops were stationed. Evidence for this is found in the inscription of Publius Acilius Pisonianus. He had been a *pater patratus*, that is, a high dignitary in the cult of Mithra, and he states that at his own expense he had reconstructed a Mithraeum and a Mithraic grotto that had been destroyed by fire on land purchased at public expense. A damaged inscription refers to a certain Gaius Gallio Atticus, who in a solemn rite had sought the divine will by casting lots. Ambrose warned his flock about the malice of such practices. Cf. *Enarrationes in xii psalmos davidicos*, 39.4 (CSEL 64.215).

[1] J. Vendyres, "La religion des Celtes," in *La religions de l'Europe ancienne* (Paris, 1948) 3:276.

[41] Peiper, *Ordo urbium nobilium* (Leipzig, 1886) 146:
    Et Mediolani mira omnia: copia rerum,
    innumerae cultaeque domus, facunda virorum
    ingenia, et mores laeti, tum duplice muro
    amplificata loci species, populique voluptas,
    circus et inclusi moles cuneata theatri;
    templa, Palatinaeque arces, opulensque moneta,
    et regio Herculei celebris sub honore lavacri,
    cunctaque marmoreis ornata peristyla signis,
    moeniaque in valli formam circumdata limbo,
    omnia quae magnis operum velut aemula formis
    excellunt, nec iuncta premit vicinia Romae.
English translation as cited in Ramsey, *Ambrose*, 21. See Calderini, *La "Forma Urbis Mediolani" nell'anno bimillenario di Augusto* (Milan: Ceschina, 1937).

[42] Idem, *L'Anfiteatro romano* (Milan: Ceschina, 1940); A. de Capitani d'Arzago, *Il Circo romano* (Milan: Ceschina, 1939).

references in Paulinus,[43] an epitaph of the gladiator Urbicus,[44] from a street well known as the Via Arena, and from possible references to an amphitheater in the writings of Saint Ambrose.[45]

As with many other cities in antiquity, it is not easy to determine the population of Milan during the fourth century. The walls of the city were two and one half miles in circumference and embraced an area of approximately two hundred and seventy-five acres. Claudius Mamertinus, in an oration in honor of Maximian, mentions the large crowds that gathered to watch the passage of Diocletian and Maximian in a carriage through the streets of the city.[46] From isolated data such as this, A. De Marchi has concluded that there were probably about 130,000 people living in Milan.[47] While we cannot know the exact number, what is certain is that the establishment of the imperial court there brought an influx of thousands. The posts in the imperial bureaucracy and army had to be staffed with many different kinds of people. There was also a flourishing labor class,[48] and then as now, Milan was an important center of commerce and trade.[49] Milan was

---

[43] Paulinus, *Vita Ambrosii*, 34 (Navoni, 112).

[44] See A. De Marchi, *Antiche epigrafi di Milano* (Milan, 1917) 83.

[45] *Enarrationes in xii psalmos davidicos*, 39.4 (CSEL 64.215); *Expositio in Psalmum cxviii*, 16.45 (CSEL 62.376).

[46] Claudius Mamertinus, *Panegyricus genethliacus Maximiano Augusto dictus II*, in G. Baehrens, *XII Panegyrici latini* (Leipzig, 1911) 284; see also 295.

[47] De Marchi, *Antiche epigrafi di Milano*, 316.

[48] The relatively few Milanese inscriptions frequently mention the *fabri* and the *centonarii*. The former were employed in the construction of buildings, and the latter made the awnings, which were soaked in vinegar and water to put out fires. This corporation was divided into twelve centuries, which were in turn divided into decuries. The metalworkers, or those employed in the treasury, were enrolled in a third corporation, which was also divided into twelve centuries.

[49] There is still extant the epitaph of a businessman who had interests on both sides of the Alps and who was at the same time the patron of the boatmen of Como. Another merchant from Apulia dealt in military cloaks, and another from Ravenna was a wholesaler of shoes. Publius Julius Macedon traded in cloth and skins. There was also a merchant from Metz who specialized in cloth for the army. Finally, there is the epitaph of a distinguished citizen who made his fortune as a banker. These various activities lead us to conclude that Milan was a center of foreign as well as local trade. Among the inscriptions there are also references to *sagarii*, or *castrensiarii*, the makers of military

also famous for its schools.[50] Peter Brown's description of fourth-century Milan provides a vivid snapshot of life in the city:

"Milan was the political capital of an important part of the Western Empire. A typical residence of Emperors in this time of constant emergency, it owed its importance to its strategic position on the roads leading over the Alps. Diplomats and secret agents came there from as far apart as Trier, to the North, and Persia, to the East. The barbarian soldiers around the palace would have been a sinister reminder of a strange, untamed world beyond the Alps. Only wooden stockades on the passes into modern Jugoslavia stood between this prosperous new city and barbarian warbands that would soon wander with impunity throughout the Balkans.

A brilliant society had grown up around the court. Poets would come to Milan from as far away as Alexandria, and the works of Greek philosophers would be read both by the clergy of the Milanese church and by great landowners in villas within sight of the Alps. Such would study the revived philosophy of Plato; they would write both classical metre and on the nature of the universe. Even the Catholicism of the town was eminently respectable: the sermons of Ambrose were "learned," his major work was modeled carefully on Cicero, his ideas betrayed the influence of contemporary exponents of Plato. Even the sarcophagi of such Christians show an exquisite classical taste."[51]

---

cloaks. Milan was an important textile center in the fourth century, as it was during the Middle Ages and still is today. Another inscription refers to a corporation of muleteers of the Porta Vercellina, and Jovia. Justus, a shoemaker of the *gens Atilia*, in addition to his name, left a picture of his worktable on his epitaph. Under the arch of the east gate one can still see the dyer or tailor of the family of the Novellii cutting a piece of cloth, the emblem of his trade. Other examples of this type can be found in epitaphs preserved in the Archeological Museum at Milan. On the tomb of his freedman, a patron wrote: "His poorest works equaled the best of other artisans, and no one could equal what he himself did well." Such esteem for manual labor indicates a society in which work was no longer despised, as it had been in ancient Rome, but regarded rather as a source of wealth and honor.

[50] Virgil left Mantua to complete his studies in this city. In a number of places in the *Confessions*, Augustine describes his own career as a professor of rhetoric in Milan.

[51] Peter Brown, *Augustine of Hippo: A Biography* (Berkeley: University of California Press, 1967) 71–72.

As governor, Ambrose's primary responsibilities were enforcing the law, supervising the collection of taxes, maintaining order, and representing "the savage and relentless face of the late Roman judiciary."[52] Ambrose's rhetorical skills were an essential tool as he carried out these duties.[53] The centralization of power in the emperor afforded governors relatively little prestige or initiative and even less coercive power in terms of directing either the army or even their own permanent staff. Imperial honors, conferred directly from the court, protected many local elites from the governor's authority. Most serious of all, representatives of the empire could never be certain that their authority would be upheld by those who had sent them. The governor therefore needed the authority of well-established local figures in order to bolster his own authority for both the collection of taxes and the maintenance of law and order. Rather than functioning autocratically, the governor was one participant among many in a shifting local situation. A governor worked most effectively through alliances with local factions. This situation was further complicated by the fact that no governor could be certain that any one alliance would endure, for there were so many groups that he might offend. Local notables could quietly but persistently withdraw their collaboration and support, rendering the governor ineffective. These ever-changing circumstances

"created a strictly delineated, but constant, role for the use of a language of persuasion. Far from being rendered unnecessary by the autocratic structure of late Roman government, rhetoric positively throve in its many intricacies. For rhetoric transformed the creaking of an unwieldy political organism into elevating, classical music. It presented educated contemporaries with the potent image of a political world held together, not by force, collusion, and favoritism, but by *logoi*, by the sure working, ancient magic of Greek words. . . . Governors did not seek allies or respect vested interests out of fear of isolation or from an instinctive sense that the late Roman tax system worked best through collusion with the rich. They did so because their own high culture enabled them to see, in the local notables . . . their 'natural' friends and soul mates."[54]

---

[52] McLynn, *Ambrose of Milan: Church and Court in a Christian Capital*, 5.

[53] In the following discussion I am indebted to Brown, *Power and Persuasion in Late Antiquity*, 23–31.

[54] Ibid., 30.

Above all, rhetoric enabled successful factions to celebrate their victories. In a political system where change occurred through the manipulation of factions and networks of patronage, rhetoric served to add momentum to these slow-working factors and to pronounce the wisdom of a change after it had been implemented.

ELECTION AS BISHOP

The details of Ambrose's election as bishop of Milan are well known and have been widely discussed.[55] When Ambrose came to Milan, the church there was governed by Auxentius. "A Cappadocian by birth and an Arian by conviction, [Auxentius] had early attached himself to the circle of Court clergy that surrounded the Emperor Constantius. When, in A.D. 355, Dionysius, the orthodox Bishop of Milan, was sent into exile, [Auxentius] was nominated by the Emperor to the vacant see."[56] Auxentius then successfully used diplomacy, moderation, and tact to win over the general population of Milan, so that only the strict Catholics remained unreconciled to their new bishop.[57]

---

[55] Paulinus, *Vita Ambrosii*, 6–9 (Navoni, 58–66); Yves-Marie Duval, "Ambroise, de son élection à sa consécration," in *Ambrosius Episcopus: atti del Congresso internazionale di studi ambrosiani nel XVI centenario della elevazione di sant'Ambrogio alla cattedra episcopale, Milano, 2–7 dicembre 1974*, ed. G. Lazzati (Milan: Vita e pensiero, 1976) 2:243–283; Otto Faller, "La date della consacrazione vescovile de sant'Ambrogio," in *Ambrosiana: scritti di storia, archeologia ed arte pubblicati nel XVI centenario della nascita di sant'Ambrogio, CCCXL–MCMXL*, ed. Arturo Faccioli (Milan: Biblioteca ambrosiana, 1942) 97–112; F. L. Ganshof, "Note sur l'élection de évêques dans l'empire romain au IVe et pendant le première moitié du Vme siècle," in *Revue internationale des droits de l'Antiquité* 4 (*Mélanges Vissher* 3, 1950) 467–498; Roger Gryson, "Les élections épiscopales en Occident au IVe siècle," in *Revue d'Histoire Ecclésiastique* 75 (1980) 257–283; Homes Dudden, *The Life and Times of Saint Ambrose*, 1:66; McLynn, *Ambrose of Milan: Church and Court in a Christian Capital*, 1–52; Paredi, *Saint Ambrose: His Life and Times*, 116–121; Moorhead, *Ambrose: Church and Society in the Late Roman World*, 15–19; 23–25; Williams, *Ambrose of Milan and the End of the Nicene-Arian Conflicts*, 112–114.

[56] Homes Dudden, *The Life and Times of Saint Ambrose*, 1:64.

[57] Ibid., 1:65. McLynn gives two reasons that the people of Milan would be reconciled to Auxentius. First, Valentinian I, who arrived in Milan in the summer of 364 and remained there for a year, publicly endorsed Auxentius while expelling Hilary, the spokesman for Nicene Christianity, from the city.

Probably in October 373, Auxentius died.⁵⁸ By this time, Dionysius was also dead, making it necessary to elect a new bishop. The Catholics were determined to capture the bishopric; the Arians were equally determined to retain it. A meeting for the election was held in the cathedral.⁵⁹ Fearing that the crowd might erupt in violence, Ambrose, in his official capacity as governor, went to the cathedral to maintain order.⁶⁰ While he was speaking to the people, a voice cried out, "Ambrose Bishop!"⁶¹ The whole congregation took up the cry as Catholics and Arians alike acclaimed Ambrose bishop.⁶²

Second, McLynn argues that Auxentius was in all likelihood the first bishop to perform his duties in Milan's Constantinian basilica, a magnificent setting that served to raise his status in the community. McLynn, *Ambrose of Milan: Church and Court in a Christian Capital*, 24–31.

⁵⁸ Homes Dudden, *The Life and Times of Saint Ambrose*, 1:66, n. 1.

⁵⁹ McLynn argues that "contested" elections seldom saw competing parties assemble together, especially when issues of doctrine were at stake. He points us to the work of R. Lane Fox, *Pagans and Christians* (Harmondsworth, Middlesex, 1986; New York: Viking, 1986) 511. Instead, all elections were designed to be "unanimous" in order to give the appointee a "mandate." Thus the Arians assembled to elect a bishop. If the Catholics were present, they were there as intruders. McLynn, *Ambrose of Milan: Church and Court in a Christian Capital*, 9–10.

⁶⁰ McLynn sees the Catholics as the guilty party in any insurgency that may have occurred, and Ambrose's response to potential violence as curious. Normal procedure would have been to single out an individual for exemplary punishment and not the governor appealing to the crowd. McLynn cites Ammianus, *Marc.*, 15.7.4, and the fact that ecclesiastical disputes threaten neither the state nor its representatives. McLynn therefore understands Ambrose's speech to the crowd not as a plea for compromise and peace but as a highly controversial assertion of the equal status of the two parties, which assisted the Catholics in the election. Ibid., 8–10.

⁶¹ Paulinus says that it was the voice of a child. Cf. Paulinus, *Vita Ambrosii*, 6 (Navoni, 58).

⁶² McLynn argues that the people's unanimous acclamation of Ambrose as bishop was not, as historians have suggested, "an overwhelming wave of popular support [for] an authentically—and exceptionally—'democratic candidate' [but] . . . a quite ordinary feature of episcopal elections, and of public life in general." Furthermore, the acclamation that Ambrose received was not the united voice of the people but that of a vocal Catholic minority. McLynn, *Ambrose of Milan: Church and Court in a Christian Capital*, 7, 44.

For his part Ambrose, who was still a catechumen, did not want to be bishop.[63] Paulinus records Ambrose's attempts to escape this honor. Ambrose first tried to tarnish his reputation by using torture to examine witnesses in his capacity as judge and by openly inviting prostitutes into his home. He then proposed to remove himself from public life for the tranquil life of the philosopher. When these efforts failed, Ambrose fled the city by night.[64] Caught by the people, Ambrose was taken into custody.[65] A report of Ambrose's election was sent to the emperor, Valentinian I. While the people awaited word from Valentinian, Ambrose fled again, this time to the estate of a noble named Leontius. When word came of the emperor's approval of Ambrose's election, along with an edict threatening anyone who hid Ambrose with arrest and confiscation of property, Leontius turned Ambrose over to the people.[66]

Whether these incidents actually occurred as Paulinus reports them, as scholars today think,[67] is beside the point. Paulinus was using the literary theme of resistance to show that Ambrose was chosen by God to be bishop of Milan.[68] That Ambrose himself understood his election as a divine call is evident from his treatise *De officiis ministrorum*, in which he describes himself as "carried off from the judgment seat, and the garb [*infulis*] of office, to enter on the

---

[63] *De officiis ministrorum*, 1.1.2 (PL 16.23); *Epistola* 14 (Maur. 63).65 (CSEL 82/3.269).

[64] Paulinus, *Vita Ambrosii*, 7 (Navoni, 60).

[65] McLynn argues that the "populace" who pursued their governor so energetically were not, in fact, the two Christian congregations of Milan, now fused together by their enthusiasm for Ambrose, but the same group of Catholics that had acclaimed him in the cathedral. Thus Paulinus describes the process by which Ambrose's election assumed the *appearance* of unanimity. McLynn, *Ambrose of Milan: Church and Court in a Christian Capital*, 44ff.

[66] Paulinus, *Vita Ambrosii*, 8 (Navoni, 60).

[67] These incidents were until recently regarded as hagiographical exaggeration. However, recent scholarship has convincingly argued that Paulinus's account of Ambrose's attempts to avoid episcopal election is too circumstantial and provides too much potentially damaging material against the bishop for it not to be accurate. Duval, "Ambroise, de son élection," 243–283.

[68] Resisting ecclesiastical office is a common feature of the biographies of saints. Cf. Pierre Courcelle, *Recherches sur saint Ambroise: "Vies" Anciennes, Culture, Iconographie* (Paris: Études Augustiniennes, 1973) 10ff.

priesthood."[69] Thus Paulinus reports that Ambrose then recognized his election as God's will and that he could no longer resist it.[70]

In a letter to Valentinian II, Ambrose himself reports that Valentinian I had assured him that if he accepted the office, the emperor would guarantee religious peace in Milan.[71] Convinced that his election was God's will and relying on Valentinian's assurance, Ambrose consented to his election but insisted that the bishop who baptized him be a Catholic. Although this condition was agreed to, when Ambrose sought to delay his ordination in order to adhere to the Nicene canon that forbade the ordination of neophytes, he was flatly refused, the bishops agreeing that in his case the canon might be set aside.[72] And so Ambrose was baptized and, eight days after his baptism, on December 7, 374, was ordained bishop.[73] Paulinus's description of the week between Ambrose's baptism and his ordination, during which he fulfilled all the ecclesiastical offices, has generally been understood as suggesting that Ambrose passed through all the ecclesiastical grades, from doorkeeper to presbyter, before receiving episcopal ordination.[74]

---

[69] *De officiis ministrorum*, 1.1.4 (PL 16.24). Basil's letter to Ambrose indicates that his contemporaries viewed these events as a divine call: "Remember, therefore, O man of God, that it was not humans who gave or taught you Christ's gospel, but the Lord himself has taken you from among the judges of the earth to place you on the seat of the Apostles." Basil, *Epistula* 197.1, as cited in Cesare Alzati, *Ambrosianum Mysterium: The Church of Milan and Its Liturgical Tradition*, trans. George Guiver (Cambridge: Grove Books, 1999) 1:4.

[70] Paulinus, *Vita Ambrosii*, 9 (Navoni, 62).

[71] *Epistola* 75 (Maur. 21).7 (CSEL 82/3.77).

[72] *Epistola* 14 (Maur. 63).65 (CSEL 82/3.269).

[73] Homes Dudden and Palanque give November 24 as the date of Ambrose's baptism and December 1, 373, as the date of his ordination. McLynn and Paredi give November 30, 374, for Ambrose's baptism and December 7, 374, for his ordination. Cf. Homes Dudden, *The Life and Times of Saint Ambrose*, 1:68; McLynn, *Ambrose of Milan: Church and Court in a Christian Capital*, 51; Paredi, *Saint Ambrose: His Life and Times*, 124; Palanque, *Saint Ambroise et l'empire romain*, 484–487.

[74] Paulinus, *Vita Ambrosii*, 9 (Navoni, 62); Homes Dudden, *The Life and Times of Saint Ambrose*, 1:68. It has been argued that Paulinus misrepresented what actually happened in order to protect Ambrose from the charge of having violated the Nicene canon and that the insistence that Ambrose had to pass through all the ecclesiastical ranks is anachronistic. Instead, the argument runs, Ambrose went simply from baptism to episcopal ordination after a week's

That Ambrose was not baptized until just prior to his ordination as bishop is not at all surprising. Postponing baptism until mature adulthood even among the sincerely devout was not at all unusual at that time.[75] Born and raised in a Christian household, Ambrose would have been initiated into the catechumenate with the rites then customary in Gaul: a priest had imposed his hand on Ambrose's forehead, traced the sign of the cross on it, and given him salt to taste. Ambrose's postponement of baptism may have been a sign of the seriousness of his Christian conviction. Holding a position of civil authority that might involve the taking of life was considered a good reason for postponing the sacrament.[76]

---

interval.[2] Stating there was nothing irregular about this procedure, McLynn labels Ambrose fulfilling all the ecclesiastical offices "an invention designed to attract publicity rather than an expedient to satisfy canonical regulations. It served to identify Ambrose with each of the groups in his church and provided a gathering liturgical momentum for his approaching consecration." McLynn, *Ambrose of Milan: Church and Court in a Christian Capital*, 51.

> [2] Paulinus tells us that during the seven days between Ambrose's baptism and consecration he fulfilled all the ecclesiastical offices, from doorkeeper to presbyter. Paulinus, *Vita Ambrosii*, 9 (Navoni, 62). McLynn labels this procedure "an invention designed to attract publicity rather than an expedient to satisfy canonical regulations. It served to identify Ambrose with each of the groups in his church and provided a gathering liturgical momentum for his approaching consecration." McLynn, *Ambrose of Milan: Church and Court in a Christian Capital*, 51.

[75] Ambrose tells us that his brother Satyrus was not baptized until he was well into his thirties or even forties, and then as an act of gratitude to God after having survived shipwreck: *De excessu fratris*, 1.43-48 (CSEL 73.232–236). Basil the Great, his brother Gregory of Nyssa, Gregory Nazianzen, and Augustine, all of whose parents enjoyed a reputation for holiness, were also not baptized until well into adulthood. For a discussion of the deferment of baptism and the motivations for it, see Moorhead, *Ambrose: Church and Society in the Late Roman World*, 22–23; Riley, *Christian Initiation: A Comparative Study*, 212–213; Edward Yarnold, "Initiation: The Fourth and Fifth Centuries," *The Study of Liturgy*, rev. ed., ed. Cheslyn Jones, Geoffrey Wainwright, Edward Yarnold, and Paul Bradshaw (New York: Oxford University Press, 1992) 130–131.

[76] See, for example, Hans von Campenhausen, *Men Who Shaped the Western Church*, trans. Manfred Hoffmann (New York: Harper and Row, 1964) 93. Yarnold, "Initiation: The Fourth and Fifth Centuries," 31.

Apart from the fact that he insisted on being baptized by a Catholic bishop,[77] we know very little of Ambrose's own baptism. Augustine relates that "when Ambrose, then bishop, had been baptized, Simplicianus had stood as father to him, and Ambrose regarded him with affection as a father indeed."[78] Yet, Ambrose never mentions his baptism. Nor do we hear that later in Ambrose's episcopacy charges were raised that his baptism was invalid or that it compromised his position as a defender of orthodoxy because it was not in accordance with the Nicene faith. Williams is therefore correct that

"the almost total lack of documentation for Ambrose's baptism and yet the absence of any question about its efficacy in the ensuing years leads to the conclusion that his baptism was a wholly unspectacular event. It was administered quickly and quietly by a presbyter of the Church in order to hurry the candidate on to the fulfillment of the requisite offices before the episcopate could legally begin."[79]

Yet, to say that there was nothing extraordinary about the event of Ambrose's baptism does not imply that Ambrose's baptism did not

---

[77] Paulinus, *Vita Ambrosii*, 9 (Navoni, 62).

[78] Augustine, *Confessions*, 8.2.3 (CCSL 27.114). On the presbyter Simplicianus preparing Ambrose for baptism, see McLynn, *Ambrose of Milan: Church and Court in a Christian Capital*, 54, n. 7. Williams presents a very strong case that Simplicianus not only prepared Ambrose for baptism but also baptized him. Ambrose need not have been baptized by a bishop, since the baptism of a catechumen could be accomplished by a presbyter in the absence of a bishop. Given the rapidity of events that followed Ambrose's election, there is a strong possibility that he was baptized not by a bishop but by Simplicianus. Williams finds in Augustine's identification of Simplicianus as the "father of Ambrose (then bishop) in receiving grace" an allusion to the imparting of a sacrament such as baptism. Such a view casts new light on the way Ambrose spoke of Simplicianus as a "parent" in his letters: "love us, as you do, with the affection of a parent." *Epistola* 36 (Maur. 2).10 (CSEL 82/1.19.96). Elsewhere Ambrose responds to Simplicianus's request for sermons on the writing of the Apostle Paul, "I realize in this complaint the result of our old friendship and, what is more, a tenderly fatherly love." *Epistola* 1 (Maur. 7).2 (CSEL 82/1.44.12–13). These passages develop the conclusion that Simplicianus was not only Ambrose's spiritual preceptor but also his baptizer in the hurried aftermath of his election as bishop. Williams, *Ambrose of Milan and the End of the Nicene-Arian Conflicts*, 117–118.

[79] Ibid., 119.

have an extraordinary impact on his life. There can be little doubt that although he never refers to it, Ambrose's baptism, occurring as it did only after his election as bishop, marked for him a decisive break in his life. The lofty phrases and intensity that Ambrose uses to expound the meaning of baptism seem to flow from his own experience. For Ambrose the significance of baptism is found in the transition from the earthly to the heavenly:

"The one who passes through the waters of this font—that is, from earthly things to heavenly (for this is the meaning of this passage, this pasch:[80] it is the passage of the person who is baptized, it is a passage from sin to life, from guilt to grace, from vileness to holiness)—the one that passes through these waters does not die, but rises again."[81]

This transition is, in fact, death and resurrection: "In this faith you died to the world and rose to God. Buried as it were in this element of the world,[82] and having died to sin, you rose to eternal life."[83] Risen again through the grace of Christ and marked with his cross,[84] the newly baptized rise in Christ's likeness so that they may live after his pattern.[85]

From the available information, we can conclude that Ambrose did not participate in a lengthy period of preparation and examination prior to being baptized; he was swept up in God's call. Thus he taught that coming to baptism is not a matter of worthiness but divine call: "So you received baptism; you believed. For it is contrary to God's command for me to judge otherwise; for you would not have been

---

[80] Cf. Exodus 12:11, 17. The Pasch commemorates how the Lord "passed over" the Israelites' homes when he slew the Egyptian firstborn. Ambrose takes the word also to mean a "transit" from the state of sin to one of grace. In this same sense John 13:1 seems to attribute to Jesus, the true Paschal Lamb, a passover from this world to the Father. Yarnold, *The Awe-Inspiring Rites of Initiation*, 104, n. 22.

[81] *De sacramentis*, 1.4.12 (SC 25bis.66).

[82] The phrase "this element of the world" (*illo mundi consepultus elemento*) refers to water, which, along with air, fire and earth, was considered by the ancients to be one of the four constitutive elements of the universe.

[83] *De mysteriis*, 4.21 (SC 25bis.166); cf. *De sacramentis*, 3.1.2 (SC 25bis.90).

[84] Ibid., 2.7.23 (SC 25bis.86); 6.2.7 (SC 25bis.140).

[85] Ibid., 6.2.7 (SC 25bis.140).

called to grace, had not Christ judged you worthy of his grace."[86] It is only after baptism that the bishop of Milan stresses the awesome responsibility that comes with their initiation and exhorts them to live a life of virtue as the fulfillment of this responsibility.[87]

THE BISHOP AND THE EMPIRE

Ambrose's reign over the church of Milan was not characterized by the peace that Valentinian had promised. Events brought the bishop of Milan into close contact with the rulers of the Western empire—Gratian, Maximus, Justina, mother of Valentinian II, and Theodosius I. In his interactions with the empire, Ambrose is famous for combating Arianism and paganism, and for maintaining the independence of the church against civil power. Ambrose is therefore best known as "a churchman who exerted extraordinary influence in the public sphere."[88] While it is beyond the scope of this project to review the complete record of Ambrose's interactions with the empire, in order to illustrate the power and influence he exerted in the political sphere, we will consider three significant events in Ambrose's ministry that his people knew about and participated in: the basilica conflict of 385 and 386, pagan attempts to reinstate the Altar of Victory in the senate, and the burning of the Jewish synagogue at Callinicum.

Although Ambrose's initial acts as bishop reveal a careful balancing of dissenting religious opinions aimed at consolidating the divided Milanese church under his leadership,[89] his evenhanded approach to

---

[86] *Ergo accepistis baptismum, credistis. Nefas est namque me aliud aestimare; neque enim vocatus esses ad gratiam nisi dignum te Christus sua gratia iudicasset.* Ibid., 1.1.1 (SC 25bis.6); cf. ibid., 6.2.5 (SC 25bis.140). In the translation provided by Yarnold, *accepistis baptismum, credistis* is translated, "So you were baptized and came to believe." Yarnold, *The Awe-Inspiring Rites of Initiation*, 100. Botte translates *accepistis baptismum, credistis* as "Vous avez reçu le baptême, vous avez la foi" (SC 25bis.62).

[87] Ibid., 6.5.26 (SC 25bis.154).

[88] Ramsey, *Ambrose*, 42.

[89] Part of a letter attributed to Basil of Caesarea seems to show that one of Ambrose's first acts as bishop was to request and obtain Basil's help in securing the return to Milan of the body of his predecessor Bishop Dionysius. For the Catholics, the return to Milan of the relics of the city's last orthodox bishop would signal the eventual return of orthodoxy to Milan. See Basil, *Epistola* 197.2 (PG 32.709–713). There is some dispute over the factuality of this request

Arianism would soon change.⁹⁰ In 378 Gratian, who succeeded his father Valentinian as emperor in the West, requested that Ambrose prepare an explanation of orthodox belief. Ambrose responded to that request with the first two books of his lengthy treatise *De fide*.⁹¹ Daniel Williams correctly concludes that "the publication of *De fide* represents a sudden and dramatic reversal in [Ambrose's] policies toward the Homoeans in Milan."⁹² This treatise is a full-scale attack that condemns Arianism as the worst of all heresies and an enemy of the truth. This abrupt transformation is best understood as Ambrose's reaction to events at Milan—most notably the arrival in the city of the empress Justina, the mother of Valentinian II, and her immediate political patronage of the Arians—that undermined Valentinian's promise that

---

for two reasons. First, there is serious doubt as to the authenticity of the part of the letter in question. Second, we have no proof of either the reception of Dionysius's remains in Milan or the existence of a monument to Dionysius in Milan in Ambrose's lifetime. What the undoubtedly authentic part of Basil's letter (197.1) shows, however, is that the strongly anti-Arian bishop of Caesarea believed that he had discovered a kindred spirit in Ambrose, which implies that Ambrose's own letter, now unfortunately lost, must have expressed anti-Arian sentiments. Cf. Ramsey, *Ambrose*, 23; Williams, *Ambrose of Milan and the End of the Nicene-Arian Conflicts*, 120–121. On the other hand, Ambrose appears to have initially pursued reconciliation with the Arians of his diocese by accepting Auxentius's Arian clergy as his own. Ibid., 121. Ramsey suggests that the practical matter of keeping his see running may have left Ambrose with little choice in the matter if the vast majority of the city's priests and deacons were Arian, which would have been very likely after nearly twenty years of Auxentius's rule. Ramsey, *Ambrose*, 23.

⁹⁰ In the following discussion of Ambrose and Arianism, I am indebted to Williams, *Ambrose of Milan and the End of the Nicene-Arian Conflicts*.

⁹¹ For a discussion of scholarship concerning *De fide*, see ibid., 128–154. For a brief analysis of Ambrose's use of the Bible in *De fide*, see Moorhead, *Ambrose: Church and Society in the Late Roman World*, 113–118.

⁹² Williams, *Ambrose of Milan and the End of the Nicene-Arian Conflicts*, 129. Though Gratian was favorably impressed with *De fide*, 1–2,³ the criticism leveled against it, especially by the Arian bishop Palladius of Ratiaria, was so severe that Ambrose expanded this work into three more books and sent them to the emperor by the end of 380. Ibid., 161.

³ *Epistola* 12.7.

Ambrose's episcopate would be peaceful.[93] In just eight short years the bishop found himself contending with the imperial court over providing a basilica for Arian worship in Milan.[94]

In the spring of 385,[95] Ambrose went before the consistory, where Valentinian, undoubtedly urged on by his mother Justina,[96] is said to have threatened Ambrose with the seizure of a basilica.[97] A crowd

---

[93] Between 376 and 378, Arian opposition to Ambrose was organized by Julian Valens along with Ursinus. On August 9, 378, the Roman army suffered a devastating defeat at the hands of the Goths at Hadrianople. Gratian's uncle, the emperor Valens, was killed, and in the aftermath many Arian refugees, including the court of Valentinian II and his mother Justina, fled to Milan. As the Arian community in Milan increased, so too did the need for religious accommodation. This need was soon expressed in a request to Gratian for the use of a basilica in the city. When Ambrose refused, Gratian responded by seizing an orthodox basilica. See *De spiritu sancto*, 1.1.19–21 (CSEL 79.23–25); Williams, *Ambrose of Milan and the End of the Nicene-Arian Conflicts*, 139–140. Concurrent with the seizure of the basilica, Ambrose was attacked for selling the church's sacred vessels in order to ransom captives from the barbarians, perhaps because this act of charity was a subtle way of erasing Milan's Arian past. Cf. *De officiis*, 2.28,136 (PL 16.139); Williams, *Ambrose of Milan and the End of the Nicene-Arian Conflicts*, 140. In the midst of these mounting hostilities, Gratian requested from Ambrose an explanation of his faith. Thus, while scholarship has generally presumed that Gratian's request was for his own instruction, it was, in fact, a demand for a clarification of Ambrose's views in the face of mounting accusations against him. Ibid., 141–144.

[94] Our treatment of the basilica conflict is perhaps a bit too detailed for a work on Ambrose's mystagogy; however, it reflects both the author's concern to accurately present what was a complicated situation and interest in this significant event in the life of Saint Ambrose. For a review of scholarship on this event, see ibid., 210–211.

[95] Though Ambrose nowhere mentions the time of year at which this first demand for a basilica occurred, Williams reasons that it was likely made sometime prior to Easter, because an unknown number of conversions to Arianism resulting from the ministry of Auxentius, the Arian bishop of Durostorum, created the need to secure baptismal facilities prior to Easter, when catechumens were baptized. Ibid., 212. Cf. Ambrose, *Epistola* 75 and 76 (Maur. 20 and 21) (CSEL 82/3.108–125; 74–81).

[96] On Justina's efforts against the Nicenes, see Williams, *Ambrose of Milan and the End of the Nicene-Arian Conflicts*, 202–203.

[97] *Contra Auxentium*, 29 (CSEL 82/3.101).

gathered outside the palace, demanding the bishop's release, and when the palace guard was unable to disperse the crowd, Ambrose was asked to go out and calm the people. This potentially explosive situation was quickly defused when the court retracted its demands. On January 23, 386, Valentinian issued a new edict proclaiming freedom of worship to adherents of that faith defined as Arianism and confirmed as heretical at Constantinople, thereby restoring Arianism to official status and ensuring the unobstructed spread of its doctrine.[98] Early in March the court renewed its demands for the Portian Basilica. Ambrose refused and was ordered to leave Milan for violating the new edict.[99] The exile does not seem to have been enforced, because shortly thereafter Ambrose received orders commanding him to appoint judges for a hearing before the consistory, orders that Ambrose flatly refused to obey.[100] On March 27 the court demanded that Ambrose give up the New Basilica, a larger building inside the walls.[101] This may have been a psychological tactic aimed at securing the Portian Basilica, because the next day the court requested it again.[102]

On Palm Sunday, Ambrose was preaching in the cathedral when word came to him that imperial functionaries had entered the (Portian) Basilica and were hanging imperial banners, in order either simply to decorate it with the imperial colors or to designate it as imperial property. While Ambrose continued the celebration of the Eucharist, a crowd made its way to the basilica to prevent it from falling completely into the emperor's hands.[103] The siege intensified when soldiers were sent to enforce the imperial sequestration on Tuesday. Although Ambrose feared that the people would be slaughtered, he refused to restrain them when asked to do so by an embassy of Gothic tribunes.[104] The emperor further responded to the uproar by imposing heavy fines and even imprisonment on Milanese businessmen sympathetic to the pro-Nicenes.

A break in the impasse finally occurred when the Catholic soldiers guarding the basilica were threatened with excommunication.[105] These

---

[98] Williams, *Ambrose of Milan and the End of the Nicene-Arian Conflicts*, 212.
[99] *Epistola* 75 (Maur. 21) (CSEL 82/3.74–82).
[100] Ibid.
[101] *Epistola* 76 (Maur. 20) (CSEL 82/3.108–125).
[102] Williams, *Ambrose of Milan and the End of the Nicene-Arian Conflicts*, 214.
[103] *Epistola* 76 (Maur. 20) (CSEL 82/3.108–125).
[104] Ibid.
[105] Ibid.

soldiers entered the church where Ambrose was presiding, abandoning the besieged basilica, and asked for prayers, presumably of forgiveness. On Maundy Thursday word came that the emperor had ordered all soldiers to withdraw from the basilica and that the symbols of imperial appropriation had been removed.

A second siege of the (probably Portian) Basilica[106] occurred sometime after Easter.[107] Ambrose was personally present on this occasion and preached his sermon *Contra Auxentium*.[108] He describes the basilica as surrounded by soldiers while inside the people "kept sleepless watch so many nights and days."[109] During this siege Ambrose taught the congregation anti-Arian hymns as a means of relieving their fears and maintaining their faith.[110] We do not know when the confrontation ended. The court evidently backed down again; however, the reasons why the court withdrew its demands are not given in Ambrose's sermon.[111]

Whatever the reason the court withdrew its demand, Ambrose's victory was enhanced when, on June 17, 386, the relics of two previously unknown martyrs, Protasius and Gervasius, were "discovered"

---

[106] This chronology, which deviates from traditional reconstructions, is based on the conclusions of J. H. van Haeringen and A. Lenox-Conyngham, who understand the events reported in Ambrose's *Contra Auxentium* as referring to a separate and second confrontation from the one Ambrose described in *Epistola* 76 (Maur. 20). J. H. van Haeringen, "De Valentinian II et Ambrosio: illustrantur et digeruntur res anno 386 gestae," *Mnemosynae*, 3rd ser. 5 (1937): (1) "Valentinianus II basilicam adornitur (de Ambrosii epistula xx), 152–158; (2) "De Ambrosii epistula xxi," 28–33; (3) "De Ambrosii epistula xx et xxi: temporum descriptio," 229–240; A. Lenox-Conyngham, "A Topography of the Basilica Conflict of AD 385/6 in Milan," *Historia* 31 (1982) 353–363; idem, "Juristic and Religious Aspects of the Basilica Conflict of AD 386," *Studia Patristica* 18 (1985) 55–58.

[107] *Contra Auxentium*, 37 (CSEL 82/3.107).

[108] For a summary of *Contra Auxentium* see below, 97.

[109] *Contra Auxentium*, 4, 7 (CSEL 82/3.84, 86).

[110] Augustine, *Confessions*, 9.7.15 (CCSL 14.141). Ambrose was one of the first to write metrical Latin hymns, many of which are still sung in Christian churches today. For the text of the four hymns unanimously considered to be Ambrose's, along with their English translation, see Ramsey, *Ambrose*, 166–173.

[111] Williams offers the threat of Maximus as the reason the court would have called off the siege a second time. Williams, *Ambrose of Milan and the End of the Nicene-Arian Conflicts*, 216–217.

in the Church of Saints Felix and Nabor.[112] The appropriation of these relics as signs of divine vindication provided Ambrose with a powerful weapon that he used most effectively against the Arianism of the court. Augustine, then a catechumen in Milan, observes: "[T]hereafter the mind of that enemy, if not turned to healing belief, was checked nevertheless from the reign of persecution."[113] Yet, in Milan, the discovery of the relics of Saints Gervasius and Protasius, while exciting, was not unique. "The Christian cemetery areas were already dotted with quite sizeable martyr's *memoriae*."[114] What was new was the speed and the certainty with which Ambrose appropriated the relics. He moved them only after two days from the shrine of Saints Felix and Nabor, where they had been unearthed, into the new basilica that

---

[112] *Epistola* 77 (Maur. 22) (CSEL 82/3.126–140); Paulinus, *Vita Ambrosii*, 14 (Navoni, 74). Ambrose's only report about the discovery of these relics is found in this letter written to his sister, in which he describes how the bones of the martyrs were found. It tells us that Ambrose was persuaded by the people to consecrate the newly built Ambrosian basilica (the original church of Sant'Ambrogio) in the same way that he dedicated the Roman basilica (Basilica Apostolorum, the present Church of Saint Nazaro), on the condition that he would find the relics of some martyrs to place in it; Paulinus tells us that Ambrose dedicated the Basilica of the Apostles with relics of Saints Peter and Paul. Paulinus, *Vita Ambrosii*, 33 (Navoni, 110). Under the inspiration of 'a kind of prophetic ardor,' he ordered the ground to be excavated near the graves of the martyrs Felix and Nabor, and in a short while the still bloody bones of two men of extraordinary size were exhumed. They were identified —we are not told exactly how—as the remains of Protasius and Gervasius, two martyrs who had died in an early persecution. The two skeletons, accompanied by an enthusiastic crowd, were brought first to the so-called Basilica of Fausta and then, on the following day, to the Ambrosian Basilica. As they were being transported to their final resting place, to the spot beneath the altar that Ambrose had originally reserved for himself, numerous miraculous cures occurred, most notably the restoration of sight to a blind man named Severus. It has been argued that all of these events were somehow staged by Ambrose in order to promote the cause of orthodoxy. See Otto Seeck, *Geschichte des Untergangs der antiken Welt* (Stuttgart, 1923) 5:207. Regardless of how this event happened, the discovery of the bones of the two men, along with the miraculous cures that accompanied it, provided a powerful means of repressing anti-Nicene harassment.

[113] Augustine, *Confessions*, 9.7.16 (CCSL 27.141).

[114] Peter Brown, *The Cult of the Saints: Its Rise and Function in Latin Christianity* (Chicago: University of Chicago Press, 1981) 36–37.

he had built for himself. He placed them under the altar, where he himself had planned to be buried, thereby inseparably linking these martyrs with the communal liturgy, with the church built by the bishop, in which the bishop would frequently preside. At the same time, the bishop restricted the random feasting that had been common at other martyrs' *memoriae* on the grounds that it too closely resembled pagan family anniversaries.[115] In this way Ambrose established his church as a holy place, elevated his status as a holy person, and promoted unity by co-opting private devotional practice. Thus Peter Brown asserts that Ambrose enhanced his reputation as an authentic representative of Christ through the cult of saints.[116]

In addition to protecting the church from the internal threat posed by Arianism, Ambrose also found himself called upon to defend the church against the attacks of paganism and Judaism. While it is true that paganism had experienced a steady decline since Constantine adopted Christianity and indicated his disfavor toward the ancient gods, the old religion was far from waning, and many pagan customs survived to Ambrose's day. Among the customs that continued into the final quarter of the fourth century was the maintenance of an altar to the goddess Victory near the entrance to the senate in Rome. The deliberations of the senate were understood by the pagans to occur under the influence of the goddess, and at certain times the senators were expected to sprinkle incense on the altar in honor of the goddess and to swear upon it.

Toward the end of his reign, the emperor Constantius II removed the altar as incompatible with the Christian faith. This change was not long-lasting. Emperor Julian restored the altar to its place in the senate at the beginning of his reign. It remained there until 382, when Gratian had it removed as part of a wider anti-paganism campaign that he and Theodosius were waging, which included the elimination of the state subsidies enjoyed by pagan temples and priesthoods.[117] The year 383 brought the enforcement of anti-pagan legislation to an end.[118]

---

[115] Augustine, *Confessions*, 6.2.2 (CCSL 27.74–75).

[116] Brown, *The Cult of the Saints*, 36–37.

[117] *Epistola* 72 (Maur. 17) (CSEL 82/3.11–33); Paulinus, *Vita Ambrosii*, 26 (Navoni, 94–96).

[118] In 383 Magnus Maximus, who was commanding Roman troops in Britain, was proclaimed emperor by his rebellious soldiers, and Gratian was assassinated at Lyons by one of his own officials. Maximus soon gained control of

In 384, Symmachus, the prefect of Rome and a man of considerable standing, sent a petition to Valentinian requesting the reinstatement of the Altar of Victory and the restoration of the public subsidies abolished by Gratian.[119] Ambrose was somehow apprised of this petition. In a letter to Valentinian he demanded a copy of it so that he could compose a suitable response.[120] Anticipating that Valentinian could easily yield to Symmachus, Ambrose threatened him, should he agree to the petition, with episcopal resistance and the reproaches of his dead brother and father. This letter seems to have been sufficient to convince Valentinian not to accede to the pagan demands. Ambrose's actual reply to Symmachus's petition indicates that by the time he had written it, Valentinian had already denied the request.[121] Some years later, in 389 or 390, the pagan senators approached the emperor Theodosius, asking him to restore the public subsidies for the cult. This time there seems to have been no mention made of the Altar of Victory. Theodosius hesitated, but Ambrose managed to convince him to turn down the request.

In addition to defending the Church against paganism, Ambrose also sought to assert Christianity's supremacy over Judaism. Sometime in the summer of 388, the bishop of Callinicum was accused of having instigated the burning of a local synagogue in reaction to an unspecified offense supposedly committed by the Jews against the Christians. When informed of this incident, Theodosius decided that those who had set fire to the synagogue should be punished and that the bishop would have to pay to rebuild it. When Ambrose was informed of the emperor's decision, he sent Theodosius a long letter urging him to change his mind.[122] He warned the emperor that if the bishop of Callinicum submitted to rebuilding the synagogue, it would be an act of apostasy, whereas if he resisted the imperial order he

---

Gaul, leaving the West in turmoil. In order to prevent the alienation of a large part of the population, Gratian's successor, Valentinian II, stopped enforcing his half-brother's anti-pagan legislation.

[119] Paulinus, *Vita Ambrosii*, 24 (Navoni, 90).

[120] *Epistola* 72 (Maur. 17) (CSEL 82/3.11–33).

[121] *Epistola* 73 (Maur. 18) (CSEL 82/3.34–53).

[122] *Epistola* 74 (Maur. 40) (CSEL 82/3.54–73). McLynn interprets this letter to show that Ambrose's concern over the synagogue was, in fact, a pretext for putting the cases of deacons and presbyters being assigned to municipal responsibilities on Theodosius's immediate agenda. McLynn, *Ambrose of Milan: Church and Court in a Christian Capital*, 302.

might become a martyr. In a kind of defense of the burning of the synagogue, Ambrose went as far as saying that he would take responsibility for the arson himself.

Although Theodosius dropped his insistence that the bishop rebuild the synagogue, Ambrose was not ready to declare the issue settled. In another letter,[123] this one to Marcellina, Ambrose describes his first encounter with Theodosius after he had written to him. The bishop was preaching a long homily in the cathedral of Milan, in which he was comparing the Jews unfavorably with the Christians, when he began to directly address the emperor, who was in the congregation. Ambrose told the emperor that he owed his position to God and that he must not allow God's enemies—the Jews—to gain the upper hand over his servants; rather, he must forgive those of God's servants who had erred and restore peace to the Church. Ambrose then came down from the pulpit, and a brief exchange took place between him and the emperor. Ambrose threatened that unless Theodosius promised to lift every sanction against all the Christians involved in the damage done to the synagogue, he would not celebrate the Eucharist. The emperor, faced with a bishop whose determination he had no reason to doubt, and surrounded by a congregation that almost surely shared their bishop's harsh sentiments about the Jews, had little choice but to acquiesce, and he did. The Eucharist was then celebrated.

In our age of religious tolerance, we are justified in being offended by Ambrose's intolerance of other religions and religious perspectives and naturally tempted to dismiss it as bigotry. Yet, we must keep in mind the fourth-century conviction that the right form of worship is essential if heaven is to be propitious. Inasmuch as bishops were believed to be instruments of divine grace, Christians considered a proper part of bishops' role to be praying for the emperor and his army. Victory in battle was understood to be the gift of heaven, and nothing was more likely to make and keep heaven favorable than the devout prayers and holy lives of the people of God. "That the right form of worship is essential if heaven is to be propitious is an axiom of ancient society. The axiom lies at the root of the pagan persecutions of the Christians, as also of the deep unpopularity of the Jews in the Greco-Roman world."[124]

---

[123] *Epistola extra coll.* 1 (Maur. 41) (CSEL 82/3.145–161); cf. Paulinus, *Vita Ambrosii*, 23 (Navoni, 88).

[124] Henry Chadwick, *The Role of the Christian Bishop in Ancient Society* (Berkeley: Center for Hermeneutical Studies in Hellenistic and Modern Culture, 1979) 10.

Christianity introduced an even greater ardor into the matter by the conviction that right worship presupposes right doctrine. A corollary of this axiom is that heresy or schism would, if long tolerated or regarded as a matter of indifference, provoke the wrath of the Lord. Henry Chadwick contends that "the ferocity of the sectarian conflicts in the fourth and later centuries cannot be understood without the centrality of this axiom."[125] Thus, Chadwick argues that when the bishop and his clergy of Callinicum burned a Jewish synagogue to the ground and Theodosius ordered the bishop to rebuild it, Ambrose's refusal to begin the eucharistic liturgy, with its solemn prayer for the emperor and his armies, until Theodosius countermanded the order[126] was not an attempt to embarrass or blackmail the emperor but the expression of Ambrose's belief that any harassment of the church at Callinicum would negate any value that the liturgy might possess in preserving the favor of heaven.[127]

Throughout the twenty-four years of his episcopate, Ambrose established a sphere in which the Church could act independently of the state and as an entity completely responsible for governing itself, though there is no clear indication from Ambrose that he set out to do so.[128] From the perspective of history, we can see that Ambrose's "guiding principle was to free the ecclesiastical power from interference by the temporal, in particular to rescind the emperors' implied claim to stand at the head of the Church."[129] His position is summarized in a letter to Marcellina, written after Valentinian had commanded Ambrose to hand over the Portian Basilica for Arian worship: "It is alleged that everything is permitted to the emperor

---

[125] Ibid.

[126] *Epistola extra coll.* 1 (Maur. 41).28-29 (CSEL 82/3.161).

[127] Chadwick, *The Role of the Christian Bishop in Ancient Society*, 11. Responding to Chadwick, Ramsey MacMullen points out a second corollary: People listened to bishops out of fear of the divine disfavor that bishops could bring upon them. "If [the bishop] was crossed, your child might die, or you yourself fall ill, and recover only when you had repented." Ibid., 29.

[128] While Angelo Paredi suggests that Ambrose "followed a definite course of action" in his ministry as bishop, it seems much more likely that, as Boniface Ramsey contends, he simply "had no alternative but to seek to shape events as he did, as the occasion presented itself." Paredi, *Saint Ambrose: His Life and Times*, 214; Ramsey, *Ambrose*, 47.

[129] Richard Krautheimer, *Three Christian Capitals*, 72.

and that all things are his. I reply: Do not so burden yourself, O Emperor, as to believe that you have any imperial right to those things that are divine . . . The palaces belong to the emperor, the churches to the bishop."[130] Ambrose was not saying that Church and state were unrelated to each other and had no responsibilities toward each other. Ideally, the Church was to instruct and judge the state by setting the moral and doctrinal perimeters within which the state might legitimately operate, and the state was to foster and protect the true religion proclaimed by the Church in such a way as not to infringe upon its independence.[131]

Our discussion of Ambrose's dealings with imperial authorities and especially with the emperor may give the impression that his relationship to the empire was overwhelmingly adversarial. However, this is by no means true.[132] Ambrose enjoyed a close relationship with Gratian, at least in the final years of his life. Ambrose was Gratian's mentor, and he remarks in his funeral oration for Valentinian that Gratian often spoke his name shortly before he was murdered in Gaul.[133] In this same funeral sermon Ambrose suggests that sometime after the basilica conflict, the young emperor, undoubtedly following the death of his domineering mother Justina in 388, had a change of heart and expressed a desire to be baptized by Ambrose.[134] Ambrose refers obliquely to the crisis of 385–386, but that was a thing of the past, and the bishop's praise of the deceased emperor is unstinting. In the course of his eulogy, Ambrose also reminds the congregation that twice he had undertaken a mission to Gaul on Valentinian's behalf.[135] When the time came for Ambrose to preach Theodosius's eulogy, Ambrose made it clear that he saw in Theodosius the ideal of the Christian ruler.

---

[130] *Epistola* 76 (Maur. 20).19 (CSEL 82/3.118).

[131] Ramsey, *Ambrose*, 48.

[132] See ibid., 54.

[133] *De obitu Valentiniani*, 80 (CSEL 73.367).

[134] Valentinian in fact never received baptism; he was a catechumen at the time of his death, but if we are to believe Ambrose's eulogy of him, his desire to be baptized was strong and persistent. Ibid., 52–53 (CSEL 73.354–355).

[135] Ibid., 28 (CSEL 73.343). These missions occurred in late 383 and again probably in 386. Their purpose was to plead with the usurper Maximus for the return of Gratian's body and, if possible, to secure peace between the two.

In addition to his personal relationships with the emperors, as bishop Ambrose had considerable secular authority.[136] Between 312 and 337, Constantine persuaded the bishops to assume and exercise some of his own prerogatives. In 318 they received the power of jurisdiction in civil proceedings when Christians were involved in the case, and no one was allowed to appeal their judgments.[137] In 316 and 321 the emperor enlisted the help of the bishops in dealing with the question of the legal force of those acts that granted emancipation to Christian slaves and the related question of granting the rights of citizenship to those who had been made free. In conjunction with these responsibilities, bishops were assigned their proper place in the carefully graded social scale of the state and granted a proper priority in the protocol of court, which included the titles, insignia, and privileges that, for the most part, corresponded to the highest dignitaries in the land, the *illustres*.[138] Within the imperial "system," Ambrose also maintained his importance and influence through his ongoing special connections, which included social exchanges, playing an important role in the marriages of Milan's Christian society, and informally recommending candidates for the imperial service. Thus the bishop was considered a *vir venerabilis*, a person deemed "worthy of reverence" by the powerful.[139]

---

[136] See Theodore Klauser, *A Short History of the Western Liturgy: An Account and Some Reflections*, 2nd ed., trans. John Halliburton (New York: Oxford University Press, 1979) 33–34.

[137] Ambrose discusses his role as judge in *De officiis ministrorum*, 2.24.125 (PL 16.136); See also *Epistola* 82 (CSEL 82/1.170–175). On bishops as holy men capable of discerning people's hearts and therefore not in need of correction by a higher court, see Chadwick, *The Role of the Christian Bishop in Ancient Society*, 6–7.

[138] Insignia included the *lorum* (the *pallium*), the *nappula* (a ceremonial napkin), the *compagi* (a special kind of footwear), the *camalaucum* (a distinctive headgear), and probably also the golden ring. Privileges included the right to a throne whose height and design were carefully prescribed, the right to be accompanied by lights and incense, the privilege of being greeted with a kiss of the hand, the right to be greeted by a choir of singers upon his arrival at church, to be waited on at the throne and the altar with covered hands, and to have people genuflect to him and kiss his foot. Theodore Klauser, *A Short History of the Western Liturgy*, 33–34.

[139] Ernst Jerf, *Vir venerabilis: Untersuchungen zur Titulatur der Bischöfe in der ausserkirchlichen Texten der Spätantike*, Beiträge zur Theologie 26 (Vienna: Herder, 1970) 94–128.

The authority of the bishop was further enhanced by the fact that, in the person of the bishop, the voice of a newly formed urban grouping, the local Christian congregation, came to be heard in the politics of the empire. One reason for this development was the bishop's concern for the poor.[140] Concern for the poor was central to Ambrose's episcopacy. In *De officiis ministrorum*, he warns that priests should not be wasteful by spending money on "expensive banquets and much wine" but instead should receive the stranger, clothe the naked, redeem the captives, and help the needy.[141] Ambrose cultivated simplicity in his diet and attire, and insisted that fine clothes were unsuitable for the clergy.[142] His writings, particularly the treatise *De Nabuthe*, indicate a passionate commitment to alleviating the misery of the poor. Ambrose believed that poverty was closer to God than wealth.[143] Nevertheless, he was aware of the vices of the poor.[144]

Ambrose's most familiar teaching with respect to wealth was that private property is a usurpation of what was intended by God in the beginning to be held in common.[145] That Ambrose not only preached his conviction that poverty is closer to God but practiced it in his own life is evident from the fact that at the time of his ordination, he gave

---

[140] In the following discussion I am indebted especially to Peter Brown's chapter "Poverty and Power" in *Power and Persuasion in Late Antiquity*, 71–118.

[141] *De officiis ministrorum*, 2.21.109 (PL 16.132).

[142] Ibid., 1.19.83 (PL 16.48). Yet, this insistence stands in stark contrast to the "relic of the dalmatics," the pair of gorgeous robes preserved by the church of Milan and traditionally thought to have been made for Ambrose. For collaboration of this claim, see H. Granger Taylor, "The Two Dalmatics of Saint Ambrose," *Bulletin de Liaison, Centre International d'Etude des Textiles Anciens* 57–58 (1983) 127–173. This paradox attests to Ambrose's awareness of the importance of outward appearance and the ease with which he functioned in both the world and his basilica. On Ambrose's concern for outward appearance, see also *De officiis*, 1.18.72 (PL 16.44), in which Ambrose recalls a presbyter whose "insolent gait" offended him.

[143] Cf. *Expositio in Psalmum cxviii*, 3.37 (CSEL 62.63).

[144] Cf. *Hexaemeron*, 5.17.57 (CSEL 38-1.183).

[145] *Expositio in Psalmum cxviii*, 8.22 (CSEL 62.163). The idea that private property is robbery appears in Basil's *Homily VI* (PG 31.261, 278) as well as in the Stoic tradition, e.g., Seneca. See Brian E. Daley, S.J., "Building a New City: The Cappadocian Fathers and the Rhetoric of Philanthropy," *Journal of Early Christian Studies* 7/3 (Fall 1999) 431–461; see esp. 436, n. 20 (Stoic) and 442–447 (Basil).

away his property to the Church and to the poor, after making certain that his sister Marcellina was provided for.[146] We know from *De officiis ministrorum* that Ambrose melted down the sacred vessels of the church at Milan in order to ransom captives, declaring that "the Church has gold, not to store up, but to lay out, and to spend on those who need."[147] Still, Ambrose felt a certain ambivalence toward wealth and property, as his other writings show. He could acknowledge that wealth was not evil on the one hand and claim that it was unnatural on the other.[148]

As "lovers of the poor," bishops could assert themselves as the most effective protectors and pacifiers of the lower classes of the cities and, speaking for the poor, comment on how wealth was spent by the rich. In this way they could both control the lower classes and sway the emperor and his servants. Bishops also used their status as "lovers of the poor" to consolidate their power within their churches. Inasmuch as the ability to care for the poor gave power to the wealthy, who could bypass the bishop and his clergy, bishops were concerned with the taint of private wealth on the Church.[149] It was therefore essential that the wealth of the Church be presented as the wealth of the Christian community as a whole, and the best way of disconnecting this wealth from its donors was to distribute it to the poor, "the nonpersons who huddled on the edge of the community."[150]

Thus, when Ambrose melted down the church plate in order to ransom prisoners,[151] he destroyed the memory of the Christian families [supporters of Auxentius] "whose names would certainly have been engraved on the edges of the great silver patens and along the rims of the Eucharistic chalices."[152] In the hands of the bishop as "lover of the poor," the wealth of the Church became public wealth. And in distrib-

---

[146] Paulinus, *Vita Ambrosii*, 38 (Navoni, 116).

[147] *De officiis ministrorum*, 2.28.137 (PL 16.140). For Ambrose's discussion of this incident, see ibid. 2.28.136–143 (PL 16.139–142).

[148] Cf. *Epistola* 14 (Maur.63).92 (CSEL 82/3.285); *Expositio evangelii secundum Lucam*, 7.246 (CCSL 14.297).

[149] Rita Lizzi, "Ambrose's Contemporaries and the Christianization of Northern Italy," *Journal of Roman Studies* 80 (1990) 164–165; idem, *Vescovi e strutture ecclesiastiche nella città tardoantica* (Como: New Press, 1989) 141–145.

[150] Brown, *Power and Persuasion in Late Antiquity*, 96.

[151] *De officiis ministrorum*, 2.28.37 (PL 16.113).

[152] Brown, *Power and Persuasion in Late Antiquity*, 96.

uting its wealth to the poor, the Church would display it in ways that put other groups to shame.[153] Thus, when Ambrose scattered gold pieces to the poor, his enemies accused him of usurping an imperial prerogative.[154] The poor quickly became part of the bishop's "symbolic retinue."[155] Their presence in the bishop's following, along with that of monks and consecrated virgins, symbolized the unique texture of the bishop's power. He was the protector of those who owed least to the city, the unmarried and the homeless.

As protectors of the poor, bishops received an even further measure of public prominence in a role that Ambrose describes as "the controllers of the crowds, upholders of peace, unless, of course, they are moved by insults to God and to his church."[156] This process began in the 380s when Theodosius, forced to tax the cities more heavily than ever before, responded to riots opposing the taxes with formidable demonstrations of his anger. Yet, the true motivation for Theodosius's anger was to restore his popularity by having it appeased, and for a number of religious and political reasons, Theodosius determined that the Christian bishops would be the most useful to him as the appeasers of his rage.[157] Thus, in the spring of 387, the emperor showed mercy to those involved in the Riot of the Statues at the request of the bishop of Antioch,[158] and, when in 388 Theodosius acquiesced to Ambrose's demand and countermanded his order that the church

---

[153] *Epistola* 73 (Maur. 18).17 (CSEL 82/3.45). For a discussion of Ambrose's use of wealth, see McLynn, *Ambrose of Milan: Church and Court in a Christian Capital*, 55–56; Yves-Marie Duval, "L'originalité du 'De virginibus' dans le mouvement ascetique occidental: Ambroise, Cyprien, Athanase," in *Ambroise de Milan . . . dix études*, ed. Yves-Marie Duval (Paris: Études Augustiniennes, 1974) 9–66. See also G. Rosso, "La 'lettera alle vergini': Atanasio e Ambrogio," *Augustinianum* 23 (1983) 421–452.

[154] *Contra Auxentium*, 33 (CSEL 82/3.104). "Only the emperor, a man raised by fortune above all concern for wealth, could scatter gold, the most precious of all metals, on the populace." Brown, *Power and Persuasion in Late Antiquity*, 97.

[155] Ibid., 97. The respectful and orderly retinue or entourage that accompanied Ambrose at the palace or elsewhere allowed him to meet people of high rank with whom he dealt on equal terms. This retinue allowed Ambrose to operate not as an individual but as the head of an organization. McLynn, *Ambrose of Milan: Church and Court in a Christian Capital*, 253.

[156] *Epistola* 74 (Maur. 40).6 (CSEL 82/3.58).

[157] Brown, *Power and Persuasion in Late Antiquity*, 105–108.

[158] Ibid.

rebuild the synagogue at Callinicum,[159] he elevated the bishop to a very powerful position.

In this context, when seven thousand inhabitants of Thessalonika were killed by order of the emperor as punishment for a riot in 390,[160] Ambrose could approach Theodosius as a spiritual guide in a long letter and invite him to do penance.[161] Theodosius submitted to Ambrose, and though his motivations for doing penance may not have been contrition and remorse,[162] in acting as he did following the massacre at Thessalonika, the bishop of Milan nevertheless established himself as the arbiter of imperial mercy.

Following his reconciliation to the Church, Theodosius issued a series of edicts against polytheism that further increased the bishops' stature.[163] For example, his prohibition of all forms of sacrifice, issued

---

[159] *Epistola extra coll.* 1 (Maur. 41).28–29 (CSEL 82/3.161).

[160] The people of Thessalonika rioted over the imprisonment of one of their favorite charioteers on a charge of immorality, and in the course of the uproar the commander of the garrison was killed along with several other officials. Theodosius, enraged by this act, ordered his soldiers to lure the citizens of Thessalonika into a public theater and to massacre them there.

[161] *Epistola* 51 (Maur. 15) (CSEL 82/3.212–218). Ambrose, as in the past, was somehow informed of the emperor's decision. He approached the emperor several times to plead with him to rescind his order. By the time Theodosius did, as many as seven thousand were dead at Thessalonika. Ambrose now wrote privately to the emperor, expressing his affection for Theodosius and inviting him to do penance.

[162] What actually took place, aside from the fact that the emperor was not permitted to receive the sacraments and that he performed public penance, is the subject of speculation.[4] The excommunication and penance imposed on Theodosius were short compared to the standards of the ancient Church: by Christmastime they were lifted. See Brown, *Power and Persuasion in Late Antiquity*, 112.

[4] See, for example, Homes Dudden, *Saint Ambrose: His Life and Times*, 1:381–391, McLynn, *Ambrose of Milan: Church and Court in a Christian Capital*, 327–330; Paredi, *Saint Ambrose: His Life and Times*, 307–310, Paulinus, *Vita Ambrosii*, 24.

[163] In late February, 391, shortly after Theodosius's reconciliation with the Church, the emperor, joined by his co-emperors, issued an uncompromising edict against paganism, which forbade not only sacrifice but even approaching or wandering through the pagan shrines, and it imposed heavy fines on

in February 391, had the result that, throughout the empire, the ceremony of the procession of welcome that marked the governor's solemn arrival in state led only to the Christian basilica and included the bishop, the public display of Christian symbols such as the processional cross and great copies of the Gospels, and the newly arrived governor making gestures of respect to the Christian churches that now marked the threshold of the city.

AMBROSE THE PASTOR

Despite the fact that history remembers Ambrose for defending the Church against Arianism and paganism and for defining the relationship between Church and state, the members of Ambrose's congregation knew him best, not through dramatic events like facing down the court as it attempted to seize a basilica or compelling the emperor to do public penance, but as a liturgical presence, preaching and presiding at the celebration of the Eucharist. Chadwick asserts that the "bishop's power-base, so to speak, lay always in the allegiance of his flock to the ministry of word and sacrament and to the ministry of pastoral care of which he is the focus."[164] In a letter to Marcellina, Ambrose tells us that he celebrated the Eucharist daily.[165] We have noted previously that the fourth century saw preaching become the official act of the bishop.[166] Ambrose regarded preaching as one of the principal duties of a bishop, never failing to preach to his people during the liturgy on Sundays and feast days, and preaching every day during Lent.[167]

As we shall see, Ambrose was a powerful preacher, and his sermons affected many, including Augustine, whom he baptized at Milan on Easter in the year 387. Ambrose was one of the first to write metrical

---

certain public officials who ignored the law. Since Theodosius was in Milan when the edict was issued, it is perfectly reasonable to assume that Ambrose had influenced the recently absolved emperor. Another law directed specifically against the pagan cult in Egypt followed in June of that year. In 392 the pagan senators asked Valentinian to restore the cult subsidies, only to be refused for a final time.

[164] Chadwick, *The Role of the Christian Bishop in Ancient Society*, 4.
[165] *Epistola* 76 (Maur. 20).15 (CSEL 82/3.116). In *De sacramentis*, 5.25 (SC 25bis.133), Ambrose encourages the daily reception of Communion.
[166] Above, 3, n. 5.
[167] Paredi, *Saint Ambrose: His Life and Times*, 259.

Latin hymns, many of which are still used in Christian churches. His introduction of the congregational singing of psalms and hymns during the basilica conflict of 386[168] became a hallmark of Milanese Christianity.[169] To the faithful Ambrose represented an instrument of divine grace, his ordination considered by them to be a sacramental act conferring a charismatic gift of grace appropriate to the office.[170]

Pastoral availability and hospitality were important characteristics of Ambrose's ministry as bishop.[171] He taught that a bishop should be easily approachable by anyone who needed advice.[172] He reports an occasion when a magistrate named Studius approached him for advice on the morality of capital punishment.[173] Augustine gives us an insight into how available Ambrose made himself to his people.[174] We are told that his home was open to anyone who wanted to enter, and none of his visitors was announced beforehand. Sometimes, as visitors arrived, they found Ambrose absorbed in his reading, trying to snatch a few moments of quiet from a busy schedule.[175] Augustine relates that on such occasions he would not interrupt Ambrose, but pastoral experience teaches that not everyone would have been so sensitive.

---

[168] See above, 55.

[169] References are usefully collected in James McKinnon, *Music in Early Christian Literature* (Cambridge, N.Y.: Cambridge University Press, 1987) 125–134. For an appreciation of Ambrose's role as "théoricien et maitre de la poésie liturgique," see Jacques Fontaine, *Naissance de la poésie dans l'occident chrétien* (Paris: Études Augustiniennes, 1981) 127–141. Ambrose's love of music and his use of hymns are also discussed in Moorhead, *Ambrose: Church and Society in the Late Roman World*, 140–143.

[170] 1 Timothy 4; 2 Timothy 1:6; Chadwick, *The Role of the Christian Bishop in Ancient Society*, 5.

[171] We are distinguishing here between pastoral availability and personal accessibility. For while Ambrose was pastorally available to his people, he was not personally accessible to them. On Ambrose exercising great control over his image, see below, 80, n. 239.

[172] *De officiis ministrorum*, 2.12.61 (PL 16.119).

[173] *Epistola* 28 (Maur. 50) (CSEL 82/1.187–194).

[174] Augustine, *Confessions*, 6.3.3 (CCSL 27.102).

[175] McLynn looks upon Ambrose's practice of admitting people to his home while he studied not as a sign of his accessibility and hospitality but as a staged event designed to allow the public to see how far Ambrose was progressing in his studies. McLynn, *Ambrose of Milan: Church and Court in a Christian Capital*, 57.

Homes Dudden reports that Ambrose kept an open table for all comers and that persons of the highest rank, as well as the poor and strangers, shared meals with him.[176]

Paulinus unintentionally testifies to Ambrose's approachability when he recounts an incident that occurred when Ambrose was a guest at the home of a distinguished Roman matron.[177] A woman of very low social standing sought Ambrose out at the matron's home because she had heard that he was nearby, and she believed that he could cure the paralysis that had disabled her. She had herself transported directly to him at the matron's home, and she clung to him as he prayed for her and placed his hands on her.[178] A further aspect of Ambrose's accessibility was his readiness to correspond with those who wrote to him, whether to answer serious theological questions or just to be friendly. Not only did Ambrose respond to these letters, it seems he usually answered them in his own hand.[179] Thus, in being pastorally available, "Ambrose presented himself as a serene and readily accessible guide to the perplexed."[180]

As bishop, Ambrose was responsible for reconciling sinners to the Church, and in this capacity he displays the essential Gospel value of forgiveness. Paulinus speaks movingly of Ambrose's sympathy for those who confessed their sins to him: "he so wept as to compel the other person to weep as well, for he seemed to himself to be cast down along with anyone else who was cast down."[181] In *De penitentia* Ambrose draws the connection between his having been elected bishop, which, as we have said,[182] he considered an experience of grace, and how he must deal with sinners:

"Preserve, O Lord, your work, guard the gift which you have given even to him who shrank from it. For I knew that I was not worthy to be called a bishop, because I had devoted myself to this world, but by your grace I am what I am. Indeed, I am the least of all the bishops

---

[176] Homes Dudden, *The Life and Times of Saint Ambrose*, 1:111; cf. *De officiis ministrorum*, 2.21.103 (PL 16.131).

[177] Paulinus, *Vita Ambrosii*, 10 (Navoni, 66).

[178] Cf. Luke 7:36-50.

[179] *Epistola* 37 (Maur. 47).1-3 (CSEL 82/2.20–21).

[180] McLynn, *Ambrose of Milan: Church and Court in a Christian Capital*, 254.

[181] Paulinus, *Vita Ambrosii*, 39 (Navoni, 118).

[182] Above, 46–47.

and the lowest in terms of merit.[183] Yet, inasmuch as I too have taken up some labor on behalf of your Church, protect this fruit, so as not to allow to perish as a bishop him whom you called to the office of bishop when he was lost. And grant first that I may know how to console sinners with profound sensitivity, for this is the highest virtue. . . . Whenever the offense of some sinner is laid bare, let me be compassionate. Let me not rebuke him proudly but mourn and weep, so that as I shed tears over someone else I may weep for myself.[184]

Although elected by his own see, no small part of the aura attached to the local bishop depended on his recognition by the bishops of neighboring churches. In councils and synods the bishop represented his people; however, to his people the bishop represented the synod, that is, the "unity and universality among the federation of local churches bonded together in eucharistic communion, spread through the Mediterranean world of the Roman Empire."[185] Their authority was further enhanced by the fact that, in the late fourth century, bishops, though in communion with one another across the Church, were supreme in their sees, accountable to no one else, except in fairly unusual circumstances. Any bishop, but especially the bishop of a city as influential as Milan, would eventually be called upon to involve himself in affairs of the greater Church. Ambrose served as the only metropolitan in northern Italy and was responsible for supervising the dioceses of the province.[186] His duties in this capacity included convening councils, hearing appeals, determining the proper day for celebrating Easter, and ordaining bishops for other cities.

Finally, as an advocate of virginity, Ambrose became one of the principal spokesmen for a movement that was shaping the Western Church.[187] By the end of the fourth century, "benches in the apse raised on steps, thrones veiled with curtains, processions and the chanting

---

[183] Cf. 1 Corinthians 15:9–10.

[184] *De penitentia*, 2.8.73 (SC 179.180).

[185] Chadwick, *The Role of the Christian Bishop in Ancient Society*, 1.

[186] On Ambrose's ministry as metropolitan, see Chadwick, *The Role of the Christian Bishop in Ancient Society*, 3–4; Homes Dudden, *The Life and Times of Saint Ambrose*, 1:126–129.

[187] In the following discussion, I am indebted especially to Peter Brown, *The Body and Society: Men, Women and Sacred Renunciation in Early Christianity* (New York: Columbia University Press, 1988), esp. chap. 13, "Daughters of Jerusalem," 259–284, and McLynn's section "Concerning Virgins," in *Ambrose*

crowds of virgins" were an integral part of a bishop's show of power.[188] For many late Roman parents, women, like wealth, were theirs to use as matrimonial pawns,[189] and the clergy's regard for virgins as "sacred vessels dedicated to the Lord" threatened the family-arranged marriages that knit together the families of a community. A gift given to the Church was "sacred," and, therefore, irrevocable. Thus, the presence of dedicated virgins, who had often dedicated themselves to Christ despite the demands of their families, provided a powerful symbol of the permanent place the Church had come to hold in Roman society. "Bodies withdrawn in perpetuity from the normal ebb and flow of marital strategies radiated the clear message that the Church led by [its] bishops . . . had every intention of holding on to the wealth and the human persons offered to it by a pious laity."[190] In the imperial laws of the period, consecrated women were spoken of with utmost respect: they were "most sacred persons."[191] Furthermore, in the West, sheltered nuns, the "brides of Christ," became the stereotypical representatives of heroic asceticism. They were thought of by their male spokesmen as harboring a deposit of values particularly precious to the Church.

Women with ascetic vocations emerged in upper-class circles, where they possessed the wealth and prestige necessary to make a permanent impact on the Christian Church. The faceless seclusion of virgins, who left the inner rooms of their family home only to participate in the ceremonies of the local church, bestowed on them a supernatural aura that attracted the interest of the entire community. Building upon this interest, Ambrose not only gave consecrated virgins a place of prominence in his preaching, but he also dramatically displayed their commitment in public through the spectacular ceremony of *velatio*, the initiation of the new virgin by the bishop into new profession.[192] Despite the scarcity of candidates in Milan, Ambrose continued these

---

of Milan: Church and Court in a Christian Capital, 259–284. On Ambrose's attitude toward women, see Moorhead, *Ambrose: Church and Society in the Late Roman World*, 40–70.

[188] Brown, *The Body and Society*, 260.

[189] *De virginibus*, 1.11.65-66 (Cazzaniga, 33–34).

[190] Brown, *The Body and Society*, 262.

[191] Ibid.

[192] For a description of this ceremony, see Nicetas Remesiana, *De lapsu virginis*, 19–20 (where the ceremony marks the climax of the Easter celebration) in A. E. Burn, *Nicetas of Remesiana: His Life and Works* (Cambridge, 1905). Cf. Ambrose,

ceremonies by bringing initiates to be sanctified at Milan from throughout northern Italy and as far as the remote parts of North Africa.[193] In this way Ambrose defined the Church's position—and hence his own—as sacred and therefore privileged.

THE MORAL LEADER

In his pastoral dealings with the members of his congregation, Ambrose felt it his duty to call his parishioners from the excesses of Milanese society to the higher calling of the Christian life. Ambrose's sermons and other writings provide us with chance encounters with his parishioners outside of worship, through which we can glean a hint of their everyday lives.[194] In particular, his treatises *De Nabuthae, De Tobia*, and *De Helia et ieiunio* respectively reflect the excessive

---

De virginibus, 3.1.1 (Cazzaniga, 57) on Marcellina's initiation at a crowded St. Peter's.

[193] Ibid., 1.10.57–59 (Cazzaniga, 30–31).

[194] Whereas Homes Dudden asserts that Ambrose's sermons and treatises shed light upon "the morals and manners of contemporary society," McLynn argues that "Ambrose's works do not give any conclusive evidence for either the social conditions prevailing in Milan or his own ideological position." Cf. Homes Dudden, *The Life and Times of Saint Ambrose*, 2:461; McLynn, *Ambrose of Milan: Church and Court in a Christian Capital*, 246.

McLynn is correct in questioning the degree to which social historians have assumed that Ambrose's writings offer a clear window upon his own beliefs and that Ambrose's observations accurately reflect the state of contemporary Italy. However, McLynn's dismissal of Ambrose's works as providing no insight into the social context of contemporary Milan is an overstatement. McLynn reasons that Ambrose's background as a wealthy assessor, his relationships with the rich and powerful, the fact that his protests against the excesses of the wealthy were lifted from his Greek sources rather than from direct observation, and Ambrose's allegorical rather than literal style together "ensured that any glass he held up to his society was riddling and dark." Ibid., 247. McLynn's comparison of Ambrose's preaching with that of Chrysostom (ibid.) seems to reveal a bias that prophetic preaching must be the direct attack upon the mighty by one who stood outside normal patterns of social intercourse. Yet, one of the most famous examples of "prophetic preaching"—the condemnation of David by Nathan (2 Sam 12:1-6)—is an indirect, allegorical message delivered by a court insider. On Ambrose's teaching that preaching is an act of subtle persuasion rather than direct confrontation, see his discussion of "sweet" and "stinging" sermons in *Epistola* 36 (Maur. 36).2.8–11, 13, 18, 26 (CSEL 82/2.6–8, 10, 12, 17). See below, 103.

luxury of the rich in contrast to the poor, the greed that characterized Milanese society, and the unrestrained habits of the people, particularly drunkenness.[195] Elsewhere Ambrose describes the Milanese's love of horse races and theatrical productions. From these works we can briefly review Ambrose's preaching on Milanese society.

The rich of Ambrose's time evidently lived in extravagant luxury. Their palaces were regal in their splendor.[196] They spent vast amounts of money on clothes. Ambrose describes the rich lords decked out, like women, in trailing garments of silk or gold brocade,[197] their bodies drenched with perfumes,[198] and their wives completely dominated by an irrational attraction to jewelry and fine clothes.[199] The palaces of the rich were filled with an incredible number of slaves. In addition to the many slaves required to carry out the work of the household, many servants were maintained purely for show or for amusement.[200]

---

[195] McLynn argues that Ambrose's contemporary audience is more likely to have recognized these sermons as variations upon his characteristic scriptural themes and not as attacks against contemporary injustices. McLynn, *Ambrose of Milan: Church and Court in a Christian Capital*, 245. While these sermons may not be as direct and pointed as McLynn seems to think is necessary for authentic preaching on social issues and are undoubtedly rhetorical exaggerations, one wonders why Ambrose would introduce attacks against avarice, drunkenness, and usury into his preaching if these issues were not relevant to his audience.

[196] For a compilation of Ambrose's works that describe the homes of the wealthy of Milan, see Homes Dudden, *The Life and Times of Saint Ambrose*, 2:462. Works cited include *De Cain et Abel*, 1.19 (CSEL 32/1.355); *De Nabuthae*, 25, 54, 56 (CSEL 32/2.480, 499, 500); *De Tobia*, 10 (CSEL 32/2.523); *Epistola* 12 (Maur. 30).4 (CSEL 82/1.94); *Expositio in Psalmum cxviii*, 2.32, 22.38 (CSEL 62.39, 506); *Hexaemeron*. 3.53, 4.32 (CSEL 32/1.95, 137).

[197] *De Nabuthae*, 3 (CSEL 32/2.470); *De Tobia*, 19 (CSEL 32/2.527); *Hexaemeron*, 5.77 (CSEL 32/1.195); *Expositio evangelii secundum Lucam*, 5.107 (CCSL 14.167).

[198] *De Nabuthae*, 3 (CSEL 32/2.470); *De Helia et ieiunio*, 36 (CSEL 32/2.432); *Expositio evangelii secundum Lucam*, 6.27, 8.14 (CCSL 14.183, 303).

[199] *De Nabuthae*, 26 (CSEL 32.2/481); *De penitentia*, 2.88 (SC 179.188); *De virginibus*, 1.29, 55 (Cazzaniga, 15, 29); *De virginitate*, 68 (PL 16.282); *De viduis*, 28 (PL 16.246); *Expositio evangelii secundum Lucam*, 8.76 (CCSL 14.327).

[200] Many slaves were required to carry out the work of the household because in Roman households during this period a minute subdivision of labor was customary. Slaves maintained for show and amusement included footmen, pages, dancing girls, and a small army of retainers, who escorted their master and mistress when they went about. See *De Cain et Abel*, 1.14 (CSEL

Especially in the morning, the palaces were crowded with throngs of clients. "Robed in their best, they attended the daily receptions of their patron, accompanied him, as a guard of honor, when he visited the law courts or the baths, lavished flatteries upon him, and were rewarded for these civilities by a trifling dole of money and an occasional invitation to dinner."[201] The owners of these grand estates took great pride in the number and breed of their dogs and horses, sometimes even providing their favorite horses with golden bits.[202] They squandered vast amounts of money to supply their overloaded tables with exquisite provisions brought from far-distant places and with wines guaranteed to be of old and famous vintages.[203]

Despite all that they possessed, the rich were never content; the more they had, the more they sought to acquire.[204] Without shame or scruple they appropriated the desirable lands of orphans and harassed defenseless widows who owned property that they coveted with litigation.[205] While many of the rich squandered their wealth on gluttony, gambling, and debauchery,[206] some were misers who, though possessing immense wealth, voluntarily lived the life of paupers, often denying themselves even enough to eat.[207] The selfishness of these rich people was extreme. They cared nothing for the general good. They dreaded times of plenty, when food was cheap, and would store up their corn during plentiful years so that when there was a shortage, they could place it on the market at an extortionate price. Thus times of scarcity that caused public suffering and distress were

---

32/1.348); *De Helia et ieunio*, 54 (CSEL 32/2.444); *De penitentia*, 2.43 (SC 179.160); *De Tobia*, 19 (CSEL 32/2.527); *De virginibus*, 3.25, 27 (Cazzaniga, 69, 70); *Enarrationes in xii psalmos davidicos*, 1.46; 48.25 (CSEL 64.38, 376); *Epistola* 4 (Maur. 27).13; 27 (Maur. 58).5; 15 (Maur. 69).7 (CSEL 82/1.18; 182; 114); *Hexaemeron*, 6.52 (CSEL 32/1.243).

[201] Homes Dudden, *The Life and Times of Saint Ambrose*, 2:463. Cf. *Enarrationes in xii psalmos davidicos*, 1.46; 48.25 (CSEL 64.38, 376); *De Tobia*, 17 (CSEL 32/2.526); *Hexaemeron*, 3.30 (CSEL 32/1.78).

[202] *De Nabuthae*, 54, 56 (CSEL 32/2.499, 500); *Enarrationes in xii psalmos davidicos*, 1.46 (CSEL 64.38).

[203] *De Tobia*, 17, 19 (CSEL 32/2.526, 527); *De Helia et ieunio*, 24, 32 (CSEL 32/2.425, 429); *Expositio evangelii secundum Lucam*, Prol. 6 (CCSL 14.5).

[204] *De Nabuthae*, 4 (CSEL 32/2.471); *De Abraham*, 1.12 (CSEL 32/1.511).

[205] *Expositio in Psalmum cxviii*, 16.7 (CSEL 62.354).

[206] *De Nabuthae*, 13 (CSEL 32/2.475).

[207] Ibid., 16–18 (CSEL 32/2.475–476).

welcomed as an opportunity for private profit.[208] Some of the rich were hypocritical as well as cruel. They came to church and kept the fasts, and all the while schemed how to legally rob their neighbors.[209] They were even impudent enough to defend their intolerance of the poor on the ground that it would be wrong to meddle with the dispensations of divine providence.[210]

The practice of usury was another scandal. The legal rate of interest was 1 percent per month, or 12 percent per annum. But the law was evaded, and sometimes as much as 50 percent per annum was exacted.[211] Money-lending was thus extremely profitable, so much so that not only lay people but even members of the clergy found this means of increasing their fortunes an irresistible temptation. The Church, on the grounds of the scriptural injunctions against usury, condemned all lending at interest and deposed members of the clergy who were guilty of it.[212] But the evil was too deep-rooted to be eradicated by ecclesiastical legislation. Ambrose, like the majority of early Christian teachers, refused to tolerate usury even in the mildest form.[213] He denounced it as an evil that produced a "viper's brood" of ever-multiplying evils,[214] calling usury a crime equal to murder and idolatry.[215]

Drunkenness appears to have been peculiarly prevalent at Milan. Ambrose describes the lower classes with hardly a shirt on their backs sitting in front of the taverns and talking grandly about politics, while they drink up a whole week's earnings in a single day. From talking they fall to quarreling, and from quarreling to fighting, until the blood of the tipsy brawlers was mingled with the wine.[216] Yet, drunkenness was not confined to persons of the lower class; it was prevalent among

---

[208] Ibid., 35 (CSEL 32/2.487); *De officiis ministrorum*, 3.41 (PL 16.149).

[209] *De Nabuthae*, 44, 45 (CSEL 32/2.492–493).

[210] Ibid., 40 (CSEL 32/2.490).

[211] Homes Dudden, *The Life and Times of Saint Ambrose*, 2:470.

[212] The seventeenth canon of the Council of Nicaea directed that any cleric who lent money at interest should be deposed and have his name struck off the canon.

[213] *De Tobia*, 7, 48, 52 (CSEL 32/2.521, 546, 548); *De officiis ministrorum*, 3.20 (PL 16.150).

[214] *De Tobia*, 41, 42 (CSEL 32/2.541, 542).

[215] Ibid., 51, 52 (CSEL 32/2.547, 548).

[216] *De Helia et ieunio*, 42, 43 (CSEL 32/2.436); *Enarrationes in xii psalmos davidicos*, 1.29 (CSEL 64.23).

all classes. Ambrose provides a lively picture of a regimental mess in which it is the ambition of every warrior to show that he can drink the most. The soldiers compete in drinking contests, and to refuse to participate in this Bacchanalian rivalry is considered a disgrace.[217] Ambrose indicates that drinking went on at all hours and in almost all places. Even at dawn there was a bustle in all the taverns.[218] At the chapels and tombs of the martyrs people drank from morning till night, as though their prayers would not be heard unless they offered them when half-intoxicated.[219] Women, who even in the recesses of their own houses ought not to be seen or heard by strangers, roamed the streets singing, dancing, tossing their hair, clapping their hands, displaying their persons, to the amusement of dissolute young men who witnessed the degrading spectacle.[220] "How can I bear to speak of such things?" Ambrose cried. "Yet how, consistently with my duty, can I pass them by in silence? How, again, can I bewail them fittingly? Wine has caused the loss of innumerable souls."[221]

Ambrose also publicly deplored the prevailing laxity in marriage.[222] A particular emphasis of the first book of Ambrose's *De Abraham*[223] is his application of Christian virtues to marriage.[224] Ambrose sees in the moral decay of the end of the fourth century, from which the common mentality was informed, an obstacle to faith that he must address with great vigor in order to establish in the conscience of his hearers the clear borders between lawful and illicit, especially in marriage. Thus the adulterer and the concubine are frequently condemned.[225] Divorce is compared to adultery, though judged a less serious offense.[226] The

---

[217] *De Helia et ieunio*, 46–50; 62–64 (CSEL 32/2.438–441, 448–449).

[218] Ibid., 55 (CSEL 32/2.444).

[219] Ibid., 62 (CSEL 32/2.448).

[220] Ibid., 66 (CSEL 32/2.450).

[221] Ibid., 67 (CSEL 32/2.451).

[222] *Hexaemeron*, 5.18, 19 (CSEL 32/1.153–154); *De Abraham*, 1.8, 23, 25 (CSEL 32/2.507, 517, 519).

[223] For a discussion of *De Abraham*, see below, 150.

[224] *De Abraham*, 1.16 (CSEL 32/1.513): the qualities of a spouse; 1.84 (CSEL 32/1.555): conditions for a good marriage; 1.91 (CSEL 32/1.561): counsel for remaining faithful. See Franco Gori, *Sant'Ambrogio: Abramo: Opere esegetiche II/II* (Milan: Bibliotheca Ambrosiana; Rome: Città nuova, 1984) 13.

[225] *De Abraham*, 1.7, 8; 1.19; 1.23, 25, 26; 1.59, 65 (CSEL 32/1.507; 517, 519, 520; 540, 544).

[226] Ibid., 1.59 (CSEL 32/1.540).

absence of morals associated with marriage particularly illustrates the disorientation that accompanied the period of transition in which the permissiveness of the pagan legal norm stood in stark contrast with the gradually increasing influence of Christian moral doctrine.[227]

Finally, Ambrose blasted the circus and the theater. Ambrose condemned the vanity of the spectacles of the circus and the fact that they kept people away from church.[228] He also warned against the corrupting influence of the theater, which he regarded as being full of evil.[229]

Ambrose's descriptions of the excessive luxury of the rich in contrast to the poor, the greed that characterized Milanese society, the unrestrained habits of the people, particularly drunkenness, the absence of morality in marriage, and the Milanese's love of horse races and theatrical productions may, in fact, be exaggerated. Nevertheless, they underscore his conviction that the everyday world in which Christians lived was a place filled with temptations that threatened their faith. He therefore thought it his duty to teach his people how to live Christian virtues in a hostile world.

In order to teach people in virtue, Ambrose felt that the bishop should surpass all others in the practice of Christian values,[230] and that in order to counsel others in Christian virtue, priests need to embody that virtue themselves. He asks, "Who seeks for a spring in the mud? Who wants to drink from muddy water?"[231] Ambrose felt that only a person of character was equipped to teach and counsel others in the life of virtue and guide them in the path of salvation. He wrote:

"Such, then, ought he to be who gives counsel to another, in order that he may offer himself as a pattern in all good works, in teaching, in trueness of character, in seriousness. Thus his words will be wholesome and irreproachable, his counsel useful, his life virtuous, and his opinions seemly. . . . He must have nothing dark, or deceptive, or

---

[227] Gori, *Abramo*, 13.

[228] *De fuga saeculi*, 4 (CSEL 32/2.165); *Hexaemeron*, 5.34 (CSEL 32/1.167); *Expositio in Psalmum cxviii*, 5.28, 16.45 (CSEL 62.97, 376); *Enarrationes in xii psalmos davidicos*, 39.4 (CSEL 64.215).

[229] *Hexaemeron*, 3.5 (CSEL 32/1.61); *De penitentia*, 2.42 (SC 179.160); *Epistola* 27 (Maur. 58).5 (CSEL 82/1.185); *Expositio evangelii secundum Lucam*, 6.8, 7.37 (CCSL 14.176, 227); *Expositio in Psalmum cxviii*, 16.17 (CSEL 62.361).

[230] *Epistola* 14 (Maur. 63).59, 64 (CSEL 82/3.265, 269).

[231] *De officiis ministrorum*, 2.12.60 (PL 16.118).

false about him, to cast a shadow on his life and character, nothing wicked or evil to keep back those who want advice.[232]

Thus in *De officiis ministrorum*, Ambrose gives specific prescriptions to his clergy for their ministry at the altar of Christ. These directives include an emphasis on celibacy so that the office is not "defiled" by conjugal intercourse and a recommendation that priests abstain from wine so that they may be upheld by the good witness not only of the faithful but also by those who have no faith. These guidelines show Ambrose's concern that the dignity of the office be maintained so that God can be glorified. He writes, "Thus he who sees the minister of the altar adorned with suitable virtues may praise their Author, and reverence the Lord who has such servants."[233]

For Ambrose, Christian character involves a rejection of the "pleasures" of this world for two reasons. First, these pleasures inhibit the development of likeness to God.[234] Moreover, the clergy cannot be entrapped by the pleasures of the world, because "raising up the likeness of Christ" involves a way of life that is counter to many cultural standards. For example, Ambrose insists that the only proper ambition for the clergy is the virtues of the office to which they are called and not either the ambition for glory, money, and power so common in Roman society or ecclesiastical success. Thus Ambrose insists on the importance of humility and a disciplined life, particularly in the area of speech. Ambrose warns that the clergy need to be careful not only in what they do but also in what they say. In all things they are to reflect the disciplined grace of a virtuous life, for as Ambrose puts it with reference to talking too much, "An overflowing river quickly gathers mud."[235]

AMBROSE'S PRIVATE SIDE

Ambrose was, of course, also a man with a personality and private side. He stood five feet four inches tall.[236] The early fifth-century

---

[232] Ibid., 2.17.86, 88 (PL 16.126).
[233] Ibid., 1.50.256 (PL 16.101).
[234] Ibid., 1.49.254 (PL 16.100).
[235] Ibid., 1.3.12 (PL 16.27).
[236] Ambrose's height is confirmed by the evidence of his bones, which were carefully examined in 1871. A. Ratti, "Il più antico ritratto di S. Ambrogio," in *Ambrosiana: Scritti vari pubblicati ne XV centenario dalla morte di sant'Ambrogio*

Figure 1 Mosaic of Ambrose, Milan, Church of Sant'Ambrogio, Chapel of San Vittore in Ciel d'Oro.

mosaic of Ambrose in the Chapel of San Vittore in Ciel d'Oro, or San Satiro, in the Church of Sant'Ambrogio in Milan (Figure 1) portrays a rather gaunt and frail figure, with a high forehead, a long melancholy face, and great eyes. Allowing for a certain desire on the part of the unknown artist to portray Ambrose as ascetic and holy, the detail of the painting prevents us from dismissing it as false. We may infer from this image that, physically, Ambrose was not a robust man. From Augustine's *Confessions* we learn something about Ambrose's health that must have preoccupied him, given the amount of public speaking that he was obliged to do. In the passage, previously cited, which relates the bishop's habit of reading silently to himself rather than aloud, as seems to have been customary in antiquity, Augustine speculates that Ambrose's reason for this practice was perhaps to save his voice, which easily grew hoarse.[237] In other words, Ambrose

---

(Milan, 1897) 5–74. Cf. Homes Dudden, *The Life and Times of St. Ambrose*, 1:114, n. 8.

[237] Augustine, *Confessions*, 6.3.3 (CCSL 27.75).

evidently suffered from some chronic malady of the throat. Ambrose himself appears to hint at this ailment toward the end of one of his mystagogical sermons when he comments that his voice grows weak.[238]

We can glean from Ambrose's behavior at crucial moments in his ministry some of the personality traits that make up his character: determination, decisiveness, fearlessness, zeal, compassion, political astuteness, commitment to law and order, reserve, and also intolerance. Ambrose enhanced these personality traits by carefully controlling his self-presentation.[239] He also enjoyed an elevated position in Milanese society due to his close contacts with court society in Milan, connections to Roman society, and links to the Roman church.

Paulinus describes Ambrose's personality in terms requisite for a saint. Immediately after his ordination Ambrose handed over his wealth to the Church and to the poor and became both an example

---

[238] *De sacramentis*, 1.24 (SC 25bis.72). Cf. *Apologia prophetae David*, 2.5.28 (CSEL 32.2.376).

[239] The underlying premise of McLynn's study of Ambrose is that whatever can be known of Ambrose depends upon literature the bishop himself carefully controlled. McLynn asserts that no body of patristic literature is as carefully controlled as Ambrose's and cites as evidence of Ambrose's control over his works the fact that he sent his work to a friend to be combed for any "barrister's pleasantries," [*Epistola* 32 (Maur. 48).3], that his exegetical treatises are collated rather than transcribed from his sermons, and that he organized his correspondence into a collection. McLynn asserts that none of Ambrose's contemporaries shows such constant attention to the form in which their works were issued or was so keenly aware that his books would have to "speak for themselves." See *Epistola* 32 (Maur. 48).3. McLynn further asserts that Ambrose's editorial hand extends even to the biography of Paulinus, whose reverence for the bishop precluded independent judgment. McLynn concludes that Ambrose's works reveal a self-constructed figure, a public persona, and that to rely upon the biography of Ambrose presented in these works "risks mistaking studio portraits of the bishop for snapshots." McLynn describes his own book as emphasizing the circumstances and forces which helped to mold the façade of Ambrose's public persona. See McLynn, *Ambrose of Milan: Church and Court in a Christian Capital*, xvi–xix. While Ambrose was undoubtedly concerned about his public image, McLynn's underlying assumption seems to be that there is a vast discrepancy between the bishop of Milan's public persona and Ambrose's true personality; this assumption leads McLynn to operate from a hermeneutic of suspicion that is deconstructive, even cynical.

and an advocate of strict asceticism.[240] Paulinus tells us that Ambrose fasted daily and was most diligent in praying day and night. Ambrose's devotion to prayer is reflected in his instructions to virgins, where he recommends a sevenfold pattern of daily prayer:

"Let frequent prayer also commend us to God. For if the prophet who was preoccupied with the demands of his kingdom said: 'Seven times a day I have praised you,' what does it behoove us to do, who read: 'Watch and pray, lest you enter into temptation'? Solemn prayers with thanksgiving should certainly be made when we arise from sleep, when we go out, when we are about to eat, when we have eaten, and at the hour of incense, when at last we are going to bed.

But even in bed I want you to join psalms with the Lord's Prayer in frequent alteration, as also when you wake up or before drowsiness floods your body. . . . Daily, too, before daybreak, we ought to make a point of going over the Creed, which is as it were the seal of our hearts. Even when something frightens us we should have recourse to it in our soul."[241]

Homes Dudden is surely correct that what Ambrose recommended to virgins he practiced himself.[242] It is particularly noteworthy that Ambrose emphasized the importance of praying during the night.[243] In fact, he even says that the greater part of the night ought to be devoted to prayer and reading.[244] The value that Ambrose placed on fasting is obvious in his treatise *De Helia et ieiunio*, in which he glorified the discipline as having physical, moral, and salvific benefits.[245]

---

[240] Paulinus, *Vita Ambrosii*, 38 (Navoni, 116). Homes Dudden asserts that this cannot be correct because Ambrose's own writings show that, years after his ordination, he still possessed private property. Homes Dudden, *The Life and Times of Saint Ambrose*, 1:107; cf. Ambrose, *Epistola* 76 (Maur. 20).8 (CSEL 82/3.114); *Contra Auxentium*, 5 (CSEL 82/3.85); *De excessu fratris*, 1.24 (CSEL 73.222).

[241] *De virginibus*, 3.4.18-20 (Cazzaniga, 65–66); cf. *Expositio evangelii secundum Lucam*, 7.88 (CCSL 14.243).

[242] Homes Dudden, *The Life and Times of Saint Ambrose*, 1:108.

[243] *Expositio in Psalmum cxviii*, 8.45-52 (CSEL 62.178–183); cf. ibid., 7.31 (CSEL 62.145); *Expositio evangelii secundum Lucam*, 7.87, 88 (CCSL 14.242–243); *De Abraham*, 1.9.84 (CSEL 32-1.555).

[244] *Expositio in Psalmum cxviii*, 7.32 (CSEL 62.145).

[245] For a fine summary of *De Helia et ieiunio*, see Homes Dudden, *The Life and Times of Saint Ambrose*, 1:108, n. 10.

Ambrose encouraged his people to fast, especially during Lent,[246] and was laborious in his own observance of this discipline.[247] Ambrose's willingness to part with his property upon ordination points not only to a concern for the poor but also to an attraction to poverty itself, which Paulinus underlines when he describes Ambrose as Christ's "stripped and unencumbered soldier," desirous of following his Lord, who had himself embraced poverty when he embraced the human condition.[248]

Ambrose's letters reveal a willingness to endure martyrdom. In letters to Marcellina, Ambrose twice expresses his readiness to shed his blood in the context of the confrontation with the imperial court in 386.[249] Two months later he wrote to her that after the discovery of the bones of the martyrs Gervasius and Protasius, he had told his congregation (with a hint of regret) that he had found the relics because he was unworthy to be a martyr himself.[250] A year after that, Ambrose wrote to the priest Horantianus that he pleads for a martyr's suffering, but when the Holy Spirit sees his weakness, the Spirit says, "This you cannot accept." Ambrose laments the fact that he has had opportunities to be a martyr, and "almost at the very brink I have been called back!"[251]

Boniface Ramsey observes that Ambrose, occasionally dropping his natural reserve, shares with his readers his deeply personal relationship with Christ.[252] For example, in his early treatise *De fide*, while discussing Christ's human nature and the sufferings that he took upon himself on behalf of humankind, Ambrose suddenly stops speaking of the Savior in the third person and begins to address him directly and with touching warmth: "Not your wounds, but mine, hurt you, Lord Jesus; not your death but our weakness, even as the prophet says: 'For he is afflicted for our sakes'—and we, Lord, judged you afflicted, when you grieved not for yourself, but for me."[253] In *De penitentia* Ambrose again addresses Christ on the theme of repentance:

---

[246] *De Helia et ieiunio*, 21.79 (CSEL 32/2.460); *De virginibus*, 3.4.17 (Cazzaniga, 65).

[247] For a discussion of Ambrose's practice of fasting see Homes Dudden, *The Life and Times of Saint Ambrose*, 1:108–110.

[248] Paulinus, *Vita Ambrosii*, 38 (Navoni, 116).

[249] *Epistola* 76 (Maur. 20).5, 28 (CSEL 82/3.110, 125).

[250] *Epistola* 22 (Maur. 77).12 (CSEL 82/3.134).

[251] *Epistola* 36 (Maur. 23).4 (CSEL 82/1.168).

[252] Ramsey, *Ambrose*, 45.

[253] *De fide*, 2.7.54 (PL 16.570).

"Would that you might reserve for me, O Jesus, the washing of your feet, which you dirtied by walking in me! . . . Would that you might deign to come to this tomb of mine, Lord Jesus, and that you might wash me with your tears! For my eyes are hard and I do not have such tears as to be able to wash away my sins. If you weep for me, I shall be saved."[254]

Further evidence of Ambrose's personal devotion to Christ is found in the great number of times he mentions Jesus in his treatises on the Old Testament, where he finds the Savior prefigured everywhere. While this is not unusual in the writings of the Fathers, what is striking in Ambrose's approach to Christ is his extensive application of the Song of Songs to him. In *De virginibus* and *De mysteriis*, Ambrose sees Christ as the bridegroom of the Song of Songs, in reference to virgins in the former and to the Church, particularly the newly baptized, in the latter.[255] Elsewhere in his writings, Ambrose presents Christ as the bridegroom of the Song of Songs as the bridegroom of the soul.[256]

Ramsey is correct that when Ambrose writes generally of the Christian soul as the bride of Christ, he is speaking of his own soul as well. The fact that in writing of the Christian soul as the bride of Christ Ambrose is borrowing directly from Origen, who had a very strong personal piety centered in Christ, indicates that the bishop of Milan found in the Alexandrian's relationship to Christ a description of his own. "It is a relationship that, with Origen, he finds perfectly appropriate to express in the erotic vocabulary of the Song of Songs. Beneath his Roman reserve, Ambrose's passion had an outlet in his highly expressive love for Christ."[257] Thus, Ambrose's genuine devotion to Christ was nourished by and found expression in what he read.

AMBROSE THE THEOLOGIAN

From his ordination Ambrose devoted himself to preparing himself to fulfill the duties of his new office. He spent his nights and his rare free daylight hours studying the doctrine of the Church and in

---

[254] *De penitentia*, 2.8.67, 71 (SC 179.178).
[255] Cf. *De virginibus*, 1.8.46–47 (Cazzaniga, 23–24); *De mysteriis*, 6.29 (SC 25bis.172), 7.35–41 (SC 174, 176, 178), 9.55–57 (SC 188, 190).
[256] *Epistola* 11 (Maur. 29).9–10 (CSEL 82/1.83).
[257] Ramsey, *Ambrose*, 46–47.

improving his scriptural training.[258] Ambrose did this because he was so completely unprepared theologically for the duties of his office. In his treatise *De officiis ministrorum* Ambrose declares of himself, "I began to teach before I began to learn. Therefore I must learn and teach at the same time, since I had no leisure to learn before."[259] In learning Christian theology Ambrose relied on his knowledge of Greek. His curriculum consisted of the Greek tradition—Origen, Basil, Hippolytus of Rome, Eusebius of Caesarea, Didymus the Blind, Gregory Nazianzus, and Athanasius, as well as Jewish writers such as Philo and Flavius Josephus.[260] McLynn contends that Ambrose had to meet the standard set by Auxentius, "a native speaker of Greek whose service to a learned bishop at Alexandria had given him a good grounding in contemporary theology," in order to meet the expectations of the Milanese congregation.[261] As we have noted previously, Ambrose's custom, attested to by Augustine, of admitting visitors to his silent study sessions certainly allowed the people of Milan to see the progress their bishop was making with his studies.[262]

In addition to providing for his own theological training, knowledge of Greek enabled Ambrose to introduce much Eastern theology into the West, making him one of the most important Latin authors of his day. By making Greek ideas accessible to Westerners who knew nothing or relatively little of the Greek language, Ambrose served as a cultural mediator, bringing the Christian spirituality of the East to the Western part of the empire. Ambrose transmitted to the Latin Churches the Alexandrian heritage by translating and paraphrasing Philo, Origen, and Athanasius; and he adopted the older Platonic tradition, as well as the more recent views of Neoplatonism, to Christian beliefs.

AMBROSE THE SAINT

Ambrose ruled the church at Milan twenty-three years, from 373 until his death on Easter Eve, April 4, 397. As he desired, Ambrose was buried in the basilica that bears his name, at the side of the martyrs Protasius and Gervasius. Paulinus reports that miracles surrounded

---

[258] Augustine, *Confessions*, 6.3.3 (CCSL 27.75).
[259] *De officiis ministrorum*, 1.1.4 (PL 16.24).
[260] Homes Dudden, *The Life and Times of Saint Ambrose*, 1:113ff.
[261] McLynn, *Ambrose of Milan: Church and Court in a Christian Capital*, 57.
[262] See above, 68. Augustine, *Confessions*, 6.3.3 (CCSL 27.75); McLynn, *Ambrose of Milan: Church and Court in a Christian Capital*, 57.

the event and, in what seems an attempt to enhance Ambrose's influence after his death, presents him as appearing in visions at strategic moments, offering much needed help with dramatic consequences.[263] Even without such miracles, Ambrose had a profound influence on the church of Milan and the Christian world.

[263] Paulinus, *Vita Ambrosii*, 49–52 (Navoni, 132–136).

Chapter 3

"I yield to my desire to teach": Ambrose: The Preacher

Among the scenes depicted on the front of the altar of the Church of Sant'Ambrogio in Milan is one of Ambrose preaching, inspired by an angel (Figure 2).[1] It is an artist's rendering of the report of one who is said to have heard the bishop of Milan preach.[2] In this chapter we will paint our own portrait of Ambrose the preacher. Our purpose is to lift up those events, circumstances, personality traits, and relationships that shaped both Ambrose as a preacher and his preaching on the sacraments. Although we begin our discussion of Ambrose's method of mystagogical preaching with Ambrose himself, this in no way implies that the preacher is the most important element in this process. We could, for example, choose the Christian assembly as our starting point.[3] Nevertheless, we choose to begin with Ambrose the preacher for two reasons. First, the primary tools that Ambrose brought to his mystagogical preaching were his personality, experience, understanding, insight, and theological agenda. This is likewise true for us as we

---

[1] For a description of the *paliotto,* or "altar frontal," of the Church of Sant'Ambrogio, see Pierre Paul Courcelle, *Recherches sur saint Ambroise: "Vies" Anciennes, Culture, Iconographie* (Paris: Études Augustiniennes, 1973) 169–172. For a description of the carving of Ambrose preaching, see ibid., 176.

[2] Paulinus, *Vita Ambrosii,* 17 (Navoni, 78–80). See below, 88; 105.

[3] For a discussion of the Christian assembly as the starting point for the proclamation of the Word, see National Conference of Catholic Bishops, *Fulfilled in Your Hearing: The Homily in the Sunday Assembly* (Washington: United States Catholic Conference, 1982) 3–8; Evangelical Lutheran Church in America, *The Use of the Means of Grace: A Statement on the Practice of Word and Sacrament* (Minneapolis: Augsburg Fortress, 1997), nos. 8–9; Thomas G. Long, *The Witness of Preaching* (Louisville: Westminster/John Knox Press, 1989) 11ff.

Figure 2 Ambrose preaching, inspired by an angel. Milan, Panel of the altar frontal of the Church of Sant'Ambrogio. Photograph by Cathy Satterlee.

endeavor to preach mystagogically. Our hope in beginning with the preacher is that, in understanding the factors that shaped Ambrose as a mystagogue, we might look at our own lives in order to become aware of and better understand the tools that we bring to the task of mystagogical preaching. Second, the preacher "works within an unusual network of trust and intimacy that makes the separation of character from performance impossible" so that "all preaching is to some extent self-disclosure by the preacher."[4] Thus, the preacher, while not the most important element, is a vital ingredient in the preaching event that cannot be overlooked.

In creating our portrait of Ambrose the preacher, we will use a very interesting "pallette." First, we will evaluate Ambrose as a preacher using the assessments provided by both Ambrose's contemporaries and modern scholars. Second, we will discuss Ambrose's own views on preaching as they are found in his works. Third, we will use the attributes of an effective preacher—faith, conviction, authority, and

[4] Fred B. Craddock, *Preaching* (Nashville: Abingdon Press, 1985) 23.

grace[5]—as the lenses through which we will look on Ambrose's life in order to explore the factors that shaped him as a preacher and contributed to his effectiveness. In the fourth and final section of this chapter, we will reflect on the pneumatic dimension of our preacher, that is, the manner in which the Holy Spirit acted in Ambrose's ministry of preaching. Throughout our discussion, we will illustrate these factors as they find expression in Ambrose's sermons, with one obvious exception. Inasmuch as we will be analyzing Ambrose's mystagogical sermons in detail in subsequent chapters, examples from *De sacramentis* and *De mysteriis* in this chapter will be restrained.

AMBROSE THE PREACHER

Although he had a soft voice, Ambrose was regarded as an outstanding preacher.[6] Augustine, himself a sophisticated speaker, refers only to Ambrose's attractive style and gives his preaching much of the credit for his own conversion.[7] Augustine reports that both ardent believers and skeptical connoisseurs "hung keenly on his lips"[8] because of both the content of his sermons and his ability as a preacher. Augustine observes that his sermons, while lacking in excitement and superficial charm, were eloquent and perceptive, full of sound learning and solid instruction, and possessing in a marked degree the power of convincing those who heard them.[9] Marcellinus calls Ambrose *orator catholicus*—a preacher for all seasons; and Cassiodorus refers to him as "a distiller of milky speech, weighty yet acute, most sweet in his power of gentle persuasion, whose teaching was not inferior to his life."[10]

Ambrose's ascetic preaching aroused a stir and some anxiety. Ambrose reports that women came to Milan from afar in order to

---

[5] Ibid., 24.

[6] Augustine, *Confessions*, 6.3.3; 5.13.23 (CCSL 27.75; 27.71). On Ambrose's voice see *De sacramentis*, 1.6.24 (SC 25bis.72); *Apologia prophetae David* 2.5 (SC 239.74); below, 293–294.

[7] Augustine, *Confessions*, 5.13.23–14.24 (CCSL 27.71–74); 6.3.4 (CCSL 27.76).

[8] Ibid., 5.13.23 (CCSL 27.71).

[9] Ibid., 5.13.23, 5.14.24 (CCSL 27.71, 74); idem, *Contra Julianum*, 2.5.11 (PL 44.681).

[10] Marcellinus, *Chron.* A.D. 398; Cassiodorus, *Instit. div. litt.*, 20; cf. ibid. 1, "planus atque suavissimus doctor." As cited in Homes Dudden, *The Life and Times of Saint Ambrose* (Oxford: Clarendon Press, 1935) 2:454–455.

receive the veil from his hand, and many parents within his congregation found it necessary to dissuade their daughters from their ascetic enthusiasm to the point that Ambrose took the more pious children under his protection against their parents.[11] Finally, as we noted above,[12] Paulinus recalls an occasion when an Arian, whom he describes as a sharp debater, hard and unyielding with regard to the Catholic faith, was in church and heard Ambrose preach. Paulinus tells us that, afterward, this Arian reported having seen an angel speaking into the bishop's ear while he was preaching, so that the bishop seemed to be proclaiming the angel's words to the people. When he saw this, the man was converted and began to defend the Catholic faith.[13] While the objectivity of this report must be questioned, it speaks to the caliber of Ambrose's preaching.

Reading Ambrose's sermons today, we cannot but feel disappointed. Scholars are correct that we do not find the conversational style, precise language, originality of thought, or dramatic presence that we might well expect of a great preacher. Most important, we do not find in Ambrose's sermons an organizing theme or focus statement. Rather, many of his surviving works that were originally sermons strike us as rambling and repetitive.[14] It is important to remember that we possess only the ponderous and intricate treatises into which Ambrose edited his sermons for publication. Yet, it is in "the extreme density of scriptural citations, allusions, and reminiscences in the tissue of the prose of Ambrose"[15] that we discover what was truly distinctive about Ambrose's preaching.

For the benefit of his hearers, Ambrose could comb the books of a brilliant new generation of Greek bishops and a whole tradition of Greek Christian scholarship, giving his congregation some of the most

---

[11] *De virginibus*, 1.10.57-59 (Cazzaniga, 30–31). See above, 71.

[12] Above, 88.

[13] Paulinus, *Vita Ambrosii*, 17 (Navoni, 78–80).

[14] Examples of assessments of Ambrose's preaching by modern scholars include Yngve Brilioth, *Landmarks in the History of Preaching* (London: S.P.C.K., 1950) 6; Neil B. McLynn, *Ambrose of Milan: Church and Court in a Christian Capital* (Berkeley and Los Angeles: University of California Press, 1994) 237; Boniface Ramsey, *Ambrose* (New York: Routledge, 1997) 49.

[15] Gerard Nauroy, "L'Ecriture dans la Pastorale d'Ambroise de Milan," *Le Monde Latin Antique et La Bible*, ed. J. Fontaine and C. Pietri (Paris: Beauchesne, 1985) 371.

learned and up-to-date sermons in the Latin world. Nor did he have
any scruples about borrowing from the pagans: he gloried in being
able to parade his spoils from the pulpit—this "gold of the Egyptians"
was fair prize . . . he could parade all the great "names" [of philosophy] and their opinions, only to dismiss them with contempt; how
could these frail quibblings stand against the word of Moses, who had
spoken "mouth to mouth" with God? In any case, what was true in
these philosophers was merely plagiarized from their predecessors in
time, the Hebrew prophets.[16] People gave Ambrose their attention
because he had something new to say. Thus Augustine, who was
initially attracted by Ambrose's talents as a speaker, came to admire
his skill as an expositor as Ambrose "drew aside the veil of mystery
and opened . . . the spiritual meaning of passages." Augustine's
complete thought is worth repeating:

"Another thing that brought me joy was that the ancient writings of
the law and the prophets were now being offered to me under quite a
different aspect from that under which they had seemed to me absurd,
when I believed that your holy people held such crude opinions, for
the fact was they did not. I delighted to hear Ambrose, often asserting
in his sermons to the people, as a principle on which he must insist
emphatically, *The letter is death-dealing, but the spirit gives life*. This he
would tell them as he drew aside the veil of mystery and opened to
them the spiritual meaning of passages which, taken literally, would
seem to mislead. He said nothing which offended me, even though I
still did not know whether what he said was true."[17]

But, in addition to listening to Ambrose because of what he said,
people listened to him because of the way he said it. Ambrose "deployed
his scholarship—his extensive adaptions from other authors and
scatterings of textual variants, Hebrew etymologies, and quotations in
Greek—almost impressionistically, to suggest the range and depth of
possible meanings [of passages of Scripture] rather than to explain

---

[16] Peter Brown, *Augustine of Hippo: A Biography* (Berkeley: University of California Press, 1967) 84.

[17] Augustine, Bishop of Hippo, *Confessions*, in *The Works of Saint Augustine: A Translation for the 21st Century*, Pt. 1, vol. 1, trans. Maria Boulding, O.S.B., and ed. John E. Rotelle, O.S.A. (Hyde Park, N.Y.: New City Press, 1997) 6.6.4 (CCSL 27.76).

them systematically."[18] Ambrose "ranged through the Old Testament, unraveling one mystery after another through application of a figurative interpretation, an exhilarating fizzling of paradoxes which conjured up the possibility that sense could be made of the whole."[19]

Yet, Ambrose's actual exegesis was of secondary importance to his distinctiveness as a preacher. More important, Ambrose's constant recourse to biblical quotations and paraphrase enabled him to "speak the Bible."[20] Convinced that the Bible's mode of expression was the most appropriate for pastoral speech, Ambrose sounded like the Bible, reproducing in his preaching the texture and rhythm of Scripture itself. Ambrose accomplishes this biblical imitation by assimilating in one homogeneous speech the wealth of hundreds of scriptural memories through multiple and thin fragments, sometimes reducing a biblical reminiscence to a single suggestive word that explodes with meaning in the ears of his hearers.

Ambrose also juxtaposes biblical quotations of disparate styles in a synthetic but eminently allusive speech.[21] While our best example of Ambrose "speaking the Bible" is his description of the wife of Potiphar's attempt to seduce innocent Joseph,[22] his scriptural *suavitas* eludes us today because of the gap that exists between Ambrose's preaching and the edited, exegetical works that we possess. Unlike Ambrose's scholarship, we cannot confirm biblical rhythm and expression through indices and concordances. Yet this *suavitas*, which informed the rhythms of Ambrose's preaching and also his hymns, is perhaps more fundamental to the spell that Ambrose cast over his hearers.[23]

---

[18] McLynn, *Ambrose of Milan: Church and Court in a Christian Capital*, 238; cf. Nauroy, "L'Ecriture dans la Pastorale d'Ambroise de Milan," 385, 404.

[19] McLynn, *Ambrose of Milan: Church and Court in a Christian Capital*, 240.

[20] Nauroy, "L'Ecriture dans la Pastorale d'Ambroise de Milan," 404.

[21] Ibid.

[22] *De Ioseph*, 5.22-23 (CSEL 32.2.88–89). For an analysis of the "scriptural harmonics" of this text, see Nauroy, "L'Ecriture dans la Pastorale d'Ambroise de Milan," 402–404.

[23] Augustine uses *suavis* to describe Ambrose's hymns in *Confessions*, 9.6.14 (CCSL 27.140). Poetic elements have often been noted in Ambrose's prose: see Nauroy, "L'Ecriture dans la Pastorale d'Ambroise de Milan," 404, for "les sondages suggestifs du poète" in his exegesis, and especially J. Fontaine, "Prose et poésie: L'interférence des genres et styles dans la création litéraire d'Ambroise de Milan," in Giuseppe Lazzati, *Ambrosius Episcopus* (Milan: Università Cattolica del Sacro Cuore, 1976) 1:124–170.

Yet, even if we could discover and reproduce the biblical rhythm of the preaching of the bishop of Milan, "sounding like the Bible" would be lost on contemporary listeners for two reasons. First, we have, unfortunately, generally lost both an intimate familiarity with the text of Scripture and the ability to perceive the coherence in Ambrose's use of hundreds of scriptural verses in the course of a single sermon. Second, we are different from Ambrose's listeners in that since the invention of the printing press, our interaction with the Bible has been through seeing rather than listening to Scripture, often even in worship. Nevertheless, there are characteristics of Ambrose's preaching that we continue to admire today.

AMBROSE ON PREACHING

Preaching was the top priority of Ambrose's ministry. In *De officiis ministrorum*, Ambrose taught his clergy that whatever else priests do, they are to be teachers concerned with educating people in the virtues of character.[24] Ambrose then goes on to declare teaching to be the priority of his own ministry:

"I do not therefore claim for myself the glory of the apostles (for who can do this save those whom the Son of God Himself has chosen?); nor the grace of the prophets, nor the virtue of the evangelists, nor the cautious care of the pastors. I only desire to attain to that care and diligence in the sacred writings, which the Apostle has placed last amongst the duties of the saints; and this very thing I desire, so that, in the endeavor to teach, I may be able to learn."[25]

Ramsey is correct that Ambrose "would certainly have agreed with Gregory Nazianzen (cf. *Oration* 2.35), although he did not say it quite so directly, that preaching was a bishop's foremost responsibility."[26] Paulinus tells us that the instruction of those who were to be baptized was especially important to Ambrose. "He was very vigorous, too, in attending to divine matters, to the extent that what five bishops could hardly accomplish after his death he had been accustomed to accomplish by himself in the case of those about to be baptized."[27]

---

[24] *De officiis ministrorum*, 1.1.1 (PL 16.23).
[25] Ibid., 1.1.3 (PL 16.24).
[26] Ramsey, *Ambrose*, 37.
[27] Paulinus, *Vita Ambrosii*, 38 (Navoni, 116).

Though versed in the Greek Fathers, Ambrose was truly Roman in that his approach to preaching was legal rather than contemplative. Ambrose appealed neither to raw emotions nor to reverence and awe, but to his hearers' legal, practical bent of mind. The ancient Romans were a law people, a people legally minded and law conscious, devoted to law and justice. In fact, there has been no other people, ancient or modern, among whom the law formed such an integral part of their lives and modes of thought as it did for the ancient Romans.[28] This legal worldview shaped Ambrose's deep preoccupation with the role of the Church in Roman society. He saw the Church as "an inviolably holy body, possessed of unchallengeable, because divine, authority."[29]

Ambrose viewed the world in black and white. His vision of human existence was built on a series of opposing forces and definite boundaries—Christian and pagan, Catholic and heretic, biblical truth and worldly speculation, Church and world, soul and body. To be a Christian was to observe these boundaries absolutely. Thus Ambrose saw the Christian as an athlete wrestling with the world.[30] For him the world "was a voracious sea, whipped by demonic gusts, across which there now drifted, in times of peace, the Siren songs of sensuality, of concern for worldly advantage, and of readiness to compromise with the great—beguiling, female figures who threatened always to 'effeminate' the male resolve of the mind."[31]

Yet, while a siege mentality may have been running in the background of Ambrose's thought, his defensiveness was tempered by a powerful longing for personal transformation. This transformation, promised to all Christians in the waters of baptism, formed the heart and was the goal of Ambrose's preaching in Milan. For Ambrose, the effective preacher leads the faithful in opposing the world and participating in divine life by teaching them to do good works and live as God's people. In a letter to Bishop Constantius (written before Lent

---

[28] C. Pharr, "Roman Legal Education," *The Classical Journal* 34 (1939) 257–258.

[29] Peter Brown, *The Body and Society: Men, Women and Sacred Renunciation in Early Christianity* (New York: Columbia University Press, 1988) 346.

[30] See, for example, *Expositio evangelii secundum Lucam*, prol. 6 (CCSL 14.5); *De sacramentis*, 1.2.4 (SC 25bis.62). For a discussion of Ambrose's use of the image of the athlete, see below, 319; Nauroy, "L'Ecriture dans la Pastorale d'Ambroise de Milan," 386–387.

[31] Brown, *The Body and Society*, 348; cf. *Expositio evangelii secundum Lucam*, 4.3 (CCSL 14.106–107).

379), which has been called Ambrose's *De doctrina christiana*,[32] the bishop of Milan writes:

"Warn the Lord's people and beg them to abound in good works, to renounce vice, not to enkindle the fires of passion—I shall not say on the Sabbath, but in every season. . . . Teach and instruct them to do what is good. . . . Let the people also shun evil deeds, even though they do not believe they can be found out. . . . Let your people not desire many things, for the reason that a few things are many to them. . . . Let no one speak deceitfully to their neighbor. . . . It is also very important that you persuade them to know how to be humbled, to know the true character and nature of humility. . . . Let them learn to search for the riches of good works and to be rich in character."[33]

In this same letter, Ambrose instructs Constantius to use three kinds of sermons in order to achieve this moral transformation in his people —the sweet, the stinging, and the milky. "Sweet sermons" are flowing, clear, and lucid, so that by appropriate argument sweetness is poured into the ears of the people and the grace of the preacher's words persuades them to follow willingly where the preacher leads. If, however, the people are stubborn or guilty of any fault, a sermon that stings the person with a guilty conscience is in order. Third, there are also sermons that are like milk, designed for those who cannot eat strong food but develop from infancy by drinking a natural milk.[34] Finally, Ambrose instructs Constantius that all sermons ought to be full of meaning. By this Ambrose means that they should shine forth as revelation, be filled with the preacher's insight, and be self-contained so that they stand on their own.[35]

In his treatise *De officiis ministrorum*, Ambrose states that the preacher's rhetoric ought to be neither too elaborate nor too unpolished, but simple, dignified, and, above all, understandable.[36] He reminds his presbyters that many of their listeners are ignorant people, and therefore they must use plain language so that their listeners can

---

[32] Nauroy, "L'Ecriture dans la Pastorale d'Ambroise de Milan," 391.
[33] *Epistola* 36 (Maur. 2).8-11, 13, 18, 26 (CSEL 82/2.6–8, 10, 12, 17).
[34] Ibid., 5–6 (CSEL 82/2.5–6).
[35] Ibid., 7 (CSEL 82/2.7).
[36] *De officiis ministrorum*, 1.21.101 (PL 16.55); *Epistola* 36 (Maur. 2).5 (CSEL 82/2.5).

understand.[37] Ambrose instructs his priests to pay proper attention to their delivery, for while not everyone is endowed with a musical voice, all can speak vigorously and distinctly, if only they will take pains to do so.[38] For Ambrose, the voice ought to be plain and clear, distinct in its pronunciation and full of life, free from a rough and rustic twang, and without a theatrical accent. In this way the voice keeps true to the inner meaning of the words it utters.[39]

Ambrose's instructions to his clergy reveal his extensive training in rhetoric.[40] Rhetoric was also an important tool in Ambrose's ministry as bishop. By the fourth century, bishops, many of whom had studied in the ancient schools of rhetoric, found themselves blessed with both large congregations and spacious new buildings in which to address them. These factors called for new and more energetic forms of eloquence. Responding to this situation, Christian preachers sought to accommodate themselves to the prevailing modes of discourse and, in so doing, to convert their hearers covertly, in particular by laying claim to past history.[41] In this process an interaction of Christianity and paganism occurred "as the schools of rhetoric informed the eloquence of the Fathers, and the eloquence of the Fathers transformed the schools."[42] In Ambrose's preaching, the most obvious examples of this interaction are his funeral sermons.[43]

---

[37] *De Isaac et anima*, 7.57 (CSEL 32-1.681).
[38] *De officiis ministrorum*, 1.23.104 (PL 16.55); cf. 1.19.84 (PL 16.49).
[39] Ibid.
[40] See above, 36–37; 43–44.
[41] Averil Cameron, *Christianity and the Rhetoric of Empire: The Development of Christian Discourse* (Berkeley: University of California Press, 1991) 121.
[42] Thomas K. Carroll, *Preaching the Word*, Message of the Fathers of the Church 11 (Wilmington: Michael Glazier, 1984) 144. See Cameron, *Christianity and the Rhetoric of Empire*, chs. 4 and 5, pp. 120–188.
[43] Ambrose introduced the Christian funeral oration into Latin literature most probably from his reading of his contemporaries in the East, Gregory Nazianzen and Gregory of Nyssa. To the forms of consolation found in the Greek *Encomium* these Fathers added the incomparably superior means of consolation of the Christian faith with its emphasis on resurrection. Furthermore, in the psalms and prophets of the Old Testament, Christian preachers found a consolation literature of power and beauty that possessed unique authority as the Word of God. Ambrose's funeral sermons reflect an intimate acquaintance with Greek theorists and practitioners in the field of rhetoric as

In addition to his funeral preaching, Ambrose employed all the weapons of rhetoric in the battle between orthodoxy and heresy. An example of Ambrose's use of rhetoric when preaching against Arianism is his *Contra Auxentium de basilicis tradendis*, which is modeled after the orations of Cicero. In this sermon Ambrose combines Cicero's famous orations against Catiline, which had been held up as models of public address for some four hundred years, with the assigned lessons for the day in order to bring the word of God to bear on a crisis that aroused tempers in Milan during Holy Week, 386, when the imperial court demanded that Ambrose hand over a basilica to the Arians.[44] In this sermon Ambrose develops his view of the emperor as a son of the Church serving Christ and subject to the advice of a bishop.[45] In his statistical analysis of Ambrose's corpus, Steven Oberhelman shows that Ambrose's use of high rhetoric is determined by such factors as an imperial or elite audience; weighty themes, such as the death of an emperor; virginity or defending the Church against heresy; and occasions when Ambrose wanted to bestow additional *gravitas* and *suavitas* or assert his social standing.[46]

In his later years Ambrose objected to the use of pretentious rhetorical effects for the purpose of self-advertisement in Christian discourse. He criticized those vain persons who parade their eloquence to roars of applause. Far superior is the apostolic preacher who holds fast to the true faith and does not seek ornamental speech, brilliant arguments,

---

well as the influence of the Latin *laudatio funebris* and *consolatio*. Yet, he did not feel as closely bound by his pagan models as his Greek contemporaries. Furthermore, his funeral orations are more thoroughly permeated with Christian thought and with scriptural quotation, phraseology, and imagery, and they are distinguished as a whole by a more personal tone and warmth of feeling. For an introduction to Christian Latin funeral sermons and Ambrose's funeral preaching, see Cameron, *Christianity and the Rhetoric of Empire*, 65–66, 144–149; Leo P. McCauley, et al., *Funeral Orations by Saint Gregory Nazianzen and Saint Ambrose* (New York: Fathers of the Church, 1953) vi–xvi, xix–xxi. Martin Biermann, *Die Leichenreden des Ambrosius von Mailand: Rhetorik, Predigt, Politik* (Stuttgart: F. Steiner, 1995). For a discussion of Ambrose's funeral sermon for Satyrus, see below, 102–103.

[44] See above, 55.

[45] *Contra Auxentium*, 37 (CSEL 82/3.107).

[46] Steven M. Oberhelman, *Rhetoric and Homiletics in Fourth Century Christian Literature: Prose, Rhythm, Oratorical Style, and Preaching in the Works of Ambrose, Jerome, and Augustine* (Atlanta: Scholars Press, 1991) 21–62.

and decorative periods for expressing his ideas.⁴⁷ "Away with the finery and paint of words," Ambrose declares, "which weaken the force of what is said!"⁴⁸ Christian teachers should place themselves on the same level as their hearers, and no matter how learned or eloquent they may be, Christian teachers should use simple, plain, and familiar speech.⁴⁹ Ambrose's criticism is valid. Trained on trivial, unreal, and timeworn subjects, rhetoricians often lost the ability to be simple and sincere, qualities Ambrose sought in Christian preaching. When they were unable to attract attention by their subject matter, rhetoricians' success often depended entirely on the manner in which they presented it. "To keep [their] hearers awake, [they] were obliged to stuff [their] speech with startling epigrams, smart antitheses, and quaint conceits. Sense was sacrificed to sound, force to brilliance, and the art of saying true things to the art of making the false appear to be the true."⁵⁰ Nevertheless, Ambrose, like all the great Christian preachers of his age, was educated in the school of rhetoric, and this training had a profound effect on the power of his preaching.

Ambrose's preaching is a tireless "rumination" of Scripture.⁵¹ Ambrose, more than any Father of the Latin West, continuously quoted Scripture, so much so that some of his works appear as a "marquetry" of scriptural references.⁵² Ambrose's scriptural citations are so numerous that the most learned and attentive scholars could not detect them all. For Ambrose the Bible is the source of all wisdom and knowledge, and therefore his only source of inspiration. In the Scriptures Ambrose finds the indisputable authority that empowers him to take a stand in the controversy with the heretics or the Jews, that informs the Christian people, and that dictates their duty with regard to the emperors. It is in the Bible that the bishop finds his own responsibility: like Aaron, he is the intermediary of the crowned Word, the mediator between Scripture and the people.⁵³

---

⁴⁷ *Expositio evangelii secundum Lucam*, 7.218; 8.15 (CCSL 14.289–290, 293). Cf. Paulinus, *Vita Ambrosii*, 7 (Navoni, 60).

⁴⁸ *Expositio evangelii secundum Lucam*, 8.70 (CCSL 14.324–325).

⁴⁹ *De Isaac et anima*, 7.57 (CSEL 32-1.680); *Expositio evangelii secundum Lucam*, 2.42 (CCSL 14.50).

⁵⁰ Frederick Homes Dudden, *The Life and Times of Saint Ambrose*, 2 vols. (Oxford: Clarendon Press, 1935) 1:11.

⁵¹ Nauroy, "L'Ecriture dans la Pastorale d'Ambroise de Milan," 371.

⁵² Ibid.

⁵³ Ibid., 381.

Although we will discuss Ambrose's use of Scripture in detail in Chapter 6, two points are worth noting here. First, Ambrose was not afraid of making intellectual demands on his listeners. His very appeal to the allegorical rather than the literal meaning of Scripture suggests this. Furthermore, his treatises that were originally sermons are scattered with difficult passages. Even if we allow that Ambrose the editor tightened and elevated certain features, we have to admit that some of Ambrose's exegetical works contain passages that would have required close attention on the part of his listeners, especially the *plebs christiana*.

Second, Ambrose did not worry about appearing original in his preaching and writing. In fact, Jerome was so outraged by the amount of borrowing from other sources that he found in Ambrose's treatise *De Spiritu Sancto* that, in his own preface to Didymus the Blind's discourse on the Holy Spirit, from which Ambrose had drawn, he compared Ambrose, without mentioning him by name, to "an ugly crow . . . adorned with others' plumage" and continued:

"A short while ago I read a certain person's books on the Holy Spirit and, in the words of the comic writer [Terence], I saw bad things in Latin taken from good things in Greek. Nothing there was closely argued, nothing was manly or firm so as to convince the reader, but everything was flaccid, soft, glistening and cute, painted here and in exquisite colors."[54]

Writing about three years after Ambrose's death, Rufinus of Aquileia defended Ambrose, meeting Jerome's charge of plagiarism head on in his *Apology Against Jerome* (2:25). He wrote:

"The holy Ambrose wrote about the Holy Spirit not only with words but also with his blood. For he offered his blood to his persecutors, having poured it out within himself, but God spared him for yet other labors. What if he followed Greek Catholic writers who belong to our camp and took something from their writings? Should it have been your chief concern . . . to make his 'thefts' known, when perhaps he was under pressure to write in response to the raving heretics of the time?"[55]

[54] As cited in Ramsey, *Ambrose*, 53.
[55] Ibid.

It is true that Ambrose continually drew upon the writings of the Greek Fathers for his sermons and treatises. He explained both entire biblical books and specific scriptural passages using the Greek commentaries. Besides Origen, from whom Ambrose derived his method of interpreting Scripture, his main source was the Jewish theologian Philo.[56] Ambrose also borrowed freely from philosophers including Plotinus, Plato, and Cicero, integrating philosophical themes into his treatises,[57] while at the same time dismissing these philosophers as inferior to Scripture.[58]

Yet, Ambrose's use of borrowed material was never uncritical. He approached his sources with discretion and exercised a measure of creativity by rearranging the material that he had at hand. His real originality is found in what he chose to emphasize from the tradition

---

[56] For *De Cain et Abel* Ambrose makes considerable use of Philo's *The Sacrifice of Cain and Abel*. *De fuga saeculi* shows particular dependence upon Philo's *On Flight and Discovery*. Ambrose's *De Noe* also owes a considerable amount to Philo. For *Hexaemeron*, Ambrose used as a model Basil's treatise by the same name, and *De Helia et ieiunio*, *De Nabuthae*, and *De Tobia* are all based on his sermons. Ambrose used Cicero's *De officiis* as his model for his *De officiis ministrorum*, following it closely but Christianizing it. The content of Ambrose's ascetic preaching barely goes beyond what was already taught by Cyprian. For a summary of Ambrose's use of Philo and the literature surrounding this issue, see David T. Runia, *Philo in Early Christian Literature: A Survey* (Minneapolis: Fortress Press, 1993) 291–311.

[57] See Pierre Courcelle, "Plotin et saint Ambroise," *Revue de Philologie* 76 (1950) 29–56; idem, "Anti-Christian Arguments and Christian Platonism from Arnobius to Ambrose," in Arnoldo Momigliano, ed., *The Conflict Between Paganism and Christianity in the Fourth Century* (Oxford: Clarendon Press, 1963) 151–192; Goulven Madec, *Saint Ambroise et la philosophie* (Paris: Études Augustiennes, 1974); Giuseppe Toscani, *Teologia della chiesa in sant'Ambrogio* (Milan: Università Cattolica del Sacro Cuore, 1974); Andrew Lenox-Conyngham, "Ambrose and Philosophy," in *Christian Faith and Greek Philosophy in Late Antiquity: Essays in Tribute to George Christopher Stead* (Leiden: Brill, 1993) 112–128.

[58] Believing that the pagan philosophers, Pythagoras and Plato in particular, borrowed the best of their ideas from the books of Moses, Ambrose understood his borrowing as the discrete recovery of something valuable that rightfully belongs to the tradition of the Church. That Ambrose does not generally name the philosophers such as Plato, from whom he indisputably borrowed entire pages, or even acknowledge his debt to ancient philosophy, but instead disputes, criticizes, subordinates, and minimizes their ideas, is because he finds in philosophy the mislaid vestiges of the doctrines of the biblical authors.

he had received. Hughes Oliphant Old is correct that the material Ambrose used

"obviously passed through his own experience and is therefore truly his own. This is of the very nature of the pastoral office. Ambrose as a minister of the Word has learned from the tradition how the Scriptures are to be understood. He has lived out these same Scriptures in his own life, and now as a preacher gives witness that these Scriptures are the Word of God."[59]

Over the course of his ministry, Ambrose revealed an increasing independence from his Greek theological models.[60] We see clearly in Ambrose's exegetical works the stages and progress of his training. As a high-ranking Roman civil servant at his election to the episcopacy, Ambrose came to his office without formation in the episcopal tasks, of which the first is to teach Scripture. Ambrose himself did not hide the difficulties that he encountered in the exercise of this ministry. He acknowledges having been obliged to teach before he had learned.[61] In the prologue of *De officiis*, the bishop of Milan professes his *humilitas*, his unworthiness to interpret: he received neither the glory of the apostles, nor the grace of the prophets, and he praises the virtue of silence before the mystery of the biblical text as the first discourse of the exegete.[62]

Initially it was necessary for Ambrose to closely follow the existing hermeneutic tradition, Jewish and Christian. Thus Philo guided his first steps, initiating him into the allegorical reading of Scripture that makes it possible to see beyond the literal meaning. He then read Origen and Hippolytus, co-founders of the Christian hermeneutic of the third century. As an independent and critical student, Ambrose drew inspiration from his teachers but then began to deviate from his model. Thus Ambrose's approach to Scripture next appears more flexible; he exercises the freedom to choose from or even reject his models. So, while Ambrose owes much to his models, it is much less

---

[59] Hughes Oliphant Old, *The Reading and Preaching of the Scriptures in the Worship of the Christian Church* (Grand Rapids: Wm. B. Eerdmans, 1998) 2:302.

[60] This section is indebted to Nauroy, "L'Ecriture dans la Pastorale d'Ambroise de Milan," 372–374.

[61] *De officiis ministrorum*, 1.1.4 (PL 16.24).

[62] Ibid., 1.1.3 (PL 16.24); 1.2.5-8 (PL 16.25–26).

than we have sometimes concluded from what are, in fact, narrow textual parallels and interpretations that share the resemblance of words more than the similarity of meaning.

Rather than being dependent on his models, the bishop of Milan, subjected to the hard discipline of the weekly sermon, even daily in certain periods of the liturgical year, and assisted by an exceptional memory, an uncommon aptitude for work, and a gift of meditation that impressed Augustine, quickly achieved a real autonomy in his role as exegete. Without expressly rejecting his Greek and Latin models but continuing to read them with an inexhaustible intellectual curiosity, Ambrose generally followed his own way, tracing a rich tradition with a freedom and vision that made his preaching both a synthesis of the exegesis of the first four centuries and an original contribution, in terms of both his interpretation and the themes and forms in which he encases it.

Ambrose's style was at times dense, due to the voluminous material he included in a single work, and at times clear and forceful, depending on his purpose and audience. In his exegetical preaching, for example, Ambrose was more concerned with plumbing the depth of meaning of a text than with providing a unifying theme or systematic approach. Gerard Nauroy makes this abundantly clear in his examination of two of Ambrose's works, *De Iacob et beata vita* and *De Isaac et anima*.[63] On the other hand, Ambrose's funeral sermons, which follow Greek and Latin models of funeral orations,[64] consist of arguments that are carefully thought out and unfold in an orderly sequence.

An example of Ambrose's detailed argument is found in the second funeral sermon that he preached for his brother Satyrus, which is modeled after the literary genre known as the consolation. As in that model, Ambrose begins with the thesis that "death is not to be mourned over; firstly, because it is common and due to all; next,

---

[63] Gerard Nauroy, "La méthode de composition d'Ambroise de Milan et la structure du *De Iacob et beata vita*," in Y.-M. Duval, *Ambroise de Milan: XVIe centenaire de son élection épiscopale: dix études* (Paris: Etudes Augustiniennes, 1974) 115–153; idem, "La structure du *De Isaac vel Anima* et la cohérence de l'allégorèse d'Ambroise de Milan," *Revue de Études Latines* 63 (1985) 210–236.

[64] For a discussion of the life of Satyrus and a brief description of these sermons, see John Moorhead, *Ambrose: Church and Society in the Late Roman World* (London and New York: Longman, 1999) 36–39. For a discussion of the literary form of the Christian funeral oration, see above, 96–97, n. 43.

because it frees us from the miseries of this life and, lastly, because when in the likeness of sleep we are at rest from the toils of this world, a more lively vigor is shed upon us."[65] Ambrose then develops each point in a step-by-step fashion using painstaking detail. In so doing he convinces his hearers—and himself—to move from immense grief to sincere hope.

Ambrose's preaching was relevant to the everyday lives of his listeners. He often illustrated his points using examples from the daily lives of his hearers—the athlete, the soldier, the boxer, the physician, the charioteer, the great lord, the social beauty, the musician, and the prostitute. His arguments were also enriched with many delightful maxims. Homes Dudden provides a full page of Ambrose's "apothegms."[66] We limit our examples to three: "The devil tempts that he may ruin; God tempts that He may crown."[67] "To flee from the world is to abstain from sins."[68] "The devil's snare does not catch you, unless you are first caught by the devil's bait."[69] Ambrose also knew how to rouse the conscience and touch the heart. In his treatise *De Nabuthe*, originally a sermon or sermons, Ambrose wonderfully speaks to his listeners' hearts and lays guilt upon their consciences as he denounces greed and calls his hearers to heed the plight of the poor. In *De Helia et ieiunio*, Ambrose uses humor to persuade his hearers when he gives an amusing account of the preparation of a big dinner.[70]

Ambrose teaches that large subjects are best dealt with in what today we call sermon series.[71] In his own preaching Ambrose preferred this practice. In addition to *De sacramentis*, examples of Ambrose's sermon series include *Hexaemeron*, which is based on nine sermons that Ambrose preached during an undetermined Holy Week between 386 and 390; the first book of *De Abraham*, composed sometime in the 380s and originally a series of sermons delivered to catechumens; and *De interpellatione Iob et David*.

---

[65] *De excessu fratris*, 2.3 (CSEL 73.252).
[66] Homes Dudden, *The Life and Times of Saint Ambrose*, 2:461.
[67] *De Abraham*, 1.8.66 (CSEL 32-1.545).
[68] *De fuga saeculi*, 4.17 (CSEL 32/2.178).
[69] *Expositio in Psalmum cxviii*, 14.37 (CSEL 62.323).
[70] *De Helia et ieiunio*, 8.24, 25 (CSEL 32-2.425–426). This satirical touch is also found in sermons of Basil, Gregory Naziansen, and Gregory of Nyssa; Ambrose seems to depend heavily on Basil. Brian E. Daley, S.J., Princeton, to Craig A. Satterlee, Notre Dame, 27 September 1999.
[71] *De officiis ministrorum*, 1.21.101 (PL 16.54).

We know precious little of Ambrose's method of sermon preparation. In his letter to Bishop Constantius, Ambrose directs him to read, saying that those who read much and also understand are filled; those who have been filled shed water upon others.[72] Augustine tells us how Ambrose read, saying that when he was not with the crowds who brought their arbitrations for him to settle, which was a very brief period of time, Ambrose restored either his body with necessary food or his mind by reading. When he was reading, his eyes ran over the page and his heart perceived the sense, but his voice and tongue were silent.[73] Elsewhere in the Roman world this kind of access would have resulted in Ambrose's explaining the text he was studying or discussing questions raised by it. While McLynn overstates the case when he says that Ambrose's preference to study silently resulted in "the blurring of the boundary usually apparent between the exegete and his subject matter,"[74] parishioners seeing their bishop silently—prayerfully, perhaps—meditating on God's word would certainly enhance the bishop's stature as a preacher.

As for Ambrose's writing, Paulinus tells us that, as a rule, he edited his sermons in the quiet of the night and did not shun the task of writing books with his own hand, except when his body was troubled by some infirmity.[75] Ambrose himself tells us that he did not dictate, particularly at night, when he did not want to trouble and burden others.[76] But there was more to Ambrose's decision to write rather than dictate than the desire to show charity toward those in his service. Ambrose continues that, while dictation requires that words roll out with a certain impetuosity and in a rapid flow, he wants to carefully select the words he uses.[77] Mohrmann is correct that in saying that Ambrose, borrowing as he did from both Greek Fathers and Neoplatonists, required the privacy of his study in order to work through his source material and lift out what was useful to him.[78] Perhaps that is

---

[72] *Epistola* 36 (Maur. 2).4 (CSEL 82/2.5).
[73] Augustine, *Confessions*, 6.3.3 (CCSL 27.75).
[74] McLynn, *Ambrose of Milan: Church and Court in a Christian Capital*, 239.
[75] Paulinus, *Vita Ambrosii*, 38 (Navoni, 116).
[76] *Epistola* 37 (Maur. 47).1 (CSEL 82/2.20).
[77] Ibid., 2.
[78] Mohrmann, "Observations sur le *De Sacramentis* et le *De Mysteriis* de Saint Ambroise," *Ambrosius Episcopus* (Milan: Università Cattolica del Sacro Cuore, 1978) 110.

what he meant by not having to be ashamed in the presence of another who is doing the writing, but conscious only of himself, without a witness, and weighing with the ear and also with the eye the things he wrote.[79]

While Ambrose nowhere discusses his method of sermon delivery, the available evidence leads to the conclusion that Ambrose preached from memory. First, preaching without a written text or even notes seems to have been the normal practice in Ambrose's time.[80] Developing the memory was part of training in rhetoric and law, and speaking from memory was expected of both trained rhetors and lawyers. Second, Paulinus's report of the Arian who saw an angel speaking into the bishop's ear while he was preaching[81] would not be at all appropriate for a bishop who was known to have preached from a manuscript. Finally, Ambrose's reputation as a preacher, the absence of sermon manuscripts and the likely presence of a tachograph or stenographer in the assembly,[82] and the detail with which Ambrose recounts sermons in his correspondence all point to his preaching from memory.

Ambrose's preaching was liturgical. From the information given by Augustine in his *Confessions* that he heard Ambrose every Lord's Day,[83] and substantiated by references in Ambrose's sermons to lessons based on a lectionary,[84] it is evident that Ambrose's preaching was set

---

[79] *Epistola* 37 (Maur. 47).2 (CSEL 82/2.20).

[80] The development of memory was apparently one of the main parts of professional rhetorical training. Augustine delivered his sermons without notes, according to his biographer, and they were written down by stenographers. Apparently Cicero gave his speeches without a written text, although they lasted several hours, and then edited the transcripts for circulation. It was understood in classical rhetoric that a speaker would carefully prepare his speech, gather and order his ideas, but that his training would allow him to actually deliver the speech with no notes in front of him. Roy J. Deferrari, "St. Augustine's Method of Composing and Delivering Sermons," *American Journal of Philology* 43 (1922) 97–123.

[81] Paulinus, *Vita Ambrosii*, 17 (Navoni, 78). See above, 87–88.

[82] Mohrmann, "Le style oral du *De Sacramentis* de Saint Ambroise," *Vigiliae Christianae* 6 (1952) 170–171.

[83] Augustine, *Confessions*, 6.3.4 (CCSL 27.76).

[84] "That passage was read by no arrangement of mine, but by chance . . ." *Lectio nempe ista nulla nostra dispositione recitata est, sed casu. Contra Auxentium,* 19 (CSEL 82/3.94). In Ambrose's mystagogical preaching, see *De sacramentis,*

within the context of the service. Certain sections of Ambrose's sermons bear the marks of having been addressed to catechumens.[85] The liturgical context of Ambrose's preaching is also evident from his use of Scripture.[86] In the sermons that are inserted in certain of Ambrose's letters we not only find very explicit references to the readings that had preceded them, but we also find points when our preacher was anxious to return to the lesson in his homily, even when the principal subject of his homily did not correspond to the readings of the day.

The strange gaps frequently experienced by the modern reader of Ambrose's works are, in fact, the implicit reference to a text that had just been read and to which our preacher returns his listeners allusively. That Ambrose is preaching on texts that have just been read explains his general supposition that his audience knows the biblical narratives. He usually makes only brief mention of them, as summarized familiar accounts. Ambrose includes the text in his homily only when to do so serves his particular purpose. Lastly, when we note in the text of the Ambrosian liturgy the richly rhetorical style of prayer, which was strongly influenced by Greek prototypes, we are led to conclude that Ambrose's preaching fit well into its liturgical context.

As regards length, Ambrose felt that a sermon should be neither very long nor very short: long sermons bore people, while very short ones fail to make a deep impression.[87] The direct examples of Ambrose's preaching that are preserved, such as sermons inserted in letters and *De sacramentis*, show that the preached sermons of the bishop of Milan seldom exceeded ten pages of a modern printed edition.

WHAT MADE AMBROSE AN EFFECTIVE PREACHER?

What made Ambrose an effective preacher? An effective preacher can be defined as a person of faith, conviction, authority, and grace.[88] In this section we will explore the ways in which these four characteristics of an effective preacher are applicable to Saint Ambrose. *Faith* is what makes the preacher believable. Craddock highlights the impor-

---

2.2.3 (SC 25bis.77); 2.7.23 (SC 25bis.86); 3.2.8 (SC 25bis.96); 6.2.9 (SC 25bis.140). See below, 211–212.

[85] For example, *De Abraham*, 1 (CSEL 32.1) and *Expositio in Psalmum cxviii*, 130–140 (CSEL 62).

[86] Nauroy, "L'Ecriture dans la Pastorale d'Ambroise de Milan," 383.

[87] *De officiis ministrorum*, 1.22.101 (PL 16.55); cf. 1.19.84 (PL 16.49).

[88] See Craddock, *Preaching*, 24.

tance of faith to preaching when he reminds us that "if the messenger is not believable, neither is the message" and that "the absence of faith is almost impossible to disguise for any period of time."[89]

If faith makes a preacher believable, Ambrose was believable, because his Christian faith, though reserved, was an integral part of his very nature. While his orthodox belief and devotion to prayer and asceticism were undoubtedly the natural reflection of his upbringing, Ambrose's election as bishop and subsequent baptism marked the decisive moment when he made these things the major concerns of his life. From his mystagogical preaching, it is apparent that Ambrose understood that in baptism he was making his home not in Roman society but in the kingdom of God. Thus Ambrose made love of Christ the center of his life, even expressing his willingness to suffer martyrdom for Christ's sake.

In order to be effective, a preacher must be regarded by his hearers as a center of meaning, power, and influence. The values derived from the Gospel that cause listeners to turn to the preacher as a center of meaning, power, and influence constitute the preacher's *conviction*.[90] In discussing Ambrose's conviction, we are attempting to discover what made him persuasive. By "persuasive" we are not speaking of the broad sense of the word but more precisely in terms of the qualities that made Ambrose an authentic Christian witness and a genuine representative of Christ. Obviously, Ambrose's congregation looked to him as a center of meaning because as bishop he was their spiritual leader. Yet, the manner in which Ambrose conducted his ministry as bishop and guided the ministry of his clergy enhanced his persuasiveness. Ambrose made worshiping God and proclaiming God's word the top priorities of his ministry. He was particularly concerned with instructing those who were to be baptized. Ambrose further understood that his office required him not only to teach but to be an example by rejecting worldly pleasures and embodying Christian values. These values included the strength to stand up to the empire, availability and hospitality, compassion and forgiveness, concern for the poor, and reverence for the saints. These values flowed from Ambrose's conviction that his chief responsibility as bishop was educating people in virtue.

Authority is what gives the preacher the right to speak. Among the types of authority that constitute the authority to preach are the

[89] Ibid., 24.
[90] Ibid.

authority of the Church, the authority that comes from the call to ministry, one's personal talents and training, and the willingness of the listeners to give their attention. Ambrose was a person of authority, first, because he was the bishop of Milan and an important figure in public life. As bishop, Ambrose wielded both sacred and secular authority formally as he discharged the duties of his office and informally through his connections with people of power and influence. Second, beyond his office, Ambrose had the authority of his personality, character, education, and social status. People listened when Ambrose preached because he was a talented speaker and trained rhetorician with new insight into the Scripture. For the newly baptized, Ambrose's authority was further enhanced by the fact that he both prepared them for and celebrated the mysteries of their initiation.

Finally, *grace* is what keeps the preacher listening to the word of God. Craddock says that "preaching, like singing, begins in the ear, and the one who has heard the word of God's grace can pronounce it properly."[91] Ambrose continued to listen to the word of God's grace, first, because of his election as bishop and call to ministry. Like all leaders of God's people, Ambrose's most profound experience of God's grace was his call to ministry. Paulinus in particular describes the events that resulted in Ambrose's election as bishop of Milan in near-biblical proportions.[92] Second, Ambrose continued to listen to God's word because his election found him theologically unprepared for the duties of his office. As he devoted himself to studying Church doctrine and improving his scriptural training, Ambrose came to regard Scripture as the source of all wisdom and knowledge and, therefore, his only source of inspiration. In the Scriptures the bishop found the indisputable authority to respond to any crisis, to teach the Christian people, and to define the relationship between Church and state. Ambrose also found in Scripture not only the message but the manner for addressing his people. Understanding his role as the intermediary between God's word and the people, Ambrose continued to listen.

REFLECTION:
THE PNEUMATIC DIMENSION OF THE PREACHER

In the previous section we used four characteristics of an effective preacher to explore the personality traits and life experiences that

---

[91] Ibid., 24–25.
[92] Paulinus, *Vita Ambrosii*, 6–9 (Navoni, 58–66).

shaped Ambrose as a preacher. In this section we reflect upon the closely related but distinct question of how the Holy Spirit was present and active in the preaching ministry of the bishop of Milan. Despite Paulinus's portrayal of Ambrose as a saintly defender of the faith whose holiness was foreshadowed in his early life and manifested itself even after his death,[93] Ambrose was not the kind of person who today we might call charismatic—someone overflowing outwardly with the Holy Spirit. Although others report seeing visions in connection with the bishop of Milan,[94] Ambrose makes no claim to any sort of miraculous revelation from God. In fact, Ambrose provides only hints at his own relationship with God, although these hints suggest a relationship that was rich, life-giving, and transforming. Even Ambrose's saintly activities—prayer, fasting, sponsoring asceticism, ministering to the poor—were the result of careful and considered planning and not spontaneous inspiration.

Ambrose's faith and ministry generally and his preaching in particular were the result of discipline—tireless study, ceaseless prayer, sincere asceticism. Ambrose worked at being a Christian, a bishop, and a preacher. He made preaching and teaching his priority, especially the instruction of those preparing for baptism. Ambrose encountered the Spirit of God through his discipline and not by some miraculous, extraordinary means. Thus the example of our preacher supports the assertion, made in Chapter 1,[95] that the Holy Spirit speaks and acts in and through a method of preaching and is not contained by it.

Ambrose also understood that he was not only the recipient of the Holy Spirit but also the vessel through whom others might receive the Spirit. We began this chapter talking about the complex relationship between preacher and listeners that makes the separation of the preacher from the message impossible. Ambrose knew this and therefore carefully guarded both his own image and that of his clergy. In fact, not only did Ambrose safeguard against anything that might diminish his message, he actively cultivated an image that blurred the distinction between his person as bishop and the word that he preached. In our age of "spin," caring for one's image has taken on negative connotations. Yet, Ambrose reminds us that the preacher is

---

[93] Ibid., 3–4; 48–52 (Navoni, 52–56; 130–136).
[94] Ibid., 17; 42; 47 (Navoni, 78; 124; 130).
[95] Above, 18–19.

the voice of the Spirit and that preachers have a responsibility in their being and living to seek to be the best person through whom the Spirit might speak. Ambrose called his clergy to virtuous living not for its own sake but for the integration of messenger and message or, from the perspective of Christian preaching, the incarnation of the message in the messenger.

APPRAISING OUR PORTRAIT

Stepping back to appraise our portrait of Ambrose the preacher, we see that the image before us is that of a committed pastor struggling to bring the truth of God's word to the very real world and the everyday lives of his hearers. Responding to God's call, Ambrose worked to hear God's word as the Spirit spoke through the Scriptures, to embody that word in his own life, and to proclaim that word to his people in order to teach them how to live as faithful Christians within the complex circumstances of fourth-century Milan. In carrying out this task, Ambrose drew upon the best resources at his disposal, which included his own faith, personality, and experience, the exegetical and theological works of others, and methods of effective communication appropriate to his audience. Our portrait of Ambrose of Milan reveals a preacher whose greatness lies in his commitment to the Lord, to the Church, to his hearers, and to his task of bringing God's word to both regular people and to the extraordinary circumstances of his time. This "ordinary" pastoral commitment certainly makes Ambrose the preacher not only a saint to be revered but also a valuable model and guide for those who are called to preach.

Chapter 4

"This family clothed in white": The Newly Baptized of Milan: The Listeners

Chanting Psalm 22 (23), the newly baptized process from the baptistry into the cathedral, now jammed with the faithful celebrating the Easter Vigil.[1] They come dressed in new linen robes, smelling of oil, still damp from the baptismal waters. The faithful greet them with the kiss of peace and welcome them as newborn members of the family. Ambrose declares that "the church rejoices in the redemption of so many and is exultant with spiritual gladness when she sees at her side this family clothed in white."[2] But who are these newest members of the household of faith? In our last chapter we painted a portrait of Ambrose the preacher as our entrée into his method of mystagogical preaching. In this chapter we go from being artists to detectives as we attempt to compile a "profile" of those who listened to Ambrose's mystagogy—the newly baptized of Milan.

Craddock correctly asserts that a sermon "is to be located as much among a particular group of listeners as with a particular speaker."[3] This is especially true of mystagogical preaching, where the goal is to draw the listeners into the rites of initiation *that they have experienced* but have not understood in all of their depth. Mystagogical preaching, then, is preaching on the *neophytes' experience of the rites*. Mystagogy must therefore be appropriate to the listeners, not a general discourse on the sacraments but sermons that explain a specific celebration of

---

[1] For a discussion of the newly baptized processing to the altar, see below, 179–180.
[2] *De sacramentis*, 5.3.14 (SC 25bis.126); cf. *De mysteriis*, 7.34 (SC 25bis.174).
[3] Fred B. Craddock, *Preaching* (Nashville: Abingdon Press, 1985) 31.

the rites to the particular group of people who participated in them. Thus the listeners' experience is essential to mystagogy's content. Moreover, because preaching is an oral event that takes place at a particular time and place and among particular participants, the listeners are not only influenced by the nature and occasion of the preaching event, but they also bring to that event personal and social factors that influence not only how they hear the sermon but also the preaching itself.

Craddock offers three statements about the nature of preaching that follow from the conviction that listeners are active participants in preaching, statements particularly applicable to mystagogy.[4] First, preaching requires that the preacher has a thorough knowledge of, and has seriously listened to, the listeners. Second, sermons should move in a way that gives the listeners something to think, feel, decide, and do during the preaching. Third, sermons should speak *for* the listeners as well as *to* them.

These three statements will provide the framework for our investigation of the newly baptized of Milan. In the first section of this chapter, we will outline how Ambrose listened to and came to know his listeners and how we might listen to and come to know them as well. In the second section of this chapter, we will conduct our "audience analysis" of the newly baptized of Milan. In section three of this chapter, we consider the listeners as participants in mystagogy by asking what Ambrose wanted his hearers to think, feel, decide, and do during their instruction on the sacraments and how he preached to achieve this goal. We include in this section a discussion of the ways that Ambrose spoke for the newly baptized as well as to them. We conclude our chapter on the neophytes of Milan with a reflection on the pneumatic dimension of the listeners.

LISTENING TO THE LISTENERS

We are obviously at a disadvantage in that we can know the newly baptized of Milan only indirectly. We cannot sit down with those neophytes and ask them about their journey to faith, their desire to be baptized, their experience of Christian initiation, and the world in which they live out their faith. Yet Ambrose did not know his neophytes intimately and individually. Rather than special interactions explicitly designed to acquaint the bishop with the newly baptized,

---

[4] Ibid., 25–27.

Ambrose came to know them in the course of his work. His years as provincial governor furnished him with countless contacts with the people of Milan in the many arenas of their daily lives. As governor, his responsibility for maintaining public order and his role as judge of first instance in all trials, whether civil or criminal, allowed Ambrose to know his people in ways far removed from their "Sunday best."[5] We have seen that, as bishop, Ambrose continued to carry out these same responsibilities and hence to have this same interaction with his people. Augustine reports on the crowds that came to Ambrose on business and describes the bishop as "habitually available to serve them in their needs."[6] We have previously discussed Ambrose's pastoral availability, which found expression in his instruction that bishops should be easily approachable by anyone seeking advice, his open home and open table, and his readiness to correspond with those who wrote to him.[7]

Finally, although we will describe the process of Christian initiation at Milan in Chapter 5, we note here that the catechumenate itself may have provided the bishop with opportunities to come to know candidates for baptism. For example, Ambrose refers to candidates for baptism as *competentes*.[8] Originally a political term for "candidates," *competentes* means that people had in some way formally applied for baptism and in that sense suggests that there was some sort of formal process by which the church came to know and evaluate candidates for baptism. Part of that process undoubtedly involved the bishop and included discerning the reason a candidate was applying for baptism. Ambrose also had regular contact with candidates for baptism in the course of their Lenten instruction.

That Ambrose did not engage in activities specifically aimed at acquainting himself with the inner lives of candidates for baptism is evident from his relationship with Augustine, who never became intimate with the bishop who opened his eyes to the truth of Christianity and baptized him into the faith.[9] In two places in his *Confessions*,

---

[5] See above, 43.
[6] Augustine, *Confessions*, 6.3.3 (CCSL 27.75).
[7] Above, 68.
[8] Below, 148–149.
[9] George E. Saint-Laurent, "Augustine's Hero–Sage–Holy Man: Ambrose of Milan," in V. Capanaga, J. Leclercq, et. al., *Word and Spirit* 9 (Petersham, Mass.: St. Bede's Publications, 1987) 22–34.

Augustine declares that Ambrose did not share in his spiritual struggles. He says that Ambrose "was unaware of my spiritual turmoil or the perilous pit before my feet. There were questions that I wanted to put to him, but I was unable to do so as fully as I wished."[10] And again, "[N]o opportunity at all was given me to find out what I longed to know from your holy oracle, Ambrose's heart. At most, I could only put a point to him briefly, whereas my inner turmoil was at such a feverish pitch that I needed to find him completely at leisure if I were to pour it all out, and I never did so find him."[11] And so, longing for a deeper abiding in God in his daily life, Augustine went to discuss his perplexities not with Ambrose but with Simplicianus.[12] Augustine's only personal contact with Ambrose prior to his baptism was an exchange of letters.

After Augustine's final crisis of conversion, which, as McLynn correctly observes, was precipitated not by pastoral attention but by a social call from a fellow African courtier,[13] he withdrew to the rural estate of Cassiciacum for what was conceived of as a long retreat in preparation for baptism.[14] Yet Augustine did not consult Ambrose regarding how he should prepare for baptism. Only toward the end of the holidays did Augustine write to Ambrose to report all that had happened to him and to inquire what he should read in preparation for baptism. Ambrose provided only the bare instruction to read Isaiah, which Augustine abandoned after finding the first part unintelligible.[15] Yet Augustine expresses neither disappointment at Ambrose's reply nor the expectation of a dialogue with Ambrose, leaving us to conclude that such interaction with the bishop was not part of a candidate's preparation for baptism.

One reason that Ambrose did not attempt to establish a heart-to-heart connection with Augustine or with any of the *competentes* may be the nature of the Church of the fourth century. Brown argues that one of the consequences that "centuries of anxious concern for the solidarity

---

[10] Augustine, *Confessions*, 6.3.3 (CCSL 27.75).

[11] Ibid., 6.3.4 (CCSL 27.76).

[12] Ibid., 8.1.1 (CCSL 27.112); 8.2.3 (CCSL 27.112).

[13] Neil B. McLynn, *Ambrose of Milan: Church and Court in a Christian Capital* (Berkeley and Los Angeles: University of California Press, 1994) 242.

[14] For Augustine at Cassiciacum, see Peter Brown, *Augustine of Hippo: A Biography* (Berkeley: University of California Press, 1967) 115–127.

[15] Augustine, *Confessions*, 9.5.13 (CCSL 27.140).

of a threatened group" had on both Judaism and early Christianity was that "what was most private in the individual, his or her most hidden feelings or motivations, those springs of action that remained impenetrable to the group, 'the thoughts of the heart,' were looked to with particular attention as the source of tensions that threatened to cause fissures in the ideal solidarity of the religious community."[16] Privacy was viewed as a shield that concealed the intentions and motivations of heart from other people; however, the heart was totally public to the gaze of God and the angels.[17] Believing that the true heart was screened from human observation, the Church was concerned with behavior rather than intention, with action rather than contemplation. Furthermore, believing that the human heart could not be hidden from God, the Church trusted the Holy Spirit to reveal "the 'hidden things of the heart' . . . as the community of the 'saints' stood undivided, their hearts unveiled, in the very presence of God."[18] Thus we will see that Lenten scrutinies included a physical examination in order to determine if anything unclean still clung to the bodies of the *competentes*.[19]

A second reason that Ambrose did not engage in personal interaction with the *competentes* may be pedagogical. Nauroy sees in Ambrose's works a spiritual hierarchy that corresponds to the stages of Christian initiation.[20] Ambrose transmits the truth of Scripture gradually. The depth of his instruction is determined not by the listeners' intellectual capacity or worldly knowledge but by their advancement toward perfect initiation. The hierarchy seems to be pagan, Jew or heretic, catechumen, *competens*, neophyte, and fully initiated, with Ambrose dedicating the majority of his efforts to the last category.

Thus, in listening to and coming to know the neophytes of Milan indirectly, we are using the same approach as Ambrose himself. The means at our disposal for listening to Ambrose's listeners include Ambrose's mystagogical catecheses and other writings and current

---

[16] Paul Veyne, *A History of Private Life: From Pagan Rome to Byzantium*, trans. Arthur Goldhammer (Cambridge: Harvard University Press, 1987) 1:254.

[17] Ibid.

[18] Ibid., 256.

[19] See below, 152.

[20] Gerard Nauroy, "L'Ecriture dans la Pastorale d'Ambroise de Milan" in *Le Monde Latin Antique et La Bible*, ed. J. Fontaine and C. Pietri (Paris: Beauchesne, 1985) 380.

scholarship on the political, social, architectural, and ecclesiastical history of Milan, particularly during the period from 380 to 390, when *De sacramentis* was most likely written.

THE NEWLY BAPTIZED OF MILAN

In this section we conduct our audience analysis of the newly baptized of Milan, first, by determining the composition of the church of Milan, of which the newly baptized were a part. We will then discuss the characteristics that the newly baptized had in common, particularly, the decision to be baptized. Lastly, we will reflect upon the "contexts" in which the newly baptized heard their mystagogical instruction.

The Church of Milan

Ambrose became bishop of what seems to have been a very large Christian community. Excavations of Ambrose's cathedral in 1943 and 1961–1962 reveal an extraordinarily large building, 223 by 149.5 feet (67.6 by 45.3 meters), that offered space, not counting chancel area and transept wings, for a congregation of close to three thousand people.[21] Yet, if we assume that there were probably about 130,000 people living in Milan, and that Ambrose's cathedral, with a capacity of three thousand, was full on Sundays, then the congregation constituted about two percent of the population of Milan. Regardless of how we judge the congregation's size, the church of Milan's influence in both the concerns of the greater Church and the politics of the empire gave this Christian community stature beyond that of its architectural home. Thus the neophytes were members of an important and impressive community.

---

[21] Ernesto Brivio, *A Guide to the Duomo of Milan*, 3rd ed., trans. Liliana Zaccarelli Fumagalli (Milan: Veneranda Fabbrica del Duomo di Milano, 1997) 57. Krautheimer gives the dimensions of Ambrose's cathedral as 80 by 45 meters. Richard Krautheimer, *Three Christian Capitals* (Berkeley: University of California Press, 1983) 76. Excavations and exploration of extant structures in Milan have yielded the remains of fourth-century church building in such quantity that Milan is the foremost city in the West next to Rome for gaining a vivid impression of early Christian architecture on a major scale. We will discuss the archeological excavations of the basilica and baptistry of Milan and this cathedral as the architectural setting for Ambrose's mystagogical preaching in detail in Chapter 8. See below, 299–304.

The congregation was composed of diverse social groups. McLynn does a remarkable job of bringing together data from disparate sources to create a sampling of the "congregational roll" of the church of Milan.[22] Members of the court, and those brought to Milan in its train, were the most dynamic elements of this congregation. On any given Sunday Ambrose would find in his cathedral men noted for successful court careers,[23] if not the emperor himself.[24]

A second element of Ambrose's congregation was the transplanted population of Milan.[25] Consecrated virgins[26] and the

---

[22] In the following discussion of the composition of Ambrose's congregation, I am indebted to McLynn's section "Constructing a Community" in *Ambrose of Milan: Church and Court in a Christian Capital*, 220–226.

[23] Members of Ambrose's congregation with successful court careers include Ponticianus, an *agens en rebus* who managed to reconcile Christian baptism with a successful court career (see Augustine, *Confessions*, 8.6.14; CCSL 27.121), the former *tribunus et notarius* Nicentius, who, despite the pain of his gout, continued to attend church (*Epistola* 56 [Maur. 5].8 CSEL 82/2.88; Paulinus, *Vita Ambrosii*, 44; Navoni, 126), and Manlius Theodorus, who retired from politics toward the end of Gratian's reign in order to pursue his philosophical interests (McLynn, *Ambrose of Milan: Church and Court in a Christian Capital*, 221). Only one *civis* of Milan can be identified with certainty among Ambrose's congregation, the *grammaticus* Verecundus, who lent Augustine his rural estate at Cassiciacum (Augustine, *Confessions*, 8.6.13; CCSL 27.121).

[24] On Ambrose preaching to Theodosius, see *Epistola extra coll.* 1 (Maur. 41) (CSEL 82/3.145–161); cf. Paulinus, *Vita Ambrosii*, 23 (Navoni, 88).

[25] Members of Ambrose's congregation who came to Milan from other places include Augustine, Alypius, and Evodius, baptized by Ambrose at Easter 387, who were all from Tagaste in Africa. See Augustine, *Confessions*, 9.6.14 (CCSL 27.140) for Alypius; 9.8.17 (CCSL 27.143) for Evodius. Augustine's mother Monica is also to be counted among this element of the congregation. Benivolus, the most senior of Ambrose's known supporters against Justina, was not a citizen of Milan. His home was Brescia, seventy miles from Milan. The discomforts of travel and local particularism meant that Brescia was exposed only intermittently to the capital's direct influence. See McLynn, *Ambrose of Milan: Church and Court in a Christian Capital*, 221.

[26] One such consecrated virgin was Daedalia, the sister of Manlius Theodorus. Daedalia's grave, which is adjacent to the twin burial places of Victor and Satyrus, suggests that she held a place of prominence in life similar to theirs. Victor is one of Milan's prized collection of imported martyrs: Satyrus is Ambrose's brother. The archeology of the present chapel of San Vittore in Ciel d'Oro is discussed by A. Palastra, "I cimitieri paleocristiani

needy[27] constituted two more social elements of Ambrose's congregation. The wealthy who gave their alms to the church's pensioners were a fifth component of the church of Milan. Those looked to for support by the truly indigent were slaveholders, landowners, tradespeople, businesspeople, educated people able to provide their families with items of luxury. On the other hand, Ambrose states that many of his listeners were ignorant people who required plain language in order to understand.[28] Still, they were a distinct minority. Ambrose's congregation overall was "a distinctively upper-class audience, enriched or impoverished, depending on one's point of view, by a less narrow sampling of the population on certain days and in special settings."[29] Thus Ambrose, like most preachers of his day, could assume that he was addressing "the most educated audience that the region could supply, meaning, of course, the well-to-do."[30] Ambrose preached to people like himself, calling them to be intermediaries between the church and the urban masses.[31]

It is important to note that although the church of Milan was diverse, in worship Ambrose preached to a united congregation. Ambrose effectively united his diverse audience through the congregational singing of psalms and hymns. Ambrose's congregation was enthralled by the exotic melodies of his Eastern-style antiphonal chants.[32] In fact, the effect was so notable that Ambrose's opponents accused him of

---

Milanesi," *Archivio Ambrosiano* 28 (1975) 25–26. For the location of Daedalia's tomb, see Ernst Diehl, *Inscriptiones Latinae Christianae Veteres* (Berlin: Apud Weidmannos, 1961–1967); for her epitaph, composed by Theodorus, see Pierre Courcelle, "Quelques symboles funéraires du néoplatonisme latin," *Revue des Études Anciens* 46 (1944) 65–73. Daedalia, "distinguished of birth and richly endowed in worldly goods," boosted the prestige of Ambrose's company of consecrated virgins.

[27] *Contra Auxentium*, 33 (CSEL 82/3.104). Ambrose describes the pensioners of the church as "the blind and the lame, the feeble and the elderly." He mentions and does not deny the charge that their devotion had been nurtured by financial assistance.

[28] *De Isaac et anima*, 7.57 (CSEL 32/1.681).

[29] Ramsay MacMullen, "The Preacher's Audience," *The Journal of Theological Studies* 40 (1989) 510.

[30] Ibid., 509.

[31] Ibid., 511; McLynn, *Ambrose of Milan: Church and Court in a Christian Capital*, 223.

[32] Augustine, *Confessions*, 9.7.15 (CCSL 14.141).

"bewitching" his congregation; he did not deny it but attributed the power of such hymns to their Trinitarian lyrics, by which "all have become teachers, who were scarcely able to be learners."[33] Singing helped to focus the congregation's attention and drown out background noise.[34] "[I]n more elevated terms, it produced a *symphonia* from the *plebis concordia*—an 'uproar in unison' of young and old, rich and poor."[35] Ambrose found in congregational singing the means to reach across the barriers of social class that separated his people in their everyday lives and to create a sense of solidarity that suppressed antisocial behavior and distracted people from their propensity to avarice.[36] Through congregational song, even the emperor could be incorporated into the community.[37]

Although the unity created by congregational singing was only experienced in church and neither changed the structures of society nor healed its divisions, even this isolated experience of community served to comfort the diverse elements of Ambrose's congregation. Thus Augustine confessed that at his baptism he was "keenly moved by the sweet singing of Your church. Those voices flowed into my ears, truth seeped into my heart, and feelings of devotion welled up; tears ran down, and it was well with me that they did."[38] In the case of his mystagogical preaching, Ambrose's audience was united by their common experience of the rites of initiation.

Finally, two comments from Augustine are insightful. First, Augustine reports that, "surveying the full assembly of the Church I observed that people's lifestyles varied."[39] Second, we have previously noted

---

[33] *Contra Auxentium,* 34 (CSEL 82/3.105). For a discussion of Ambrose's hymns, see Frederick Homes Dudden, *The Life and Times of St. Ambrose* (Oxford: Clarendon Press, 1935). 1:270–293; Boniface Ramsey, *Ambrose* (New York: Routledge, 1997) 65, 166–173.

[34] On singing as a tool for focusing the congregation's attention, see *Expositio in Psalmum cxviii*, 7.25 (CSEL 62.144); on drowning out background noise, see *Enarrationes in xii psalmos davidicos,* 1.9 (CSEL 64.7).

[35] McLynn, *Ambrose of Milan: Church and Court in a Christian Capital,* 225. Cf. *Hexaemeron,* 3.29 (CSEL 32/1.78); *Explanatio evangelii secundum Lucam,* 7.237-238 (CCSL 14.295–296).

[36] *Expositio in Psalmum cxviii,* 7.29 (CSEL 62.144); cf. *Enarrationes in xii psalmos davidicos,* 1.9 (CSEL 64.7).

[37] Ibid.

[38] Augustine, *Confessions,* 9.6.14 (CCSL 27.140).

[39] Ibid., 8.1.2 (CCSL 27.112).

Augustine's remark that ardent believers and skeptical connoisseurs "hung keenly on [Ambrose's] lips."[40] These details lead us to conclude, first, that the members of Ambrose's audience had different degrees of commitment to Christianity and, second, that they "were remarkably patient of rhetoric pitched at a high level of stylistic and exegetical sophistication."[41] In the church of Milan the preacher's erudite speech was matched by his audience's ability to listen. The challenge was to speak to people at various places on the spectrum of faith and commitment to the Church. While this may be true for Ambrose's congregation generally, we can assume that the newly baptized shared at least some level of faith and commitment that led them to seek baptism and undergo the process of Christian initiation.

The Decision to Be Baptized

The characteristics that the newly baptized of Milan shared in common were their decision to be baptized and their experience of the process and rites of initiation. As we have said, we will discuss initiation in Milan in detail in our next chapter. We will, therefore, concentrate here on the neophytes' decision to be baptized. Ambrose makes clear that deciding to be baptized was not the norm. Preaching on the text "We toiled all night and took nothing,"[42] Ambrose compares the lack of response to his request for names for baptism to the apostles' unsuccessful night of fishing.[43]

Why was this so? In the time of Ambrose, more and more Christians found themselves unable to answer the questions and reconcile the conflicts posed by peace with the empire. The necessity of leading a responsible life in the world previously rejected by the Church made the baptismal demand of radical obedience to the Gospel a seemingly impossible ideal best postponed until one's involvement with the world was over. For this reason, baptism in the time of Ambrose stood on the brink of becoming "a purely eschatological sacrament, an individualistic act often postponed until the death bed, which would wash away all one's sins, and at the most convenient moment, when the struggle and doubt as to what it meant to be a Christian in the world was well-nigh over, would throw open the gates of heaven to

[40] Ibid., 5.13.23 (CSEL 27.71). See above, 89.
[41] MacMullen, "The Preacher's Audience," 504.
[42] Luke 5:5.
[43] *Expositio evangelii secundum Lucam*, 4.76 (CCSL 14.134).

the fortunate recipient."[44] Ambrose's criticism of the practice of deferring baptism is evident in his commentary on the parable of the prodigal son, where he asserts that the error of the son lay not in asking for his portion of the inheritance but in removing himself from the house of the father.[45]

While we know that the decision to be baptized was a momentous one, W.H.C. Frend notes that the motives that led people to transfer their allegiance from paganism to Christianity, let alone to commit to the level of faith that accompanied baptism, remain obscure.[46] One of the "more reputable"[47] motives for conversion to Christianity was certainly the power of the Christian message. Sozomen tells how in Phoenicia, "prominent individuals were converted after conversations with bishops" and after signs and dreams.[48] We have previously noted that Augustine claims to have been brought to faith by the power of Ambrose's message.[49]

If we look at the sarcophagi and catacomb paintings of the fourth century, we see that the hope of the resurrection through Christ was a second factor that led to serious conversion. The raising of Lazarus, prominent on a number of Roman sarcophagi, was the type of the individual's own resurrection, while the three holy children symbolized the Christian's deliverance from malevolent powers.

A third motivation for baptism was "the romance of the church's heroic past, the long-term influence of the martyrs of the previous generation."[50] We have previously discussed Ambrose's use of martyrs'

---

[44] Hugh M. Riley, *Christian Initiation: A Comparative Study of the Interpretation of the Baptismal Liturgy in the Mystagogical Writings of Cyril of Jerusalem, John Chrysostom, Theodore of Mopsuestia, and Ambrose of Milan* (Washington: Catholic University of America Press, 1974) 22.

[45] *Expositio evangelii secundum Lucam*, 7.213 (CCSL 14.288). See Adriano Caprioli, "Battesimo di Agostino, Imagine di Chiesa e Figura di Christiano," in *Agostino a Milano: Il Battesimo: Agostino Nelle Terre di Ambrogio*, ed. M. Sordi (Palermo: Edizioni Augustinus, 1988) 68.

[46] W.H.C. Frend, *The Rise of Christianity* (Philadelphia: Fortress Press, 1984) 561.

[47] Ibid., 564. In this discussion we are concerned with the motives that led to baptism as opposed to the conforming Christianity that was replacing conforming paganism as the mark of an educated provincial. See above, 2, n. 3.

[48] *Ecclesiastical History*, 2.5.6 as cited in Frend, *The Rise of Christianity*, 564.

[49] Above, 89; cf. Augustine, *Confessions*, 6.6.4 (CCSL 27.76).

[50] Frend, *The Rise of Christianity*, 565.

memoriae to enhance his reputation as a holy person, combat Arianism, and promote unity within his church.[51] A further consequence of the memory of these martyrs, enhanced as it was by reports of miraculous cures associated with their relics, was that people were moved to make a serious commitment to the Christian faith.

Fourth, recovery from sickness was among the best motivations for baptism and was used by bishops for this purpose. Thus in two letters[52] Ambrose attempted to persuade Bellicius to see his recovery from illness as the occasion for baptism. Ambrose wrote:

"You tell me that while you lay very ill you believed in the Lord Jesus and soon began to grow better. This sickness was intended for your health and brought you more gain than peril, since you were long postponing the fulfillment of your promise. This is the meaning of the words: 'I will not strike, and I will heal.'[53] God struck you with illness; He healed you with faith. God saw the inward desire of your soul, not void of pious longing, but troubled with delays, and God chose to admonish you in such a way as not to harm your health and yet to incite your devotion."[54]

Finally, others were hastened in their decision to be baptized by some apparently miraculous event. Ambrose's brother Satyrus was baptized as an act of gratitude to God after having survived shipwreck.[55] It is noteworthy that these motivations for baptism are all profound religious experiences, a characteristic that the newly baptized certainly had in common.

Mystagogy in Context

Craddock rightly describes a sermon as "but a gathering of paragraphs until placed in its various contexts."[56] Stated simply, preachers not only need to know who their audience is, but they also need to know what is happening in their audience's lives. Ambrose viewed the world of the newly baptized of Milan as a place hostile to Christian faith. Recalling Ambrose's descriptions of the excessive luxury of

---

[51] Above, 55–57.
[52] *Epistola* 9, 67 (Maur. 79, 80) (CSEL 82/1.71–72, 82/2.165–168).
[53] Deuteronomy 32:39.
[54] *Epistola* 9 (Maur. 79) (CSEL 82/1.71–72).
[55] *De excessu fratris*, 1.43-48 (CSEL 73.232–236).
[56] Craddock, *Preaching*, 32.

the rich in contrast to the poor, the greed that characterized Milanese society, the unrestrained habits of the people, particularly drunkenness, the absence of morality in marriage, and the Milanese's love of horse races and theatrical productions,[57] we see how the everyday world in which Christians lived was a place filled with temptations that threatened their faith. Ironically, these temptations gained power because of the threat of complacency brought about by the Church's peace with the empire. Not only was an ever-increasing number of Christians no longer hostile toward the empire; they were, in fact, officials in that empire, responsible for the secular city. Ambrose perceived that this new relationship between Church and state threatened individual Christians.

Christians and even the Church were also threatened by the very real struggle against the paganism and Judaism that threatened the Church from the outside and the heresy, particularly Arianism, that threatened it from within. Thus Ambrose felt the need to protect his congregation from both internal and external threats to their faith. Whether confronted by paganism, Judaism, or Arianism, Ambrose sought to stoutly defend the Church and, as we shall see, this agenda naturally found expression in his mystagogy.

Summary

From our audience analysis, we can conclude that the newly baptized of Milan came from a population that was socially, economically, educationally, and spiritually diverse. While the vast majority of Ambrose's congregation may have been upper class, the poor and the uneducated were present as well. Ambrose's congregation was also diverse in terms of its commitment to Christ. Members' commitment ranged from consecrated virgins to nonbelievers, whose attendance was due to their appreciation of Ambrose's rhetoric. Ambrose overcame the diversity of his audience in part by uniting the congregation through an overriding common experience and in part by his rhetorical skill. In Sunday worship the unifying experience was the congregational singing of hymns. In the case of mystagogy, the newly baptized were united by two additional experiences. First, they had all experienced something that led them to submit their names for baptism. Second and more important was their experience of the process of Christian initiation.

---

[57] Above, 72–77.

Despite the Milanese church's influence and status, and even if we assume that the three-thousand-seat cathedral of Milan was full on Sundays, baptized Christians constituted but a minuscule part of Milanese society. As such, their faith and Christian commitment were constantly challenged by the excessive greed and moral laxity of the culture and the competing claims of other religions, most notably paganism. Catholic and Orthodox Christians were even confronted by Arians, who threatened their faith with incorrect doctrine. Thus Ambrose viewed the day-to-day world in which the newly baptized lived as hostile to their status as baptized Christians.

THE NEWLY BAPTIZED AS PARTICIPANTS IN MYSTAGOGY

Convinced that the neophytes were about to face a world hostile to their status as baptized Christians, Ambrose understood mystagogy as the opportunity for his hearers to discover how they would engage in this struggle. More than passively receiving the information he provided, Ambrose therefore called upon his hearers to participate fully in their instruction on the sacraments.[58] In this section we consider the neophytes as participants in mystagogy using Craddock's observations about preaching that understands the listeners as participants.[59] First, we will ask what Ambrose wanted his hearers to think, feel, decide, and do during their instruction on the sacraments. Second, we will attempt to describe the newly baptized's *ability to listen* and the influences that shaped this ability. Third, we will explore how Ambrose

---

[58] From the perspective of classical rhetoric, in *On Rhetoric*, 1.3.2-3, Aristotle states that the hearer is "either a spectator *[theoros]* or a judge *[kritēs]*, and [in the latter case] a judge of either past or future happenings. He then distinguishes "three genera of rhetorics; *symbouleutikon* ['deliberative'], *dikanikon* ['judicial'], *epideiktikon* ['demonstrative']." Deliberative speech is either exhortation or dissuasion, and its goal is to show the better or the worse course of action. Judicial speech is either accusation or defense, and the goal is a just verdict. Demonstrative speech is either praise or blame, and its goal is to show either honor or shame. Mystagogy is closer to deliberative speech than to judicial and demonstrative speech. George A. Kennedy, *Aristotle: On Rhetoric: A Theory of Civic Discourse*, Newly translated with Introduction, Notes and Appendixes (New York: Oxford University Press, 1991) 47–50.

[59] Craddock, *Preaching*, 25–27. See above, 112.

shaped his sermons to involve the neophytes as participants. Among these methods we include a discussion of how Ambrose spoke for the newly baptized as well as to them.

Think, Feel, Decide, and Do

As we said, Craddock asserts that one of the consequences of understanding the listeners as participants in preaching is that "the sermon should proceed or move in such a way as to give the listener something to think, feel, decide, and do during the preaching."[60] For Ambrose it was not enough simply to understand the world of the neophytes in order to make the rites "applicable" to their lives. Ambrose wanted the neophytes to participate in their mystagogical instruction in such a way that they would enter more fully and deeply into their encounter with Christ in the rites of initiation. This level of participation leads the newly baptized to both rightly appreciate the meaning and significance of this encounter and allow it to become the guiding force of their lives. For Ambrose this happens when the neophytes move beyond worldly perception and see using the eyes of faith, which they received at baptism.[61] In this way the newly baptized come to understand the depth of the meaning of the mysteries and view the events of their lives not in terms of things temporal but of things eternal, a perspective that "is not grasped by the eyes but perceived by the spirit and the mind."[62]

Thus Ambrose wanted his hearers to both think about and feel the power of the sacraments, to re-experience the rites of initiation or, better yet, to experience them more fully, even profoundly, so that, as newborn Christians, the neophytes might cherish the gift of faith and union with Christ that they received at baptism by deciding to live as mature Christians in the world. Candidates for baptism learned how they were to live as Christians in the world as part of their Lenten preparation for baptism.[63] From the mysteries they received the faith, desire, and ability to do so. Ambrose wanted to bring his listeners to embrace this power and live the new life of faith.

---

[60] Craddock, *Preaching*, 25. See above, 112.
[61] *De sacramentis*, 3.2.15 (SC 25bis.100). See below, 140; 318.
[62] *De mysteriis*, 3.15 (SC 25bis.162).
[63] See below, 140–141.

The Neophytes' Ability to Listen

Getting the neophytes to participate in mystagogical preaching was not a difficult task. The newly baptized of Milan had a very acute ability to listen, that is, they were active, attentive, interested, and involved listeners. Three influences contributed to this ability. First, the fact that rhetoric held a prominent place in the culture made the newly baptized skilled listeners. We have previously discussed the important role that rhetoric played in preaching.[64] Ambrose's hearers considered rhetoric one of the greatest forms of art. In order to appreciate this art form, people needed to be cultivated listeners.

Second, the neophytes had high expectations of the preacher. When people expect to hear a good preacher, they listen carefully and, due in great part to the fact that they listen carefully, they hear a good preacher. As an educated, upper-class congregation that included members of the imperial court, Ambrose's listeners expected to hear a good preacher. McLynn goes as far as to argue that when it came to preaching, "Ambrose had to meet the standard set by Auxentius, a native speaker of Greek whose service to a learned bishop at Alexandria had given him a good grounding in contemporary theology; the Milanese congregation will therefore have had certain expectations."[65] In Chapter 3 we discussed at length Ambrose's effectiveness as a preacher. Add to this effectiveness the fact that Ambrose prepared the neophytes for baptism and initiated them into the mysteries and we cannot doubt that Ambrose's hearers expected great things of their bishop as they gathered to hear him throughout the week following Easter.

Third, the newly baptized of Milan were highly invested in the message. They had undergone some sort of profound religious experience that led them to accept the Church's demand of radical obedience to the Gospel and submit their names for baptism. As we will see in Chapter 5, they endured a long and rigorous catechumenal process in preparation for baptism and were initiated into the mysteries without prior explanation of the rites. Now they were expected to live a new and different life in a culture that was often in conflict with, if not openly hostile to, their newfound faith. Ambrose was answering their questions, explaining the mysteries, and telling the newly baptized

---

[64] Above, 95–98.
[65] McLynn, *Ambrose of Milan: Church and Court in a Christian Capital*, 57.

how they were to live as Christians in the world. Certainly they wanted to hear what he had to say.

Involving the Neophytes in Mystagogy

Despite the fact that Ambrose could expect the newly baptized to participate in mystagogy, he did not take their involvement for granted. Instead, he structured his sermons in ways that fostered his listeners' participation. In this section we will explore the methods that Ambrose used to engage the neophytes in order to bring them to deeper participation in the rites of initiation and his explanation of them. We group these methods under three headings: (1) catechetical style, (2) recreating the neophytes' experience of the rites, and (3) speaking for his hearers as well as to them.

Catechetical Style. The first group of methods that Ambrose employs to engage his hearers comprise what Christine Mohrmann defines as a "catechetical style," a style with "le caractère même de la catéchèse."[66] Catechesis is distinct from teaching in that it involves more than conveying information. Its purpose is the formation of Christians. In order to bring about this "change," catechetical preaching requires both a higher degree of intimate contact between the preacher and the listener and a clearer and simpler form than do sermons preached to the community of the faithful. Thus catechetical preaching aims at engaging the listeners in a dialogue so that they do not remain passive.[67] In order to accomplish this task, these sermons breathe with

---

[66] Christine Mohrmann, "Le style oral du *De sacramentis* de saint Ambroise," *Vigiliae Christianae* 6 (1952) 172. In the following discussion of Ambrose's catechetical style, we are indebted to Mohrmann, "Le style oral du *De sacramentis* de saint Ambroise"; idem, "Observations sur le *De sacramentis* et le *De mysteriis* de saint Ambroise," in *Ambrosius Episcopus* (Milan: Università Cattolica del Sacro Cuore, 1978); G. Lazzati, "L'autenticità del De sacramentis e la valutazione letteraria delle opera di S. Ambrogio," *Aevum* 29 (1955) 17–48; and the summary of Mohrmann's work found in Steven M. Oberhelman, *Rhetoric and Homiletics in Fourth Century Christian Literature: Prose, Rhythm, Oratorical Style, and Preaching in the Works of Ambrose, Jerome, and Augustine* (Atlanta: Scholars Press, 1991) 101–108. Our purpose here is to describe the components of Ambrose's catechetical style. The reader is directed to these sources for a detailed analysis of the Latin text of *De sacramentis*.

[67] Mohrmann, "Le style oral du *De Sacramentis* de saint Ambroise," 172–173.

spontaneity and improvisation and contain a very free, loose structure.[68] Mohrmann points to the repetitions, omissions, loose syntax, use of questions, and dialogue form. The tone is paternal and familiar. The vocabulary, though simple, does not approximate vulgar spoken Latin. As Mohrmann has noted, the diction gives the impression of a cultivated man speaking frankly and clearly.[69]

Finally Ambrose avoids formal rules of rhetoric in favor of an oral homiletic style to present the mysteries to the newly baptized.[70] Thus *De sacramentis* gives the impression of the urgency and spontaneity characteristic of a speaker who is sufficiently confident to adapt his speech to his audience as he goes on, something Ambrose would no doubt have been well able to do after his long experience in secular politics before becoming bishop of Milan. The elements of Ambrose's catechetical style are presented in the following paragraphs and illustrated with examples from *De sacramentis*.

---

[68] Ibid., 173ff.; Lazzati, "L'autenticità del De sacramentis e la valutazione letteraria delle opera di S. Ambrogio," 28–29, 33; Oberhelman, *Rhetoric and Homiletics in Fourth Century Christian Literature*, 102.

[69] Mohrmann, "Le style oral du *De sacramentis* de saint Ambroise," 174; Lazzati, "L'autenticità del De sacramentis e la valutazione letteraria delle opera di S. Ambrogio," 27; Oberhelman, *Rhetoric and Homiletics in Fourth Century Christian Literature*, 102.

[70] Mohrmann, "Le style oral du *De sacramentis* de saint Ambroise," 175; Lazzati, "L'autenticità del De sacramentis e la valutazione letteraria delle opera di S. Ambrogio," 27; Oberhelman, *Rhetoric and Homiletics in Fourth Century Christian Literature*, 102. For example, the classical Greek oratorical form of argument, which the Roman lawyer Cicero (first century B.C.) polished in his orations and outlined in *De oratore*, is not used in Ambrose's mystagogical works. The structure set forth by Cicero, Quintilian, and their followers is that of the modern essay. Using the traditional Latin headings, this structure is summarized as follows: *exordium* (introduction), *narratio* (general description of subject and background), *propositio* (thesis), *partitio* (statement of how the thesis is to be divided and handled), *confirmatio* (chief evidence in support of the thesis), *reprehensio* (enumeration and refutation of the opposition's claims), *digressio* (discussion of matters related but not essential to the subject), *peroratio* (summary of the discussion and call for adoption of the thesis). For a quick and useful summary of classical rhetoric and its application to contemporary literary genres, see Sheridan Baker, *The Complete Stylist and Handbook*, 3rd ed. (New York: Harper and Row, 1984) 451–453.

First, Ambrose addresses the newly baptized directly.[71] In both *De sacramentis* and *De mysteriis* we regularly find Ambrose using the second-person singular form of the verb. Examples include *ingressus es, unctus es*,[72] *abrenuntiasti mundo, abrenuntiasti saeculo*,[73] and *Venisti ad fontem, descendisti in eum, adtendisti summum sacerdotem, leuitas, presbyterum in fonte uidisti*.[74] Elsewhere Ambrose uses the second-person singular pronoun to address the neophytes: *Quando te interrogavit*,[75] *Tuum est . . . credere*,[76] and *Ergo, tibi ut respondeam*.[77] Through this implied *you*, Ambrose seems to address only one person while speaking to the entire community. Additionally, Ambrose uses the first-person plural form of verbs to express his solidarity with his hearers. Examples include: *Ergo quid egimus sabbato?*,[78] *Miramur mysteria Iudaeorum*,[79] and *recipimur et demergimur resurgimus, hoc est, resuscitamur*.[80] By his use of "you," Ambrose addresses the neophytes individually rather than as a group. By his use of "we," he asserts his connection to them. Both these forms of direct address serve to establish an atmosphere of familiar conversation or dialogue between the bishop and the newly baptized.

Second, the tone of *De sacramentis* is familiar and paternal. The text reveals a certain intimacy between the bishop and the neophytes that distinguishes *De sacramentis* from Ambrose's other sermons. Our aristocratic bishop, cultivated and erudite, who made intellectual demands on his hearers by including elements of philosophy and Greek exegesis in his sermons and whose eloquent rhetoric led Augustine to praise him, uses simple sentences, elementary Latin, and forgoes a

---

[71] Mohrmann, "Observations sur le *De sacramentis* et le *De mysteriis* de saint Ambroise," 119.

[72] *De sacramentis*, 1.2.4 (SC 25bis.62). "you went in, you were anointed"

[73] Ibid., 1.4.8 (SC 25bis.64). "you have renounced the world, you have renounced this age"

[74] Ibid., 2.6.16 (SC 25bis.82). "You came to the font, you went down into it, you turned toward the bishop, you saw the levite and the presbyter in the font."

[75] Ibid., 1.2.5 (SC 25bis.62). "When you were asked"

[76] Ibid., 1.6.21 (SC 25bis.72). "Yours is to believe"

[77] Ibid., 4.4.16 (SC 25bis.110). "Therefore, to answer your question"

[78] Ibid., 1.1.2 (SC 25bis.60). "Therefore, what did we do on Saturday?"

[79] Ibid., 1.4.11 (SC 25bis.66). "We marvel at the Jewish mysteries"

[80] Ibid., (SC 25bis.90). "we are received, and plunged, and we emerge, that is, we are raised up"

certain "literary ardour"[81] to communicate with the newly baptized. This distinctiveness becomes obvious when one compares *De sacramentis* with *De mysteriis*, which was edited for publication. Here we provide parallel passages on the *ephphatha*:

Ergo quid egimus sabbato? Nempe apertionem: quae mysteria celebrata sunt apertionis quando tibi aures tetigit sacerdos et nares. Quid significat? In evangelio dominus noster Iesus Christus, cum ei oblatus esset surdus et mutus, tetigit aures eius et os eius, aures quia surdus erat, os quia mutus, et ait: Effetha. Hebraicum uerbum est quod latine dicitur adaperire. Ideo ergo tibi sacerdos aures tetigit ut aperirentur aures tuae ad sermonem et ad alloquium sacerdotis.

Sed dicis mihi: Quare nares? Ibi quia mutus erat os tetigit, ut quia loqui non poterat sacramenta caelestia uocem acciperet a Christo. Et ibi quia uir, hic quia mulieres baptizantur et non eadem puritas serui quanta et domini, —cum enim ille peccata concedat, huic peccata donentur, quae potest esse comparatio?—ideo propter gratiam operis et muneris non os tangit episcopus sed nares. Quare nares? Vt bonum odorem accipias pietatis aeternae, ut dicas: Christi bonus odor sumus deo, quemadmodum dixit apostolus sanctus, et sit in te fidei deuotionisque plena flagrantia (*De sacramentis*, 1.1.2–3).[82]

---

[81] Mohrmann, "Observations sur le *De sacramentis* et le *De mysteriis* de saint Ambroise," 114.

[82] SC 25bis.60–62. "What, then, did we do on Saturday? The opening. These mysteries of opening were celebrated when the bishop touched your eyes and nostrils. What does this mean? Our Lord Jesus Christ, in the gospel, when the deaf and mute man was brought to him, touched his ears and his mouth, his ears because he was deaf; his mouth because he was mute; and said: *Effetha*. It is a Hebrew word which in Latin means *be opened*. The reason, therefore, that the bishop touched your ears was that your ears might be opened to the sermon and the discourse of the bishop.

"But you say to me: Why the nostrils? In that case, because he was mute, he touched his mouth, that, since he was unable to speak the heavenly mysteries, he might receive the ability to speak from Christ. And in that case because it was a man; here, women are baptized, and the purity of the servant is not as great as that of the Lord,—For what comparison can there be, when one forgives sins and the other's sins are forgiven?—therefore, out of respect for the grace of the action and the function, the bishop does not touch the mouth but the nostrils. Why the nostrils? That you may receive the good odor of eternal goodness, that you may say, "We are the good odor of Christ for God," as the holy apostle said, and there may be in you the full fragrance of faith and devotion."

> *Aperite igitur aures et bonum odorem uitae aeternae inhalatum uobis munere sacramentorum carpite. Quod uobis significauimus cum apertionis celebrantes mysterium diceremus: Effetha, quod est adaperire, ut uenturus unusquisque ad gratiam quid interrogaretur cognosceret, quid responderet meminisse deberet.*
>
> *Hoc mysterium celebrauit Christus in euangelio, sicut legimus, cum mutum curaret et surdum. Sed ille os tetigit quia et mutum curabat et uirum, in altero ut os eius infusae sono uocis aperiret, in altero quia tactus iste uirum decebat, feminam non deceret (De mysteriis, 1.3–4).*[83]

In comparing Ambrose's mystagogical works, we find that the vocabulary of *De sacramentis* is very simple without ever being popular, and the sentence structure lacks oratorical ornamentation. In *De mysteriis*, however, we occasionally encounter passages with a certain oratorical flair. This flair is found not only in the vocabulary, which is more colorful and flowery; it also appears in the sentence structure of *De mysteriis*, which is less elementary than that of *De sacramentis*. These differences are in keeping with Ambrose's views on preaching. As we have said, Ambrose reminded his presbyters that many of their hearers are simple people. Therefore, they needed to use plain language in order to be understood. He calls this kind of preaching "milky speech," intended to nourish those who, like infants, cannot digest strong food.[84]

A third characteristic of Ambrose's catechetical style is his frequent use of questions. As we noted in Chapter 1, questions occur so often in *De sacramentis* that they are a prominent feature of the text.[85]

---

[83] Ibid., 158. "Open your ears, then, and lay hold of the good odor of eternal life that was breathed upon you by the gift of the sacraments. This was signified to you when we celebrated the mystery of the opening and said: 'Ephphatha—that is, open up,' so that each one who was advancing to grace would know what was being asked and would remember how to respond.

"Christ celebrated this mystery in the gospel, as we read, when he healed the deaf man. But, because the mute whom he healed was also a man, he touched his mouth. He did this, on the one hand, in order to open his mouth for the sound of a voice that was now being given to it, and, on the other hand, because a touch was appropriate for a man but would have been inappropriate for a woman."

[84] See above, 95.

[85] Above, 26–27.

Mohrmann is correct that these questions are of two types.[86] First, there is the oratorical device characteristic of popular preaching, which is found frequently in both *De sacramentis* and *De mysteriis*, as well as in Ambrosian works generally. These oratorical questions serve both to move the argument and to aid the speaker in holding the attention of his audience by prompting the hearers and involving them in the argumentation. In the treatises that Ambrose edited for publication, these questions seem to be a residue of the sermons on which these works were based. Examples from Ambrose's mystagogical works include: *Lux quid est nisi ueritas quia apertum et planum lumen effundit? Columna lucis quis est nisi Christus dominus qui tenebras infidelitatis depulit, lucem veritatis et gratiae spiritalis adfectibus infudit humanis?*,[87] *Ex his igitur omnibus non intellegis quantum opertur sermo caelestis? Si operatus est in fonte terreno, si operatus est sermo caelestis in aliis rebus, non operatur in caelestibus sacramentis?*,[88] and *Non agnoscis quis iste sit? Potest homo esse rex iustitiae, cum ipse uix iustus sit? Potest rex pacis cum uix possit esse pacificus?*[89] In *De sacramentis*, we also find a second type of question that is absent in *De mysteriis*.[90] These are short questions consisting of one, two, or three words. Examples of this type of question include *Ergo quid egimus sabbato? Quid significat?*,[91] *Quare*

---

[86] Mohrmann, "Observations sur le *De sacramentis* et le *De mysteriis* de saint Ambroise," 117–118.

[87] *De sacramentis*, 1.6.22 (SC 25bis.72). "What is the fire except truth, which gives a clear and visible light? What is this column of light except Christ the Lord, who has scattered the darkness of infidelity and poured into human hearts the light of spiritual truth and grace?"

[88] Ibid., 4.4.19 (SC 25bis.112). "From all of this do you not understand the power that is contained in the heavenly word? If it was effective in the earthly spring, if the heavenly word was effective in the other cases, why should it not be so in the heavenly sacraments?"

[89] *De mysteriis*, 8.46 (SC 25bis.182). "Do you not recognize who this is? Can a man be king of righteousness if he is barely righteous? Can he be king of peace if he can barely be peaceable?"

[90] Lazzati, "L'autenticità del De sacramentis e la valutazione letteraria delle opera di S. Ambrogio," 32; Mohrmann, "Observations sur le *De sacramentis* et le *De mysteriis* de saint Ambroise," 117–118; Oberhelman, *Rhetoric and Homiletics in Fourth Century Christian Literature*, 105. On this second type of question as a "tic" of Ambrose's delivery, see below, 292.

[91] *De sacramentis*, 1.1.2 (SC 24bis.60). "What did we do on the Saturday? . . . What does this mean?"

hoc dico?,⁹² Quare? dicam, accipe,⁹³ Quid ergo significat?,⁹⁴ Quid lectum est heri?,⁹⁵ and Quare angelus?⁹⁶ Once again, these questions serve to engage a listening audience in dialogue and instruction. Both types of questions emanate from Ambrose's constant effort to establish a direct contact with his listeners.

Fourth, Ambrose uses dramatic narrative as a teaching tool to make the meaning of the mysteries accessible and concrete. The elements of narrative that Ambrose employs include direct discourse and dialogue. Comparing parallel passages from *De sacramentis* and *De mysteriis* on the episode of Naaman make these dramatic elements clear:

Neman ergo leprosus erat. Ait puella quaedam uxori illius: Dominus meus, si uult mundari, uadat in terram Israhel et ibi inueniet eum qui possit ei lepram tollere. Dixit illa dominae suae, uxor marito, Neman regi Syriae, qui eum quasi acceptissimum sibi misit ad regem Israhel. Audiuit rex Israhel quod missus esset ad eum cui lepram mundaret et scidit uestem suam. Tunc Helisaeus propheta mandat ei: Quid est quod scidisti uestem quasi non sit deus potens qui mundet leprosum? Mitte illum ad me. Misit illum, cui aduenienti ait propheta: Vade, descende in Iordanem, merge et sanus eris.

Ille coepit cogitare secum et dicere: Hoc est totum? Veni de Syria in terram iudaeam et dicitur mihi: Vade in Iordanem, merge et sanus eris? Quasi flumina meliora non sint in patria mea. Dixerunt ei serui: Domine, quare non facis uerbum prophetae? Magis fac et experire. Tunc ille iuit in Iordanem, mersit et surrexit sanus.

Quid ergo significat? Vidisti aquam, sed non aqua omnis sanat, sed aqua sanat quae habet gratiam Christi. Aliud est elementum, aliud consecratio, aliud opus, aliud operatio. Aquae opus est, operatio spiritus sancti est. Non sanat aqua nisi spiritus sanctus descenderit et aquam illam consecrauerit, sicut legisti quod, cum dominus noster Iesus Christus formam baptismatis daret, uenit ad Iohannes, et ait illi Iohannes: Ego a te debeo baptizari et tu uenis ad me. Respondit illi Christus: Sine modo, sic enim decet nos inplere omnem iustitiam. Vide quia omnis iustitia in baptismate constituta est (De sacramentis, 1.5.13–15).⁹⁷

⁹² Ibid., 1.2.6 (SC 25bis.64). "Why do I say this?"
⁹³ Ibid., 1.3.9 (SC 25bis.64). "Why? I will tell. Listen."
⁹⁴ Ibid., 1.5.15 (SC 25bis.68). "What, then, does it mean?"
⁹⁵ Ibid., 2.2.3 (SC 25bis.74). "What was read yesterday?"
⁹⁶ Ibid., 2.2.4 (SC 25bis.74). "Why an angel?"
⁹⁷ SC 25bis.64–68. "As I was saying, Naaman was a leper. One of his slave-girls said to his wife: 'If my lord wishes to be cured, he should go into the

Denique doceat te decursa Regnorum lectio. Neman Syrus erat et lepram habebat nec ab ullo mundari poterat. Tunc ait puella ex captiuis quoniam esset propheta in Israhel qui posset eum a leprae contagione mundare. Sumpto, inquit, auro et argento perrexit ad regem Israhel. Qui cognita aduentus eius causa scidit uestimenta sua dicens quod temptaretur magis cum de se ea quae non essent potestatis regiae poscerentur. Helisaeus autem regi intimauit ut ad se dirigeret Syrum quo cognosceret quod esset deus in Israhel. Et cum uenisset mandauit ei ut septies mergeret in Iordane fluuio.

Tunc ille secum tractare coepit quod meliores aquas flumina haberent patriae suae in quibus saepe mersisset et numquam a lepra esset ablutus, eoque reuocatus non oboediebat mandatis prophetae. Sed admonitu et persuasionibus seruulorum adquieuit et mersit, mundatusque ilico intellexit non aquarum esse quod unusquisque mundatur, sed gratiae (De mysteriis, 3.16–17).[98]

---

country of Israel, and there he will find someone who can cure his leprosy.' This is what she said to her mistress; and the wife told her husband Naaman, who told the King of Syria. The king sent him, as one of his most highly favored subjects, to the King of Israel. When the King of Israel was told that a man had been sent to him to have his leprosy cured, he rent his garments. Then the prophet Elisha sent a message to him: 'What is this? Do you rend your garments as though there were no God powerful enough to heal leprosy? Send the man to me.' The king sent him. The moment Naaman came, the prophet told him: 'Go down to the river Jordan; bathe there and you will be cured.'

"Then he began to reflect within himself and to say: 'Is that all? I come from Syria to the land of the Jews and someone says to me: "Go to the Jordan, bathe there and you will be cured." As though there were not better rivers in my own country!' Then his servants said to him: 'Lord, why not do what the prophet says? Do it and see what happens.' Then he went to the Jordan, bathed there and came out cured.

"What is the meaning of this? You saw the water, but not all waters have a curative power; only that water has it which has the grace of Christ. There is a difference between the matter and the consecration, between the action and its effect. The action belongs to the water, its effect to the Holy Spirit. The water does not heal unless the Spirit descends and consecrates the water. So you have read that when our Lord Jesus Christ instituted the rite of baptism, he came to John and John said to him, 'I need to be baptized by you, and do you come to me?' Christ answered: 'Let it be so now; for thus it is fitting for us to fulfill all righteousness.' See how the righteousness is established in baptism."

[98] Ibid., 164. "Let the passage from the Book of Kings that was read also teach you (2 Kgs 5:1-14). Naaman was a Syrian and he had leprosy and could

In *De sacramentis* the episode is related in direct discourse, dramatic dialogue, paratactic constructions, and oral elements. In *De mysteriis*, however, the entire episode is in indirect speech, with subordinate clauses and without dialogue.

Fifth, Ambrose uses repetition to help the neophytes remember, the most obvious example being his treatment of the Lord's Prayer.[99] Ambrose reserved teaching the Lord's Prayer and its meaning until after baptism.[100] In his instructions he begins by reciting the prayer in its entirety.[101] Ambrose then begins a phrase-by-phrase exposition of the prayer,[102] repeating not only the phrase that he is explaining but every phrase that has preceded it. For example, we find *Pater noster. . . . Pater noster, qui es in caelis. . . . Pater noster, qui es in caelis, sanctificetur nomen tuum.*[103]

Sixth, the introductions and conclusions of the sermons contained in *De sacramentis* are indicative of Ambrose's concern that the neophytes participate in mystagogy. Like a good teacher, he begins his first sermon by stating the subject matter of his discourse and explaining the underlying assumptions of his pedagogical approach.[104] In beginning

---

not be cleansed by anyone. Then a girl who was a captive said that there was a prophet in Israel who could cleanse him of the contamination of the leprosy. Taking gold and silver, it says, he went off to see the king of Israel. When he was apprized of the reason for his coming he rent his garments, declaring that he was being put to the test because what was being requested of him did not fall under his royal power. Elisha, however, told the king to send the Syrian to him so that he might know that there was a God in Israel. And when he came he ordered him to bathe seven times in the River Jordan.

"Then [Naaman] began to think to himself that the rivers of his own homeland had better water and that he had often bathed in them without ever being washed of his leprosy; changing his mind on that account, he did not obey the prophet's orders. But, thanks to the admonition and persuasion of his attendants, he gave in and bathed, and when he was cleansed then and there he understood that it is not water but grace that cleanses a person."

[99] *De sacramentis*, 5.4.18–30 (SC 25bis.128–136).

[100] Due to the *disciplina arcani* [see below, p. 155] the newly baptized most likely would not have heard the Lord's Prayer until they participated in the Easter Eucharist after their initiation. See below, 180.

[101] *De sacramentis*, 5.4.18 (SC 25bis.128).

[102] Ibid., 5.4.19–30 (SC 25bis.128–136).

[103] Ibid., 5.4.19, 20, 21 (SC 25bis.128–130). "Our Father. . . . Our Father in heaven. . . . Our Father in heaven, hallowed be your name."

[104] Ibid., 1.1.1 (SC 25bis.60).

subsequent sermons, Ambrose places the sermon in context by reminding the neophytes where they had left off the previous day.[105] In concluding these sermons, Ambrose shows his awareness of the constraints of the available time, tailoring his instruction accordingly, and previews the next day's instruction.[106] In these ways Ambrose helps his hearers understand how each sermon fits into both the overall scheme of his mystagogy and their experience of the rites of initiation.

Using these six methods—(1) direct address, (2) a familiar and paternal tone, (3) questions, (4) dramatic narrative, (5) repetition, and (6) placing his instructions in context— Ambrose employs a catechetical style to engage the newly baptized in a dialogue, thereby helping them to participate in mystagogy. This is particularly noteworthy because, as Nauroy correctly observes, we do not find in the aristocratic and refined speech that characterizes Ambrose's treatises either a warm tone or direct contact with the audience, striking features of the sermons of Saint Augustine. Nor does Ambrose recapitulate his thought for those of simple spirit. Even if the link between the preacher and his audience was lost when his sermons were edited into treatises, Ambrose's exegetical preaching required a level of listening on the part of his hearers not required in *De sacramentis*.[107] Yet, there is more to mystagogical preaching than being a good teacher. Ambrose wants the neophytes to experience the rites of initiation more fully so that they comprehend the depth of their meaning and respond with a life of faith. We now turn to a discussion of the ways that Ambrose used his dialogue with the neophytes to lead them to experience the mysteries at a deeper level.

Recreating the Neophytes' Experience. Ambrose himself makes clear to the neophytes that he wants them to re-experience the mysteries so that they perceive the depth of their meaning. Ambrose tells the newly baptized that they need to have their ears prepared and their minds ready so that they are able to retain what he declares to them and have the grace of the Trinity.[108] He explains that this is possible because the neophytes received the necessary faith in baptism. Ambrose says, "You received baptism, you believed."[109] "You came there [the font],

---

[105] *De sacramentis*, 2.1.1; 3.1.1; 5.1.1 (SC 25bis.74; 90; 120).

[106] Ibid., 1.6.24; 3.2.15; 4.6.29 (SC 25bis.72; 100; 119).

[107] Nauroy, "L'Ecriture dans la Pastorale d'Ambroise de Milan," 379.

[108] *De sacramentis*, 1.6.24 (SC 25bis.72).

you washed, you came to the altar, you began to see what you had not seen before."[110] For Ambrose the grace and faith necessary to experience the mysteries in all their fullness and to comprehend them in all their depth come from God through the sacraments.[111] Thus, in a concluding blessing, Ambrose prays that the Lord God will preserve in the neophytes the grace that God has given them and may deign to illuminate the eyes God has opened.[112] Yet Ambrose does not believe that efforts to open the neophytes' eyes, to prepare their ears, and to ready their minds to receive God's gift of grace and faith are limited to prayer.

Ambrose calls upon the neophytes to see beyond what they saw—to see not only a levite but an angel and know that their promises are kept not on earth but in heaven,[113] to see not only the baptismal font but a tomb and know that they were buried with Christ,[114] to see not just bread and wine but the body and blood of Christ and know that they receive the forgiveness of sins.[115] This challenge demonstrates that Ambrose understands that seeing through the eyes of faith is not a passive process; rather, the newly baptized have a responsible role to play in experiencing God's grace in the mysteries. Ambrose therefore cultivates the eyes of faith of the newly baptized by recreating their experience of the rites of initiation at a deeper level.

The methods that Ambrose employs to assist the newly baptized in experiencing the rites on the level of faith include: (1) calling upon the neophytes to remember what they experienced, (2) emphasizing the neophytes' active involvement in the mysteries, (3) appealing to the neophytes' senses and emotions, as well as to their minds, (4) telling the newly baptized how to respond, and (5) spelling out the implication of initiation for life in the world.

First, Ambrose appeals to the neophytes to remember their experience. Ambrose tells the newly baptized to recall specific, concrete things. Then he reminds them of what they saw and said, of where they were, and of the people that they were with. For example, in

[109] Ibid., 1.1.1 (SC 25bis.62).
[110] Ibid., 3.2.15 (SC 25bis.100).
[111] Ibid., 4.2.7 (SC 25bis.104).
[112] Ibid., 4.6.29 (SC 25bis.118).
[113] Ibid., 1.2.6 (SC 25bis.62).
[114] Ibid., 2.6.19; 3.1.1 (SC 25bis.84; 90).
[115] Ibid., 4.14, 20, 28 (SC 25bis.108, 112, 116).

describing their entrance into the baptistry, Ambrose says, "Think whom you saw, think what you said: recall it carefully."[116] Then he reminds them that they were received by a levite and a presbyter and asked if they renounce the devil and his works, the world and its pleasures, and that they answered, "I do renounce them."[117] Again, in his explanation of the renunciation Ambrose tells the newly baptized to "think of the place where you made your promise, think of those to whom you made it." He then reminds them that they saw a levite, a minister of Christ's altar and therefore a representative of heaven.[118] In discussing the neophytes being clothed in white robes, Ambrose gives his hearers a scriptural "hint" that the angels see them coming up from the wilderness in white[119] and then tells them to recall what they have received—not only a new robe but the new life of grace.[120] By instructing his hearers to recall specific, concrete elements of their initiation and helping them to do so, Ambrose engages his hearers with their own experience and then uses that experience to move them from physical words and actions to the meaning of these ritual formulas and movements at the level of grace.

A second method used by Ambrose to recreate his hearers' experience of initiation is to emphasize their active involvement by positioning the verb at the beginning of the sentence for stress.[121] In some instances the verb is the first word in the sentence. Examples include: *venimus ad fontem, ingressus es, unctus es. . . . Occurrit tibi levita, occurrit presbyter, unctus es quasi athleta Christi;*[122] *uidisti fontem, uidisti et sacerdotem;*[123]

---

[116] Ibid., 1.2.4 (SC 25bis.62). *Considera quos uideris, quid locutus sis considera, repete diligenter.*

[117] Ibid., 1.2.4–5 (SC 25bis.62).

[118] Ibid., 1.2.6 (SC 25bis.62). *Ubi promiseris considera uel quibus promiseris.*

[119] Song of Songs 8:5.

[120] *De sacramentis*, 4.2.5, 6 (SC 25bis.104).

[121] Mohrmann, "Le style oral du *De sacramentis* de saint Ambroise," 175; Lazzati, "L'autenticità del De sacramentis e la valutazione letteraria delle opera di S. Ambrogio," 28; Oberhelman, *Rhetoric and Homiletics in Fourth Century Christian Literature*, 103.

[122] *De sacramentis*, 1.2.4 (SC 25bis.62). "We arrived at the font. You went in. You were anointed. . . . You were received by a levite, you were received by a presbyter. You were anointed as Christ's athlete."

[123] Ibid., 1.3.9 (SC 25bis.64). "You saw the font, you saw also the bishop . . ."

Ingressus es, vidisti aquam, vidisti sacerdotem, vidisti levitam;[124] *Tangit ergo sacerdos calicem, redundat aqua in calice, salit in vitam aeternam, et bibit populus dei qui dei gratiam consecutus est;*[125] *venisti ergo ad altare, accepistis gratiam Christi.*[126] Beginning a sentence with the verb is very exceptional in Latin.[127] For this reason it catches the attention of the hearer and seems to confer on the verb a preeminent value. In *De sacramentis* the initial position of the verb almost always confers a preeminent value on the verb, that is, it highlights the verbal action.

Third, rather than describing, Ambrose evokes. Rather than appealing to the mind, Ambrose appeals directly to the senses and, through them, to the emotions. *De sacramentis* is filled with bodily images—seeing, hearing, touching, smelling, tasting. Ambrose reminds the neophytes that they were touched and were perhaps a bit embarrassed by it. Their ears and nostrils were touched by the bishop.[128] They were rubbed down with oil like an athlete.[129] They were immersed, plunged, buried in the water and were undoubtedly anxious and perplexed.[130] Entering the baptistry, they saw the font, the water, the bishop, and the levite and were perhaps disappointed.[131] Entering the cathedral, they saw the altar and were perhaps filled with wonder.[132] The neophytes heard the congregation singing and at least one of them reports being moved to tears.[133] When they were anointed after baptism, they smelled the fragrance of the *myron* as they felt it running down their faces.[134] At the altar the newly baptized ate the bread and drank from the cup and tasted sweetness and joy and became drunk with the

---

[124] Ibid., 1.3.10 (SC 25bis.64). "You went in, you saw the water, you saw the bishop, you saw the levite."

[125] Ibid., 5.1.3 (SC 25bis.122). "The bishop touched the chalice, water flowed into the chalice, it welled up to eternal life, and the people of God who have received grace drank from it."

[126] Ibid., 5.3.14 (SC 25bis.126). "You have come, then, to the altar, you have received the grace of Christ. . . ."

[127] Mohrmann, "Le style oral du *De sacramentis* de saint Ambroise," 176.

[128] *De sacramentis*, 1.1.2–3 (SC 25bis.60–62).

[129] Ibid., 1.2.4 (SC 25bis.62).

[130] Ibid., 2.7.20; 3.1.3 (SC 25bis.84; 91).

[131] Ibid., 1.3.9–10 (SC 25bis.64).

[132] Ibid., 3.2.15; 4.3.8 (SC 25bis.101; 107).

[133] Augustine, *Confessions*, 9.6.14 (CCSL 27.140).

[134] *De sacramentis*, 3.1.1 (SC 25bis.91); *De mysteriis*, 6.29 (SC 25bis.172).

spirit.[135] By appealing to the neophytes' senses and building upon their emotions, Ambrose does something more important than explain the mysteries. He places his hearers back in their experience of the mysteries. From here Ambrose moves them to a deeper level of experience, namely, their encounter with Christ and reception of grace.

To be immersed once again in their experience of Christian initiation was for the newly baptized moving, perplexing, inspiring, and confusing. They had been initiated without any prior explanation of what was about to happen to them, let alone of what it all meant. As we will see in our next chapter, the rites were magnificent. Their place, time, characters, words, objects, and actions were carefully crafted to create a drama that was not designed to be readily understood but to have a lasting emotional impact. During the week following Easter, the neophytes were therefore sorting out their experience and struggling to respond to it. Knowing this, the fourth method that Ambrose uses to draw his hearers into a deeper experience of the mysteries is to tell them how to respond. For example, after reminding his hearers that they renounced the devil and the world, he tells them that they must keep their answers in mind so that the terms of their guarantee never fade from their memory.[136] If the newly baptized keep in mind what they promised, they will keep faith with Christ, guard that faith, and be prudent and alert in the world.[137] In another sermon Ambrose tells the newly baptized that when they come to the altar, they come with desire because they will receive the sacrament there.[138] Further, they ought to come to the altar and receive the sacrament often so that their sins may be forgiven.[139] In his exposition of the Lord's Prayer, Ambrose tells his hearers to be bold in prayer, not on account of their own merits but because of the grace of Christ.[140]

In addition to telling his hearers how to respond to the rites themselves, Ambrose's fifth method of drawing the neophytes into a fuller experience of the mysteries is to spell out the implications of Christian initiation for life in the world. As we shall see, *De sacramentis* both portrays the world as a hostile place and specifically attacks paganism,

---

[135] *De sacramentis*, 5.3.17 (SC 25bis.128).
[136] Ibid., 1.2.5 (SC 25bis.49).
[137] Ibid., 1.2.8 (SC 25bis.56).
[138] *De sacramentis*, 4.2.7 (SC 25bis.106).
[139] Ibid., 4.6.28 (SC 25bis.116).
[140] Ibid., 5.4.19 (SC 25bis.128).

Judaism, and Arianism.[141] Ambrose also tells the neophytes that baptism obliges them to resist the world, and he provides instructions on how they are to do so. Ambrose tells his hearers that just as they passed safely through the waters of baptism, so they are to believe that they will come out safely when they are in difficulties; they are not to murmur but to implore, to pray and not complain.[142] As the neophytes clung to Christ in the font, so they are to cling to Christ in order that the devil cannot tear them away, and their own human nature cannot call them back to their former life.[143] Anointed to eternal life, the newly baptized are not to prefer temporal life to eternal life or to make life in the world their priority over eternal life, even if they are threatened with death.[144] In prayer they are to put divine things—the riches of chastity, purity, faith, devotion, and mercy—before human concerns such as money, gain, honor, or avarice. Within a marriage, the serious demeanor, chastity, and good conversation of a wife will summon her husband to faith and devotion, and a husband's wise words will do the same for his wife.[145] Ambrose does not engage in direct moral exhortation. Instead, he spells out the type of life that follows naturally from participation in the mysteries.

By calling upon his hearers to recall their experience of the rites of initiation and then recreating that experience by emphasizing their active involvement and appealing to their senses and emotions, Ambrose places his hearers *in* the mysteries rather than talking to them *about* the mysteries. Ambrose then assists his hearers in formulating a response to their experience, both in terms of understanding both the individual rites and their implications for life in the world. In this way the bishop of Milan leads the newly baptized to actively see with the eyes of faith.

Speaking for the Neophytes. The third way that Ambrose facilitates the neophytes' participation in mystagogy is by giving them a voice in their instruction. Ambrose accomplishes this by crafting his sermons so that they "speak *for* as well as *to* the congregation," as Craddock

---

[141] Below, 193–195.
[142] *De sacramentis*, 1.6.21 (SC 25bis.70).
[143] Ibid., 2.7.24 (SC 25bis.88).
[144] Ibid., 1.7.24 (SC 25bis.72).
[145] Ibid., 6.5.20 (SC 25bis.148).

says.[146] Ambrose includes in his mystagogy what his hearers want to *say*—their faith, their doubt, their anger, their love, their joy, their gratitude.[147] The first technique used by Ambrose to speak for the newly baptized is to put into words the questions that are in his hearers' minds. In *De sacramentis* we find: "But why, you may ask, the nostrils?"[148] "And what is this but death? 'How can this be?', you ask."[149] "Perhaps someone will say, . . ."[150]

Second, Ambrose gives voice to his hearers' likely reaction to the rites, even when it is negative. Of the neophytes' entrance into the baptistry Ambrose observes, "And if anyone should perhaps be thinking of saying: 'Is that all?'"[151] Explaining the miracle of the Eucharist, Ambrose says, "Perhaps you say: 'The bread I have here is ordinary bread.'"[152]

Third, Ambrose voices his hearers' objections to his explanations. In response to his assertion that the wine of the Eucharist is the true blood of Christ, Ambrose says, "Perhaps you will say: 'How can this be true? I see the likeness of blood, but I cannot see real blood.'"[153] By giving voice to his hearers' questions, reactions, and even their objections, the bishop of Milan invites the newly baptized to hear themselves in the mystagogy so that they say, "Yes, that is what I have wanted to say."[154]

REFLECTION:
THE PNEUMATIC DIMENSION OF THE LISTENERS

We find in *De sacramentis* the conviction that the newly baptized could neither come to faith nor live as Christians in the world apart from the gracious presence of Christ. Ambrose summarizes this conviction well when he says, "You cannot follow Christ unless he draws

---

[146] Craddock, *Preaching*, 26.

[147] Ibid., 26–27.

[148] *De sacramentis*, 1.1.3 (SC 25bis.60). *Sed dicis mihi: Quare nares?* Cf. ibid., 5.1.2 (SC 25bis.120).

[149] Ibid., 2.6.17 (SC 25bis.82). *Quid illud est nisi mors? Quaeris quomodo?*

[150] Ibid., 4.3.9 (SC 25bis.106). *Forte aliquis dixerit:* cf. ibid., 4.7.20 (SC 25bis.112).

[151] Ibid., 1.3.10 (SC 25bis.64). *Ne forte aliqui dixerit: Hoc est totum?*

[152] Ibid., 4.4.14 (SC 25bis.108). *Te forte dicis: Meus panis est usitatus.*

[153] Ibid., 6.1.2 (SC 25bis.138). *Forte dicas: Quomodo uera? Atqui similitudinem video, non video sanguinis veritatem.*

[154] Craddock, *Preaching*, 27.

you to himself."¹⁵⁵ Our study of the neophytes of Milan confirms the Christian conviction that Christ calls people to himself through the Spirit at work in the various contexts—pastoral, historical, theological, and (as we shall see) liturgical—through personal encounters in order to transform their everyday lives. Our study shows that both the circumstances that brought the neophytes to submit their names for baptism and the circumstances in which they were to live as Christians following their week of postbaptismal catechesis are specific, concrete, and real. For them faith is not a matter of intellectual assent but of choosing a way of life. As baptized Christians, Ambrose's hearers are expected to live as new, different people. Most important, as real as the arena in which Milanese Christians were expected to live out their faith and the expectation of a new way of life brought about by faith is the transformation that has taken place within them. This conversion was not theoretical but actual, not intellectual but holistic, not theological reflection but divine manifestation. This transformation was brought about by God and could only be sustained and brought to completeness by God.

In order to persevere in faith and live as Christians in the world, the neophytes need to understand and experience their transformation. Seeing the mystagogical encounter as an opportunity for the Spirit to bring the newly baptized to this fuller, deeper level, Ambrose crafted his sermons by using a catechetical style, recreating the experience of initiation, and speaking for the newly baptized as well as to them in order to create a dialogue not only between bishop and congregation but between heaven and earth, between Christ and his Church. His aim was that his hearers experience God's grace, Christ's presence, and the Spirit's power in such a way that they open themselves to God by remembering their promise, clinging to Christ, learning to pray, and viewing the world through eyes of faith so that when they observe the events of their lives, they see beyond the temporal to the eternal, "which is not apprehended by the eye, but discerned by the mind and the spirit."¹⁵⁶ The newly baptized received this vision at baptism. For it is through the rites of initiation that God brings God's people "from earthly things to heavenly things, from sin to life, from guilt to grace, from vileness to holiness."¹⁵⁷ What these rites

---

[155] *De sacramentis*, 5.2.10 (SC 25bis.124).
[156] *De mysteriis*, 15 (SC 25bis.162).
[157] *De sacramentis*, 1.3.12 (SC 25bis.66).

entail and how this change is understood to occur are the subject of our next chapter.

Chapter 5

"I shall begin now to speak of the sacraments which you have received": Initiation in Milan: The Text

"I shall begin now to speak of the sacraments which you have received."[1] So Ambrose begins his first sermon to the newly baptized. With these words the bishop declares what is truly distinctive about mystagogical preaching: mystagogy is preaching "on the sacraments." In mystagogy the "text" on which the sermon is based is not a passage of Scripture but the rites of initiation in which the neophytes have participated. When we say that Scripture is not the "text" upon which mystagogy is based, we in no way imply that Scripture is not essential to mystagogical preaching. In our next chapter we will present the essential role that Scripture plays in mystagogy.

Nevertheless, the goal of mystagogy is to draw the hearers more deeply into sacramental acts and not scriptural texts. In this regard, mystagogy is more like thematic preaching, where Scripture serves to illuminate a given topic, than preaching from a lectionary, where a given pericope determines the message.[2] Also, when we say that the rites of initiation in which the neophytes have participated provide the "text" on which mystagogy is based, we are defining *text* not as an ancient document but as a living experience that encompasses not only words but actions, objects, place, and time as well.

Rather than artists or detectives, in this chapter we become candidates for baptism. We begin in section one by attempting to reconstruct

---

[1] *De sacramentis*, 1.1.1 (SC 25bis.60).
[2] See below, 211–212; Fred B. Craddock, *Preaching* (Nashville: Abingdon Press, 1985) 101.

the rites of initiation that provide the "text" for *De sacramentis* and *De mysteriis*. Although we will consult studies of the liturgy and sacramental theology of the fourth century in general and of Saint Ambrose and Milan in particular,[3] the mystagogical writings of Ambrose are the chief evidence for liturgical practices at Milan, and this fact presents us with certain difficulties. As Paul Bradshaw rightly observes, "Since his audience were generally Christians already familiar with the rites to which he was alluding, Ambrose is not always very explicit about the precise details, and his extensive use of metaphor also makes it difficult to know if and when references to such things as incense and anointing are to be taken literally."[4] In reconstructing each of the rites that Ambrose "explains" in his mystagogical preaching, we will therefore first attempt to reconstruct them in terms of their words, actions, time, and location.

Second, we will discuss Ambrose's theology of each rite, that is, Ambrose's understanding of what each rite means. In determining Ambrose's theology of the process of Christian initiation, we must remember that his mystagogical homilies are not in fact a "sacramental theology" of these rites in the strict sense of that term. Enrico Mazza regards mystagogy "not so much a form of catechesis or spiritual theology as it is a way of doing theology in the true and proper sense of the term."[5] He claims that the mystagogical catecheses of the Fathers belong not only to the sphere of catechesis or spirituality but are "a true and proper theology: a liturgical theology."[6] From *De sacramentis* Mazza argues that "theology is directly produced by the consistent typological application of Old Testament passages to the Christian sacraments. Since this is the specific and proper method of Ambrose's mystagogy, it follows that mystagogy as such is theology or, better, a

---

[3] We are especially indebted to Hugh Riley's excellent study *Christian Initiation: A Comparative Study of the Interpretation of the Baptismal Liturgy in the Mystagogical Writings of Cyril of Jerusalem, John Chrysostom, Theodore of Mopsuestia, and Ambrose of Milan* (Washington: Catholic University of America, 1974).

[4] Paul F. Bradshaw, *The Search for the Origins of Christian Worship: Sources and Methods for the Study of Early Liturgy* (New York: Oxford University Press, 1992) 115.

[5] Enrico Mazza, *Mystagogy: A Theology of Liturgy in the Patristic Age*, trans. Matthew J. O'Connell (New York: Pueblo, 1989) 6.

[6] Ibid., 3.

way of doing theology."[7] Placing *De sacramentis* in the genre of sacramental theology, Mazza follows the work of Giampietro Francesconi[8] in assigning precise and technical definitions to Ambrose's vocabulary, namely the terms *mysterium, sacramentum, figura, umbra, forma, typus, imago, species,* and *similitudo*.[9] Mazza insists that although the meaning of each word partially overlaps that of the others, "it would be a mistake to let this objective proximity of meanings lull us into thinking that the words are simply interchangeable synonyms, all expressing the idea of *sacramentality*."[10]

Yet in his efforts to find in mystagogy a developed liturgical theology, Mazza sets aside the original purpose of these works: to give introductory instructions on the sacraments to the newly baptized and not to create a treatise for theologians. It is unreasonable to think that Ambrose would use and expect his hearers to understand such precise and technical definitions. Furthermore, it seems inconsistent that such careful technical language is found in a document that displays the characteristics of spontaneous, oral speech. We have seen that Ambrose was not reading a carefully crafted theological treatise but making extemporaneous remarks on the meaning of the sacraments.[11] Thus Hugh Riley is correct that "the mystagogical catecheses are not theological treatises as such, but rather *ad hoc* explanations of a given liturgical process to specific hearers on a specific occasion."[12] The theology of the rites is not presented in "the closed, ordered form of the theological treatise"[13] but, like the rites themselves, must be analyzed and uncovered.

Having reconstructed the rites of initiation and determined their meaning, we will in the second part of this chapter develop ten principles that govern how Ambrose employs the liturgical text in order to interpret the rites of initiation to his congregation. We

---

[7] Ibid., 6.

[8] Giampietro Francesconi, *Storia e Simbolo: "Mysterium in Figura": La Simbolica Storico-Sacramentale nel Linguaggio e Nella Teologia di Ambrogio di Milano* (Brescia: Morcelliana, 1981).

[9] Mazza, *Mystagogy*, 15–23.

[10] Ibid., 15.

[11] See above, 26-27; below, 288–293.

[12] Riley, *Christian Initiation*, 40.

[13] Ibid.

conclude our discussion of the "text" in section three with a reflection on the pneumatic dimension of the rites of initiation.

INITIATION IN MILAN

In the fourth century, Christian initiation was not limited to a single rite or even a series of rites. It was an intense process that spanned months or even years. In this section we gather with the *competentes* of Milan and experience the process of Christian initiation with them. The pattern described by Saint Ambrose is composed of five stages: (1) enrollment, (2) a period of Lenten formation, (3) the rites of initiation themselves, (4) the celebration of the Easter Eucharist, and (5) a period of mystagogy or daily instruction on the meaning of the sacraments during the week following Easter. While, properly speaking, the "text" of Ambrose's mystagogy is stages three and four, the rites of initiation and the celebration of the Easter Eucharist, he places those rites in context by referring to the period of Lenten instruction.[14] As we seek to uncover not only the texts and meaning of the rites but the experience of the participants, we will also place the "text" on which Ambrose's mystagogy is based in context by here describing the first four stages of the process of initiation, from enrollment through Easter Eucharist. We will discuss stage five, the period of mystagogy, in detail as part of our discussion of sermon delivery in Chapter 8.[15]

Stage One: Enrollment

Catechumens were divided into two classes, hearers and elect.[16] Hearers became members of the elect when they determined themselves ready for baptism and turned in their names. Ambrose's reference to the *competentes* having "signed for the competition for the crown"[17] may suggest that they confirmed their desire with their own signature. Ambrose tells us that, as early as Epiphany, he began to ask his hearers to turn in their names for baptism.[18] Preaching on the text

[14] *De mysteriis*, 1.1 (SC 25bis.156).
[15] Below, 295–299.
[16] *De Helia et ieiunio*, 10.34 (CSEL 32/3.430).
[17] Ibid., 21.79 (CSEL 32/3.460).
[18] *Expositio evangelii secundum Lucam* 4.76 (CCSL 14.134). The practice of enrolling the *competentes* on the feast of Epiphany rather than at the beginning of Lent is also attested to in Maximus of Turin (near Milan). It is possible that we have here a connection with Alexandrian practice and that at some point in its

"We toiled all night and took nothing,"[19] Ambrose compares the lack of response to his request for names for baptism to the apostles' unsuccessful night's fishing. Ambrose explains that those who turned in their names were known as *competentes*—those whose "applications" for baptism were accepted.[20] Reminding the neophytes of when they gave in their names for baptism, Ambrose says that Christ anointed the candidates' eyes with clay.[21] There is no evidence that the candidates' eyes were anointed when they gave in their names. The clay must therefore stand for the spiritual sight of faith.

Stage Two: Lenten Formation

In Milan the period of Lenten formation consisted of daily moral instruction, fasting, scrutinies, and learning the Creed. This formation was carried out in an atmosphere of secrecy called the *disciplina arcani*. Together these components served to make Lent an intense time that produced both anxiety and anticipation in the *competentes*.

Lenten Instruction. In Milan Lenten instruction was one part of a worship service that also included readings and psalms. This instruction was held twice daily, Monday through Friday, at the third and ninth hours.[22] Excavations under Piazza Duomo in Milan[23] have uncovered the vestiges of a hall having perhaps two apses and dating to the end of the fourth century that is believed to have constituted the

---

history, Milan knew a baptismal day and season of preparation unrelated to Easter. See Bradshaw, *The Search for the Origins of Christian Worship*, 180; Maxwell E. Johnson, *The Rites of Christian Initiation: Their Evolution and Interpretation* (Collegeville, Minn.: The Liturgical Press, 1999) 135; Thomas J. Tally, *The Origins of the Liturgical Year*, 2nd ed. (Collegeville, Minn.: The Liturgical Press, 1991) 217.

[19] Luke 5:5.

[20] *Epistola* 76 (Maur. 20).4 (CSEL 82/2.110). See above, 120.

[21] *De sacramentis*, 3.2.12 (SC 25bis.98).

[22] Leonel Mitchell, "Ambrosian Baptismal Rites," *Studia Liturgica* (1962) 242. Mitchell calls this worship service a "pro-anaphora." Frederick Homes Dudden, *The Life and Times of St. Ambrose* (Oxford: Clarendon Press, 1935)1:337, calls this service *missa catechumenorum*; however, this term dates from a period later than Ambrose and refers to the first part of the Mass and not a gathering for catechetical instruction.

[23] See below, 156–157; 300–301.

catechumeneum, a place for the instruction of catechumens.[24] Paulinus tells us that Ambrose handled the instruction of the *competentes* himself.[25] Unlike Cyril and Theodore, Ambrose did not use the Creed as his Lenten syllabus. In fact, as we shall see, he gave only a single instruction on the Creed. Rather the curriculum that Ambrose used for his daily instructions was the same curriculum that he used on Sundays: sermons, often in series, focused on exemplary Old Testament figures or books. In *De Abraham* we have a series of these daily sermons.[26] In *De mysteriis*, Ambrose (belatedly) explained the rationale that had guided his Lenten instruction:

"We have given a daily sermon on morals, when the deeds of the Patriarchs or the precepts of the Proverbs were read, in order that, being informed and instructed by them, you might become accustomed to enter upon the ways of our forefathers and to pursue their road, and to obey the divine commands, whereby renewed by baptism you might hold to the manner of life which befits those who are washed."[27]

Ambrose recognized that in order to learn the way of life appropriate to the baptized, the *competentes* needed two things: (1) appropriate models to imitate, and (2) basic moral principles to follow. For both, he turned to the Scriptures: the Patriarchs provided the models, while Proverbs provided the moral principles.[28] Moreover, both could be

[24] Ernesto Brivio, *A Guide to the Duomo of Milan*, 3rd ed., trans. Liliana Zaccarelli Fumagalli (Milan: Veneranda Fabbrica del Duomo di Milano, 1997) 62. On the other hand, Ambrose tells us that his instruction on the Creed took place in the baptistry. *Epistola* 76 (Maur. 20).4 (CSEL 82/2.110). See below, 156–157.

[25] Paulinus, *Vita Ambrosii*, 38 (Navoni, 116).

[26] In *De Abraham* Ambrose addresses those "qui ad gratiam baptismatis tenditis." See *De Abraham*, 1.4.23, 25; 7.39; 9.89 (CSEL 32/1.517, 519; 531; 560). On *De Abraham*, 1 as sermons, see Franco Gori, *Sant'Ambrogio: Abramo: Opere esegetiche* II/II (Milan: Bibliotheca Ambrosiana (Rome: Città nuova, 1984) 12.

[27] *De mysteriis*, 1.1 (SC 25bis.156).

[28] On Ambrose's moral instructions, see Gori, *Abramo*, 11–12; V. Monachino, *S. Ambrogio e la cura pastorale a Milano nel secole IV* (Milan: Centro Ambrosiano di Documentazione e Studi Religione, 1973) 63–68; Bonaventura Parodi, *La catechesi di Sant'Ambrogio, Studio di pedagogia pastorale* (Genoa, 1957) 98–109. Of *De Abraham* Parodi writes: "We can therefore rely on this book in order to know the weft of the formative-didactic thought, by which Ambrose habitually worked out his moral catechesis" (ibid., 100).

presented in an easy-to-remember medium: narrative (the Patriarchs) and aphorism (Proverbs).[29] Thus, Ambrose saw Lent as a time for moral education. Champion of orthodoxy that he was, Ambrose was concerned that the *competentes* have orthodox views; however, this apparently was not his focus, at least to the degree that it was for Cyril and Theodore.

Fasting. Fasting was the second component of the *competentes'* Lenten preparation for baptism. Ambrose's *De Helia et ieiunio* is a sermon (or sermons) delivered at the beginning of Lent, sometime between 387 and 390. On this occasion Ambrose inaugurated Lent by exhorting the whole assembly—faithful, catechumens, and *competentes*—to adopt a proper fast. First, he set out Elijah as a model of true fasting and listed the benefits that Elijah enjoyed from his forty-day fast. Ambrose implied that his hearers, especially the *competentes*, would also enjoy these same benefits by their fasting. In his chapter on Augustine's Lenten preparation for baptism, William Harmless summarizes Ambrose's presentation of the benefits of fasting:

"Elijah 'raised the widow's son from the dead' (just as the *competentes* would rise from the dead at baptism); 'he drew down fire from heaven' (just as the *competentes* would draw down the fire of the Spirit); 'while fasting he was snatched in a chariot to heaven and . . . gained the presence of God' (just as the *competentes* would be swept, after baptism, into the presence of heavenly mysteries)."[30]

After extolling the benefits of fasting, Ambrose entertained his audience by satirizing the feasting and drinking habits of the Milanese elite.[31] He then set Christian ideals in stark contrast to the Milanese elite by quoting Isaiah 58:7, which says that one should share one's "bread with the hungry, and bring the homeless poor into your house; when you see the naked . . . cover them."[32] For Ambrose, true fasting was inseparable from the work of justice. Ambrose directed his closing

---

[29] William Harmless, *Augustine and the Catechumenate* (New York: Pueblo, 1995) 95.

[30] Ibid., 94.

[31] *De Helia et ieiunio*, 8.4.24-14.50 (CSEL 32/3.425–441). On the feasting and drinking habits of the Milanese elite, see above, 72–74.

[32] *De Helia et ieiunio*, 10.34 (CSEL 32/3.430).

remarks to the *competentes*. He compared them to wrestlers and insisted that, like all such athletes, they were to follow a rigorous discipline: train daily; adhere to a strict diet; and abstain from sex: "We are athletes, we strive, as it were, in a spiritual stadium. . . . Even an athlete's diet is given him, discipline is demanded, continence is observed. And you have given [in] your name for the contest of Christ, you have signed for the competition for the crown. . . ."[33] Ambrose admitted the discipline was hard, but encouraged the *competentes* to persevere: "When you have come into the wrestling place, the heat is severe, but the victory is sweet."[34]

Scrutinies. Sometime during Lent, perhaps during vigils on the third, fourth, and fifth Saturdays,[35] the *competentes* went through an exorcism (or exorcisms). Ambrose calls this "the mysteries of the scrutinies."[36] Unfortunately, he gives no specifics about the rite, except that it included a physical examination: "There was a search—lest anything unclean still cling to the body of anyone of you. Using exorcism we sought and brought about a sanctifying not only of your body, but of your soul as well."[37] As we have said,[38] the Church believed that the human heart was concealed from human observation but could not be hidden from God and the angels. The Church therefore trusted the Holy Spirit to use physical manifestations to reveal the intentions of the heart.

As in Milan, Lenten preparation in North Africa also included three scrutinies, which could be quite severe. Based on several scattered references in Augustine and elsewhere, Thomas Finn gives the following description of a North African scrutiny:

"In the eerie light of first dawn the candidates stood barefoot on the coarse animal skins *(cilicium)*, naked and with head bowed. Invoking the power of Christ and the Trinity, voicing vituperative biblical condemnations of Satan, and imposing hands, the exorcist hissed in

---

[33] Ibid., 21.79 (CSEL 32/3.460).

[34] Ibid.

[35] Thomas M. Finn, *From Death to Rebirth: Ritual and Conversion in Antiquity* (New York: Paulist Press, 1997) 223 and 235, n. 45.

[36] *Explanatio symboli ad initiandos*, 1 (SC 25bis.46).

[37] Ibid.

[38] Above, 115.

the faces of *competents*, peremptorily commanding the Evil One to depart. There followed a physical examination to determine whether the *competentes* showed evidence of a disease, which signaled the continued inhabitation of Satan. Granted that they passed scrutiny, each in her or his own voice, then renounced Satan, his pomps, and his service."[39]

Creed. On the Sunday before Easter, after the readings and dismissal of the catechumens, Ambrose and the *competentes* went to the baptistry, where he would personally deliver the Creed to them and give a brief instruction on it.[40] Not only do we know what Ambrose said about the Creed from his *Explanatio symboli ad initiandos*, but the form of *Explanatio symboli* suggests that it is not so much a sermon delivered at the *traditio symboli* as a stenographic report of the rite itself.[41]

From the *Explanatio symboli* we can therefore conclude that the rite contained certain elements.[42] The *traditio symboli* began with (1) an introduction in which Ambrose announced the reason for this special instruction: "It is now the time and the day for us to hand over the Symbol: a Symbol which is a spiritual seal, a Symbol which is our heart's meditation and, as it were, an ever-present guard, a treasure within our breast."[43] Harmless points out that here Ambrose quickly touches upon the images and themes that will run throughout his

---

[39] Finn, *From Death to Rebirth*, 155.

[40] *Epistola* 76 (Maur. 20).4 (CSEL 82/2.110).

[41] Indications that the *Explanatio symboli* is a stenographic summary of the *traditio* include (1) skeleton citations of the Creed at those points in the text where Ambrose apparently recited an entire article or combination of articles (*Explanatio*, 5.1–2, 7–9, 22, 35; 6.15; 8.4, 7, 11, 18); (2) at those two points in the text where the entire Creed is recited without interruption there are simply notations to the effect that the Creed was recited (ibid., 3.3, 20); (3) rather than a single sermon explaining the Creed, the *Explanatio* is a series of commentaries each of which follows or accompanies a recitation of the Creed (ibid., 3.4–19; 4.1–6, 22; 8.1–16); and (4) the style of the *Explanatio* indicates a stenographer's record (cf. ibid., 4.1–12). Bernard Botte, *Ambroise de Milan: Des Sacrements; Des Mystères; Explication du Symbole*, SC 25bis (Paris: Les Éditions du Cerf, 1980) 22. Robert Stanislaus Campbell, "The Explanatio Symboli ad Initiandos of St. Ambrose of Milan: A Comparative Study" (Thesis, University of Notre Dame, 1974) 5–9.

[42] For a summary of these elements see ibid., 9.

[43] *Explanatio symboli*, 1 (SC 25bis.46).

instruction: that the Creed was something precious; that it had to be interiorized; that it guarded one against error.[44] Ambrose then used an analogy from fourth-century finance to explain the meaning of the Greek term *symbolum* to his Latin-speaking audience:

"First then we must have an explanation of the name itself. Symbolum is a Greek word which in Latin means 'contribution.' Business people especially are used to speaking of their symbols when they contribute their money, which—when it is lumped together, so to speak, into one sum from their individual contributions—is kept whole and inviolable, so that no one may attempt any fraud, neither with the sum contributed nor in his business dealings. Finally, among such business people this is the custom: that if anyone has committed fraud, he is tossed out as a cheat."[45]

The image behind *symbolum* is that of a kind of "mutual fund," a credit union. The creedal formula was a *symbolum* in the sense that it contained the "treasure" that the Church had built up and drew on for its communication of the faith.[46] Ambrose also used this image both to warn the *competentes* that creedal fraud resulted in expulsion from the community and to introduce a popular legend—that the Creed had been a joint composition of the twelve apostles: "The holy Apostles gathered as one and made a brief summary of the faith, so that it might always be held in memory and be remembered."[47] After this, Ambrose had (2) the *competentes* sign themselves with the sign of the cross.[48] Then (3) Ambrose recited the Creed,[49] after which he gave (4) general remarks on the Trinity and the Incarnation.[50] Next, Ambrose (5) recited the Creed a second time,[51] followed by (6) an explanation of the Creed phrase by phrase.[52] Ambrose then (7) instructed the candidates to sign

---

[44] Harmless, *Augustine and the Catechumenate*, 96.

[45] *Explanatio symboli*, 2 (SC 25bis.46).

[46] Brian E. Daley, S.J., Princeton, to Craig A. Satterlee, Notre Dame, February 7, 2000.

[47] *Explanatio symboli*, 3 (SC 25bis.48).

[48] Ibid.

[49] Ibid.

[50] Ibid., 3–4 (SC 25bis.48–50).

[51] Ibid., 5 (SC 25bis.50).

[52] Ibid., 5–7 (SC 25bis, 50–56).

themselves a second time.[53] After this, the bishop (8) recited the articles of the Creed a third time, this time in groups of four with a brief comment following each group.[54] The rite concluded (9) with the bishop instructing the candidates that the Creed should not be written down and that the *competentes* should repeat it every day. In this way they would enjoy its power to ward off shocks to mind and body and to shield one from demonic temptations.[55] Finally, he asked them to recite it silently so that no catechumen would hear it.[56] Ambrose makes no explicit mention of the *redditio symboli*, the practice of the candidates "handing back" the Creed to the bishop shortly before their baptism in order to demonstrate that they had learned it.[57] He does, however, mention that the candidates "have yet to deliver it."[58]

Disciplina Arcani. The *disciplina arcani*, or "discipline of secrecy,"[59] the practice of preserving the central elements of the faith as a secret from outsiders, became universal by the fourth to the first half of the fifth century. The liturgy reflects the precautions taken to preserve this secrecy: those who were not baptized had to leave the church before the eucharistic portion of the liturgy. In his *Expositio evangelii secundum Lucam*, Ambrose jumps from 10:42 to 11:5.[60] Yarnold suggests that Ambrose does this in order to avoid having to quote and explain the Lord's Prayer and in so doing violate the *disciplina arcani*.[61] For Ambrose,

---

[53] Ibid., 8 (SC 25bis.56).

[54] Ibid.

[55] Ibid., 9 (SC 25bis.56).

[56] We need to remember that ancients both read and prayed out loud. See Pieter W. van der Horst, "Silent Prayer in Antiquity," *Numen* 41 (1994) 1–25.

[57] Edward Yarnold, *The Awe-Inspiring Rites of Initiation: The Origins of the R.C.I.A.*, 2nd ed. (Collegeville, Minn.: The Liturgical Press, 1994) 13.

[58] *Explanatio symboli*, 9 (SC 25bis.56).

[59] Yarnold, *The Awe-Inspiring Rites of Initiation*, 55–58. See also Christoph Jacob, "Arkandisziplin," *Allegorese, Mystagogie: Ein Neuer Zugang zur Theologie des Ambrosius von Mailand*, Theophaneia 32 (Frankfurt am Main: Anton Hain, 1990). In Chapter 1 Jacob deals with scholarship on the definitions and origins of the *disciplina arcani*, which include Hellenistic mystery religions, gnosticism, "unwritten" apostolic traditions, and the awe-inspiring nature of the rites of initiation. The explanations are manifold but inconclusive.

[60] CCSL 14.241–242.

[61] Edward Yarnold, "Baptism and the Pagan Mysteries in the Fourth Century," *Heythrop Journal* 13 (1972) 259.

the rationale for this discipline of secrecy was twofold: the desire to show reverence for the mysteries, as suggested by Matthew 7:6, and the sound educational principle that truth must be conveyed gradually and adapted to the circumstances and apprehensions of the hearers.[62] Ambrose states that "every mystery ought to be hidden and, so to speak, concealed in a holy silence so as not to be inconsiderately published to profane ears."[63] In another passage he warns that the mysteries should be kept secret "lest by premature speech you should commit them half baked, so to speak, to faithless or weak ears and the hearer be repelled and feel repugnance and loathing: if he tasted them more fully baked, he would enjoy a taste of spiritual food."[64] We can deduce from a remark of Ambrose that the secrecy was not perfectly observed,[65] leading us to wonder whether there was, in fact, a certain fiction about the catechumens' ignorance of the rites. What is important is that the catechumens did not receive a public instruction on these mysteries until after their baptism.[66] Thus, regardless of whether the *disciplina arcani* was an authentic part of Church life or an artificial, liturgical practice, it was in fact part of the *competentes'* Lenten preparation.

Stage Three: The Rites of Initiation

The rites of initiation, for which the *competentes* so arduously prepared, were celebrated at the great Easter Vigil.[67] These rites include: *ephphatha*, prebaptismal anointing, renunciation, exorcism and consecration of the water, baptism, postbaptismal anointing, footwashing, vesting with white robes, "spiritual seal," and procession to the altar. At Milan the candidates received no more than hints of what went on during this celebration. It was not until after they were baptized and had participated in the celebration of the Eucharist that they were judged ready to receive a full explanation of the sacraments.

The *competentes*, who were generally adults,[68] did not assemble in the baptistry. *De sacramentis* tells us that they are brought in later.[69] The

---

[62] *Expositio evangelii secundum Lucam*, 6.105 (CCSL 14.212).

[63] *De Abraham*, 1.5.38 (CSEL 32/1.521).

[64] *De Cain et Abel*, 1.35-37 (CSEL 32/1.369–371).

[65] *Expositio in Psalmum cxviii*, 2.26 (CSEL 62.35).

[66] See below, 186–187.

[67] *De sacramentis*, 1.1.2 (SC 25bis.60).

[68] *De Helia et ieiunio*, 34 (CSEL 32/2.430); *Hexaemeron*, 1.1.4–4.14 (CSEL 32/1.5–13).

[69] *De sacramentis*, 1.2.4 (SC 25bis.62).

competentes may have gathered in the *catechumeneum* where they had been instructed, moved to the baptistry after the *ephphatha*,[70] finally entering the cathedral to celebrate the Easter Eucharist after their baptism. In this way they would have physically enacted their change in status from *competentes* to *fideles*, highlighting baptism as the means by which they enter the Church.[71] The order and contents of this journey, as it was celebrated in Milan at the time of Saint Ambrose, may be summarized as follows:

Ephphatha. The *ephphatha* or "opening" is found in *De sacramentis*, 1.1.2–3 and *De mysteriis*, 1.3–4.[72] The account in *De mysteriis* only refers in general terms to the opening and its significance, the details of which are more fully dealt with in *De sacramentis*. From *De sacramentis* we learn that the *ephphatha* took place on Saturday, that is, Easter Eve. The *ephphatha* derived its name from the word and actions of Jesus in the healing of the deaf and dumb man recorded in Mark 7:34. The rite was performed by the bishop *(sacerdos)*, who touched the ears and nostrils of the candidate and said, "*Ephphatha*, that is, be opened, to an odor of sweetness."[73]

Ambrose explains this ceremony in two ways. First, it is the opening of the faculties to understand the questions and answers in the renunciations that follow. Second, its purpose is to facilitate the fruitful reception of the sacraments.[74] Bradshaw is undoubtedly correct in saying that "the very existence of multiple explanations and interpretations is itself a very good indication that no authoritative tradition with regard to the original purpose and meaning of the custom had survived, and [Ambrose] felt free to use his imagination."[75]

This rite differs from the biblical passage on which it is based in two important ways. First, according to Ambrose, the nostrils were touched instead of the mouth, because it was not considered seemly for the bishop to touch the mouths of women. Yarnold understands this

---

[70] Ambrose reminds the *neophytes* that they "arrived" *(venimus)* at the baptistry and went in. Ibid. This seems to imply that they were at a place other than just outside the baptistry for the *ephphatha*.

[71] Alberto Rocca, Archdiocese of Milan, Interview, June 2, 1999.

[72] SC 25bis.60, 156.

[73] *De sacramentis*, 1.2.4 (SC 25bis.62).

[74] *De mysteriis*, 1.3 (SC 25bis.156); *De sacramentis*, 1.1.2 (SC 25bis.60).

[75] Bradshaw, *The Search for the Origins of Christian Worship*, 71.

statement as evidence of Ambrose's delicacy or even prudery.[76] E. C. Whitaker argues that Ambrose gives this "most unconvincing account of the reason why the nostrils have been substituted for the mouth" because he was "embarrassed by the discrepancies between the gospel account of the miracle and its liturgical performance."[77] Second, there is no mention in Ambrose's description of the use of saliva or oil. Based on evidence from other Western rites, specifically the *Apostolic Tradition, Gregorian Sacramentary,* and Gothic Missal, Whitaker concludes that Ambrose is so embarrassed by the use of oil rather than spittle that he avoids a specific mention of it, although it is clear that it was used.[78] Yarnold states that it is arguable that Ambrose's sensibilities about the use of saliva led him to preserve a discreet silence over this detail of the ceremony.[79] The most that we can say is that the question of whether Ambrose used anything to touch the *competentes'* nostrils and what that might be remains open.

Entrance into the Baptistry. Pietro Borella contends that the *ephphatha* was accompanied by the opening of the baptistry door, or those of an inner baptismal chamber, to admit the *competentes*.[80] Though Ambrose does not describe such a ritual act, he does tell us that after the *ephphatha* the *competentes* entered the baptistry.[81] Excavations before the present cathedral in Milan have revealed the ground plan of Ambrose's cathedral and baptistry.[82] The baptistry, which Ambrose started to build in 378 and where in 387 he baptized Augustine, is octagonal in shape and has a central font (See Figure 3).[83] The baptistry's octagonal structure

---

[76] Edward Yarnold, "The Ceremonies of Initiation in the *De Sacramentis* and *De Mysteriis* of St. Ambrose," in F. L. Cross, *Studia Patristica* 10 (Berlin: Akademie-Verlag, 1970) 454.

[77] Edward C. Whitaker, *Documents of the Baptismal Liturgy*, rev. ed. (London: S.P.C.K., 1970) 44.

[78] Ibid.

[79] Yarnold, *The Awe-Inspiring Rites of Initiation*, 17, n. 80.

[80] Pietro Borella, "Il Battesimo nel secole IV," in Mario Righetti, *Manuale di Storia Liturgica*, 2nd ed. (Milan: Ancora, 1959) 4:569.

[81] *De sacramentis*, 1.2.4 (SC 25bis.62); *De mysteriis*, 1.4 (SC 25bis.156).

[82] Below, 299–301.

[83] The following description of the baptistry is based on my visits to the archeological site of the Battistero di San Giovonni alle Fonti and the Chapel of Saint Aquilino on June 3, 1999. Literature on the excavation and baptistry includes Brivio, *A Guide to the Duomo of Milan*, 57–62; Mario Mirabella Roberti

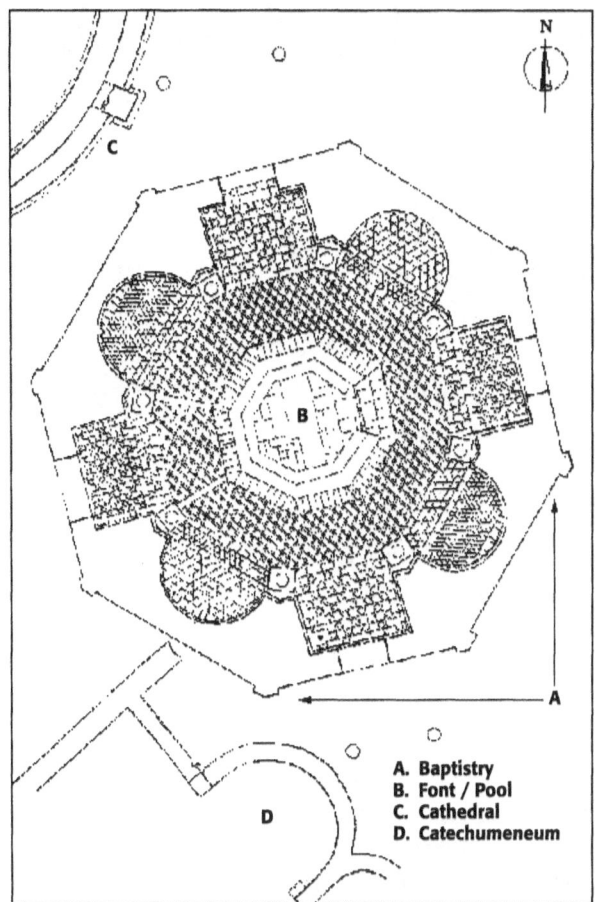

Figure 3 Reconstruction of the Battistero di San Giovanni alle Fonti, Milan. Adapted from Mirabella, *Il Battistero Ambrosiano di San Giovanni alle Fonti*. Reprinted with permission.

and Angelo Paredi, *Il Battistero Ambrosiano di San Giovanni alle Fonti* (Milan: Veneranda Fabbrica del Duomo di Milano, 1974), esp. 9–34. Later in this chapter we will see how Ambrose uses the physical construction of the baptistry to provide mystagogical interpretation of the rites (see below, 166; 196–197). Offering a different perspective, Cesare Alzati contends that *De sacramentis* reflects the older Santo Stefano alle Fonti (3rd–5th century) and *De mysteriis* reflects the Battistero di San Giovanni alle Fonti. Alzati cites as evidence the description of the bishop standing *supra fontem* in *De sacramentis*, 1.3.9 (SC 25bis.64), an arrangement identifiable in the older baptistry. Cesare Alzati, *Ambrosianum Mysterium: The Church of Milan and Its Liturgical Tradition*, trans. George Guiver (Cambridge: Grove Books, 1999) 25.

Figure 4 The large octagonal baptismal font. Photograph by Chelsey Grace Satterlee.

had a diameter of 63.7 feet (19.3 meters). Its perimeter was lined with alternating rectangular and semicircular niches, the rectangular niches containing doors. The niches were adorned with eight large columns, each of which was placed in front of the shafts of masonry between two niches. These columns supported the dome. This plan follows the same dimensions, plan, and architectural style as the mausoleum (or imperial tomb) of Maximianus, which was rediscovered under the Basilica of San Vitore al Corpo and dates to the first decade of the fourth century. Judging from the Chapel of Saint Aquilino, another imperial mausoleum discovered near the Basilica of San Lorenzo Maggiore that dates from the late fourth or early fifth century and has the same plan and structure as the baptistry and is still Roman as far as its roof, the baptistry was covered by a segmented roof that could have been as high as 59.4 feet (18 meters) and with all probability was illuminated by small windows arranged around a high ambulatory through which light pierced the building.

In the center of the baptistry stands the large, octagonal-shaped pool or font (See Figure 4). The baptismal pool is 20.1 feet (6.1 meters) in diameter and had three marble steps by which the catechumens descended into the water. The font's source of water, an inflow canal, can still be seen. The water came gushing into the font through many spouts distributed along its sides along a hidden pipeline (partly still existing) and then flowed down to a well, the water level remaining constant thanks to a flood-way. The floor of the baptistry was made of black and white marble in three different geometric patterns. The walls were also lined with fine marble, at least up to a certain level. No adjacent rooms have been discovered, and except for the *ephphatha*, all the rites described in *De sacramentis* and *De mysteriis* until the procession to the altar seem to have taken place in this single baptismal room. Ambrose considered the baptistry the "holy of holies" and the "sanctuary of rebirth."[84] The *competentes* remained a little distance removed from the baptismal pool itself.[85]

By his interpretation of the *competentes'* entrance into the baptistry, Ambrose sets the stage for the drama to follow. By distinguishing the baptistry from the place where the *ephphatha* had occurred, "Ambrose indicates thereby a graduated dramatic introduction into the mystery based on the physical appointments of the baptistry, a mystagogy which occurs again, and more importantly, in explaining the baptismal act itself, where the resemblance of the baptistry to a tomb is indicated."[86] Ambrose sees in the fact that the candidates stand somewhat removed from the font, facing west and therefore unable to see it,[87] a kind of combat arena where the struggle with the devil will be acted out. The area between the door of the baptistry and the edge of the font is the place where the devil, the antagonist in the drama of salvation, is present in a quasi-physical way.[88]

Prebaptismal Anointing. Once inside the baptistry, the candidates removed their clothes.[89] A priest and deacon anointed their entire bodies

---

[84] *De mysteriis*, 2.5 (SC 25bis.158) for *sancta sanctorum* and *sanctuarium regeneratonis*.

[85] *De sacramentis*, 1.3.9 (SC 25bis.64).

[86] Riley, *Christian Initiation*, 48. On the baptistry as tomb, see below, 166; 265.

[87] Riley is correct that, given the baptistry of the church of Milan, it seems physically impossible that the candidates would not see the font upon their entrance until one notes that they faced west and then, after the renunciation, turned east to see the font, at least "ritually," for the first time. Ibid., 49, n. 77. On the candidates turning from east to west, see below, 197.

[88] *De mysteriis*, 2.7 (SC 25bis.158).

[89] See *Enarrationes in xii psalmos davidicos*, 61.32 (CSEL 64.396).

with olive oil. Ambrose describes this anointing in *De sacramentis*, 1.1.4,[90] though it is not mentioned in *De mysteriis*.[91] He does not mention either the stripping or the fact that the whole body was anointed. Yarnold characterizes this omission as typical of Ambrose's delicacy.[92] We conclude that the whole body was anointed because Ambrose describes it as the anointing of an athlete.[93] Additionally, the need of the services of a deacon as well as a presbyter to perform the anointing suggests that the ceremony was complicated and even messy.

In comparing this anointing to that of the athlete, Ambrose speaks of the *competentes* as Christ's athletes "about to wrestle in the fight of the world."[94] According to Ambrose, this anointing constituted a strengthening of the candidates for the struggle with the devil to follow: "The wrestler has something to hope for; every contest has its trophy."[95] Once again, Ambrose does not mention exorcism in connection with this rite. Nevertheless, Kilian McDonnell and George Montague describe this anointing as being preparatory and having "the character of purgation/exorcism: the oil cleanses from the traces of sin and chases away the invisible powers of Satan."[96] This descrip-

---

[90] SC 25bis.62.

[91] Inasmuch as this anointing is found in the Roman rite but is not in the later Milanese forms, it has been suggested that its presence in *De sacramentis* shows the influence of Roman custom and implies a difference of rite from *De mysteriis*. A more probable explanation for this difference is the *disciplina arcani*. The anointing of the body, or parts of the body other than the head, would be performed on women candidates as well as on men. There was no order of deaconesses in the West, as there was in the East, where deaconesses assisted in the case of women. As the candidates were stripped before entering the font, Jews and pagans might criticize the unction on the ground of decency. This would account for the silence of *De mysteriis*, a work intended for publication.

[92] Yarnold, "The Ceremonies of Initiation in the *De Sacramentis* and *De Mysteriis* of St. Ambrose," 456.

[93] *De sacramentis*, 1.1.4 (SC 25bis.62). Ambrose seems to allude to this anointing by his use of the image of a fighter who comes to meet his adversary in *De mysteriis*, 2.7 (SC 25bis.158).

[94] *De sacramentis*, 1.1.4 (SC 25bis.62).

[95] Ibid.

[96] Kilian McDonnell and George T. Montague, *Christian Initiation and Baptism in the Holy Spirit: Evidence from the First Eight Centuries* (Collegeville, Minn.: The Liturgical Press, 1991) 267.

tion is not in keeping with Ambrose's explanation, which emphasizes strengthening rather than the removal of sin and evil. In Ambrose's description this is the first of two anointings and is followed by the renunciation.[97]

Renunciation. After the anointing comes the renunciation, which Ambrose describes in *De sacramentis*, 1.2.5 and *De mysteriis*, 2.5, 7.[98] Once again the description in *De sacramentis* is fuller and more exact. While *De mysteriis* summarizes the content of the renunciation, *De sacramentis* gives the formula. The renunciation was twofold, given in interrogatory form.[99] The *competentes* were asked if they renounced, first, the devil (not Satan) and his works and, second, the world and its luxury and pleasures. The answer in each case was "I renounce." There follows in *De sacramentis* the admonition, "Keep what you said in mind. The terms of the guarantee you gave must never fade from your memory." In his interpretation Ambrose indicates that the candidates' answers, though uttered in the tomb of the dead, that is, the baptistry,[100] are recorded in the book of the living.[101]

In the account of the renunciations in *De mysteriis*, the questions are put to the *competentes* by the bishop, who also consecrates the water.[102] In *De sacramentis*, 1.1.2 and 1.2.4, there is a certain ambiguity. The ministers mentioned immediately before the anointing are "levite" and "presbyter." The section on the renunciation begins without any reference to the change of subject and without any explicit mention of the speaker. We get, "When he asked you." But the bishop's presence and action in the *ephphatha* have already been indicated and are again stated in connection with the consecration of the font.[103] The use of the singular "When *he* asked you," when levite and presbyter have been

---

[97] Yarnold places this anointing as one of three after the renunciation of sin and profession of faith. Yarnold, *The Awe-Inspiring Rites of Initiation*, 21.

[98] SC 25bis.62, 158.

[99] Botte notes that only the Milanese formula, with its two interrogations, parallels this one. Botte, *Des Sacrements; Des Mystères*, 26. See Marcus Magistretti, *Monumenta veteris Liturgiae Ambrosianae* (Milan: Apud U. Hoepli, 1897–1904) 2:160.

[100] *De sacramentis*, 3.1.1 (SC 25bis.90).

[101] *De mysteriis*, 2.5 (SC 25bis.158).

[102] Ibid., 3.8 (SC 25bis.158).

[103] *De sacramentiis*, 1.2.8 (SC 25bis.64).

mentioned, is consistent with the words being spoken by the bishop, who has been present throughout. *De mysteriis* may here be clearing up the ambiguity of *De sacramentis*. In his interpretation, Ambrose likens the figures of bishop, priest, and deacon and their ministry to the work of angels.[104]

Botte dismisses as improbable the suggestion of G. Morin that *De mysteriis*, 2.7 should be amended to read ". . . and by way of renouncing him to spit in his face."[105] Botte bases his conclusion on both manuscript and liturgical grounds. First, Botte reports that the foundation of this hypothesis is the variant *sputaris* of one manuscript. He reminds us that Faller already stated that all the rules of criticism necessitate rejecting this reading and confirms his judgment. Botte sees this variant as an accident due to reduplication. Additionally, in order for the sentence to be acceptable, it is necessary to introduce an unsupported change in the manuscript tradition (*renuntiando* in place of *renuntiandum*).[106] Second, this emendation would introduce a custom for which there is no Western evidence.[107]

Although we must necessarily conclude that *De mysteriis*, 2.7 provides no proof of *sputation*, this passage does provide us with an important detail: the renunciation of the devil was done facing west, then the *competens* turns to the east, "turns to Christ, looks at him with direct gaze."[108] Thus the devil is present on one side and Christ appears on the other. Ambrose makes no other reference to words of adhesion to Christ by the *competentes* at this point. He does explain that in renouncing the devil and his works, the *competentes* are giving by their words a solemn pledge, which is kept in heaven, that they are binding themselves to Christ.[109] The renunciation completed, the *competentes* drew near the font to see the water, priest, and a levite.[110]

---

[104] Ibid., 12.6 (SC 25bis.64); *De mysteriis*, 2.6 (SC 25bis.158).

[105] Botte, *Des Sacrements; Des Mystères*, 27.

[106] Ibid.

[107] Riley, *Christian Initiation*, 28, n. 27.

[108] *De mysteriis*, 2.7 (SC 25bis.158). While Ambrose does not explicitly state that the *competens* faces the west for the renunciation, and no mystagogical "explanation" is provided for this position, the fact that the turning to the east with an accompanying mystagogy is explicitly mentioned makes it clear.

[109] *De sacramentis*, 1.2.7 (SC 25bis.64); *De mysteriis*, 2.5-7 (SC 25bis.158).

[110] *De sacramentis*, 1.3.9, 10 (SC 25bis.160).

Exorcism and Consecration of the Water. The consecration of the water is found in *De sacramentis*, 1.3.9, 18 and 2.5.14 and in *De mysteriis*, 3.8, 3.14 and 4.20.[111] Here again the details of the blessing are derived almost entirely from *De sacramentis*, in which Ambrose speaks of "an exorcism over the element of water" and of "an invocation and prayer, that the font may be hallowed and the presence of the eternal Trinity may come upon it."[112] Standing "over the font" and using "heavenly words," the bishop "invokes the name of the Father, and the presence of the Son and the Holy Spirit. What heavenly words?"[113] Answering his own question, Ambrose quotes Matthew 28:19.[114]

To these details *De mysteriis*, 3.14 adds the signing of the water with the cross. Finn understands the form of this signing as Ambrose tracing the sign of the cross over the waters and, perhaps, plunging a cross (his shepherd's staff) into them. Both Finn and Yarnold understand the reference to Moses' rod sweetening the bitter water of Marah in *De mysteriis*, 2.5.14 as suggesting that the cross is not the sign traced by the bishop's hand but the cross that he carries in his hand.[115] *De mysteriis*, 3.8 gives the impression that when the candidates arrive at the font, the bishop is already consecrating the water. Riley may therefore be correct that this ceremony was not one in which the candidates actively participated but may have already been in progress when they arrived at the font.[116]

The baptismal water is consecrated by the grace of Christ and the descent of the Holy Spirit consecrating the water to heal, by the presence of the Trinity, and by the mystery of the cross. In *De sacramentis*, 1.5.15 Ambrose says: "Not all waters have a curative power; only that water has it which has the grace of Christ . . . The water does not heal unless the Spirit descends and consecrates the water." Speaking of the

---

[111] SC 25bis.64, 70, 81, 158, 162, 166.

[112] *De sacramentis*, 1.3.18 (SC 25bis.70).

[113] Ibid., 1.3.9; 2.5.14 (SC 25bis.64; 81).

[114] Ibid.

[115] Thomas M. Finn, *Early Christian Baptism and the Catechumenate*, Vol. 2: *Italy, North Africa, and Egypt*, Message of the Fathers of the Church 6 (Collegeville, Minn.: The Liturgical Press, 1992) 60; Finn, *From Death to Rebirth*, 227; Yarnold, "The Ceremonies of Initiation in the *De Sacramentis* and *De Mysteriis* of St. Ambrose," 458.

[116] Riley, *Christian Initiation*, 149, n. 26. Riley's assertion that the consecration of the water has no liturgical significance or mystagogical importance fails to recognize Ambrose's use of this rite to teach Nicene Christianity.

Trinity, Ambrose says in *De sacramentis*, 1.6.19, "Therefore Christ descended into the water, and the Holy Spirit descended as a dove. Also, God the Father spoke from heaven. You have the presence of the Trinity." Finally, Ambrose implies that the purpose of the signing of the waters is to signify that the passion of Christ is the source of baptism's effectiveness. In *De mysteriis*, 3.14 he says: "For water without the proclamation of the Lord's cross serves no purpose of future salvation; but when it has been consecrated by the mystery of the saving cross, then it is fitted for the use of the spiritual washing and the saving cup."[117] In *De mysteriis*, 4.20 Ambrose asks, "For, without the cross of Christ, what is water but an ordinary element without any sacramental effect?"[118]

Baptism: Descent into the Font, Baptismal Profession and Immersion, Coming Out of the Pool. Ambrose discusses what we might consider "Baptism Proper" in *De sacramentis*, 2.7.20 and *De mysteriis*, 4.21, 5.28.[119] The font was sunk into the floor of the baptistry, and Ambrose describes its appearance as "somewhat like that of a tomb in shape."[120] At the font the *competentes* found the bishop, a priest, and deacons.[121] Into this pool each descended in turn. The font was two to four feet deep, surrounded by a wall. The *competens* stood waist deep in water.

Ambrose gives a summary of his mystagogy of baptismal profession and immersion in *De sacramentis*:

"You were asked, 'Do you believe in God, the Father almighty?' You said: 'I believe,' and you submerged, that is, you were buried. Again you were asked: 'Do you believe in our Lord Jesus Christ and in his cross?' You said: 'I do believe,' and you submerged. So you were also buried together with Christ.[122] For those who are buried with Christ rise again with Christ. A third time you were asked: 'Do you believe in the Holy Spirit?' You said: 'I do believe,' you submerged a third time, so that the threefold confession absolved the multiple lapse of the previous life."[123]

---

[117] SC 25bis.162.
[118] Ibid., 166.
[119] Ibid., 114, 134.
[120] *De sacramentis*, 3.1.1 (SC 25bis.90).
[121] Ibid., 2.6.16 (SC 25bis.82); *De mysteriis*, 2.6, 3.8 (SC 25bis.158).
[122] Cf. Romans 6:4.
[123] *De sacramentis*, 2.7.20 (SC 25bis.84).

We see that the baptismal profession was made in response to three questions. To each question the *competens* replied, "I believe." Immersion followed each response. The addition of the phrase "and in his cross" to the second question, quoted in *De sacramentis*, and referred to in *De mysteriis*,[124] is not found in any of the Creeds or in any of the baptismal rites,[125] though there is a reference to it in *Expositio evangelii secundum Lucam*, 5.23.[126] In both *De sacramentis* and *De mysteriis*, Ambrose states that we are baptized in one name—the name of the Father and of the Son and of the Holy Spirit—because Christ spoke of only one name.[127] However, this need not imply that the bishop quoted a Matthean formula of baptism. Based on the evidence, the three questions were in all likelihood the words spoken at baptism.

According to Ambrose, when the *competentes* are immersed, they die and rise with Christ. Riley shows how Ambrose develops this theme by the significance that he attaches to the triple immersion.[128] In the *first immersion*, Ambrose sees death and burial in its deepest aspects. Making use of Romans 6, he explains that the baptismal act is a representation of death, linking it to the liturgical act of immersion into the water.[129] Ambrose further develops this theme by showing how the baptistry is a tomb and how immersion in water is similar to burial in the earth.[130]

In his treatment of the *second immersion*, Ambrose uses Romans 6 to connect the candidate's death, first, to the death of Jesus and, then, to his cross and passion. Ambrose's unique insertion of the words "and in his cross"[131] into the baptismal profession indicates the emphasis of his mystagogy, relating the baptismal act to the passion and death of Christ. Using Romans 6, Ambrose asserts that not only were the

---

[124] ". . . you said that you must believe in the cross of Jesus, our only Lord." *De mysteriis*, 5.28 (SC 25bis.134).

[125] T. Thompson, *On the Sacraments and On the Mysteries*, rev. ed. (London, S.P.C.K., 1950) 5.

[126] CSEL 14.29.

[127] See *De sacramentis*, 2:7.22 (SC 25bis.86) and *De mysteriis*, 4.20 (SC 25bis.166). Cf. Matthew 28:19.

[128] Riley, *Christian Initiation*, 243–261.

[129] *De sacramentis*, 2.6.17–18 (SC 25bis.84). Cf. Romans 6:7. We will discuss Ambrose's use of Scripture in detail in Chapter 6.

[130] Ibid., 3.1.1; 2.6.19 (SC 25bis.90, 84). We will discuss Ambrose's use of cultural and natural symbols in Chapter 7. See below, 267–269.

[131] Ibid., 2.7.20 (SC 25bis.84); cf. *De mysteriis*, 5.28 (SC 25bis.170).

candidates buried in baptism, they were "buried together with Christ."[132] Ambrose explains the significance of being buried with Christ: "What does 'in the death' mean? That, just as Christ died, so you also taste death;[133] just as Christ died to sin and lives to God, so you, too, died to the former allurements of sins through the sacrament of baptism and rose again through the grace of Christ."[134] In baptism the candidate dies to sin's allurements just as Christ died to sin. In baptism the candidate also shares in the passion and cross of Christ, because in baptism the candidate shares in the struggle against sin that the crucifixion of Christ represents.[135]

In his treatment of the third immersion, Ambrose does not expressly develop a relationship to the Third Person of the Trinity or interpret the third immersion as a single act.[136] Instead, he links it with the other two and treats the *triple immersion*. Ambrose connects the candidates to the scene in John 21 where Christ asks Peter if he loves him; the triple questioning reflects Peter's triple denial.[137] Ambrose sees in the triple question-and-answer formula and the triple immersion the multiple lapses in the previous life of the baptismal candidate. He reinforces the christological emphasis of his interpretation of baptism through his use of Acts 4:12. Ambrose notes that the "Name" in which

---

[132] *De sacramentis*, 2.7.23 (SC 25bis.86). Romans 6:8.

[133] Cf. Matthew 16:28; Mark 8:39; Luke 9:27; John 8:52.

[134] *De sacramentis*, 2.7.23 (SC 25bis.86).

[135] Ibid.

[136] *De Spiritu Sancto* (CSEL 79.15-222), Ambrose's treatise on the Holy Spirit was published in 381. In it Ambrose seeks to prove the divinity of the Holy Spirit by applying four characteristics of divinity to the Holy Spirit: (1) sinlessness, (2) the ability to forgive sin, (3) creativity rather than createdness, and (4) the receiving rather than the giving of worship (cf. 3.18.132). In at least one place in the treatise (1.15.152) and perhaps in two others (1.11.119; 1.11.120), Ambrose can be understood as asserting the procession of the Spirit from the Son as well as from the Father. This assertion runs counter to the Greek view that the Spirit proceeded from the Father through the Son. See Boniface Ramsey, *Ambrose* (New York: Routledge, 1997) 62. That Ambrose articulated such a developed theology of the Holy Spirit at roughly the same time as or even prior to preaching the sermons in *De sacramentis* suggests that the fact that he does not treat the third immersion is because he understands baptism more as identification with Christ rather than on account of a less developed pneumatology.

[137] Ibid., 2.7.21 (SC 25bis.86).

we are baptized contains the power of Jesus, the Name by which humanity is saved.[138] The triple immersion as the symbol of the triple fall of Peter and the threefold question and answer as the representation of Christ and Peter after the fall suggest to Ambrose that the three Persons named in the questions forgive the baptized's sins. At the same time, Ambrose upholds the unity of the divine action.[139] In addition to the forgiveness of sins,[140] we can glean other effects of dying and rising with Christ in baptism from various places in Ambrose's mystagogy. Botte lists salvation, healing, purification, new creation, new birth, transformation, and illumination.[141]

Just as Ambrose saw in immersion in the baptismal water the representation of death, so he sees in the *competentes'* coming out of the baptismal pool the symbol of resurrection. Ambrose says: "Yesterday we discussed the font, whose likeness is a kind of sepulcher into which, believing in the Father and the Son and the Holy Spirit, we are received, and immerse, and come up out of it again, that is, we are resuscitated."[142] Again Ambrose says: "Because baptism is a likeness of death, without doubt, when you immerse and when you come back out again there is a likeness of the resurrection."[143] Thus, Ambrose clearly states that coming out of the font symbolizes the resurrection of the candidate.

Riley also demonstrates that, having established that coming out of the baptismal pool is a symbol of the baptized participating in Christ's resurrection, Ambrose next shows that Christ's resurrection was also a new birth and that this new birth is valid not only for Christ but for the whole human race.[144] Ambrose explains how baptism is a regeneration by using the words of Psalm 2 to argue that, in the resurrection, Christ's status as Son of God is affirmed.[145] Ambrose interprets the words "You are my son: this day I have begotten you" as a reference to the resurrection of Christ. "If that resurrection was a regeneration, this resurrection from the font is also a regeneration."[146]

---

[138] Ibid., 2.7.22 (SC 25bis.86).
[139] Ibid.
[140] Ibid.
[141] Botte, *Des Sacrements; Des Mystères*, 35.
[142] *De sacramentis*, 3.1.1 (SC 25bis.90).
[143] Ibid., 3.1.2 (SC 25bis.90).
[144] Ibid. Riley, *Christian Initiation*, 305–312.
[145] Cf. Romans 1:4.
[146] *De sacramentis*, 3.1.2 (SC 25bis.90); cf. Acts 13:33.

Therefore, the resurrection is Christ's "birth" as the Son of God, a regeneration into divine life. Inasmuch as Christ is "the firstborn from the dead,"[147] the Christian's adoption as a child of God in baptism is likewise itself a regeneration with Christ's risen power, a sharing in the resurrection. "The resurrection was not merely a coming back to life but a birth into a new life that Christ did not have in his bodily humanity. Before the Christian can have a regeneration, Christ must have one."[148] Christ is firstborn from the dead, says Ambrose; if Christ's resurrection was a regeneration so must baptism be, as the "imitation" of the resurrection.[149] If Christ's resurrection is a new birth, then the baptized, who participate in this resurrection, symbolically manifested in their rising from the baptismal pool, the symbol of Christ's and their tomb, also participate in that "regeneration" as God's children. Ambrose further argues that just as water generates creatures to life, so baptismal water regenerates the baptized to grace.[150] Finally, in *De mysteriis*, Ambrose asserts that in the blessing of the font, the Holy Spirit comes upon the font, or upon those receiving baptism, in the same way that Spirit came upon the Virgin Mary. As the Holy Spirit brought forth a miraculous birth in the womb of the Virgin, so too in the womb that is the baptismal pool the Spirit brings forth the birth of a new creation in a miraculous way.[151]

Postbaptismal Anointing. Ambrose discusses the postbaptismal anointing in *De sacramentis*, 2.7.24 and 3.1.1 and in *De mysteriis*, 6.29, 30.[152] After the baptism the neophytes come up from the font and approach the bishop.[153] He spreads the *myron* on their heads[154] and prays:

---

[147] *De sacramentis*, 3.1.2 (SC 25bis.90); Colossians 1:18.

[148] William Ledwich, "Baptism, Sacrament of the Cross: Looking Behind St. Ambrose," in Bryan Spinks, *The Sacrifice of Praise: Studies on the Themes of Thanksgiving and Redemption in the Central Prayers of the Eucharistic and Baptismal Liturgies: In Honour of Arthur Herbert Couratin* (Rome: C.L.V. Edizioni Liturgiche, 1981) 201.

[149] *De sacramentis*, 3.1.2 (SC 25bis.90).

[150] Ibid. We will discuss Ambrose's use of natural symbols in Chapter 7. See below, 266–267.

[151] *De mysteriis*, 9.59 (SC 25bis.190). We will discuss Ambrose's use of biblical images in Chapter 6. See below, 234ff.

[152] SC 25bis.88, 90, 172.

[153] *De mysteriis*, 6.29 (SC 25bis.172).

[154] *De sacramentis*, 3.1.1 (SC 25bis.90).

"God the Father Almighty, who has regenerated you by water and the Holy Spirit, and has forgiven you your sins, Himself anoint you unto eternal life."[155] We know that this anointing was performed by the bishop because Ambrose uses the Latin word *sacerdos*, his word for "bishop,"[156] to describe this rite in both *De sacramentis* and *De mysteriis*. From *De sacramentis* we learn that this anointing was performed with *myron*. J. H. Srawley assumes that *myron* is chrism; Deferrari calls it myrrh.[157] All that we know for certain is that *myron* is oil with a scent. The allusion to ointment running down Aaron's beard in *De mysteriis*, 6.29 suggests that the oil was poured over the head rather than traced on the forehead. The prayer quoted by *De sacramentis* as used by the bishop is the first time we see this particular prayer used anywhere. It resembles, with a few changes of wording, the prayer found in the Gelasian Sacramentary in connection with the first postbaptismal anointing at Rome.

Ambrose interprets this anointing as the enrichment of the senses by grace and the embodiment of the effects of the baptismal rite. Ambrose's description of the anointing speaks of the whole rite as "regeneration."[158] Ambrose explains to the neophytes that they were anointed unto eternal life, contrasting eternal life with temporal life. Ambrose instructs the neophytes that even temporal death is to be preferred to loss of this eternal life, should some enemy attempt to destroy their faith.[159] The baptized were anointed on their *heads*, because "the wise have eyes in their head,"[160] and when this seat of natural wisdom receives grace, a more perfect form of life begins, which is called regeneration and resurrection.[161] Drawing from Song of Songs, Ambrose further connects this anointing with the resurrection by comparing the fragrant smell of the ointment with the odor of the resurrection.[162] The ointment, in its fragrance, is itself a symbol of the resurrected Christ. "In His association with the baptized, symbolized

---

[155] Ibid., 2.7.24 (SC 25bis.88).

[156] See above, 1, n. 1.

[157] Thompson, *On the Sacraments and On the Mysteries*, 22; Roy J. Deferrari, *Saint Ambrose: Theological and Dogmatic Works*, The Fathers of the Church 44 (Washington: Catholic University of America Press, 1963) 289.

[158] *De sacramentis*, 3.1.1 (SC 25bis.90).

[159] *De sacramentis*, 2.7.24 (SC 25bis.88).

[160] Ecclesiastes 2:14.

[161] *De sacramentis*, 2.7.24 (SC 25bis.88).

[162] *De mysteriis*, 6.29 (SC 25bis.172). Cf. Song of Songs 1:2-3.

by the anointing with the perfumed ointment, [Christ] is drawing them from temporal life into eternal life."[163]

Ambrose also sees in the unction a parallel to the anointing of Aaron[164] and the priestly character of the people of God.[165] He therefore understands it as the consecration of the newly baptized to their place in the priestly body of the Church.[166] In *De sacramentis* the same language is used in the fourth sermon: here the baptized are "anointed to the priesthood" and "the kingdom."[167]

Washing of the Feet of the Neophytes. After the anointing the bishop and presbyters wash the feet of the neophytes. Ambrose describes this rite of footwashing in *De sacramentis*, 3.1.4–7 and alludes to it in *De mysteriis*, 6.31–33.[168] John 13 is read; then the bishop girds himself and begins to wash the feet of a few of the newly baptized. The presbyters do the same for the rest. Ambrose is aware that the rite was not practiced at Rome[169] and defends its use at Milan. In *De sacramentis* he says, "In all things I desire to follow the Roman Church. Yet we too are not without discernment; and what other places have done well to retain, we too do well to maintain."[170] This statement is not found in *De mysteriis*, where Ambrose, writing for a general public, would naturally avoid language that seemed to involve criticism of other churches, including possibly Rome. Preaching to his own neophytes, Ambrose spoke more freely because he had no such fears.

As regards the significance of the footwashing, Ambrose, while recognizing its value as a lesson in humility,[171] assigns it a sacramental

---

[163] Riley, *Christian Initiation*, 390.

[164] Psalm 133:2.

[165] 1 Peter 2:9.

[166] *De mysteriis*, 6.30 (SC 25bis.173).

[167] *De sacramentis*, 4.1.1 (SC 25bis.102).

[168] SC 25bis.90–96, 172. Botte is correct that although *De mysteriis* does not speak of this rite, the reading of John 13 at this point does not make sense if it did not exist. Botte, *Des Sacrements; Des Mystères*, 28.

[169] While the washing of feet was not practiced by the Roman Church in conjunction with baptism, it was current in Africa, Spain, Gaul, and Ireland. It is found in service books of Gallican and Irish origin, such as the *Missale Gothicum*, *Missale Gallicanum Vetus*, Bobbio Missal, and Stowe Missal, as well as in the Ambrosian rite. Thompson, *On the Sacraments and On the Mysteries*, 23f.

[170] *De sacramentis*, 3.1.5 (SC 25bis.94).

[171] Ibid., 3.1.7 (SC 25bis.94); *De mysteriis*, 6.33 (SC 25bis.174).

efficacy. While all guilt is washed away in baptism, there remains the transmitted hereditary tendency to sin, and for this there is needed a "reinforcement of sanctification" supplied by footwashing.[172] The language in *De mysteriis* is similar. Ambrose says of Peter, ". . . his foot is washed that hereditary sins may be removed, for our own sins are loosed through baptism."[173] Our own sins are remitted in baptism. The hereditary sin, that is, the tendency to sin transmitted by Adam, needs to be cleansed. Thus Ambrose insists that it is a *mysterium* and a *sanctificatio*, which deserves a place in the initiatory rites.[174] Based on Ambrose's understanding of the words of Christ effecting the "change" in the Eucharist,[175] one must wonder whether the purpose of the reading of John 13 was to effect the cleansing of hereditary sin.[176]

---

[172] *De sacramentis*, 3.1.7 (SC 25bis.94).

[173] *De mysteriis*, 6.32 (SC 25bis.172).

[174] *De sacramentis*, 3.1.5–7 (SC 25bis.94–96); *De mysteriis*, 6.32 (SC 25bis.172).

[175] *De sacramentis*, 4.4.14–5.23 (SC 25bis.108–114); *De mysteriis*, 9.50–54 (SC 25bis.184–188).

[176] In a compelling study Martin Connell applies a detailed literary, text critical, and redactional analysis to the received Greek text of John 13:1-20 and its variant readings and concludes that the original narrative comprised only verses 6-10. Connell argues that the final redactors of John's Gospel added verses 7-20 to this "original narrative," which reinterpret the footwashing in terms of servanthood and humility. This interpretation is not present in verses 6-10. Rather, it appears as a necessary rite ("If I do not wash you . . .") done, like baptism elsewhere, in order to give the recipient a participatory "share" in Christ himself. Connell asks, "Might not the footwashing itself, especially as this is captured in 13:6-10, have been the initiatory rite of some Johannine communities? Might it not have been the rite of sanctification which wiped away one's sin or, to take from the Gospel, 'made one entirely clean'? Recall the text's 'Unless I wash you, you have no share with me' (13:8) and 'One who has bathed does not need to wash, except for the feet' (13:10). With these verses the footwashing takes on far more gravity than any of the same Gospel's few references to baptism." Martin F. Connell, "*Nisi Pedes*, Except for the Feet: Footwashing in the Community of John's Gospel," *Worship* 70, no. 4 (1996) 20–30, quotation: 24. For a summary and evaluation of this study and its implications for the New Testament origins of Christian initiation, see Johnson, *The Rites of Christian Initiation*, 20ff. For footwashing as a postbaptismal rite in the Gallican tradition, see Gabriele Winkler, "Confirmation or Chrismation? A Study in Comparative Liturgy," in Maxwell E. Johnson, *Living Water, Saving Spirit: Readings on Christian Initiation* (Collegeville, Minn.: The Liturgical Press, 1995) 202–219.

Vesting with White Robes. After the washing of feet, the neophytes received a white garment as a symbol of their baptismal transformation. This robe is alluded to in *De sacramentis*, 4.1.5–6 and 5.1.4.[177] Ambrose describes the neophytes vesting in white robes in *De mysteriis*, 7.34.[178] In *De sacramentis*, the first allusion to the white robe occurs when Ambrose describes the approach of the neophytes to the altar and imagines the angels repeating the question from the Song of Songs: "Who is that coming up from the wilderness dressed in white?"[179] The question would have little relevance except in connection with the white robe. The second allusion is found when Ambrose returns to the neophytes' approach to the altar and speaks of the joy of the church when she sees her *familia candidata*, her white-robed household, pressing around her.[180] Perhaps Ambrose does not discuss the vesting with white robes in the place it occurred in the initiation process because the neophytes were still wearing their robes as they listened to *De sacramentis*. Therefore, they did not need to be reminded that they had dressed in them after emerging from the font.

In *De mysteriis* Ambrose describes the white robe as a reminder of the shining garments of the resurrected Christ.[181] Combining the psalm dialogue of the entrance of the King of Glory into heaven (with the angels' question, "Who is this King of Glory?")[182] and another Old Testament reference to the fact that the King of Glory came dressed in a white robe,[183] Ambrose endeavors to show that the white robes worn by the neophytes signify their participation in the resurrection and ascension of Christ, the King of Glory, also depicted in a white robe. For Ambrose the white robe of the resurrected and ascended Christ and the white baptismal robe are one symbol signifying the newly baptized's incorporation into the mystery of the resurrection and ascension of Christ.

Closely related to the mystical association of the neophyte with the resurrection and ascension of Christ is the personal union of living intimacy that this association implies. Riley sees Ambrose under-

---

[177] SC 25bis.104, 122.
[178] SC 25bis.174.
[179] *De sacramentis*, 4.1.5-6 (SC 25bis.104).
[180] Ibid., 5.3.14 (SC 25bis.126).
[181] Matthew 28:3.
[182] Psalm 24.
[183] Isaiah 63:1.

scoring this personal intimacy by interpreting the baptismal robe "as a bridal garment, along with the reminiscences of the cultural preparations for wedding which this bridal garment imply, namely the bridal bath and the use of perfumes."[184] Riley notes that such a mystagogy fits well with the fact that baptism was a bath and was followed by an anointing with perfumed *myron*. Thus, following Song of Songs, Ambrose declares that Christ, upon seeing his Church in white vestments, pure and washed in the bath of regeneration, calls the Church his fair love.[185] Ambrose then shows that the baptized are attractive to Christ and moving to closer union with him. The bridal imagery of Song of Songs is used both to express the union of the baptized with the risen Christ and as a mystagogical explanation of the white robe in *De sacramentis*. As we have seen, Ambrose describes the neophytes processing to the altar for the eucharistic celebration as "this family clothed in white."[186] Ambrose then relates the image of apple trees in bloom with their white blossoms in Song of Songs 5:1 to the neophytes standing at the altar "dressed in white" in order to suggest the flowering of the grace brought about by baptism, a flowering that could not have been expected to produce such attractive fruit.[187]

Ambrose also understands the baptismal robe as symbolizing the forgiveness of sins.[188] Here he contrasts removing the garments before baptism, the "covering of sins," with putting on the shining white garment after baptism and sees a sign of the return to primitive innocence.[189] The shining whiteness of the robe represents the cleansing of the soul from defilement. Ambrose supports this interpretation of the baptismal robe by using biblical references to washing that makes whiter than snow[190] and to Moses cleansing the people with the blood of the lamb.[191] Ambrose shows that this cleansing takes place in baptism by relating to the Gospel scene of the transfiguration of Christ, a prefiguring of the resurrection, where Christ's garments were white as snow.[192] Further Old Testament reference is provided by the allusion to

---

[184] Riley, *Christian Initiation*, 439.
[185] *De mysteriis*, 37 (SC 25bis.176). Cf. Song of Songs 4:1.
[186] *De sacramentis*, 5.3.14 (SC 25bis.126).
[187] Ibid. See Riley, *Christian Initiation*, 440.
[188] *De mysteriis*, 37 (SC 25bis.176).
[189] Ibid. Cf. Psalm 50:9.
[190] Ibid.
[191] Exodus 12:22.
[192] Cf. Matthew 17:2.

sins that were once scarlet but now are white as snow.¹⁹³ The black-to-white imagery for sin and forgiveness is also provided by the picture of the Church, the *familia candidata* standing in white robes before the altar, once black with sin but now white by the grace of forgiveness.¹⁹⁴

Finally, Ambrose sees in the shining radiance of the baptismal garment a reflection of the life to be lived in partnership with Christ, who dwells within the neophytes as a seal on their heart, moving them to live a life that will reflect the image of God, the image in which the neophytes were created, which has been restored through baptism and which will shine forth in Christian conduct, like the baptismal garments themselves.¹⁹⁵

Spiritual Seal. The "spiritual seal" is described by Ambrose in *De sacramentis*, 3.2.8–10 and 6.2.6–8, and in *De mysteriis*, 7.41, 42.¹⁹⁶ In neither *De sacramentis* nor *De mysteriis* does Ambrose describe any liturgical action in connection with the spiritual seal,¹⁹⁷ except that in *De sacramentis* he prefaces the enumeration of the sevenfold gifts with the words "when, at the invocation of the bishop the Holy Spirit is bestowed."¹⁹⁸ Thus all that we are able to conclude from Ambrose is that this rite involves an invocation by the bishop that in some way bestows the Holy Spirit and its virtues.¹⁹⁹

---

[193] Isaiah 1:18.

[194] *De mysteriis*, 35 (SC 25bis.174).

[195] Ibid., 42 (SC 25bis.178). Cf. Song of Songs 8:6.

[196] SC 25bis.96, 140, 178.

[197] There are three possible reasons that Ambrose did not describe a ritual action in connection with the spiritual seal: (1) he felt that the neophytes would recall the rite and therefore did not need a description, (2) respect for the *disciplina arcani*, and (3) there was no ritual action to describe.

[198] *De sacramentis*, 3.2.8 (SC 25bis.96).

[199] Explanations of the "spiritual seal" have traditionally been based on the supposition that Ambrose's description contains clues that point to understanding the spiritual seal as the ceremony that will in time become the rite of confirmation. See, for example, Finn, *Early Christian Baptism and the Catechumenate*, 60–61; idem, *From Death to Rebirth: Ritual and Conversion in Antiquity*, 228; Yarnold, *The Awe-Inspiring Rites of Initiation*, 38. First, inasmuch as Ambrose's list of the seven gifts of the Spirit (*De sacramentis*, 3.2.8 [SC 25bis.96]; *De mysteriis*, 7.42 [SC 25bis.178]) is in a form differing from the biblical text, it is assumed to be a "liturgical formula." This formula is further assumed to be part of the formula employed by the bishop. This formula appears to corre-

spond structurally to the post-chrismational episcopal hand-laying prayer of *Apostolic Tradition* 21 (cf. *Hippolytus, La tradition apostolique de Saint Hippolyte,* Liturgiewissenschaftliche Quellen und Forschungen 39, trans. Bernard Botte [Münster: Aschendorff, 1963] 58.) and parallels the language of this prayer in the later Roman rite. The effect of this prayer is therefore understood to be a bestowal of the Holy Spirit in a way distinct from the bestowal of the Spirit in the water bath.

Second, Ambrose's description is alleged to contain hints of a signing of the cross and anointing. In *De sacramentis*, 6.2.7 (SC 25bis.140), a summary of the baptismal rites, Ambrose says, "Therefore God anointed you, the Lord signed you. How? Because you were signed with the image of the cross itself into his passion, you received a seal unto his likeness, that you may rise unto his image, and live after his pattern." This passage is assumed to indicate a signing of the cross in the giving of the "seal," as in later Ambrosian and Roman usage. Yarnold contends that Ambrose considered the anointing in this ceremony too secret even to be hinted at in *De mysteriis*. Yarnold, "The Ceremonies of Initiation in the *De Sacramentis* and *De Mysteriis* of St. Ambrose," 462. The anointing is assumed to be the anointing after baptism, which is said to mark the beginning of the rite that will become confirmation. This rite is understood to be completed by the subsequent "signing" or "seal." In this connection of postbaptismal anointing and signing or seal scholars find "a discrete entity separated from a water-rite understood as effecting forgiveness of sins, which has a different meaning or effect than that rite." Pamela Jackson, "The Meaning of 'Spiritale Signaculum' in the Mystagogy of Ambrose of Milan," *Ecclesia Orans* 7, no. 1 (Rome, 1990) 81.

Third, Ambrose describes this rite as *perfectio* (*De sacramentis*, 3.2.8 [SC 25bis.96]). He also says of the spiritual seal, "God the Father has sealed you, Christ the Lord has *confirmed* you, and has given the earnest (or pledge) of the Spirit in your heart, as you have learned from the apostolic lesson" (*De mysteriis*, 7.42 [SC 25bis.178]). Scholars have seen in these descriptions the "completion" or "perfection" of baptism. Thus, from these clues they have constructed an independent rite administered by the bishop that involves prayer for the bestowal of the Holy Spirit in a special way and the signing of the cross and anointing. This rite brings baptism to completion.

Building upon the work of Pamela Jackson, Maxwell Johnson correctly cautions that "Ambrose's 'spiritual seal' is 'elusive,' and we simply do not know 'what ritual action—if any—accompanied the bishop's prayer.'" Maxwell E. Johnson, "The Postchrismational Structure of Apostolic Tradition 21, the Witness of Ambrose of Milan, and a Tentative Hypothesis Regarding the Current Reform of Confirmation in the Roman Rite," *Worship* 70 (January 1996) 25; idem, *The Rites of Christian Initiation*, 137–138. Aidan Kavanagh suggests that it might simply be a general prayer for the neophytes or a concluding prayer for the entire process of initiation. Aidan Kavanagh, *Confirmation: Origins and*

Reform (New York: Pueblo Publishing Co., 1988) 55. Furthermore, neither the tenth-century *Ambrosian Manual* nor the twelfth-century *Ordo of Beroldus* have any corresponding rites beyond the one postbaptismal anointing and footwashing (Johnson, *The Rites of Christian Initiation*, p. 37).

That the list of the seven gifts of the Spirit is a formula is conjecture and cannot be regarded as certain, as it is not expressly stated by Ambrose that this list constitutes a formula. That the effect of this prayer is the bestowal of the Holy Spirit in a unique way, we must remember that Ambrose, as mystagogue, assigns both several meanings to a single rite and a single meaning to several rites. Jackson reminds us that "Ambrose attributes to those who have been water-baptized eyes like those of the one who has descended upon them: the Spirit (M, 37), and speaks of them as imbibing the gift of spiritual grace (M, 20); it is not easy to see how such work of the Spirit is separable from His indwelling. Similarly, Ambrose asserts that the Spirit comes on those in the font as He came upon Mary in the conception of Christ (M, 13); this seems to imply that believers are indwelt by the Spirit at their regeneration even as Christ was indwelt by the Spirit from his conception. Ambrose even uses the gift of the Spirit at Pentecost (a favorite pericope for those who argue for a separate, post-immersion gift of the Spirit) in discussing the consecration of the font (S, 11, 15)." Jackson, "The Meaning of 'Spiritale Signaculum' in the Mystagogy of Ambrose of Milan," 85–86.

In response to the argument that the spiritual seal imparts not the presence but additional graces of the Spirit, we must remember that Ambrose ascribes many kinds of activity to the Spirit in the font. Furthermore, his explanations are more often direct citations of Scripture than theological interpretations of those citations. Jackson notes that "scriptural texts which were later used as proof texts for various theories of the Spirit's presence in separate initiatory rites had not yet acquired this function in Ambrose, the presence of such a text does not demonstrate that Ambrose intended the same thing by his use of it intended by later authors." Ibid., 86. As we have seen, the content of Ambrose's mystagogy is a response to the Trinitarian controversies of his day. In *De sacramentis*, 6.2.6 and *De mysteriis*, 7.42 (SC 25bis.140, 178), Ambrose may not be assigning specific actions to specific persons of the Trinity but raising up their equality (cf. *De sacramentis*, 6.2.8 [SC 25bis.140]). Jackson asserts: "That Ambrose's concern that his neophytes believe the orthodox teaching on the equality and unity of the Persons of Trinity may have shaped his mystagogy of *spiritale signaculum* seems clear in S, VI, 5–10. Here it is apparently Ambrose's eagerness to assign a coequal function to each of the Persons of the Godhead which leads him to alter the Scriptural text which he cites, 2 Cor. 1: 21-22." Jackson, "The Meaning of 'Spiritale Signaculum' in the Mystagogy of Ambrose of Milan," 87.

Second, as for the postbaptismal anointing marking the beginning of a self-contained rite of confirmation, which is completed by the subsequent

Procession to the Altar. The procession to the altar followed the completion of the above rites. This procession is described in *De sacramentis,* 3.2.15; 4:2.5, 7; 3.8; and *De mysteriis,* 8.43.[200] Both works refer to the use of Psalms 42 and 23[201] in this procession.[202] Finn sees in *De sacramentis,*

"signing" or "seal," in neither *De sacramentis* nor *De mysteriis* does Ambrose describe an anointing or any other liturgical action in connection with the spiritual seal. Johnson conjectures that if any liturgical gesture was used in connection with the spiritual seal, it was probably a hand-laying prayer. Furthermore, in *De sacramentis* the postbaptismal anointing and spiritual seal are clearly distinct. In explaining the significance of the postbaptismal anointing in *De sacramentis,* 3.1.1 (SC 25bis.90), Ambrose concludes: "This is called regeneration," thereby seeming to connect it with the preceding rite of baptism. In view of the fact that *De mysteriis* is based upon *De sacramentis* (above, 12–14), this fact determines the interpretation of the vaguer language in *De mysteriis.*

Third, Jackson reminds us that Ambrose's use of *perfectio* to describe the spiritual seal (*De sacramentis,* 3.2.8 [SC 25bis.96]) may be nothing other than the nontechnical sense of "to bring an end." In this sense the spiritual seal is the last action before the neophytes' first Eucharist. It marks the conclusion of the process of initiation to an end. Thus the spiritual seal is not the rite of confirmation.

What, then, is the purpose of the spiritual seal described by St. Ambrose? Jackson speculates that, for Ambrose, "the spiritual seal was, with the other post-immersion rites (anointing, footwashing, clothing) part of the 'symbolic overflow' of water baptism, i.e., there are so many dimensions to what God effects in human beings when they become Christians that theological reflection on conversion and salvation over the course of time may result in the symbolic association of various of these dimensions with particular extra-immersion rites. Since human beings exist in time, it is often easier for them to grasp a number of concepts when they are presented in sequence rather than simultaneously; associating various dimensions of salvation with various ritual acts would enable converts and the Christian community to appreciate more clearly the manifold aspects of God's grace in Christ. Thus, in Ambrose, . . . *spiritale signaculum* gives expression to one's reception of the Spirit of God which makes a person 'one of His.'" Jackson, "The Meaning of 'Spiritale Signaculum' in the Mystagogy of Ambrose of Milan," 90–91.

[200] SC 25bis.100, 104–105, 178–179.

[201] What Ambrose calls Psalm 22 is what the Hebrew Psalter, along with most modern translations, calls Psalm 23.

[202] For Psalm 42, see *De sacramentis,* 4.2.7 (SC 25bis.104–105) and *De mysteriis,* 8.43 (SC 25bis.178–179). For Psalm 23, see *De sacramentis,* 5.3.13 (SC 25bis.126) and *De mysteriis,* 8.43 (SC 25bis.178–179).

5.3.13 the hint that Ambrose, who introduced responsorial singing in the West,[203] indicates that the neophytes chanted Psalm 23 in this procession to the altar for the Eucharist.[204] Regardless of whether it was chanted by the neophytes, in Ambrose's hands this psalm beautifully summarizes baptism and the Eucharist in a series of types:

"How often have you heard Psalm 22 [23] and not understood it! See how it is applicable to the heavenly sacraments: 'The Lord feeds me and I shall want nothing; he has set me in a place of pasture; he has brought me upon the water of refreshment; he has converted my soul. He has led me on the paths of justice for his own name's sake. For though I should walk in the midst of the shadow of death, I will fear no evils, for you are with me. Your rod is power, the staff suffering, that is, the eternal divinity of Christ, but also corporeal suffering; the one created, the other redeemed. You have prepared a table before me against them that afflict me. You have anointed my head with oil; and my chalice which inebriates me how goodly it is!'"[205]

Stage Four: Easter Eucharist

Ambrose also includes the eucharistic liturgy and the Lord's Prayer in *De sacramentis*. Until their baptism, the catechumens were dismissed after the liturgy of the Word in order to preserve the secrecy of the Eucharist. Thus the celebration of the Eucharist at the Easter Vigil was not only the neophytes' first reception of Communion but also their first experience of the celebration of the Eucharist. Ambrose's explanation of the Eucharist[206] is of prime importance for our knowledge of the eucharistic practice of the fourth century in Milan.

Although there is no allusion to the offering of the faithful in *De sacramentis*, we learn elsewhere from Ambrose[207] that though the neophytes communed with the faithful, they were not allowed to participate in the people's offering of bread and wine before the octave of Easter. Recalling the eight days of the Jewish period for purification, Ambrose gives as the reason for this exclusion the fact that this cere-

---

[203] Above, 118–119.

[204] Finn, *From Death to Rebirth: Ritual and Conversion in Antiquity*, 229.

[205] *De sacramentis*, 5.3.13 (SC 25bis.126).

[206] *De sacramentis*, 4.4.13–5.3.17 (SC 25bis.108–128) and 6.1.1–4 (SC 25bis.138); *De mysteriis*, 8.43–9.54 (SC 25bis.178–188).

[207] *Expositio in Psalmum cxviii*, prol. 2 (CSEL 62.3).

mony can be performed only by people who know its meaning and have become established as Christians.[208]

Yarnold asserts that "it is hard to imagine why the neophytes who had been initiated into many more precious mysteries should be debarred from this far more commonplace rite."[209] He asks, "Why does participation in the offertory require more careful preparation than communion?"[210] Yarnold answers his own question when he asserts that "the Fathers frequently saw the Offertory as the congregation's offering of themselves."[211]

Ambrose's understanding of both the process of initiation and the consecration of the bread and wine is that they are divine works. The role of the neophytes throughout the Easter Vigil is to receive God's grace. They do not need to understand what is happening to them in order to receive it. On the other hand, the offering is a response to God's grace: it is the ritual expression by which the faithful offer themselves to God. A sincere response requires understanding, which the neophytes will receive during the week following Easter. It is, therefore, appropriate for the neophytes to wait to participate in the offering until the Sunday after Easter. There is an allusion to the mingling of water and wine.[212] In his correspondence, Ambrose mentions "the kiss of Communion."[213]

The anaphora began with praise and intercession.[214] Ambrose explains that "praise is offered to God, prayer is offered up, petitions for the people, for kings, for all others."[215] The prayer "for kings" is an allusion to 1 Timothy 2:2. Scholars have attempted to find in this simple phrase references to earlier parts of the canon,[216] but this seems

---

[208] Ibid.
[209] Yarnold, *The Awe-Inspiring Rites of Initiation*, 40.
[210] Ibid.
[211] Ibid., 42.
[212] *De sacramentis*, 4.1.2 (SC 25bis.142).
[213] *Epistola extra coll.* 1 (Maur. 41).14–15 (CSEL 82/3.154).
[214] Kenneth W. Stevenson, *Eucharist and Offering* (New York: Pueblo Publishing Company, 1986) 74.
[215] *De sacramentis*, 4.4.14 (SC 25bis.109). "Laus deo, defertur oratio, petitur pro populo, pro regibus, pro caeteris."
[216] Yarnold translates the text "Laus deo, defertur oratio, petitur pro populo, pro regibus, pro caeteris." He argues that, with this reading, "praise" is the preface, "the prayer" is the prayer over the gifts, and "petitions" are the prayers for the various needs of the congregation. Alternatively, Yarnold suggests that

less likely.[217] Ambrose then supplies us with a series of prayers used in the liturgy,[218] which, when read consecutively, exhibit a general correspondence in order and contents with some sections of the *canon Missae* of the Roman Rite. These prayers include the prayer that precedes the consecration and corresponds to the *Quam oblationem* of the canon,[219] the institution narrative,[220] and the anamnesis,[221] which corresponds simultaneously to the *Unde et memores,* the *Supra quae,* and to the *Supplices* of the canon. These are, in fact, the most ancient vestiges we have of this canon; however, the two are not identical.[222]

Finally came Communion. The bishop says: "Corpus Christi." The community answers: "Amen."[223] There was an analogous formula for the cup.[224] Ambrose seems to include the recitation of the Lord's Prayer as part of the liturgy, though its position is less certain.[225] We have a double commentary on it in *De sacramentis,* 5.4.18–29 and 6.5.24.[226]

---

it is possible that the "praise" is not the preface but a special Easter prayer of rejoicing like the Alleluia. Cf. *Apologia David*, 1.8.42 (CSEL 32/2.324). In *Expositio in Psalmum cxviii*, prologue 3 (CSEL 62.4), Ambrose explains that Alleluia means "laus dei." Yarnold, *The Awe-Inspiring Rites of Initiation*, 132, n. 30. Chadwick's reading eliminates the prayer over the gifts. "Laus deo defertur, oratio petitur pro populo." Henry Chadwick, ed., *Saint Ambrose: On the Sacraments* (Chicago: Loyola University Press, 1960) 32. Cf. Josef A. Jungmann, *The Mass of the Roman Rite* (Westminster, Md.: Christian Classics, 1986) 1:53.

[217] R.C.D. Jasper and G. J. Cummings, *Prayers of the Eucharist: Early and Reformed,* 3rd ed. (Collegeville, Minn.: The Liturgical Press, 1975) 143.

[218] *De sacramentis,* 4.5.21–23; 6.26 (SC 25bis.114, 154).

[219] Ibid., 4.5.21–22 (SC 25bis.114).

[220] Ibid.

[221] Ibid., 4.6.27 (SC 25bis.116).

[222] Enrico Mazza, *The Origins of the Eucharistic Prayer,* trans. Ronald E. Lane (Collegeville, Minn.: The Liturgical Press, 1995) 246f.; idem, *The Eucharistic Prayers of the Roman Rite,* trans. Matthew J. O'Connell (Collegeville, Minn.: The Liturgical Press, 1986) 58ff. The text is the same with the exception of minor variations characteristic of a "living " text that is altered somewhat with use. G. Morin hypothesizes that Ambrose, motivated by his desire to follow Rome in all things, brought the Roman canon to Milan. *De sacramentis,* 3.1.5 (SC 25bis.94). See G. Morin, "Depuis quand und canon fixe à Milan? Restes de ce qu'il remplacé, " *Revue bénédictine* 51 (1939) 101–108.

[223] *De sacramentis,* 4.5.25 (SC 25bis.118).

[224] *De mysteriis,* 9.54 (SC 25bis.188).

[225] Yarnold, *The Awe-Inspiring Rites of Initiation,* 51, n. 259.

[226] SC 25bis.128–134, 150–152.

In addition to the liturgical formulae that they provide, *De sacramentis* and *De mysteriis* are important due to Ambrose's pronounced teaching on the conversion of the elements into the body and blood of Christ.[227] Ambrose emphasizes the words of Christ as effecting this "conversion" or "change." Ambrose says:

"Perhaps you say: 'The bread I have here is ordinary bread.' Yes, before the sacramental words are uttered, this bread is nothing but bread. But at the consecration [*consecratio*] this bread becomes the body of Christ. Let us reason this out. How can something which is bread be the body of Christ? By what words is the consecration [*consecratio*] effected, and whose words are they? The words of the Lord Jesus."[228]

He understood the bread and wine of the Eucharist to be the "figure" (*figura*) or "representing" (*repraesentare*) of the flesh and blood. The Latin words *figura* and *repraesentare* have a more definite sense than the corresponding English words and suggest the idea of exhibiting or making present the sacred realities of which they speak. In other words, there is no distinction between the real or symbolic presence of Christ. The bread of the Eucharist is the same flesh that was crucified and buried.[229] Ambrose's witness to this is the first in the West to be so clear and unambiguous. He was also the first of the Latin Fathers to attempt an explanation of the change.

For Ambrose, the change of the bread and wine into the body and blood of Christ can only be understood by faith. One must go beyond what is perceivable by the senses. Ambrose asserts that the power of the word of Christ causes this conversion.[230] The crossing of the Red Sea, the waters of Marah, and the incident of Elisha making the

---

[227] *De sacramentis* 4.4.14–5.23 (SC 25bis.108–114); *De mysteriis* 9.50–54 (SC 25bis.184–188). For discussions of Ambrose's eucharistic doctrine, see Mazza, *The Eucharistic Prayers of the Roman Rite*, 69–71; Ramsey, *Ambrose*, 68–70; Thompson, *On the Sacraments and On the Mysteries*, 37–42; Luisa Teresa Coraluppi Tonzig, "The Teaching of St. Ambrose on Real Presence, Its Misunderstanding in Later Tradition, and the Significance of Its Recovery for Contemporary Eucharistic Theology" (Ph.D. dissertation, Duquesne University, 1988); Madeline Grace, "Lest We Forget," *Emmanuel* 100 (September 1994) 409–413.

[228] *De sacramentis*, 5.4.14 (SC 25bis.108).

[229] *De mysteriis*, 9.53 (SC 25bis.186–188).

[230] *De sacramentis*, 4.4.14 (SC 25bis.108–110).

axe-head to swim reveal the possibility of the eucharistic miracle.[231] Furthermore, the body of Christ that the Christian receives was miraculously born from the Virgin.[232] Yet it is above all the word of Christ, "which was able to make out of nothing that which was not," that is capable of "changing things which exist into that which they were not"[233] that "proves" the change. Finally, Ambrose illustrates the realism of his doctrine from the Eucharistic Prayer itself.[234] In *De mysteriis*, Ambrose states that this transformation comes about through the words of Christ at the Last Supper recited by the priest:

"The Lord Jesus himself proclaims, 'This is my body.'[235] Before the blessing of the heavenly words another nature is spoken of, after the consecration the body is signified. He himself 'speaks of' his blood. Before the consecration it has another name, after it is called blood. And you say, Amen, that is, it is true."[236]

The conception of a "conversion" of the elements into the body and blood of Christ was probably derived by Ambrose, as was so much else in his theology, from Greek sources.[237]

In remembrance of Christ's passion, resurrection, and ascension, the bishop offers the bread and cup to God, calling them "this spotless sacrifice, this spiritual sacrifice, this bloodless sacrifice, this holy bread

---

[231] *De sacramentis*, 4.4.18 (SC 25bis.128).

[232] Ibid., 4.4.17 (SC 25bis.128).

[233] *De mysteriis*, 9.51–52 (SC 25bis.184–186); cf. *De sacramentis*, 4.4.16 (SC 25bis.128).

[234] Ibid., 4.5.21–23 (SC 25bis.114). In *De fide* Ambrose refers to the transformation of the bread and wine into the body and blood of Christ as taking place through the efficacy of prayer: "Now we, as often as we receive the sacramental elements which by the mysterious efficacy of holy prayer are transformed into the flesh and the blood, do show the Lord's death. " *De fide*, 4.10.125 (CSEL 78.201).

[235] Matt 26:26.

[236] *De mysteriis*, 9.54 (SC 25bis.188); *De sacramentis*, 4.5.23 (SC 25bis.114).

[237] The conception of a "conversion" of the elements into the body and blood of Christ appears for the first time (apart from some anticipation of it in Gnostic writers) in the Catecheses of Cyril of Jerusalem, and was elaborated by Gregory of Nyssa, who had a special theory of his own (*Oratio Catechetica*, c. 37), with whose language Ambrose exhibits occasional parallels. Thompson, *On the Sacraments and On the Mysteries*, xxxiv.

and chalice of eternal life" and asking God to accept this offering as God accepted the gifts of Abel and the sacrifices of Abraham and Melchizedek.[238] Thus, the eucharistic offering is conceived of as commemorative. It is a "thank-offering."[239] Ambrose looked upon the Eucharist as spiritual food by which Christ is sealed within us, a seal that we dare not violate by sin.[240] He explains that this gift is far superior to the treasures bestowed upon the Jews in their journey to the Promised Land.[241] Ambrose's understanding of the benefits of the Eucharist include the forgiveness of sins,[242] the strengthening of the soul,[243] and eternal life.[244] He also used the bridal imagery of the Song of Songs to describe the intimate relationship that the communicant shared with Christ in the Eucharist.[245] Finally, Ambrose emphasizes that the Church, aware of the great spiritual strength of the sacrament, exhorts its members to come together and partake of the Eucharist. Thus Ambrose encourages the daily reception of Communion.[246]

LITURGY AND MYSTAGOGY

Having reconstructed the rites of initiation that comprise the "text" of Ambrose's mystagogy and determined their meaning, we turn now to an exploration of Ambrose's use of this "text" in his preaching to the newly baptized. From *De sacramentis* and *De mysteriis* we can outline ten general principles that govern Ambrose's use of the liturgical "text" in his mystagogical preaching.

The Rites Are Inseparable from Scripture

First, we must acknowledge that to separate Ambrose's use of the rites from his use of Scripture, as we are doing by discussing the former

---

[238] *De sacramentis*, 4.6.27 (SC 25bis.116).

[239] Ibid., 4.6.27 (SC 25bis.116). Mazza argues that inasmuch as the bread and wine are already the *figura* of Christ's body and blood, the offering is made so that it may become "approved, spiritual, acceptable " and not "that it may become for us the Body and Blood." Mazza, *The Eucharistic Prayers of the Roman Rite*, 68–69.

[240] *De mysteriis*, 9.55 (SC 25bis.188).

[241] *De sacramentis*, 4.3.10 (SC 25bis.106); *De mysteriis*, 8.48 (SC 25bis.182).

[242] *De sacramentis*, 4.6.28 (SC 25bis.116).

[243] *De mysteriis*, 9.55 (SC 25bis.188).

[244] *De sacramentis*, 4.5.24.

[245] Cf. *De mysteriis*, 9.55-58 (SC 25bis.188–190). See below, 268–269.

[246] *De sacramentis*, 5.4.25 (SC 25bis.132).

in this chapter and the latter in the next, is an artificial division designed to facilitate our understanding of Ambrose's method of mystagogy. Ambrose interprets the meaning of the rites of initiation in terms of scriptural images, stories, admonitions, and portions of psalms. Botte notes that we do not find in Ambrose's mystagogical works neat divisions or learned definitions but a wealth of images.[247] Ambrose intertwines passages from Scripture with the step-by-step flow of sacramental actions in such a way that the two become the expression of a single reality.

"God is still visiting his people. Just as the New Testament reveals God's saving power among us in such a way that the New is discovered to be the fulfillment of the Old Covenant, so also 'the sacred liturgy is the ongoing *Sitz in Leben* of Christ's saving pattern in every age.' The economy of salvation is still going on in our midst, and it is in our liturgical celebrations that we recognize in faith and celebrate God's saving activity which continues in our daily life."[248]

Although we are currently attempting to unravel the "skeins"[249] of Ambrose's mystagogy in order to examine the liturgical strand, in Chapter 6 we will explore in great detail this inseparable link of liturgy and Scripture as it is expressed in Ambrose's mystagogy.

Explanation Follows Experience

Second, the most striking feature of Ambrose's use of the rites of initiation is that the explanations of the ritual actions are given only after the neophytes have participated in the sacraments. Like Cyril, Ambrose reserved instruction not only on baptism and the Eucharist but also on the Lord's Prayer[250] until after the candidates had been initiated. In keeping with Cyril's philosophy that the sacraments could be discussed only after initiation, Ambrose states:

"Now is the time to speak of the mysteries and to reflect systematically on the sacred ritual actions. We would not have considered it helpful

---

[247] Botte, *Des Sacrements; Des Mystères*, 33ff.
[248] Mary Pierre Ellebracht, "Today This Word Has Been Fulfilled in Your Midst," *Worship* 60, no. 4 (July, 1986) 348.
[249] Ibid., 350.
[250] *De sacramentis*, 5.4.18–29; 6.5.24 (SC 25bis.128–134, 150–152). Ambrose treats the Lord's Prayer in the course of his comments on the Eucharist.

to those not yet initiated, but rather a betrayal of them, if we had decided to give such a detailed explanation before baptism. Indeed it is better for the light of the mysteries themselves to have inundated you as a surprise than it would have been for us to have given an explanation beforehand."[251]

Ambrose here gives two reasons for this pedagogical approach. "[F]irst, to speak to the uninitiated about the sacraments would be to 'betray' rather than 'portray' them; second, the rites themselves had an inherent pedagogy, not so much in the visible play of symbols as in the inner light which 'infuses itself better in the unsuspecting.'"[252] Theologically speaking, an encounter with God comes as a surprise awareness of a new meaning of life, and it is clear that Ambrose looks upon the rites of initiation as just such an encounter with God. Pedagogically, one learns more easily if one has seen and experienced before being instructed. In *De sacramentis*, Ambrose gives a third reason for delaying explaining the rites of initiation until after they have been received. Faith is needed to understand the sacraments, and faith is not given until baptism.[253]

Ambrose gives further reasons for postponing sacramental catechesis until after one has participated in the rites in two other places,[254] both of which relate to Abraham's instructions to Sarah about making cakes.[255] In the Greek version of the biblical text, the word for cakes can also mean "hidden," presumably because the cakes were baked by being covered with hot ash.[256] From this fact Ambrose asserts that "every mystery ought to be hidden and, so to speak, concealed in a faithful silence so as not to be inconsiderately published to profane ears."[257] In other words, the Christian mysteries are too sacred for general publication. In his other comment on this passage, Ambrose says that the mysteries should be kept secret "lest by premature

---

[251] *De mysteriis*, 1.2 (SC 25bis.156).

[252] Harmless, *Augustine and the Catechumenate*, 100.

[253] *De sacramentis*, 1.1.1 (SC 25bis.60). Cf. Genesis 15:6; Romans 4:1-25. See below, 188–190.

[254] *De Abraham*, 1.5.38 (CSEL 32/1.521); *De Cain et Abel*, 1.35-37 (CSEL 32/1.369-371). See Yarnold, *The Awe-Inspiring Rites of Initiation*, 57-58.

[255] Genesis 18:6.

[256] The Greek word for "cakes" is ἐγκρύφιας, which means "hidden."

[257] *De Abraham*, 1.5.38 (CSEL 32/1.521).

speech you should commit them half-baked, so to speak, to faithless or weak ears and the hearer be repelled and feel repugnance and loathing; if he tasted them more fully baked, he would enjoy a taste of spiritual food."[258] Those interested in Christianity should not be given knowledge until they are able to receive it profitably.

The Rites Are God's Means of Giving Faith

Third, Ambrose understands that the rites are God's means of giving faith. Thus the goal of his mystagogy is not that the newly baptized merely understand the rites but that they enter more deeply into them by faith. In Chapter 4 we discussed the ways that Ambrose engaged his hearers in order to draw them more deeply into the mysteries. In our discussion of initiation in Milan we explored how Ambrose understood the rites themselves as leading the neophytes into a deeper experience and understanding of the mysteries. The mysteries were not intended to be readily understood by the neophytes as they participated in the rites. The rites were meant to have a deep emotional impact and to leave a lasting impression on those being initiated.

This emotional impact can be seen throughout the process of initiation. For example, despite the *disciplina arcani*, the *competentes* undoubtedly "heard mysterious hints of great secrets and privileges that await them."[259] Throughout Lent daily moral instruction, fasting, and examination and scrutinies all conspired to fill the candidates with excited anticipation. Finally, on Holy Saturday they are touched and "opened," commanded to renounce the devil, and—only half understanding—stripped, anointed, questioned, and plunged into the water. Gasping for breath, they emerge from the font and are greeted with joy, dressed in white, and led into the cathedral, where they see for the first time the secret rites of the Eucharist and receive for the first time the sacred bread and cup.

In addition to being overwhelmed, the neophytes are brought to faith. Ambrose says, "You received baptism; you believed."[260] He explains that in the *ephphatha* the bishop touches the *competentes'* nostrils so that they may receive "the full fragrance of faith and devotion."[261]

---

[258] *De Cain et Abel*, 1.35–37 (CSEL 32/1.369–371).

[259] Yarnold, "Baptism and the Pagan Mysteries in the Fourth Century," 259. Cf. *De sacramentis*, 1.3.10 (SC 25bis.64), 3.2.11 (SC 25bis.98).

[260] De sacramentis, 1.1.1 (SC 25bis.60).

[261] Ibid., 1.1.3 (SC 25bis.62).

In his comments on the neophytes' admission to the Eucharist, Ambrose shows how the rites themselves gave the neophytes the faith to see the deeper meaning of the sacraments. Ambrose first explains that Jesus' healing the man born blind as it is recorded in John's Gospel[262] prefigures the mysteries.[263] Ambrose then continues: "Now think of your own eyes, the eyes of your heart. With your bodily eye you saw bodily things, but you were not yet able to see sacramental things with the eyes of your heart. So when you gave in your name, he took mud and spread it over your eyes? What does this mean?"[264] Ambrose's answer is that "you had to confess your sins, examine your conscience, do penance for your faults, you had to acknowledge, that is to say, the lot of humankind."[265] As a result of this, "you went there [to the font], you washed, you came to the altar, you began to see what you had not seen before, that is to say, through the font of the Lord and the preaching of the Lord's passion, at that moment your eyes were opened. Before, you seemed to be blind of heart, but now you began to perceive the light of the sacraments."[266] Ambrose tells the neophytes that through the sacraments they began to see with the eyes of faith.[267]

Then, in his mystagogical homilies, Ambrose provides the neophytes an opportunity to see the mysteries through the eyes of faith by inviting them to retrace their journey of initiation or, better yet, to take it a second time. This time, however, the purpose is not emotional impact but comprehension through faith. That Ambrose's mystagogy is a second journey through the rites is reflected in the fact that Ambrose's mystagogy generally follows the sequence of the rites of initiation.[268] He breaks the process of initiation down into its component parts, discussing the *ephphatha*, entrance into the baptistry, prebaptismal anointing, and renunciation in *De sacramentis*, 1; the exorcism and consecration of the water in *De sacramentis*, 1 and 2; baptism proper in *De sacramentis*, 2; postbaptismal anointing in *De sacramentis*, 2 and 3; washing of the *neophytes'* feet in *De sacramentis*, 3; vesting with white

---

[262] John 9:6-7.
[263] *De sacramentis*, 3.2.11 (SC 25bis.98).
[264] Ibid., 3.2.12 (SC 25bis.98).
[265] Ibid.
[266] Ibid., 3.2.15 (SC 25bis.100).
[267] Cf. above, 136–137.
[268] See below, 250–252.

robes in *De sacramentis,* 4 and 5; spiritual seal in *De sacramentis,* 6; the Eucharist in *De sacramentis,* 4–6; and the Lord's Prayer in particular and prayer in general in *De sacramentis,* 6.

That Ambrose is calling his hearers to enter more deeply into the mysteries and see through the eyes of faith is evident from the emphasis that he places on the candidates' first sight of the baptismal font and the Eucharist. Speaking of their first sight of the baptismal font, Ambrose reminds his hearers, "You saw all that you could see with the eyes of the body, all that is open to human sight. You saw what is seen, but not what is done."[269] They saw only the appearance; they did not see the effect. Thus, for Ambrose, the goal of mystagogy is to lead the neophytes to enter more deeply into the mysteries so that they see them through the eyes of faith, which they received by participating in the rites.

The Rites Are Specific and Authentic

Fourth, Ambrose's use of the rites is *specific*. He invites particular people into a deeper understanding, experience, and appreciation of the specific rites of Christian initiation in which they have participated. Yarnold states that the sermons of Cyril of Jerusalem, Ambrose of Milan, John Chrysostom, and Theodore of Mopsuestia describe a common pattern of Christian initiation.[270] On the contrary, in these sermons the Fathers describe unique processes of initiation with distinctive features and meanings. Comparing the process of Christian initiation described by Ambrose with either those described by the other Fathers or with Yarnold's "detailed picture of the stages by which a person entered the Church"[271] in the fourth century reveals that while the pattern of Christian initiation may be common in very broad terms, the details describe a process of initiation that is unique in terms of both its rites and their meanings.[272]

[269] *De sacramentis,* 1.3.10 (SC 25bis.64).
[270] Yarnold, *The Awe-Inspiring Rites of Initiation,* 1.
[271] Ibid. For a description of Yarnold's common pattern, see 1–54.
[272] For a comparison of the processes of Christian initiation described by the Fathers, see Riley, *Christian Initiation,* esp. 78–83, 101–103, 132–138, 170–172, 179–180, 183, 207–211, 292–298, 341–348, 407–412, 445–451. Elsewhere I have made a comparative study of the process of Christian initiation described by Saint Ambrose and Yarnold's common pattern. Craig A. Satterlee, "The Process of Christian Initiation Described by Ambrose of Milan" (Ph.D. Candidacy Research Essay, University of Notre Dame, March 6, 1998).

The most distinctive feature of Christian initiation in Milan is the washing of the neophytes' feet, which is found only in Ambrose and which, according to Ambrose, is not practiced in Rome. A second unique feature of Ambrose's process of initiation is contained in the short interrogative Creed at baptism in which the *competentes* are asked, "Do you believe in the Lord Jesus Christ *and in his Cross?*"[273] The words in italics are not found in any of the Creeds or in any of the baptismal rites,[274] though there is a reference to them in *Expositio evangelii secundum Lucam,* 5.23.[275] Third, though the neophytes receive the Eucharist at the Easter Vigil, they are prohibited from participating in the offering. Ambrose is also unique in interpreting the *ephphatha* as facilitating a fruitful reception of the sacraments rather than driving out evil, and the prebaptismal anointing as strengthening and not exorcism. Thus Ambrose describes specific rites and not general patterns.

That Ambrose "explains" the mysteries as they were actually celebrated and not in some idealized way is evident from the way he uses the details of the neophytes' participation as part of his instruction. "Think what you saw," Ambrose tells his hearers, "think what you said: recall it carefully."[276] The bishop touched their ears and their nostrils, even though it was inconsistent with the biblical text. They listened to a reading and their feet were washed; even though this rite had raised objections and was not practiced at Rome. In an idealized retelling of the rites, such inconsistencies and objections would be eliminated. In fact, in *De mysteriis,* Ambrose's polished commentary on the rites, he eliminates them. That Ambrose is describing an actual celebration of the rites is also evident from the fact that he provides a detailed description of his hearers' participation. He reminds his hearers of what they saw, said, and did. If Ambrose is to draw his hearers into the mysteries, his description of their participation must be authentic. Thus Ambrose describes the specific rites in which his hearers have actually participated.

The Rites Are Means and Not Ends

Fifth, Ambrose does not look upon the rites as ends in themselves but as the means to a new life. He does not "explain" the rites for the

---

[273] *De sacramentis,* 2.7.20 (SC 25bis.84).
[274] Thompson, *St. Ambrose: On the Sacraments and On the Mysteries,* 5.
[275] CSEL 14.29.
[276] *De sacramentis,* 1.1.4 (SC 25bis.62).

sake of doing so, but in order to draw from them the appropriate lessons for Christian life. Baptism is not an end in itself but a beginning, and the newly baptized must understand the transformation that has taken place in them. Through baptism they "come to believe."[277] By the *ephphatha* they are opened to the word and the homily of the priest and "receive the sweet fragrance of eternal goodness . . . so that the full fragrance of faith and devotion may dwell in [them]."[278] They are anointed in preparation for their struggle in the world.[279] In the waters of baptism they passed "from sin to life, from guilt to grace, from vileness to holiness. Those who pass through these waters do not die; they rise again."[280] This death and resurrection serves to "break the hold of the devil in this world as well."[281]

Having been freed from the devil's hold and given eternal life, the neophytes are to "choose eternal life rather than this life."[282] For Ambrose, choosing eternal life is not an abstract theological concept but a matter of making hard choices in everyday life. The neophytes already learned what this means through their Lenten instructions on the obligations of the moral life. Now, by penetrating the depths of the Christian mysteries, they learn that they have received the faith and strength to fulfill these obligations. Thus after emerging from the font, the neophytes are "anointed to the priesthood,"[283] sanctified in the footwashing,[284] sealed to live a life reflective of the image of God,[285] and receive the Holy Spirit and its virtues.[286] Finally, when the neophytes receive the Eucharist, Christ himself is sealed within them,[287] and they receive forgiveness, strength for their souls, and eternal life.[288]

Ambrose's mystagogy illustrates his understanding of the everyday world of the newly baptized as a place hostile to their faith and new

---

[277] Ibid., 1.1.1 (SC 25bis.60).
[278] Ibid., 1.1.2–3 (SC 25bis.60).
[279] Ibid., 1.1.4 (SC 25bis.62).
[280] Ibid., 1.4.12 (SC 25bis.108).
[281] Ibid., 2.6.19 (SC 25bis.84).
[282] Ibid., 2.7.24 (SC 25bis.88).
[283] Ibid., 4.1.1 (SC 25bis.102).
[284] Ibid., 3.1.7 (SC 25bis.94).
[285] *De mysteriis*, 7.42 (SC 25bis.178).
[286] *De sacramentis*, 3.2.8 (SC 25bis.96).
[287] *De mysteriis*, 9.55 (SC 25bis.188).
[288] *De sacramentis*, 4.6.28 (SC 25bis.116); *De mysteriis*, 9.55 (SC 25bis.188); *De sacramentis*, 4.5.24 (SC 25bis.116).

status as members of the Church. In *De sacramentis* he describes the Christian as "an athlete . . . about to wrestle in the fight of this world."[289] The newly baptized are crowned by Christ for contests in the world. Though this reward is in heaven, the baptized earn this reward by their struggles in the world.[290] Ambrose reminds the newly baptized that in preparation for baptism, they renounced "the world and its pleasures," which means that they renounced life in this world.[291] He further reminds his hearers that their baptismal promises are kept not on earth but in heaven and that the mysteries they received are heavenly; therefore, they are to shun earthly things and pursue heavenly things.[292]

Ambrose directs the newly baptized to approach their life in this world with care and caution.[293] In one place he compares the world to a sea with diverse billows, heavy waves, and fierce storms and instructs his hearers to imitate the fish, which swims over the waves and does not sink in the storm, so that the world does not sink them.[294] In another place Ambrose, reminding the neophytes that they were anointed to eternal life, instructs them not to set this earthly life before that life, even if some enemy, desiring to take away their faith, threatens them with death.[295] In a third passage Ambrose compares the neophytes to good eagles, which seek heaven and scorn earthly things.[296] That Ambrose recognized that both the Church and the Christian had to live in this world and could not totally alienate themselves from it is evident in his editing of *De mysteriis*, which, as we have said, was intended for publication. Ambrose eliminated the images of the athlete, the storm and the fish, and downplayed the world in his treatment of the renunciation, and wrote instead of the newly baptized renouncing an adversary to his face.[297]

Specifically, Ambrose addresses the triple threat of Arianism, paganism, and Judaism in his mystagogy. In responding to what he perceived as exterior threats to the Church, Ambrose used his teaching

[289] Ibid., 1.2.4 (SC 25bis.62).
[290] Ibid.
[291] Ibid., 1.2.5, 8 (SC 25bis.62, 64).
[292] Ibid., 1.2.5 (SC 25bis.62).
[293] Ibid.
[294] Ibid., 3.1.3 (SC 25bis.100).
[295] Ibid., 2.7.24 (SC 25bis.88).
[296] Ibid., 4.2.7 (SC 25bis.104).
[297] *De mysteriis*, 2.5; 3.8 (SC 25bis.158).

on the sacraments to assert Christianity's superiority over paganism and Judaism. He argued that the sacraments of the Christians are more divine and more ancient than those of the Jews.[298] Ambrose ridiculed the Jews for baptizing pots and cups, as if inanimate objects were capable of committing sin or receiving grace.[299] Turning to paganism, Ambrose asserts that, while the baptism of the Jews is a figure of Christian baptism,[300] pagan baptism is simply a bath.[301] Ambrose declares that "the baptism of the faithless does not heal or cleanse but pollutes."[302] "The flesh is washed, but guilt is not wiped out;[303] rather, in that washing, new guilt is contracted."[304]

In responding to the internal threat of heresy, *De sacramentis* and *De mysteriis* make clear that Ambrose used the sacraments to teach orthodox Christianity to the newly baptized. In *De sacramentis* Ambrose challenges the Arians by name:

"The Arians believe that they are diminishing the status of the Holy Spirit if they call him [the Spirit] the Paraclete. But if Paraclete means anything, it means 'Comforter.'[305] And have you not heard in the reading that the Father himself is the 'God of Comfort'?[306] So, you see, they

[298] *De sacramentis*, 1.4.11–12; 4.3.9–12 (SC 25bis.66; 106–108); *De mysteriis*, 3–9 (SC 25bis.160).

[299] *De mysteriis*, 4.5.23 (SC 25bis.114).

[300] The examples of Jewish baptisms that Ambrose gives in *De sacramentis* are the bathing of Naaman and of the sick at the pool of Beth-zatha, and the baptism administered by John.

[301] *De sacramentis*, 2.1.2 (SC 25bis.74).

[302] *De mysteriis*, 4.23 (SC 25bis.166).

[303] The exact phrase is found in *Enarrationes in xii psalmos davidicos* 40.5 (CSEL 65.232), where Ambrose contrasts Christian baptism with the *taurobolium*, the pagan rite in which a candidate is initiated by being showered with the blood of a bull or ram. See Homes Dudden, *The Life and Times of Saint Ambrose*, 1:246; Yarnold, *The Awe-Inspiring Rites of Initiation*, 61.

[304] *De sacramentis*, 2.1.2 (SC 25bis.74).

[305] Scholars generally agree that Ambrose's understanding of the title "paraclete" is not correct. In general usage the term applied to one who was called in as a helper, especially as an advocate to plead on one's behalf.

[306] Ambrose is referring to 2 Cor 1:3. Eunomius, a follower of Arius, preferred to speak of the "Paraclete" rather than the "Holy Spirit" because he thought that to do so made the Spirit seem inferior to the Father. Cf. Gregory of Nyssa, *Contra Eunomium*, 185 (PG 43.159), a passage on which Ambrose

think they can diminish the Holy Spirit's status in the very point in which the eternal Father's power is proclaimed so devoutly."[307]

Ambrose repeatedly asserts the equality of the Persons of the Trinity.[308] He shows that all three Persons of the Trinity are present in the waters of baptism, and that the forgiveness that God extends in baptism comes from the Father, the Son, and the Holy Spirit, who are "one Substance, one Divinity, one Majesty."[309] In a clear strike against Arianism, Ambrose declares in *De mysteriis* that the profession of faith that the candidates made "is not a case of, I believe in a greater, a less, and a least."[310] For Ambrose, the sacraments show the operation of the Trinity and the equality of the three Persons, thereby refuting Arianism.[311]

The Rites Are the Continuing Drama of Salvation

Sixth, the overall structure of Ambrose's mystagogy, together with his explanation of the rites, reveals that he finds an obvious sense of drama in the process of Christian initiation. His recounting of the journey that brought the neophytes from their entrance into the baptistry to their entrance into eucharistic fellowship reflects his conviction that what Riley calls "the central core of the Christian experience as recorded in the *NT*, one believes and is baptized,"[312] is ritually enacted in the rites of initiation. Riley is correct that

"this 'believing' implies an event, a dynamic passage from one state to another, a turning, a *metanoia,* and introduction into a new world of consciousness, insertion into a history which absorbs past, present and future, and recapitulates it interiorly and transcendentally in the mystery of Christian Initiation. This drama of Christian Initiation is described in various ways, from its simplest form, as, for example, in the story of the meeting of the Jerusalem-Gaza road of the deacon

---

seems to be drawing. Gregory wrote about 383, some eight years before the date normally assigned to *De sacramentis*.

[307] *De sacramentis*, 6.2.10 (SC 25bis.142).

[308] Cf. Ibid., 5.1.1; 6.1.1; 6.1.2; 6.2.10 (SC 25bis.120, 138, 142).

[309] Ibid., 1.5.17–19. Cf. 2.5.14; 2.7.22 (SC 25bis.68–70. Cf. SC 25bis. 82, 86); *De mysteriis* 4.24, 25 (SC 25bis.168).

[310] *De mysteriis*, 5.28 (SC 25bis.170).

[311] *De sacramentis*, 6.2.5–10 (SC 25bis.140–142).

[312] Riley, *Christian Initiation*, 37.

Philip with the Ethiopian eunuch on pilgrimage to Jerusalem,[313] or in the conversion of Saul on the road to Damascus[314] to its more elaborately developed rituals. The ritual manifestations of this event . . . had passed from simple forms to ritual forms suited to the changed conditions in which the Good News was preached and the act of belief, and its negative counterpart, the act of renunciation of unbelief took place. The dramatic elements, the time of day, the pilgrimage, the road, the encounter, obvious in the portrayal of the conversion of the Ethiopian eunuch or Saul, remain present, however, even in the more highly developed ritual, because of the very nature of the mystery of Christian Initiation as a passage into a new world of consciousness, the world of salvation history. Place, time, characters, dialogue, event: all continue to play their role in describing the process of this mystery of initiation.[315]

Riley uses the rite of renunciation to show how Ambrose conceived of Christian initiation as a drama.[316] First, by his remarks on the renunciation, Ambrose sets a stage. In calling the baptistry the "holy of holies," he interpretively distinguishes the place where the renunciation takes place from the place where the *ephphatha* occurred. Thus Ambrose indicates "a graduated dramatic introduction into the mystery based on the physical appointments of the baptistry."[317] Ambrose sees a dramatic meaning in the fact that the candidates have not yet been allowed to come close to the font and have not yet turned to see it. By remaining somewhat removed from the font and facing away from it, the candidates establish a kind of combat arena where the struggle with the devil will be acted out. "You entered, then, in order to confront your adversary, whom you had to renounce to his face."[318]

Thus Ambrose sees the devil as antagonist present in a drama that takes place between the door to the baptistry and edge of the font. Ambrose's understanding of the renunciation as a dramatic combat is further reinforced by his interpretation of the prebaptismal anointing,

---

[313] Acts 8:26-40.
[314] Acts 9:1-19.
[315] Riley, *Christian Initiation*, 37.
[316] Ibid., 48–50.
[317] Ibid., 48.
[318] *De mysteriis*, 2.7 (SC 25bis.158).

where he uses the image of an athlete being rubbed down in preparation for combat with his adversary. Finally, Ambrose understands the candidates' turning from west to east as a dramatic action when he explains that the devil was present on one side and Christ on the other. Ambrose's interpretation of the setting and actions of a simple liturgical act elevate it to the level of the drama of salvation.

The Rites Speak Symbolically

Seventh, the rites speak not logically or systematically but through their symbolism. Their logic is more associative than discursive, more poetic than philosophical.[319] It is important to note that, for Ambrose, the rites are the starting point for understanding God's saving activity. Ambrose does not begin with a theological concept and understand the rites as illustrating that point. Instead, he begins with the rites themselves and asks, in effect, "What did we do?"[320] and "Why did we do what we did?"[321] In order to answer these questions, Ambrose looks to the images and symbols contained in the rites.

We will explore Ambrose's use of image and symbol in great detail in Chapters 6 and 7. For now it is enough simply to provide examples of their scope. As we have previously noted, the structure of the rites is not a logical argument but an unfolding drama. Within this drama, meaning is not reasoned out but ritually enacted. The *competentes* are oiled like an athlete in order that they will hold their own with the enemy. Facing west, the direction of the setting sun, they renounce the devil. Then, turning to the east, the direction of the new day, they turn to Christ. The candidates descend into and emerge from the font, which is tomblike in shape, and so share in Christ's death and resurrection. Thus participation in the mysteries and coming to faith is not a matter of comprehension and intellectual assent but of experiencing, reflecting, and re-experiencing with the new sight and insight that comes through faith.

The Rites Are a Mystery

Eighth, Ambrose's use of the rites takes seriously their nature as mystery. While a mystery can be pointed to, hinted at, and even

---

[319] Cf. Harmless, *Augustine and the Catechumenate*, 367.
[320] Cf. *De sacramentis*, 1.1.2; 3.1.4; 3.2.11 (SC 25bis.60; 94; 98).
[321] Cf. Ibid., 1.1.3; 1.5.15; 3.1.1; 3.1.3 (SC 25bis.60; 68; 90).

glimpsed, it can never be defined and certainly never exhausted.[322] So, rather than providing precise definitions, Ambrose piles up meanings. He says, for example, that baptism heals,[323] cleanses,[324] washes away sins,[325] cancels guilt,[326] is a burial,[327] an absolution,[328] death and resurrection,[329] and a new birth.[330] Thus, as a mystery, the meaning of the rites is a matter of "both/and" rather than "either/or." Ambrose also takes the rites as mystery seriously when he stresses their inner dynamic: the invisible action of God. He tells his hearers that there is more going on in baptism than what is perceivable by human sight. He says that the things that are effected cannot be seen, but they are much greater than those that are seen because they are eternal.[331] Similarly, the Eucharist, though it looks like ordinary bread and wine, becomes the body and blood of Christ through God's invisible activity in the consecration.[332]

Interpretation of the Rites Is in Keeping with Their History, Structure, and Theology

Ninth, although Ambrose's understanding of the rites is multi-dimensional, it is not indiscriminate. Ambrose's use of the rites is based on a solid understanding of the history, structure, and theology of the sacraments that he is describing. For Ambrose, the history of the mysteries is found in the Bible, where the sacraments are prefigured. For example, Israel's crossing of the Red Sea,[333] the cleansing of Naaman the leper,[334] and the flood[335] all prefigure baptism.[336] Similarly,

---

[322] Harmless, *Augustine and the Catechumenate*, 367.
[323] *De sacramentis*, 1.5.15 (SC 25bis.68).
[324] Ibid., 1.5.16 (SC 25bis.68).
[325] Ibid., 2.1.1 (SC 25bis.74).
[326] Ibid., 2.4.14 (SC 25bis.80).
[327] Ibid., 2.6.19 (SC 25bis.84).
[328] Ibid., 2.7.20 (SC 25bis.84).
[329] Ibid., 2.7.23 (SC 25bis.86).
[330] Ibid., 3.1.2 (SC 25bis.90).
[331] Ibid., 1.3.10 (SC 25bis.64).
[332] Ibid., 4.4.14, 20 (SC 25bis.108, 112).
[333] Ibid., 1.6.20–22 (SC 25bis.70–72).
[334] Ibid., 1.5.13–15 (SC 25bis.66–68).
[335] Ibid., 1.4.23; 2.1.1 (SC 25bis.72, 74).
[336] Ibid., 2.3.8 (SC 25bis.78).

Melchizedek's offering of bread and wine to Abraham,[337] God's raining down manna in the wilderness,[338] and Moses' striking the rock and bringing forth water[339] all prefigure the Eucharist. Yet Ambrose asserts that the Christian sacraments are both more ancient and more divine than the Jewish mysteries.[340] Ambrose also sees baptism prefigured in Jesus' healing of the paralytic at the pool of Beth-zatha[341] and in the risen Christ's asking Peter three times if he loves him.[342]

Ambrose also finds that the structure of the rites is laid out in the Bible. He sees the pattern of our baptism established and the pattern of our faith set forth by Jesus when he was baptized by John in the Jordan.[343] The structure of the consecration of the Eucharist is taken from the expressions of the evangelists and the words of Christ.[344]

Ambrose's theology of the mysteries is that the presence of the Triune God added to ordinary elements brings about the sacramental effect. Ambrose declares that not all waters have a curative power: only that water has it which has the grace of Christ.[345] Ambrose also states that the consecration of the water is brought about by the descent of the Spirit[346] and the presence of the Trinity.[347] Thus Ambrose distinguishes between the element and the consecration, between the water and the working of the Holy Spirit.[348] For this reason the bishop "first performs an exorcism over the element of water, and then utters invocation and prayer that the water may be sanctified and the eternal Trinity may dwell there."[349] Similarly, when the words of consecration are added to ordinary bread, it becomes the flesh of Christ. The words of consecration are those of the Lord Jesus.[350] Therefore, the word of Christ consecrates this sacrament.

---

[337] Ibid., 4.3.10–12 (SC 25bis.106–108).
[338] Ibid., 4.5.24 (SC 25bis.116).
[339] Ibid., 5.1.3 (SC 25bis.120).
[340] Ibid., 1.4.11, 23; 4.3.10; 4.5.24 (SC 25bis.106; 116).
[341] Ibid., 2.2.3–7 (SC 25bis.74–76).
[342] Ibid., 2.7.21 (SC 25bis.86).
[343] Ibid., 1.5.15, 16, 18 (SC 25bis.68, 70).
[344] Ibid., 4.5.22 (SC 25bis.114).
[345] Ibid., 1.5.15 (SC 25bis.68).
[346] Ibid., 1.5.15, 17 (SC 25bis.68).
[347] Ibid., 1.5.19 (SC 25bis.70).
[348] Ibid., 1.5.15 (SC 25bis.68).
[349] Ibid., 1.5.18 (SC 25bis.70).
[350] Ibid., 4.4.13, 14, 16–19 (SC 25bis.108–112).

A Variety of Methods Is Used to Incorporate and Interpret the Liturgical "Text"

Tenth, Ambrose employs a variety of methods to interpret the liturgical "text" to his hearers. Craddock suggests six methods for interpreting Scripture to a congregation that are equally valuable for including and interpreting the liturgy as the "text" on which mystagogy is based. Craddock's methods are: (1) direct and uncritical transfer of the text, (2) allegory, (3) typology, (4) interpretation of the intent of the text, (5) thematic interpretation, and (6) interpretation by translation of the text.[351] Ambrose employs all of these methods in his mystagogy. Here we provide an example of each method in order to illustrate his usage. It is important to remember that these methods are often employed consecutively, even simultaneously, and frequently in conjunction with various methods of scriptural interpretation.

Direct and Uncritical Transfer of the Text to the Listener. This method consists simply of reading and then treating the "text" as if it had been written with this audience in mind.[352] Ambrose's most striking example of direct and uncritical transfer of the liturgical text is his recitation of and commentary on the consecratory prayers of the Eucharist.[353] He first recites the words of consecration and distinguishes between the words of the evangelists and the words of Christ. He then uses the words of consecration phrase by phrase to show how these "heavenly words" change ordinary bread and wine into the body and blood of Christ in the celebration of the Easter Eucharist.[354] Continuing, Ambrose asserts that the sacrament is so great that it is prefigured and then recites more of the prayer to provide examples from the Old Testament.[355]

Allegorical Interpretation of the Text. Craddock defines an allegory as "a literary form by which one says something other than what one seems to be saying. To allegorize is to find a message behind the generally understood meaning of the words and phrases. By this means a text is cut loose from its moorings of time, place, and historical

---

[351] Craddock, *Preaching*, 136f.
[352] Ibid., 138.
[353] *De sacramentis*, 4.5.21–23; 6.26–27 (SC 25bis.114, 116).
[354] Ibid., 4.5.21–23 (SC 25bis.114).
[355] Ibid., 4.6.26–27 (SC 25bis.116).

circumstance and given a timeless, spiritual meaning."[356] Ambrose asserts that the promises that the candidates make during the renunciation are kept in heaven and not on earth.[357] One way that Ambrose proves that the neophytes' word "is not kept in the tomb of the dead but in the book of the living"[358] is by using a series of liturgical allegories to prove that the bishop and priests are angels. The priests are angels, first, because they are ministers of Christ; the neophytes know this because they have seen them ministering at the altar. Second, since the baptistry is the place where the heavenly mysteries are received, then Christ is present here. If Christ is present, angels must be stationed here as well. Heaven is the realm of angels. Thus, if the angels are present where the candidates renounce the devil, the candidates' answers are kept not on earth but in heaven.

Typological Interpretation of the Text. Craddock defines typology as "a way of addressing present listeners with an ancient text by discerning in that text events or conditions having clear correspondence to those of the listeners."[359] In his commentary on the first immersion, Ambrose argues that baptism is a type of death in part because the font is a type of tomb.[360] Ambrose reminds his hearers that the baptismal font looks somewhat like a tomb.[361] He argues further that the font is a type of grave, because when the neophytes were in the font, they were buried with water, which is of the earth and therefore satisfies the death sentence, "You are dust and to dust you shall return."[362] It therefore follows that, if the candidates are baptized in a type of tomb, baptism must be a type of death.

Interpretation of the Intent of the Text. This interpretive method seeks to authorize the sermon not by the content of the text but by its intent.[363] Ambrose's argument for retaining footwashing as a part of baptism rests on the fact that his understanding of the intent of the rite

---

[356] Craddock, *Preaching*, 138.
[357] *De sacramentis*, 1.2.6 (SC 25bis.62).
[358] *De mysteriis*, 2.5 (SC 25bis.158).
[359] Craddock, *Preaching*, 141.
[360] Ibid., 3.1.1 (SC 25bis.90).
[361] Ibid.
[362] Ibid., 2.6.19 (SC 25bis.84).
[363] Craddock, *Preaching*, 143.

differs from those who want to see it removed. Ambrose asserts that there are some who argue that footwashing ought not to be done as a sacrament, not at baptism, but as an act of humility. He then asserts that footwashing is a sacrament, and its intent is sanctification. He makes his point by arguing from the biblical account of Jesus washing the disciples' feet, which was read as part of the rite, where Jesus says, "Unless I wash your feet, you shall have no part with me."[364] Thus, Ambrose reasons, while footwashing is indeed an act of humility, the intent of the rite of footwashing is that those whose feet are washed will be sanctified.

Thematic Interpretation. By thematic interpretation we mean interpreting the text in light of major themes of the Bible or of the Christian faith.[365] We have previously noted that Ambrose explains the *ephphatha* in two ways. First, it is the opening of the faculties to understand the questions and answers in the renunciations that follow. Second, its purpose is to facilitate the fruitful reception of the sacraments.[366] Both Whitaker and Yarnold connect the opening with exorcism and conclude that Ambrose lost sight of the rite's original meaning.[367] We have previously shown that Ambrose understood the rites as God's means of giving faith.[368] Thus, rather than losing sight of this rite's original meaning, Ambrose, who downplayed the scrutinies in his description of Lenten preparation while emphasizing instruction, and who described the handing on of the Creed to the *competentes* while omitting a description of the *competentes*' handing the Creed back, chose to reinterpret this rite according to an understanding of the process of initiation as the means by which the *competentes* receive the faith. Ambrose says, "*Ephphatha*, that is, be opened, to an odor of sweetness." Could this "odor of sweetness" be Christ or the sacraments? Inasmuch as Ambrose's emphasis is on the *competentes* receiving Christ rather than driving out of the demonic, an understanding of *ephphatha* as opening the *competentes* to God rather than as exorcism is logical.

Botte supports this hypothesis. For him, the *ephphatha* shows that baptism is a supernatural gift because the candidates' mouths have to

---

[364] *De sacramentis*, 3.1.5 (SC 25bis.94).

[365] Craddock, *Preaching*, 145.

[366] *De mysteriis* 1.3 (SC 25bis.156); *De sacramentis* 1.1.2 (SC 25bis.60).

[367] Whitaker, *Documents of the Baptismal Liturgy*, 43–44; Yarnold, *The Awe-Inspiring Rites of Initiation*, 18.

[368] Above, 188–190.

be opened so that they can respond to the bishop, that is to say, in order to renounce the devil and confess their faith. For Botte, the *ephphatha* thereby indicates that baptism is God's gift of new life because the candidates cannot renounce the devil apart from God's grace. Similarly, the candidates' nostrils must be opened so that they can breathe the good scent of eternal life.[369]

In this same way, Ambrose understands the prebaptismal anointing as giving strength rather than as an exorcism. In comparing this anointing to that of the athlete, Ambrose speaks of the *competentes* as Christ's athletes "about to wrestle in the fight of the world."[370] According to Ambrose, this anointing constituted a strengthening of the candidates for the struggle with the devil to follow: "He who wrestles has something to hope for; where the contest is, there is the crown." Though Ambrose does not mention exorcism in connection with this rite, McDonnell describes this anointing as being preparatory and having "the character of purgation/exorcism: the oil cleanses from the traces of sin and chases away the invisible powers of Satan."[371] This description is not in keeping with Ambrose's explanation, which emphasizes strengthening rather than the removal of sin and evil. Once again, Ambrose interprets an individual rite according to his understanding of the overall theme of baptism.

Interpretation by Translation of the Text. This method seeks to interpret by freeing the text to speak to the listener by removing the barriers that are due to difficulties with language. The task in this approach is not to transform, explain, or apply the text, but to release the text upon the listener's ear by translating it into the language of the listener. In this way the text will speak for itself.[372] An obvious example of Ambrose interpreting by translations is his treatment of the *ephphatha*.[373] He explains that *ephphatha* is a Hebrew word, which rendered into Latin is *adaperire*, that is "be opened." With this translation it becomes clear that the reason the bishop touched the ears of neophytes was so that they might be opened. Ambrose then explains that they are opened to the word and to the homily of the bishop.

---

[369] Botte, *Des Sacrements; Des Mystères*, p. 35.
[370] *De sacramentis*, 1.1.4 (SC 25bis.62).
[371] McDonnell, *Christian Initiation and Baptism in the Holy Spirit*, 267.
[372] Craddock, *Preaching*, 147–148.
[373] *De sacramentis*, 1.1.2 (SC 25bis.60).

REFLECTION:
THE PNEUMATIC DIMENSION OF THE RITES

To reflect upon the pneumatic dimension of the rites of Christian initiation is to ask how God acts in and through these rites. For Ambrose, the liturgy of initiation is God's means of making us participants in the mystery of salvation. Through the rites of initiation Christians enter into the different dimensions of the saving activity of Christ, hoped for in the Old Testament, accomplished once and for all in Jesus' suffering, death and resurrection, and awaiting complete fulfillment in Christ's return. Ambrose sees the life, death and resurrection of Christ contained in the sacraments of the Church, which are the means by which we participate in Christ's saving work in the time in which we live—the interval between Christ's resurrection and his return. In and through the rites of initiation God brings the candidate face to face with "the drama of the whole Christ, active in himself and in history, the Christ of the *OT*, the Messiah, Jesus of Nazareth in His life, death, and resurrection, the glorified Lord, Christ united here and now"[374] with the candidates in their own conversion, their *metanoia*, their transformation from not seeing to seeing, from unbelief to faith. For it is by the very words of Christ that one baptizes.[375] When the bishop invokes the Father, calls for the coming of the Son and Holy Spirit, when he uses the very words of Christ, the Holy Spirit acts.

For Ambrose, in this encounter the candidate both shares in Christ's death and, more than being brought back to life, receives new life. Thus baptism is womb as well as tomb, rebirth as well as resurrection.[376] In this same way, the bread and wine of the Eucharist are changed into the body and blood of Christ by the power of the word of Christ,[377] "which was able to make out of nothing that which was not" and is capable of "changing things which exist into that which they were not."[378] This transformation comes about through the words of Christ at the Last Supper recited by the priest[379] and can only be

---

[374] Mazza, *Mystagogy*, 41.

[375] *De sacramentis*, 2.4.14 (SC 25bis.80).

[376] Ledwich, "Baptism, Sacrament of the Cross: Looking Behind St. Ambrose," 201–202.

[377] *De sacramentis*, 4.4.14 (SC 25bis.108).

[378] *De mysteriis*, 9.51–52 (SC 25bis.184–186); cf. *De sacramentis*, 4.4.16 (SC 25bis.128).

[379] *De mysteriis*, 9.54 (SC 25bis.188); *De sacramentis*, 4.5.23 (SC 25bis.186–188).

perceived by faith. Through this gift Christians receive spiritual food by which Christ is sealed within them.[380] The benefits of the Eucharist include forgiveness of sins,[381] strengthening the soul,[382] and eternal life.[383] Thus Ambrose understands the rites as themselves embodying the mystery of salvation.

This sacramental encounter with Christ is profoundly interpersonal. Ambrose's use of quotations and images from the Song of Songs to celebrate the nuptial character of this encounter[384] demonstrates that God always takes the initiative. The Church is the bride of Christ washed clean in the waters of baptism, clothed in the garments of the resurrection, and anointed with the rich aroma of the Holy Spirit. When she is mature in her love, the Church is invited to a bridal banquet. The Eucharist is the full consummation of union bringing forth new growth.

All this belongs to the realm of invisible things and has no meaning apart from faith. It is necessary to perceive the spiritual realities beyond sensible appearances. Water does not have in itself magic virtue. It must be impregnated by the Spirit, sanctified by Christ, who went down into it at the time of his baptism. The cross of Christ must be plunged into it, so that the Trinity might be present. But this presence, once manifested through signs, today is perceptible only through faith. For Ambrose, the mystagogical task is to reveal the pneumatic dimension of the rites of initiation; that is, to show how the mystery of God's saving activity in Christ is contained in the liturgical action. Whether he is employing biblical, cultural, or natural symbolism, and regardless of whether his subject matter is the activity of the Spirit occurring within the candidate or the transcendental or eschatological repercussions of the rites of initiation, Ambrose's message is that Christ encounters the neophytes here and now and, through the mystery of his life, death, and resurrection, joins them to the full scope of salvation history as it is understood in the Scriptures. Exploring the inseparable union of biblical narrative and the rites of initiation as it is expressed in *De sacramentis* is the subject to which we now turn.

---

[380] *De mysteriis*, 9.55 (SC 25bis.188).
[381] *De sacramentis*, 4.6.28 (SC 25bis.116).
[382] *De mysteriis*, 9.55 (SC 25bis.188).
[383] *De sacramentis*, 4.5.24 (SC 25bis.116).
[384] Ibid., 5.2.5–11 (SC 25bis.122–124). See below, 268–269.

Chapter 6

"Gather from the holy scriptures": Interpreting the Rites

Concluding his first sermon to the newly baptized, Ambrose instructs his hearers that their ears must be attentive and their minds properly disposed so that they "can grasp what I am able to gather from the holy scriptures and offer to you."[1] In this chapter we join Ambrose in his study and attempt to discover, first, how and what he gathered from the Scriptures in order to interpret and illuminate the sacraments and, second, how he offered this interpretation and illumination to his hearers.

Much scholarship has been devoted to biblical interpretation in the early Church and Ambrose's approach to and use of Scripture.[2] Rather than attempting to cover this entire topic, we will limit our discussion

---

[1] *De sacramentis*, 1.6.24 (SC 25bis.72).
[2] Studies include Leslie W. Barnard, "To Allegorize or Not to Allegorize," *Studia Theologica* 36, no.1 (1982) 1–10; Mark E. Chapman, "Early Christian Mystagogy and the Formation of Modern Christians," *Currents in Theology and Mission* 21 (August 1994) 284–293; Jean Daniélou, *The Bible and the Liturgy* (Ann Arbor: Servant Books, 1979); David Dawson, *Allegorical Readers and Cultural Revision in Ancient Alexandria* (Berkeley: University of California Press, 1992); Yves-Marie Duval, "L'Ecriture au Service de la Catechese," in J. Fontaine and C. Pietri, *Le Monde Latin Antique et La Bible* (Paris: Beauchesne, 1985) 261–288; Mary Pierre Ellebracht, "Today This Word Has Been Fulfilled in Your Midst," *Worship* 60, no. 4 (July 1986) 347–361; Karifried Froelich, *Biblical Interpretation in the Early Church*, Sources of Early Christian Thought (Philadelphia: Fortress Press, 1984); Frederick Homes Dudden, *The Life and Times of St. Ambrose* (Oxford: Clarendon Press, 1935) 2:455–459; Pamela Jackson, "Ambrose of Milan as Mystagogue," *Augustinian Studies* 20 (1989) 93–107; Christoph Jacob, "Der Antitypos als Prinzip Ambrosianischer Allegorese: Zum Hermeneutischen Horizont der Typologie," in E. Livingstone, ed., *Studia Patristica* 25 (Louvain:

of scriptural interpretation to the three areas germane to our purpose of formulating a method of mystagogical preaching: the importance of Scripture, selecting the text, and methods of interpretation.[3]

In the first part of this chapter, we attempt to define the importance of Scripture to Ambrose's preaching on the sacraments by determining the place of Scripture in these sermons.

In the second section of this chapter, we explore how Ambrose selected his Scripture texts. Were they lectionary-based, related to the season or the sermon content, or a matter of personal choice?

Peeters, 1993) 107–114; August Jilek, "Symbol und Symbolisches Handeln in Sakramentlicher Liturgie: Ein Beitrag an Hand der Mystagogischen Katechesen," *Liturgisches Jahrbuch* 42, no. 1 (1992) 25–62; William Ledwich, "Baptism, Sacrament of the Cross: Looking Behind St. Ambrose," in *The Sacrifice of Praise: Studies on the Themes of Thanksgiving and Redemption in the Central Prayers of the Eucharistic and Baptismal Liturgies: In Honour of Arthur Herbert Couratin*, ed. Bryan Spinks (Rome: C.L.V. Edizioni Liturgiche, 1981); John Moorhead, *Ambrose: Church and Society in the Late Roman World* (London and New York: Longman, 1999); Gerard Nauroy, "L'Ecriture dans la Pastorale d'Ambroise de Milan," in *Le Monde Latin Antique et La Bible*, ed. J. Fontaine and C. Pietri (Paris: Beauchesne, 1985); Hughes Oliphant Old, *The Reading and Preaching of the Scriptures in the Worship of the Christian Church* (Grand Rapids: William B. Eerdmans, 1998) 2:320–324; Angelo Paredi, *Saint Ambrose: His Life and Times*, trans. M. Joseph Costelloe (Notre Dame: University of Notre Dame Press, 1964) 257–277; Domingo Ramos-Lisson, "Tipologia de Jn 9:6-7 en el De sacramentis," in G. Lazzati, ed., *Ambrosius Episcopus: atti del Congresso internazionale di studi ambrosiani nel XVI centenario della elevazione di sant'Ambrogio alla cattedra episcopale, Milano, 2–7 dicembre 1974* (Milan: Vita e pensiero, 1976) 2:336–344; Hervé Savon, *Saint Ambroise devant l'exégèse de Philon le juif* (Paris: Études Augustiniennes, 1977); idem, "Le Temps de l'exégèse allegorique dans la Catechese d'Ambroise de Milan," in *La Temps Chrétien de la fin de l'Antiquité au Moyen Age: IIIe–XIIIe siècles: Actes du Colloque, 9–12 mars, 1984* (Paris: Centre National de la Recherche Scientifique, 1984) 345–361; Samuel Edward Torvend, *The Typology of the Basilica Conflict Between Ambrose of Milan and the Imperial Court: A Study in the Use of Biblical 'Exempla' in Ambrosian Sermons Preached Between 385–386* (Ph.D. dissertation, Saint Louis University, 1990); Joseph W. Trigg, *Biblical Interpretation*, Message of the Fathers of the Church 9 (Wilmington, Del.: Michael Glazier, 1988); Frances M. Young, *The Art of Performance: Towards a Theology of Holy Scripture* (London: Darton, Longman & Todd, 1990); idem, *Biblical Exegesis and the Formation of Christian Culture* (Cambridge; New York: Cambridge University Press, 1997).

[3] Fred B. Craddock, *Preaching* (Nashville: Abingdon Press, 1985) 99–153.

In the third section of this chapter, we ask how Ambrose determined the meaning of the scriptural text or, more accurately, how he used Scripture to determine the meaning of the sacraments. In other words, what was Ambrose's exegetical method? In this section we will also explore how Ambrose incorporates Scripture into his preaching on the sacraments. We conclude this chapter with a reflection on the role of the Spirit in using Scripture to interpret the rites.

THE IMPORTANCE OF SCRIPTURE

One way of determining the importance of Scripture to preaching is by distinguishing between two types of sermons. In what we might call *thematic preaching*, sermon content is primarily derived from topics, issues, and occasions. In this kind of preaching, Scripture texts "serve much like background music or the national anthem at a public function."[4] They contribute to the atmosphere of the occasion and provide historical continuity. Alternatively, in what we might call *text-based preaching*, Scripture determines the subject of the sermon, its governing image, or its basic vocabulary.[5] In the case of his mystagogical preaching, Ambrose would disagree with this distinction because these sermons are both thematic and text-based.

We are justified in calling Ambrose's preaching to the newly baptized *thematic* in that the topic of these sermons is the sacraments, and this topic does not emerge directly from a scriptural text but is determined by an occasion—the instruction of the newly baptized on the meaning of the mysteries during the week after their initiation at the Easter Vigil. Ambrose himself declares that this is the case when he says, "I shall begin now to speak of the sacraments which you have received."[6] He is even more explicit in declaring that the content of mystagogy is determined by the occasion in *De mysteriis* where he writes: "Now the time has come to speak of the mysteries and to explain the very structure of the sacraments."[7] Thus the mysteries are the theme. Easter week is the occasion. The sacraments are explained; the rites rather than Scripture provide the framework and direction for these sermons.

---

[4] Ibid., 100.
[5] Ibid.
[6] *De sacramentis*, 1.1.1 (SC 25bis.60).
[7] *De mysteriis*, 1.2 (SC 25bis.156).

Nevertheless, Ambrose could not have fathomed the possibility of preaching in which Scripture was not an integral part. The bishop of Milan was essentially a scriptural preacher.[8] As we have said, recourse to Scripture is constant in his sermons.[9] For Ambrose, Scripture is "the spiritual home of the Christian, it constitutes [the Christian's] intellectual world."[10] He understood Scripture to be the source of all knowledge and wisdom, from which pagan philosophers, Pythagoras and Plato in particular, borrowed the best of their ideas.[11] Therefore, though he borrowed from philosophy, in Ambrose's mind the Bible was his sole authority, the true and indisputable source of his inspiration. Profoundly versed in Scripture, Ambrose found it natural to express his ideas in the language of the Bible. Regardless of the occasion—Sunday sermon, funeral oration, controversy with the Arians, or explaining the sacraments—his sermons, which are packed with scriptural quotations and allusions, are in many cases merely expositions on various portions of the Bible.

Thus we reiterate here what we said in Chapter 5, namely, that in Ambrose's mystagogy the rites are inseparable from Scripture.[12] *De sacramentis* and *De mysteriis* are text-based in that, far from incidental, Scripture is an integral part of Ambrose's mystagogy. Even a cursory review of *De sacramentis* and *De mysteriis* reveals that these works are loaded with scriptural quotations, images, and allusions.[13] Ambrose interprets the rites of Christian initiation almost exclusively in terms of scriptural stories, images, admonitions, and segments of psalms. Botte notes that we do not find in these works neat divisions or

---

[8] Above, 98.

[9] Ibid.

[10] Goulven Madec, *Saint Ambroise et la philosophie* (Paris: Études Augustiniennes, 1974) 245.

[11] Nauroy, "L'Ecriture dans la pastorale d'Ambroise de Milan," 381. For an examination of the claim that the Greeks got their best ideas and insights from Moses, see Young, *Biblical Exegesis and the Formation of Christian Culture*, 51–57; Arthur J. Droge, *Homer or Moses? Early Christian Interpretation of the History of Culture*, Hermeneutische Untersuchungen zur Theologie 26 (Tübingen: J.G.B. Mohr, 1989).

[12] Above, 185–186.

[13] For an index of the scriptural passages used in Ambrose's mystagogical works, see Bernard Botte, *Ambroise de Milan: Des Sacrements; Des Mystères: Explication du Symbole*, Sources Chrétiennes 25bis (Paris: Les Éditions du Cerf, 1980) 18–21.

learned definitions but a wealth of images.[14] "Ambrose intertwines passages of Scripture with the step-by-step flow of sacramental actions in such a way that the two become a single reality."[15] Ambrose's mystagogical preaching is, therefore, both thematic and text-based. It is thematic in that the sacraments and the occasion of their explanation determine the content, form, and direction of these sermons. Yet these sermons are text-based in that Scripture images, lessons, and passages provide the lenses used to interpret and explain the meaning of the sacraments.

SELECTING THE TEXT

How did Ambrose choose the particular passages of Scripture that he used to explain the rites of initiation? Selection of scriptural texts "ordinarily occurs in one of two ways: by the preacher or by following the lectionary."[16] For Ambrose, explaining Scripture is, above all, a liturgical act that follows a lectionary. For the majority of Christian people of the early Church, Scripture was oral expression, liturgical word. Scripture as a book was only available to a minority of intellectuals or bishops, such as Ambrose. Understanding Scripture was not a matter of individual meditation but of corporate prayer.

In Ambrose's mystagogical works, we find references to and explanations of the lessons that were read during the liturgy of which postbaptismal instruction was a part. Ambrose asks, "What was read yesterday?"[17] He speaks of "what you have just heard in the reading."[18] Ambrose also refers to what was read "the day before yesterday."[19] Botte and Hervé Petit have each compiled the indices of the scriptural lessons found in these works and compared them with the lessons found in the Milanese liturgy in order to show that the readings from Scripture cited in *De sacramentis* and *De mysteriis* are based on a lectionary.[20] Inasmuch as the documents of the Ambrosian

---

[14] Ibid., 33ff.

[15] Ellebracht, "Today This Word Has Been Fulfilled in Your Midst," 348.

[16] Craddock, *Preaching*, 101.

[17] *De sacramentis*, 2.2.3 (SC 25bis.74); cf. *De mysteriis*, 4.22 (SC 25bis.166).

[18] *De sacramentis*, 2.7.23 (SC 25bis.86). Cf. ibid., 3.2.8 (SC 25bis.96); *De mysteriis*, 7.42 (SC 25bis.178).

[19] *De sacramentis*, 6.2.9 (SC 25bis.140).

[20] Botte, *Des Sacrements; Des Mystères*, 30–31; Hervé Petit, "Sur les catéchèses postbaptismals de S. Ambroise," *Revue bénédictine* 68 (1958) 256–264.

Rite[21] that provide the lectionary are too far removed chronologically from Saint Ambrose to have escaped reworking, it is certainly not surprising that the cycle of readings found there is not identical with that of *De sacramentis* and *De mysteriis*. Nevertheless, the comparison is interesting, and one cannot find any liturgy more closely related to the cycle of readings attested to or supposed in Ambrose's mystagogical works than that of the church of Milan.

There are seven readings explicitly mentioned in *De sacramentis* and *De mysteriis*. Based on manuscript evidence, Petit and Botte conclude that the six sermons contained in *De sacramentis* were preached from Monday through Saturday.[22] The cure of the paralytic (John 5:1-10) was probably read Monday.[23] We find this pericope listed for the Tuesday of Easter week in the Ambrosian rite. According to *De sacramentis*, 2.7.23, Romans 6:3 was read the same day.[24] This reading is also found listed for the Tuesday of Easter week in the Milanese liturgy. There is a reference to a reading as being read "today" in *De sacramentis*, 3.2.8:[25] "The spiritual seal follows. You heard about this in the reading today."[26] Although this reference is not very clear, we are probably not dealing with Isaiah 11:3, where there is nothing to suggest the idea of "seal" (*signaculum*). Rather, the text referred to is most likely 2 Corinthians 1:21-22, which is mentioned as a reading in *De mysteriis*, 7.42.[27] In the Milanese liturgy we do not find evidence of either this reading or of 2 Corinthians 12:4-6, mentioned in *De sacramentis*, 6.2.9 as having been read "the day before yesterday."[28] *De mysteriis*, 3.16[29] states that 2 Kings 5:1-14, which is discussed in *De sacramentis*, 1.9.13-14[30] and, according to the Milanese rite, is read on the Tuesday of Easter week,

---

[21] The readings for the *Missa pro baptizatis* are found in Ratti and Magistretti, eds., *Missale ambrosianum* (Milan: R. Ghirlanda, 1913) 255–284, which also provides earlier witnesses, two of which come from the ninth century.

[22] Petit, "Sur les catéchèses postbaptismals de S. Ambroise," 256–264; Botte, *Des Sacrements; Des Mystères*, 210–211.

[23] *De sacramentis*, 2.2.3 (SC 25bis.74): *Quid lectum est heri?* ("What was read yesterday?").

[24] SC 25bis.86: *in lectione praesenti* ("in the lesson just read").

[25] Ibid., 96.

[26] *Sequitur spiritale signaculum quod audistis hodie legi.*

[27] SC 25bis.178.

[28] Ibid., 140: *ut lectum est nudiustertius.*

[29] Ibid., 164.

[30] Ibid., 66–68.

was a lesson read during this time of instruction. *De mysteriis*, 6.45[31] also states that the episode of Melchizedek in Genesis 14:14-18, which is explained in *De sacramentis*, 4.3.10[32] and is read on the Friday of Easter week according to the Ambrosian rite, was read as well. Finally John 13, which is read on the Saturday *in albis* in the Milanese rite, is mentioned in both *De mysteriis*, 6.31 and *De sacramentis*, 3.1.4 as being read immediately after baptism.[33]

In addition to the readings that are explicitly mentioned, others are presupposed. These are also found in the Milanese lectionary. The miracle of Elisha's floating axe-head (2 Kings 6:5-6), quoted in both *De sacramentis* and *De mysteriis*,[34] was read on Wednesday of Easter week in the Ambrosian rite. 1 Corinthians 10:1-4, also cited in *De sacramentis* and *De mysteriis*,[35] was also read on Wednesday. The Milanese rite states that on Thursday and Friday the Gospel was taken from extracts of the discourse on the bread of life, certain quotes from which are found in *De sacramentis*, 6.1.1, 2, 4 and *De mysteriis*, 8.47–48.[36]

We must not overemphasize the importance of these correspondences, because some of these texts contain catechetical themes that are not unique to Milan. Nevertheless, taking these correspondences in total is suggestive, particularly because other texts cited in Ambrose's mystagogical works, such as Genesis 14 and 2 Kings 6, are included in the readings for Easter week and yet do not have obvious catechetical themes; nothing particularly links these pericopes to either Easter or the sacraments. We can therefore conclude that during the time of Saint Ambrose there were texts assigned to the liturgies for the newly baptized during the week after Easter.

Along with the texts from the lectionary, throughout his mystagogical works, Ambrose interprets the rites of initiation using a vast amount of material drawn from Scripture. He uses specific verses to describe and explain the rites, as when he interprets the bishop

---

[31] Ibid., 180.

[32] Ibid., 106.

[33] Ibid., 172; 92.

[34] *De sacramentis*, 2.4.11; 4.4.18 (SC 25bis.78; 112); *De mysteriis*, 9.51 (SC 25bis.184).

[35] *De sacramentis*, 16.20; 5.1.3 (SC 25bis.70; 120); *De mysteriis*, 12.49, 58 (SC 25bis.182; 190).

[36] SC 25bis.138; 182.

touching the *competentes'* nostrils in the *ephphatha* by quoting 2 Corinthians 2:15.[37] In explaining that David prophesied about baptism in Psalm 51 and the Eucharist in Psalms 23, 34, and 104,[38] Ambrose shows that he understands the rites of initiation to have been prophesied in the Old Testament. The bishop of Milan draws upon scriptural types or figures to explain the mysteries. Baptism is prefigured in the creation of the world and in the flood.[39] He notes that Paul considered the crossing of the Red Sea a figure of baptism.[40] Ambrose also sees baptism prefigured in Moses' casting wood into the bitter waters of Marah,[41] in Naaman's cleansing in the Jordan,[42] in Elisha's axe-head, which rose from the water,[43] and in the healing of the paralytic in the pool of Beth-zatha.[44] Finally, Ambrose states that Jesus deliberately prefigured baptism in his healing of the man born blind.[45] Ambrose understands Melchizedek's bread and wine as figures of the Eucharist,[46] which was also prefigured in the manna in the wilderness.[47] Both the water that flowed from the rock[48] and the water that flowed from the side of Christ are figures of the water mixed with wine in the eucharistic cup.[49]

Ambrose's inclusion of these scriptural texts is in keeping with a well-established Christian tradition of using Scripture to explain the meaning of the sacraments. Much has been written concerning whether Ambrose is dependent directly or indirectly on Cyril of Jeru-

---

[37] *De sacramentis*, 1.1.3 (SC 25bis.60).

[38] Ibid., 4.2.6; 5.3.12 (SC 25bis.104; 124); *De mysteriis*, 7.34; 9.58 (SC 25bis.174; 190).

[39] *De sacramentis*, 1.1.3; 3.1.3; 3.2.9 (SC 25bis.60; 90; 96); *De mysteriis*, 3.9–11; 4.24–25 (SC 25bis.160; 168).

[40] *De sacramentis*, 1.4.12; 1.6.20; 2.6.19 (SC 25bis.66; 70; 84); *De mysteriis*, 2.12–13 (SC 25bis.162).

[41] *De sacramentis*, 2.4.12–13 (SC 25bis.80); *De mysteriis*, 2.14 (SC 25bis.162).

[42] *De sacramentis*, 1.3.9–5.15; 2.3.8 (SC 25bis.64–68; 78); *De mysteriis*, 5.16–18 (SC 25bis.164).

[43] *De sacramentis*, 2.4.11 (SC 25bis.78).

[44] Ibid., 2.2.3-7 (SC 25bis.74–78); *De mysteriis*, 4.22–24 (SC 25bis.166–168).

[45] *De sacramentis*, 3.2.11 (SC 25bis.98).

[46] Ibid., 4.3.10; 5.2.1 (SC 25bis.106; 124); *De mysteriis*, 8.45–46 (SC 25bis.180–182).

[47] *De sacramentis*, 4.5.25 (SC 25bis.116); *De mysteriis*, 8.47–49 (SC 25bis.182–184).

[48] Ibid., 8.48–49 (SC 25bis.182–184).

[49] *De sacramentis*, 5.1.3–4 (SC 25bis.120–122).

salem for his mystagogy.⁵⁰ If the *Mystagogical Catecheses* traditionally attributed to Cyril are, in fact, the work of his successor, John of Jerusalem, this would place them too late to have influenced Ambrose. In all likelihood, the *Mystagogical Catecheses* are, in fact, the work of Cyril, later used and expanded by John,⁵¹ and this work could have influenced Ambrose.

We have previously noted that Ambrose was a studious reader of and a borrower from Greek Christian theologians.⁵² Yarnold argues that Ambrose's mystagogical works demonstrate that he was familiar with Cyril's *Mystagogical Catecheses*.⁵³ On the other hand, Botte emphatically

---

⁵⁰ Literature on this subject includes Botte, *Des Sacrements; Des Mystères*, 36–40; Old, *The Reading and Preaching of the Scriptures in the Worship of the Christian Church*, 2:320; Edward J. Yarnold, "Did St. Ambrose Know the Mystagogical Catecheses of St. Cyril of Jerusalem?" *Studia Patristica* 12 (1975) 184–189; idem, "The Authorship of the Mystagogical Catecheses Attributed to Cyril of Jerusalem," *Heythrop Journal* 19 (1978) 143–161.

⁵¹ For a helpful summary of the arguments, see Kent J. Burreson, "The Anaphora of the Mystagogical Catecheses of Cyril of Jerusalem," in Paul F. Bradshaw, ed., *Essays on Early Eastern Eucharistic Prayers* (Collegeville, Minn.: The Liturgical Press, 1997) 131–133.

⁵² Above, 100–102.

⁵³ Yarnold cites the following similarities as evidence that Ambrose had read Cyril's *Mystagogical Catecheses:* (1) similarities in the comments on the Lord's Prayer given by Ambrose and Cyril; (2) the fact that both Ambrose and Cyril adopt the practice of instructing the neophytes about the meaning of the rites of initiation only after these sacraments have been received; (3) both authors have an emphatic belief in the transformation of the bread and wine into the body and blood of Christ; (4) both explain sacramental efficacy in terms of both epiclesis and consecration; (5) the form of renunciation in *De sacramentis* is much more like Cyril's than is generally supposed; (6) both authors make much use of the distinction between symbol and reality; (7) both speak of the baptistry as the "holy of holies"; (8) both speak of "regeneration" in connection with postbaptismal anointing; (9) both apply the language of contracts to the renunciation and adhesion; (10) both authors explain the significance of Christ's baptism in partly similar terms; (11) in both Cyril and Ambrose there is an almost medieval tenderness concerning the Passion; (12) both authors make use of the text 2 Corinthians 2:15; (13) similarity in explaining the meaning of the "anointing" of the ears; (14) both authors compare baptism to the crossing of the Red Sea and the drowning of the Egyptians with the drowning of sin; (15) Ambrose's insistence that the dove which descended on Jesus at his baptism was only an appearance might well be a correction of Cyril's statement

asserts that neither the overall outline nor aspects of style betray any dependence. Botte argues further that the similarity in explanation of baptism could in fact be coincidental. After all, Botte asks, is it astonishing that Cyril and Ambrose each discovered in Saint Paul that baptism is a death and resurrection with Christ?[54] Even if Ambrose may have borrowed from Cyril, this does not necessarily mean that he simply copied Cyril's ideas and presented them to his neophytes. There are instances when the explanations of the two mystagogues differ. For example, Botte notes that while Ambrose compares the prebaptismal anointing to the anointing of athletes, for Cyril it is a rite of exorcism.[55]

Thus it appears that if Ambrose was familiar with Cyril's sermons, rather than borrowing directly from them, he provided the Latin Church with his interpretation of Cyril's mystagogical catecheses. Defining mystagogy as "describing the specific rites of the given community in sequence, exegeted by means of material drawn from Scripture,"[56] Pamela Jackson argues that the ways in which Ambrose, Cyril of Jerusalem, and John Chrysostom use Scripture in their mystagogy are distinct from one another.[57] Jackson summarizes the situation this way:

"At first reading, the mystagogical preaching of Ambrose, Cyril of Jerusalem and John Chrysostom can leave a predominant impression of the similarities of their mystagogy, but this impression can be misleading. While these contemporary masters of the mystagogical genre did share common assumptions concerning its general purpose and

---

that the Spirit's descent on Jesus was "substantial"; (16) both authors say "for the third time" in connection with the three immersions when what they really mean is three times; (17) accepting the less well attested reading *"recto nomine"* instead of the usual *"et Romae"* in *De sacramentis,* 1.1.1 recalls *Mystagogical Catecheses,* 3.5. Yarnold, "Did St. Ambrose Know the Mystagogical Catecheses of St. Cyril of Jerusalem?" 184–189.

[54] Botte, *Des Sacrements; Des Mystères,* 37.

[55] Ibid. Cf. *De sacramentis,* 1.1.4 (SC 25bis.62); Cyril of Jerusalem, *Mystagogical Catecheses,* 2, 3 (SC 126.84–86).

[56] Jackson, "Ambrose of Milan as Mystagogue," 93.

[57] Ibid., 94. Cyril uses typological material to portray his listeners as identified with their scriptural forebears to such an extent that they almost seem to reenact certain events in salvation history. Chrysostom uses Scripture to present dazzling images of the redeemed life in order to arouse in his listeners overwhelming resolve of moral transformation that will enable them to live that life. See ibid., 94–96.

method as just described, each had his own distinctive techniques of using Scriptural material in mystagogy which were shaped both by his personal homiletic gifts and what he found most pastorally effective in his community."[58]

It is also important to note that the practice of using Scripture to "explain"[59] the sacraments was not invented in the fourth century but goes as far back as the New Testament Church. As early as the New Testament we find biblical typology used to explain the sacraments.[60] Baptism, for example, was described using the Old Testament rite of circumcision and various rites of purification that involved washing or sprinkling with blood.[61] The great flood in the days of Noah and the Red Sea are also used to illuminate baptism in the New Testament.[62] The Lord's Supper was interpreted in relation to Passover, the feeding with manna, the covenantal feast on the mountain, and the wedding feast in the Song of Songs.[63] Turning to the early Church, at the end of the second century, Tertullian generously employed typology in his treatise on baptism, and even before that it seems to have been the Church's practice to "read through the Old Testament types of our redemption in Christ at the long vigil service on the night before Easter. The stories of the Passover and the Exodus were prominent in these readings, as were other stories that were regarded as types of baptism."[64] Thus Botte argues that rather than concluding that Cyril invented mystagogical catechesis and that a link between Cyril and Ambrose indicates a direct borrowing on the latter's part, it is possible that both drew upon a common source.[65]

Botte's discussion of this common source or tradition is most helpful.[66] He suggests that the issue is not whether Ambrose copied his

---

[58] Ibid., 93–94.

[59] See above, 4 n. 9.

[60] Old, *The Reading and Preaching of the Scriptures in the Worship of the Christian Church*, 2:321.

[61] Colossians 2:11-17; Revelation 1:5-6.

[62] 1 Peter 3:20-21; 1 Corinthians 10:1-5.

[63] Matthew 26:17-29 and parallels; John 6:1-70; 1 Corinthians 11:25; John 2:1-11.

[64] Old, *The Reading and Preaching of the Scriptures in the Worship of the Christian Church*, 2:321.

[65] Botte, *Des Sacrements; Des Mystères*, 38.

[66] Ibid., 38–39.

sermons from others but where he obtained the material he utilized. To what extent is it original? What themes did he borrow from a tradition? Which ones did he discover himself and which ones did he transform? As we have seen, some themes have a biblical origin. Others, such as the connection between baptism and the cure of the paralytic at the pool of Beth-zatha, are self-evident. Still others, such as the relationship between baptism and the iron of the axe-head or the prayer of Elijah when he made fire rain from the sky, are not so obvious.

In order to distinguish between what comes from a tradition and what is original, Botte is correct that the history of each of these themes would have to be determined and Ambrose's interpretations compared with those of the exegetes he read, particularly with those of Origen, but also with the themes developed in the prayers over both the font and the bread and wine and then with the various systems of Lenten readings that candidates for baptism would have heard.[67] Such an undertaking is beyond the scope of this study;[68] our purpose is to acknowledge Botte's assertion that Ambrose was dependent on an oral tradition, traces of which are evident in both liturgical formulas and the choice of readings used in the Lenten and Easter liturgies. Ambrose not only received general principles from this tradition, namely, "what has been written was done so for the purpose of serving as an example,"[69] but the applications themselves were often suggested to him, if not imposed, by the tradition. While Ambrose undoubtedly gave this material his own personal stamp, we cannot look upon his mystagogical catechesis as a profoundly original work. Above all, it is a testimony to the great Christian tradition which, beginning with Christ and the apostles, continues in the Church.

---

[67] See H. Scheidt, *Die Taufwasserweihegebete* (Münster: Verlag der Aschendorffschen Verlagsbuchhandlung, 1935), especially the table, pp. 80–81, which compares the Old and New Testament types used in sixteen different baptismal rites; Per Lundberg, *La typologie baptismale dans l'ancienne Église* (Uppsala; A.-B. Lundequistska, 1942); Daniélou, *The Bible and the Liturgy*. The connections are particularly remarkable between the *De baptismo* of Tertullian, the *De Trinitate* of Didymus the Blind, and *De sacramentis*.

[68] Even if this kind of study was successfully undertaken, drawing conclusions about which types are part of a tradition and which are original to Ambrose would largely remain a matter of conjecture.

[69] 1 Corinthians 10:11.

One final word about Ambrose's selection of scriptural texts is in order. Although we possess a treatise based on Ambrose's sermons on Luke's Gospel and the bishop himself tells us that he delivered a number of sermons on the Pauline Epistles,[70] Ambrose generally took his subject matter from the Old Testament.[71] Like ancient commentators generally, Ambrose preferred to preach from the Old Testament, partly because the available commentaries on the Old Testament seemed to him better than those on the New,[72] partly because the Old Testament was more in need of popular interpretation,[73] and partly because the Old Testament afforded ample opportunities for the exercise of the art of allegorical exegesis.[74] Christ was always the key to typological interpretation; in dealing with the Old Testament, it was clear that everything needed to be transformed. Interpreting the New Testament was more difficult because it was less clear what should be interpreted typologically and what should be interpreted literally. Thus Ambrose may have included some of the Old Testament images and texts found in his mystagogical works because of his affinity for the Old Testament.

SCRIPTURE AND MYSTAGOGY

In this section we will explore how Ambrose went about bringing his personal interpretation to the assigned texts and scriptural tradition that surrounded instruction on the sacraments. We will first review the difficulties that confront us as we attempt to uncover Ambrose's exegetical method. Turning to *De sacramentis* and *De mysteriis*, we will then outline five methods employed by Ambrose to interpret Scripture in his mystagogical preaching. Finally, we will explore five ways that Ambrose incorporates Scripture into the content of his preaching on the sacraments.

---

[70] *Expositio evangelii secundum Lucam* (CCSL 14.1–400); *Epistola* 7 (Maur. 37).1 (CSEL 82/1.43–44).

[71] Ambrose's exegetical works formed from sermons based on Old Testament books include *Hexameron, De Cain et Abel, De Abraham, De fuga saeculi, De Iacob et vita beata, De Ioseph, De patriarchis, De Helia et ieiunio, De Nabuthae, De Tobia, De interpellatione Iob et David, Apologia prophetae David, Enarrationes in xii psalmos davidicos, Expositio in psalmum cxviii*. For a description of these works, see Boniface Ramsey, *Ambrose* (New York: Routledge, 1997) 56–59.

[72] *Epistola* 75 (Maur. 75).1 (CSEL 82/2.156).

[73] *Epistola* 7 (Maur. 37).1 (CSEL 82/1.43–44).

[74] See below, 230–234.

The Mystery of Scripture

Uncovering Ambrose's method of exegesis is difficult because, unlike the exegesis of Origen or Jerome, there is nothing systematic about how Ambrose determined the meaning of a passage of Scripture. For Ambrose, a given passage of Scripture might be applied to every pastoral situation and all the events of the spiritual life.[75] Nauroy gives as an example Ambrose's use of Canticles.[76] In *De Isaac vel anima*, Ambrose uses Canticles as a commentary on the love of Isaac and Rebecca described in Genesis 24:62-67.[77] In *Expositio in Psalmum cxviii*, this same book is used to explain the psalm; elsewhere, it is used both to encourage virginity and to praise the moral virtues of the young emperor Valentian II, who has just died tragically.[78] In *De sacramentis*, the bishop of Milan uses Canticles to describe Christ and the Church and to illustrate the blessings of the Eucharist.[79]

Yet, despite the fact that few books of Scripture influenced Ambrose's reflection on the Christian person, the history of salvation, and major themes of his spirituality as did Canticles, the bishop of Milan never wrote a complete and systematic commentary on this short book. The reason that he did not is simple. For Ambrose, exegesis is not a particular genre; it is the substance of all the literary genres required of the Christian pastor, a fundamental way of thinking necessary for every aspect of a bishop's ministry. Thus it is not surprising that Ambrose finds Canticles applicable to all the speeches of a bishop. For the bishop of Milan, interpreting Scripture therefore cannot be confined to a single literary category but involves every genre of pastoral writing and speech.

The reason that Ambrose could not confine his use of Scripture to a single literary category but applied the same passage to a variety of pastoral situations is that he viewed Scripture as a mystery. Borrowing from Origen, he uses the image of the well to describe the enigmatic nature of the word of God.[80] The well cleared by Isaac[81] and the well of

---

[75] Nauroy, "L'Ecriture dans la pastorale d'Ambroise de Milan," 377.

[76] Ibid., 379.

[77] *De Isaac vel anima*, 3.8-10 (CSEL 32/1.647–650).

[78] See *Expositio in psalmum cxviii* (CSEL 62); *De virginibus*, 6.33–16.98 (Cazzaniga, 15–46); *De obitu Valentiniani*, 5–9, 58–77 (CSEL 73.332–334, 357–365).

[79] *De sacramentis*, 2.2.5–7; 5.2.5–11, 3.14–17 (SC 25bis.76; 120–124, 126–128).

[80] Nauroy, "L'Ecriture dans la pastorale d'Ambroise de Milan," 384–385.

[81] Cf. Genesis 26:19f.

Sychar, where Jesus asked a drink from the Samaritan woman,[82] are for Ambrose figures of *profundae altitudo doctrinae*, a depth of profound instruction.[83] In his letter to the church of Vercelli, Ambrose describes the Old Testament as "a deep and obscure well, from where one can draw water only with sorrow."[84]

For Ambrose, understanding Scripture as a mystery means that a passage of Scripture cannot be reduced to a single meaning. Ambrose compares Scripture with the sea, "which conceals within it profound meanings and the mysterious depths of the prophets."[85] Into this sea many diverse rivers have entered. Thus the bishop of Milan is free to admit his embarrassment, his perplexity, or his hesitation when interpreting the mystery of Scripture. In Ambrose's works we may encounter at any exegetical turn expressions such as "What does that mean?" and "I think that it is not far from the truth if we adopt the following interpretation."[86] More often Ambrose reassures his listeners or his reader that he has solved a difficulty in interpretation.[87] Ambrose does not gloss over the variants, contradictions, and difficult, even ridiculous sayings that abound in the Bible. He does not even attempt to overcome them by resorting to a single, unifying answer. Instead, he often adopts a kind of "explanatory pluralism,"[88] which allows the reader the freedom to choose from among alternative interpretations or even to retain two or three.[89] While we would be embarrassed by the uncertainty of interpretation brought about by a plurality of

---

[82] John 4:6-12.

[83] *De Isaac vel anima*, 4.21 (CSEL 32/1.656).

[84] *Epistola* 14 (Maur., 63).78 (CSEL 83/3.276). *Vetus scriptura quasi putcus profunda et obscurior, unde cum labore bauries.*

[85] *Epistola*, 36 (Maur. 2).3 (CSEL 82/2.4–5).

[86] See, for example, *De Iacob et vita bona*, 2.6.27 (CSEL 32/2.47): *Quid istud sibi uult?*; *De Ioseph*, 10.58 (CSEL 32/2.110): *puto autem quod a vero non sit alienum, si illud intellegamus.* See Nauroy, "L'Ecriture dans la pastorale d'Ambroise de Milan," 385, n. 53.

[87] See, for example, *De Abraham*, 1.7.60 (CSEL 32/1.541); *De Isaac vel anima*, 4.25, 26 (CSEL 32/1.658, 659); *De Ioseph*, 7.39 (CSEL 32/2.100). See Nauroy, "L'Ecriture dans la pastorale d'Ambroise de Milan," 385, n. 54.

[88] Savon, *Saint Ambroise devant l'exégèse de Philon le juif*, 1:303; Nauroy, "L'Ecriture dans la pastorale d'Ambroise de Milan," 385.

[89] See, for example, *De Cain et Abel*, 1.5.19 (CSEL 32/1.356); *De Isaac vel anima*, 4.15 (CSEL 32/1.653): *De fuga saeculi*, 4.23–24 (CSEL 32/2.183). See Nauroy, "L'Ecriture dans la pastorale d'Ambroise de Milan," 385, n. 56.

possible meanings, Ambrose, understanding that the word of God is a mystery, knows that one can find hidden within a passage of Scripture several equally valid interpretations.

Specifically, Ambrose distinguishes a threefold meaning in the text of Scripture. "All divine Scripture," Ambrose writes, "is either natural or mystical or moral."[90] For him, as for the other Church Fathers, along with the historical value of the biblical narratives, along with the moral lesson one can draw from them, there exists in Scripture a symbolic meaning. "Corresponding with the threefold meaning was a threefold interpretation—the literal which expounded the simple, evident import of the passage, the moral which drew out its practical teaching for the regulation of conduct, and the mystical or spiritual which brought to light the latent references to Christ, Christ's Kingdom, and the mysteries of the Christian faith."[91]

The mystical sense of Scripture assumes that the Scriptures were composed through the Spirit of God and therefore not only have the meaning that is obvious but also another meaning that is hidden from the majority of readers. The contents of Scriptures are the outward forms of certain mysteries and images of divine things. This spiritual meaning unites Scripture as testimony to the revelation of God in Christ. The unity of the Bible and its witness to Christ furnished the assumption underlying how Scripture was "received" by readers and hearers in the "public" assembly of the community.[92]

While Ambrose took pains to elucidate the literal meaning, the investigation of "the moral and the mystical or divine wisdom"[93] is

---

[90] *Enarrationes in xii psalmos davidicos*, 36.1,2 (CSEL 64.70–71): *Omnis scriptura divina vel naturalis, vel mystica, vel moralis est*. Origen also distinguishes a threefold meaning of Scripture. See Origen, *On First Principles*, trans. G. W. Butterworth (London: S.P.C.K., 1936), 4.2.4. For Origen, Scripture has a body, a soul, and a spirit. These correspond to the corporeal sense for history, psychical sense for morality, and spiritual sense for allegory. See Henri De Lubac, S.J., *Medieval Exegesis: The Four Senses of Scripture*, trans. Mark Sebanc (Grand Rapids: William B. Eerdmans, 1998) 1:142–150. Of particular interest on the subject of Origen's approach to the exegesis of Scripture is the study of Karen Jo Torjesen, *Hermeneutical Practices and Theological Method in Origen's Exegesis* (Berlin and New York: Walter de Gruyter, 1986).

[91] Homes Dudden, *The Life and Times of St. Ambrose*, 2:457–458.

[92] On the inspiration of Scripture and the proper mode of its interpretation, see Young, *Biblical Exegesis and the Formation of Christian Culture*, 19–24.

[93] *Epistola* 2 (Maur. 65).7 (CSEL 82/1.17).

what really interested him. He described the moral and mystical interpretations as both the two eyes with which Christ is seen[94] and the two kinds of nutrition by which the inner life is sustained—the former sweet and soothing, the latter strong meat, strengthening the human heart.[95] Ambrose considered both modes of interpretation necessary, but he deemed the mystical to be more valuable. Comparing them with the sisters of Bethany, he did not hesitate to exalt the mystical Mary above the moral and practical Martha.[96]

The neophytes did not yet know the mystical meaning of Scripture. They had heard the biblical narratives as part of their Lenten instruction, but up to this point only the moral teachings had been explained to them.[97] Frances Young argues that the Creed provided the hermeneutic key to discerning the mystical sense by articulating the unity necessary for a Christian reading of Scripture.[98] Now that the neophytes are fully initiated, Ambrose teaches them to use this key to unlock the mystical sense. As we have said, Ambrose transmits the truth of Scripture gradually, according to a spiritual hierarchy that corresponds to the stages of Christian initiation.[99]

Thus Botte argues that the "mysteries" referred to in the title *De mysteriis* are not the rites but the mysteries of Scripture that will be used to give the explanation of the sacred rites *(rationem sacramentorum)*.[100] "See the mystical sense," Ambrose tells his hearers.[101] By this, he is inviting the neophytes to learn that the facts of the Old Testament are, in relation to the New Testament, type, figure, and shadow. The

---

[94] *Expositio in Psalmum cxviii*, 11.7; 16.20 (CSEL 62.236–237; 363).

[95] Ibid., 13.23; 17.19 (CSEL 62.387).

[96] *Enarrationes in xii psalmos davidicos*, 1.42 (CSEL 64.35–36).

[97] See above, 149–151.

[98] The Creed taught Christians the proper way to receive Scripture: "the proper reading of the beginning and the ending, the focus of the plot, and the relations of the principle characters, so enabling the 'middle' to be heard in bits as meaningful." The Creed articulated the essential hermeneutic key without which texts and community would disintegrate into incoherence. This hermeneutic key provided the "closure" to Scripture, something contemporary theory prefers to leave open. Young, *Biblical Exegesis and the Formation of Christian Culture*, 21. Cf. idem, *The Art of Performance*, 49ff.

[99] Nauroy, "L'Ecriture dans la pastorale d'Ambroise de Milan," 380. Cf. above, 115.

[100] Botte, *Des Sacrements; Des Mystères*, 33; *De mysteriis*, 1.1 (SC 25bis.156).

[101] *De sacramentis*, 2.2.6 (SC 25bis.76).

patterns of the institution of the Christian sacraments pre-exist in Old Testament symbolism, which reveals divine thought. Thus the Christian sacraments are not only more divine but older than those of the Jews.[102] Baptism, for example, was planned in advance, at the very beginning of the world, by the Spirit who moved over the waters and cooperated in creation and who still descends upon it to render it fruitful and produce new life. The waters that gave birth to fish now give a new birth and regeneration.[103] The flood, in which the sinner was swallowed up while the righteous emerged safe and sound, is also a figure of baptism where sin is drowned. The raven that does not return to the ark is another image of sin abolished.[104] The passage through the Red Sea, where the Egyptians died while the Hebrews escaped, symbolizes the passage through the waters of baptism from sin to life, from fault to grace, from stain to sanctity.[105] The spring of Marah, whose bitterness Moses removed by plunging wood into it, is the baptismal font, where the bishop's prayer plunges the cross of Christ in order to give the water the power to forgive sins.[106] The purification of Naaman the leper in the waters of the Jordan is the image of what is produced by baptism, the cure from vice.[107] The iron axe that rose to the surface of the water when Elisha plunged the wooden handle into it prefigures the transformation of the Christian who was heavy like iron and has become as light as the wood of a fruit tree.[108] From the image of Aaron's rod that bloomed the neophytes learn that though they were dried up by sin, when they were plunged into the font, they began to bloom again and to bear fruit.[109] Jesus' curing the paralytic at the pool of Beth-zatha is also a figure of baptism. The angel for whom the sick wait is the angel of good counsel; the

---

[102] Ibid., 1.4.11; 4.3.8–11 (SC 25bis.66; 106–108).

[103] Ibid., 3.1.3 (SC 25bis.90–92); *De mysteriis*, 3.9 (SC 25bis.160).

[104] *De sacramentis*, 2.1.1(SC 25bis.60); *De mysteriis*, 3.10 (SC 25bis.160).

[105] *De sacramentis*, 1.6.20–22 (SC 25bis.68–70); 4.4.18 (SC 25bis.112); *De mysteriis*, 3.12, 13 (SC 25bis.162); 9.51 (SC 25bis.184–186).

[106] *De sacramentis*, 2.4.12; 4.4.18 (SC 25bis.80; 112); *De mysteriis*, 3.14; 9.51 (SC 25bis.162; 184–186).

[107] *De sacramentis*, 1.3.9, 5.13–14; 2.3.8 (SC 25bis.64, 66–68; 78); *De mysteriis*, 3.16-17; 4.21(SC 25bis.164; 166).

[108] *De sacramentis*, 2.4.11; 4.4.18 (SC 25bis.78–80; 112); *De mysteriis*, 9.51 (SC 25bis.184–186).

[109] *De sacramentis*, 4.1.2 (SC 25bis.102).

man whom the paralytic waits for to carry him is Christ Jesus.[110] The cure of the man born blind is also another figure, which shows that in baptism God gives the eyes of faith.[111]

In this section we have seen how Ambrose, understanding Scripture as a mystery, is able to find hidden within a passage of Scripture several equally valid interpretations applicable to a variety of pastoral situations. Opening the neophytes' eyes to the Scripture as a mystery was an important part of Ambrose's mystagogy. We now turn to the methods that the bishop of Milan used to discover this mystical meaning of Scripture.

Methods of Interpretation

Although he was convinced that Scripture is a mystery containing a wealth of meanings, Ambrose was also confident that one can discover the truth of Scripture through serious study.[112] Yet, precisely because he viewed Scripture as a mystery, Ambrose could not confine his study to a single method of interpretation. In this section we will outline five methods that Ambrose uses to interpret Scripture in his mystagogical works. These methods are: (1) typology, (2) allegory, (3) construction of intricate chains of reasoning, (4) interpretation by translation, and (5) direct and uncritical transfer of the text. After describing each method, we will illustrate how Ambrose employs it, using examples from *De sacramentis* and *De mysteriis*. We will postpone our discussion of the values of these methods for interpreting Scripture today until Chapter 9.[113]

Typology. In order to explain the ritual or theological aspects of the rites of initiation, Ambrose uses biblical *figurae*.[114] His presupposition

---

[110] Ibid., 2.2.3–7 (SC 25bis.74–76); *De mysteriis*, 4.22–24 (SC 25bis.166–168).

[111] *De sacramentis*, 3.2.11–14 (SC 25bis.98–100).

[112] *Expositio evangelii secundum Lucam*, 7.189 (CCSL 14.280).

[113] Below, 332–336.

[114] In the following discussion I am indebted especially to Daniélou, *The Bible and the Liturgy*, 4ff.; Jackson, "Ambrose of Milan as Mystagogue," 100–103; Enrico Mazza, *Mystagogy: A Theology of Liturgy in the Patristic Age*, trans. Matthew J. O'Connell (New York: Pueblo, 1989) 25–26; Hugh Riley, *Christian Initiation: An Comparative Study of the Interpretation of the Baptismal Liturgy in the Mystagogical Writings of Cyril of Jerusalem, John Chrysostom, Theodore of Mopsuestia, and Ambrose of Milan* (Washington: Catholic University of America

is that inasmuch as the rites of initiation are a re-enactment of salvation history,[115] the realities of the Old Testament are figures of both Jesus' actions in the New Testament and the sacraments of the Church. Jean Daniélou calls this "science of the similitudes between the two Testaments" *typology*.[116] Types contribute to the prophetic understanding of Scripture by showing how past narratives point to present fulfillment, or present instances are prophetic reality. In this way types relate to the Christian sense of a providential history leading to the fulfillment of God's kingdom.

The foundation of typology as a method of interpreting Scripture was laid in the Old Testament, when, during the Babylonian Captivity, the prophets proclaimed to the people of Israel that in the future God would perform for their benefit deeds analogous to, and even greater than, those that God performed in the past: a new flood, in which the sinful world would be annihilated and a faithful "remnant" preserved to inaugurate a new humanity; a new exodus, in which God would act powerfully to set humanity free from bondage to idols; and a new

---

Press, 1974) 38–52; Young, *Biblical Exegesis and the Formation of Christian Culture*, 152–154.

[115] See above, 195–197.

[116] Daniélou, *The Bible and the Liturgy*, 4. Typology is a modern construct. Whereas modern readers differentiate between "historical" events that foreshadow later ones (typology) and textual elements that are taken as referring to other, usually spiritual realities (allegory), ancient exegetes did not distinguish between typology and allegory. In patristic texts it is often difficult to make the distinction, the one shading into the other all too easily. Allegory was often required to turn a scriptural oracle into a prophecy; allegory was also required to make a type prophetic in its various respects. What the patristic texts describe as a *type* is a mimetic, imitative or representational "impress" or figure in the narrative or action described. In patristic texts the word "type" may be used for any "model" or "pattern" or "parable" foreshadowing its fulfillment, whether an event or a ritual. Thus the modern distinction of typology as distinct from allegory, an affirmation that requires the historical reality of an event as a foreshadowing of another event, its "antitype," is born of historical consciousness and has no basis in the patristic material. Nevertheless, typology is a useful term for discerning and describing an interpretive device whereby texts are shaped or read, consciously or unconsciously, so that they are invested with meaning by correspondence with other texts of a representational kind. See Young, *Biblical Exegesis and the Formation of Christian Culture*, 152–154, 193, esp. n. 20.

paradise, into which God would introduce the people God had redeemed.[117] The New Testament shows that these events are fulfilled in the person of Jesus of Nazareth. Jesus is the new Adam with whom the time of the paradise of the future has begun.[118] In Jesus that destruction of the sinful world of which the flood is the figure is already realized. Jesus accomplished the true exodus, which delivered the people of God from the power of the devil.[119] Typology was used in the preaching of the apostles to show that Christ continues and goes beyond the Old Testament in order to establish the truth of their message. Thus Paul writes: "These things happened to them to serve as an example, and they were written down to instruct us."[120]

Yet, the typology of the Old Testament is not only accomplished in the person of Jesus; it finds fulfillment in the Church as well. Consequently, in addition to christological typology or figures that point to Christ, the Old Testament also contains sacramental typology or figures that are fulfilled in the Church's sacraments. We find this sacramental typology in the New Testament, where manna is presented as a figure of the Eucharist[121] and both the crossing of the Red Sea and the flood are understood as figures of baptism.[122] This biblical typology shows how the sacraments carry on in our midst the great works of God found in the Old and New Testaments. "For example, the Flood, the Passion and Baptism show us the same divine activity as carried out in three different eras of sacred history, and these three phases of God's action are all ordered to the Judgment at the end of time."[123]

Ambrose sees the events that comprise the history of salvation, including the rites of initiation, as objectively bound together to form a coherent whole. "There is a movement from lesser to the greater, from sketch to full reality, terminating finally in the revelation proper to the eschaton. As a result the various stages in the history of salvation refer to one another and are mirrored each in the others."[124] Ambrose can

---

[117] Ibid., 4–5; Riley, *Christian Initiation*, 39.
[118] Romans 5:16.
[119] Daniélou, *The Bible and the Liturgy*, 5.
[120] 1 Corinthians 10:11.
[121] John 6:31-49.
[122] 1 Corinthians 10:1-2; 1 Peter 3:19.
[123] Daniélou, *The Bible and the Liturgy*, 5.
[124] Mazza, *Mystagogy*, 25–26.

apply the characteristics and attributes of one reality or event to another that corresponds to it because the two events constitute the single reality of God's saving work. Thus the dove sent forth from the ark not only points to the Holy Spirit who descended upon the person of Jesus at his baptism, but that dove is actually a beginning revelation of the presence of the Holy Spirit in the life of the members of the Church.[125] Inasmuch as the entire mystery of salvation is climaxed in the death and resurrection of Jesus, the blood and water that flowed from his pierced side become the sacrament of the whole Church.[126]

Conversely, Ambrose uses typology to show that ritual actions of Christian initiation contain the mystery that resides in the historical actions of Jesus and that participating in the rites is the way that we share in those historical actions. Thus, in explaining the *ephphatha*, Ambrose says explicitly that this ritual, which the newly baptized experienced on the eve of their initiation, is the same mystery that Christ performed when he cured the man who was deaf and unable to speak.[127] Ambrose can therefore exhort the neophytes to be like that man whom Jesus cured, saying, "Open your ears and take in the good odor of eternal life that has been breathed into you during the ritual actions of the sacraments."[128] In this same way, Ambrose uses typology to explain that the washing of the neophytes' feet by the bishop is the means by which they share in Christ's washing the feet of the disciples.[129]

The sacraments are therefore to be understood as the expression of constant modes of divine action, and the form of the sacraments provides the symbolism by which the meaning of this divine action is to be understood.[130] For Ambrose, "'the invisible things of God are understood by way of the things that have been made. God's eternal power and also his divinity'[131] are known through God's works."[132] Thus it is appropriate, in explaining Christian baptism, to examine the figurative "baptisms of the Jews," such as the flood, because "the mere figure helps us, since it is the herald of reality."[133]

---

[125] *De mysteriis*, 4.24 (SC 25bis.168).
[126] *De sacramentis*, 5.1.4 (SC 25bis.122).
[127] Ibid., 1.1.2 (SC 25bis.60); cf. Mark 7:34.
[128] *De mysteriis*, 1.3 (SC 25bis.156).
[129] *De sacramentis*, 3.1.4–7 (SC 25bis.92–96); cf. John 13:9-10.
[130] Daniélou, *The Bible and the Liturgy*, 7.
[131] Romans 1:20.
[132] *De mysteriis*, 3.8 (SC 25bis.158–160).
[133] *De sacramentis*, 2.1.2 (SC 25bis.74).

By studying the *figurae* one can discern the pattern of how God acts and perceive that baptism and the Eucharist fit this particular pattern and therefore are a continuation of God's work of salvation. Ambrose understands Jesus himself as intending the rites to be understood through this kind of interpretation of Scripture. He speaks of Jesus giving the pattern of baptism in his own baptism and of wishing to prefigure the mystery of baptism in his healing of the man born blind.[134] Biblical typology, therefore, reveals that the event of Christ's life, death, and resurrection is contained in the sacraments of the Church, which are God's means of salvation in the interval that exists between Christ's ascension and his return.[135]

Consequently, in explaining baptism, Ambrose concludes his treatment of the flood: "Is not this flood baptism, by which all sins are wiped out and only the spirit and the grace of the righteous are revived?"[136] His interpretation of the pillar of light that led Israel safely through the sea as the presence of Christ allows Ambrose to reflect: "What is the light but truth, since it sheds a full and open brightness? What is the pillar of light but Christ the Lord, who scattered the shadows of unbelief and poured the light of truth and spiritual grace on human hearts?"[137] He uses Israel passing through the Red Sea to explain that the Christian passing through the font is the passage from earthly things to heavenly things, from sin to life, from guilt to grace, from vileness to holiness.[138] Elisha's floating axe prefigures the removal of sin in baptism that enables humanity to rise.[139] The bitter waters of Marah, made sweet when Moses cast wood into them, teach that although water without the proclamation of the cross cannot save, when it has been consecrated by "the cross of Christ, the heavenly sacrament," it can be the vehicle for salvation. Ambrose argues that the bitterness of the water signifies the corruptibility of creatures, the fact that they cannot ultimately satisfy or take away sin. He concludes: "Water, therefore, is bitter. But when it has received the cross of Christ, the heavenly sacrament, it begins to be sweet and pleasant; and rightly sweet, because guilt is thereby canceled. Therefore, if baptism

---

[134] Ibid., 1.5.15; 3.2.11 (SC 25bis.68; 98).
[135] Riley, *Christian Initiation*, 39–40.
[136] *De sacramentis*, 2.1.1 (SC 25bis.74).
[137] Ibid., 1.6.22 (SC 25bis.72).
[138] Ibid., 1.4.12 (SC 25bis.66).
[139] Ibid., 2.4.11 (SC 25bis.78–80).

by way of figure could do so much, how much more can baptism in reality do?"¹⁴⁰ The story of Naaman confirms that it is not water that cleanses, but grace.¹⁴¹ Thus God's actions involving water, whether the waters of the primeval chaos, the waters of the flood, the waters of the Red Sea or those of the Jordan, are all united with the water in the font into which the neophytes have been plunged.

Turning to the Eucharist, Ambrose explains why water is poured into the cup by, first, recounting the figure of the water which flowed from the rock that followed the people through the wilderness. Ambrose then continues,

"You also must drink, so that Christ may follow you. Consider this mystery. Moses, that is, as a prophet; touched the rock with his staff that is, with the word of God; as a priest he touched the rock with the word of God, and water flowed forth, and the people of God drank. Therefore the priest touches the cup, the water streams into the cup, and it 'springs up to eternal life,'¹⁴² and the people of God who have obtained God's grace, drink from it."¹⁴³

Ambrose then gives as an additional reason for the water mixed with the wine—the blood and water flowing from the side of Christ, "water to cleanse, blood to redeem."¹⁴⁴

Allegory. An allegory is best understood as a series of metaphors. For Ambrose, allegory is a method of interpretation which, when applied to the text of Scripture, reveals its moral and mystical meanings. Allegory unveils the spiritual value of the text by enabling the exegete to see through the opacity of the letter to the underlying truth.¹⁴⁵ This allegorical method was, of course, not new. Plato used it in treating Homer, Philo in expounding the Pentateuch, the grammarians in interpreting Virgil, the Neoplatonists in rationalizing and harmonizing the pagan myths. Among the Christians it had been adopted and systematized by Origen. Ambrose learned the method from Philo and

---

¹⁴⁰ Ibid., 2.4.13 (SC 25bis.80).
¹⁴¹ Ibid., 1.3.9–5.15 (SC 25bis.64–68); *De mysteriis*, 3.16–18 (SC 25bis.164).
¹⁴² John 4:14.
¹⁴³ *De sacramentis*, 5.1.3 (SC 25bis.120–122).
¹⁴⁴ Ibid., 5.1.4 (SC 25bis.122).
¹⁴⁵ Nauroy, "L'Ecriture dans la Pastorale d'Ambroise de Milan," 399.

Origen, of whose works he was a diligent student.[146] Although he was not the first in the West to use allegory—Hilary of Poitiers had already done so—Ambrose applied it with extraordinary consistency and thoroughness.[147] In his expositions of scriptural passages he was seldom content with the literal meaning, even when this meaning was most clear and elevated, but delighted in exercising his ingenuity in subtle interpretation; he could not rest until he had discovered beneath the letter a deeper sense.[148]

Ambrose used allegory to demonstrate the essential agreement between the Old and New Testaments and to explain away whatever in the literal narrative might seem to be either unworthy of God or discreditable in the conduct of the ancient saints—for example, Noah's drunkenness,[149] Abraham's adultery,[150] the relations of Boaz with Ruth,[151] Gideon's want of faith,[152] Job's curse,[153] or David's unseemly dancing.[154] Allegorically interpreted, every sentence of Scripture is rich in religious and moral instruction. Not a word is superfluous or devoid of force. Profound meanings are attached even to the most minute and apparently trivial textual details. Numbers are regarded as having symbolic meaning.[155] For example, in explaining the healing of the paralytic at the pool of Beth-zatha,[156] where whoever stepped

[146] See above, 100–102.

[147] See especially the elaborate allegorization in the treatises *De paradiso* (CSEL 32/1.265–336), *De Cain et Abel* (CSEL 32/1.339–409), *De Abraham*, 2 (CSEL 32/1.564–638), and *De Isaac et anima* (CSEL 32/1.641–700). Even in his treatment of the New Testament, Ambrose regularly suggests allegorical interpretations; see, e.g., *Expositio evangelii secundum Lucam*, 2.70, 71; 5.31; 7.160ff.; 10.76 (CCSL 14.61; 146–147; 269ff.; 368).

[148] See, e.g., *De Noe*, 33, 34, 37, 38, 46, 49, 50, 51, 52, 53, 45, 55, 57, 59, 61, 62, 69, 70, 77, 79, 87, 91, 93, 97, 102, 106, 107, 111, 115, 117, 125, 126, 128 (CSEL 32/1.433–497).

[149] Ibid., 111–113 (CSEL 32/1.488–490).

[150] *De Abraham*, 1.28 (CSEL 32/1.522–524).

[151] *De fide*, 4.70 (CSEL 78.181).

[152] *De Spiritu Sancto*, 1.6ff. (CSEL 79.18ff.).

[153] *Expositio evangelii secundum Lucam*, 4.40 (CCSL 14.120–121).

[154] *Epistola* 27 (Maur. 58) 5–8 (CSEL 82/1.182–183).

[155] Cf. *Epistola* 31 (Maur. 44).3ff. (CSEL 82/1.217); *De Abraham*, 2.65 (CSEL 32/1.619–621); *De excessu fratris*, 2.108 (CSEL 73.310–311); *Expositio in Psalmum cxviii*, Prologue 2 (CSEL 62.3–4); *De Noe*, 52, 123 (32/1.449–450, 495); *De fide*, 1.3 (CSEL 78.5–6). This biblical numerology is suspect today.

[156] John 5:1–9.

into the pool first after the stirring of the water was made well from whatever disease that person had,[157] Ambrose finds in the word *first* both the people of Israel and those who fear God.[158] The triple confession and immersion in baptism absolve the manifold lapses of the past in the same way that Jesus asked Peter if he loves him three times to absolve his triple denial.[159] Names also are held to be peculiarly significant and are regularly made the starting points of elaborate trains of allegorizing.[160]

In his mystagogical works Ambrose is particularly interested in using allegory to enable his hearers to see beyond an object's physical characteristic in order to discover its symbolic meaning. Ambrose calls upon his hearers to see that the pillar of light leading Israel was, in fact, truth, since it sheds a full and open brightness, and Christ, who scattered the shadows of unbelief and poured the light of truth and spiritual grace on human hearts. Similarly, the pillar of cloud is the Holy Spirit.[161] Ambrose sees in the wood that Elisha threw into the water, which made the axe rise,[162] the cross of Christ, which raises the weakness of all humanity.[163] As a third example, Ambrose uses the description of the appointments of the second tabernacle, into which the high priest entered once a year,[164] to show that the second tabernacle is the baptistry.[165] In Ambrose's mind, the fact that the high priest entered the second tabernacle once a year parallels the fact that Easter

---

[157] John 5:4.

[158] *De sacramentis*, 2.2.5 (SC 25bis.76).

[159] Ibid., 2.7.20–21 (SC 25bis.64–66). Cf. John 21:15f.; *De Spiritu Sancto*, 2.10.105 (CSEL 79.126).

[160] One method adopted by Ambrose was first to determine the meaning of the name of some scriptural character, then to take the person as representing the idea expressed by the name, and then to interpret the person's life and acts accordingly. For example, Isaac means "laughter"; laughter is the sign of joy, the fount of joy is Christ; Isaac, therefore, is the figure of Christ. But if Isaac represents Christ, then Rebecca must represent the Church or the devout soul. Thus the story of Isaac and Rebecca illustrates phases of the relationship between Christ and the Church, the Savior and the soul, the spouse and the bride. *De Isaac et anima*, 1, 2 (CSEL 32/1.642–643) and *passim*.

[161] *De sacramentis*, 1.6.22 (SC 25bis.72).

[162] 2 Kings 6:4-6.

[163] *De sacramentis*, 2.4.11 (SC 25bis.78).

[164] Hebrews 9:4-7.

[165] *De sacramentis*, 4.1.1 (SC 25bis.102).

was the normal time for baptism.[166] The rod of Aaron, which blossomed after it had withered, was the baptized, who had withered and began to blossom again in the streaming font.[167] The censer also represents the baptized, who in baptism become a sweet savor of Christ.[168]

Allegorical interpretation is in keeping with Ambrose's conviction that in baptism God gives the faith to see beyond the physical to the spiritual. In *De mysteriis*, before he considers three classic stories in which water becomes a type of baptism, Ambrose emphasizes that the neophytes must not contemplate water as an object but must see God's intention beneath the actions that involve water. "In what might be considered a lament, he expresses the fear that they might possibly miss the presence of God entirely if they do not recognize the power and divinity of God who has come to be known precisely through his visible works.[169] He even quotes Jesus' word, 'If you do not believe me, believe my works.'"[170] Using allegory makes it possible for the bishop of Milan to immediately replace the literal reading of Scripture with a mystical interpretation, almost without transition. Ambrose passes from literal to mystical interpretation seamlessly, without transition or notification that he is changing his hermeneutical technique, and in so doing moves his hearers from the physical to the spiritual.

Leslie Barnard correctly notes that until the last decade or so, the allegorical interpretation of Scripture was thought to imply imposing a foreign, subjective meaning on a text that bears no relation to the text's original meaning. This view of allegory has, for example, been the cause of the denigration that the patristic interpretations of the parables have received.[171] Yet this view is changing as people become less hopeful that historical-critical exegesis can tell us anything of much value for faith and as postmodern approaches to reading Scripture make people aware of the value of a less "historical," artificially "objective" approach.[172] Barnard is also correct that "Ambrose's interpretation, strange though it reads to modern interests, is thoroughly

---

[166] Ibid., 4.1.2 (SC 25bis.102).

[167] Ibid.

[168] Ibid., 4.1.4 (SC 25bis.102).

[169] 2 Corinthians 4:18; Romans 1:20.

[170] John 10:38; Ellebracht, "Today This Word Has Been Fulfilled in Your Hearing," 350. See *De mysteriis*, 3.8 (SC 25bis.158–160).

[171] Barnard, "To Allegorize or Not to Allegorize," 1.

[172] See below, 334–335.

christological and is rooted in history. The reader is directed back to the change wrought in history by the incarnation and sacrificial death of Christ."[173]

Construction of Intricate Chains of Reasoning. Reading Ambrose's works, we can see in his dense and intense use of Scripture his legal mind employing Scripture as his body of law, citing biblical precedent in order to prove his case. Like a lawyer's brief, which contains all the facts and points of law pertinent to a case, Ambrose's sermons are constructed to a great degree on collated Scripture passages. As we have said, Ambrose found in Scripture, more than anywhere else, a witness to the divine truth he sought to espouse and a weapon against the evil powers that he sought to resist. From the perspective of a lawyer, Ambrose's mystagogical preaching in many ways corresponds to the arguments of an attorney presenting a case to a jury.

Pamela Jackson and Mary Pierre Ellebracht each demonstrate how Ambrose uses the many scriptural images found in his mystagogical works as components in the construction of intricate arguments[174] in order to prove to his hearers the greatness and worth of the sacraments.[175] Ambrose is always careful to remind the neophytes that while the biblical *figura* helps them to understand the reality, it is not greater than the reality or, phrased another way, if the figure is great, how much greater must the reality be.[176] Ambrose's use of scriptural *figurae* to spin out elaborate chains of reasoning in order to overwhelm his hearers with the magnitude of the sacraments is so extensive that at times it obscures the fact that he is trying to present a sequential explanation of the rites.[177]

In order to prove the greatness and worth of the sacraments, Ambrose first points to the unseen activity of God in the sacraments.

---

[173] Barnard, "To Allegorize or Not to Allegorize," 7.

[174] While rhetoric is the art of persuasive argument, what is distinct here is Ambrose's method or means of argument; he employs biblical images rather than syllogisms.

[175] For the following discussion, I am indebted to Jackson, "Ambrose of Milan as Mystagogue," 97–103; Ellebracht, "Today this Word Has Been Fulfilled in Your Midst."

[176] *De sacramentis*, 5.1.1 (SC 25bis.120); ibid., 2.4.13 (SC 25bis.80); cf. *De mysteriis*, 8.48–49 (SC 25bis.182–184).

[177] For example, *De sacramentis*, 4.5.25–6.26; 5.1.1–2 (SC 25bis.116; 120).

In both *De sacramentis* and *De mysteriis* he bases his scriptural explanations on the principle: "The things that are not seen are far greater than the things that are seen; since 'the things that are seen are temporal, the things that are not seen are eternal.'"[178] Whereas God worked with the Jews through visible signs, God imparts the truth (which the visible signs only pointed to) invisibly in the sacraments.[179]

Second, Ambrose explains the meaning of the rites by drawing so heavily on Old Testament figures that the listeners are led to compare Christian and Jewish mysteries.[180] For example, Ambrose says, "Perhaps someone will say: 'To the Jews God granted such grace, he rained down manna upon them from heaven; what more has he given to his faithful, what more has he bestowed on those to whom he promised more?'"[181] Ambrose then sets himself to the task of proving "that the sacraments of Christians are more divine and older than those of the Jews."[182] To demonstrate the greater antiquity of the Christian sacraments, he cites the flood as a figure of baptism[183] and Melchizedek as a figure of the Eucharist, since Melchizedek predates both Judah and the giving of the Law.[184] In proving that Christian baptism is "more divine" than "baptisms of the Jews," he points out that while those who passed through the Red Sea later perished, Christians who pass through the font never die.[185] Similarly, while only one who descended into the pool of Beth-zatha could be healed, all are saved who descend into the font of the Church.[186]

Third, Ambrose then demonstrates that although it is invisible, God's saving power is in fact at work in the waters of baptism.[187]

---

[178] Ibid., 1.3.10 (SC 25bis.64–66); *De mysteriis*, 8.15 (SC 25bis.162). Cf. 2 Corinthians 4:18.

[179] *De sacramentis*, 2.5.14–15 (SC 25bis.80–82); cf. ibid., 2.2.4 (SC 25bis.74); *De mysteriis*, 4.22, 5.27 (SC 25bis.166; 170).

[180] On Ambrose's attitude toward the Jews, see above, 58–59.

[181] *De sacramentis*, 4.3.9 (SC 25bis.106); *De mysteriis*, 8.44 (SC 25bis.180).

[182] *De sacramentis*, 1.4.11 (SC 25bis.66); ibid., 5.2.10 (SC 25bis.124); *De mysteriis*, 8.44 (SC 25bis.180).

[183] *De sacramentis*, 1.1.2 (SC 25bis.60); *De mysteriis*, 3.9 (SC 25bis.160).

[184] *De sacramentis*, 4.3.10; 4.4.13; 5.1.1 (SC 25bis.106; 108; 120); *De mysteriis*, 8.45–46 (SC 25bis.180–182).

[185] *De sacramentis*, 1.4.12 (SC 25bis.66). Cf. 1 Corinthians 10:5.

[186] *De sacramentis*, 2.2.5 (SC 25bis.76); *De mysteriis*, 4.23 (SC 26bis.166).

[187] Cf. ibid., 4.19 (SC 25bis.164).

"Ambrose does this by (a) citing many instances where God saved through water in the past, thus revealing how [God] works; (b) showing that baptism corresponds to these instances; (c) citing the words of Jesus (Mt. 28) to show that Christian baptism is indeed such an instance where the power of God saves through water. To establish the presence of the Trinity in baptism (*ergo,* the power of God), Ambrose cites Jesus' own baptism (which he considers a pattern, *forma* of Christian baptism, and the *figura* of the pillars of light and cloud at the Red Sea.[188] To underline the presence and power of the cross, he cites the wood Elisha cast into the water to raise up the sunken iron, and the wood Moses cast into the bitter waters of Marah to make them sweet,[189] to establish the presence of the Holy Spirit, he cites Christ's baptism and Pentecost."[190]

The structure and intricacy of Ambrose's argument from Scripture are more easily seen in his treatment of the story of the paralytic at the pool of Beth-zatha[191] in *De mysteriis.*[192] After stating that no one was healed in the pool unless the angel descended from heaven to move the water, Ambrose juxtaposes elements of each event to bring out the excellence of the sacrament. Ellebracht summarizes Ambrose's argument in schematic fashion:

God's Action at the Pool		*God's Action in Baptism*
for them, a sign	but	for you, faith
for them, an angel	but	for you, the Holy Spirit
for them, the creature	but	for you, Christ the Lord of creation works
for them, one was healed	but	now, all are healed[193]

In the end Ambrose brings rite and biblical narrative together again with the statement that what occurs at the pool takes place so that the

---

[188] *De sacramentis,* 1.5.15–6.22 (SC 25bis.68–72); *De mysteriis,* 3.12 (SC 25bis.162).

[189] *De sacramentis,* 2.4.11–13 (SC 25bis.80); *De mysteriis,* 3.14 (SC 25bis.162).

[190] Jackson, "Ambrose of Milan as Mystagogue," 98. *De sacramentis,* 2.5.14 (SC 25bis.80); cf. *De mysteriis,* 4.24 (SC 25bis.163); *De sacramentis,* 2.5.15 (SC 25bis.82); cf. ibid., 2.3.9 (SC 25bis.78).

[191] John 5:1-9.

[192] *De mysteriis,* 5.22–24 (SC 25bis.166–168).

[193] Ellebracht, "Today This Word Has Been Fulfilled in Your Midst," 354.

neophytes will know in faith that divine power has descended into the font.

In order to complete his task of convincing his hearers that the sacraments are superior to the mysteries of the Old Covenant, Ambrose demonstrates that the Eucharist is "more divine" than its Jewish precedents. In proving that the Eucharist is "more excellent than manna,"[194] Ambrose notes that while those who ate manna died, those who eat the Eucharist will have forgiveness of sins and never die.[195] Once again, Ambrose's logic is more easily observed in *De mysteriis*:

Old Testament Wonders Are:	The Sacraments Are:
Bread of angels	The flesh of Christ
from heaven	above heaven
of heaven	of the Lord of the heavens
subject to decay	free from corruption, even preserving those who eat it
Water from a rock	The blood of Christ
satisfied thirst for a time	blood floods you forever
Jews drank and thirsted	you drink and never thirst again
There foreshadowing	Here reality[196]

Ellebracht's schematic presentation makes it easy to both see Ambrose's argument and comprehend the superiority of the Christian sacraments. This procedure is certainly not stereotyped; however, Ambrose never moves away from the principle: "If you marvel at the foreshadowings, how much more will you be in awe of the realities!"[197]

Third, as in his treatment of baptism, Ambrose demonstrates that God is indeed present to save in the bread and wine of the Eucharist. Anticipating his hearers' reaction, Ambrose says, "Perhaps you say, 'The bread I have here is ordinary bread,'" and asks, "How can something that is bread be the body of Christ?"[198] Ambrose sets out to "reason this out"[199] by documenting biblical precedents to prove that

---

[194] *De mysteriis*, 8.44 (SC 25bis.180).

[195] *De sacramentis*, 4.5.24 (SC 25bis.116); *De mysteriis*, 8.47 (SC 25bis.182); cf. John 6:49-51.

[196] Ellebracht, "Today This Word Has Been Fulfilled in Your Midst," 354.

[197] Ibid.

[198] *De sacramentis*, 5.3.14 (SC 25bis.126); ibid., 6.1.2. (SC 25bis.138); *De mysteriis*, 9.50 (SC 25bis.184).

[199] Ibid.

throughout salvation history God has in fact acted to change nature.[200] These precedents include Moses' rod becoming a serpent, the rivers of Egypt turning to blood, the parting of the Red Sea, the water flowing from the rock, the bitter water of Marah turning sweet, Elisha's floating axe-head, and the turning back of the Jordan.[201] The bishop then asks, "If the heavenly word can change nature in such earthly things as the spring of Marah, can it not in the heavenly sacraments?"[202] Similarly, if human words such as Elijah's calling fire from heaven are powerful enough to change nature, is not the word of Christ powerful enough to change the elements of the Eucharist?[203] Ambrose's crowning example is the incarnation: "Why do you seek the natural order here in the case of the body of Christ, when the Lord Jesus himself was born of the Virgin in a way beyond nature?"[204] Ambrose then recites and explains the words of Christ by which the change occurs.[205] Since the neophytes "can see the ways in which the word of Christ is powerful enough to change all things," when Christ himself testifies that they receive his body and blood, "should we doubt his authority and testimony?"[206]

Ambrose thus demonstrates that eternal salvation comes through God's presence in baptism and the Eucharist. The divine presence is effected through the repetition of Christ's words in the consecration of the font and in the eucharistic prayer. By this demonstration Ambrose emphasizes the greatness of what the neophytes have received in the rites. "The very Word that changed material things has also, through those rites, changed them."[207] In this section we have seen that Ambrose's method of proving the greatness of the Christian sacraments is to use biblical images to construct intricate chains of argument.

Interpretation by Translation. Perhaps less significant than the methods we have discussed thus far, Ambrose occasionally uses translation to

---

[200] *De mysteriis*, 9.50 (SC 25bis.184).

[201] *De sacramentis*, 4.4.15, 18 (SC 25bis.110, 112); *De mysteriis*, 9.51–52 (SC 25bis.184–186).

[202] *De sacramentis*, 4.4.19 (SC 25bis.112).

[203] *De mysteriis*, 9.52 (SC 25bis.186).

[204] *De mysteriis*, 9.53 (SC 25bis.186–188); cf. *De sacramentis*, 4.5.17 (SC 25bis.110).

[205] *De sacramentis*, 4.5.21–23 (SC 25bis.114).

[206] Ibid., 4.5.23 (SC 25bis.114); cf. *De mysteriis*, 9.54 (SC 25bis.188).

[207] Jackson, "Ambrose of Milan as Mystagogue," 100. See *De sacramentis*, 4.4.16 (SC 25bis.110); cf. 2 Corinthians 5:7; cf. *De mysteriis*, 9.59 (SC 25bis.190).

interpret the meaning of a passage. His approach to Scripture differs from that of modern scholars in that, rather than seeking an original text by setting aside inaccurate versions and incorrect variants, Ambrose's exegetical approach is to draw from the plurality of versions and diversity of textual variants an enriched meaning. Unlike modern scholars, he does not believe that there is an original text to which it is advisable to turn. Ambrose uses multiple versions[208] and variants of a text not to eliminate but to add meaning. "Thus, if the verse were taken from the Old Testament, he would carefully note variations in the Greek and Latin versions,"[209] sometimes explaining the cause of a

---

[208] Ambrose's undisputed works supply evidence of the sources available to him for the text of Scripture. He was unacquainted with the Hebrew text of the Old Testament but familiar with the Greek Septuagint, the chief authority in the Church. See *Expositio in Psalmum cxviii*, 9.13 (CSEL 62.196–197). Ambrose was also familiar with the Greek versions of Aquila and Symmachus. Sometimes he quotes both versions, as in ibid., 15.12; 22.41, 45 (CSEL 62.336–337; 507–508, 510) and *Enarrationes in xii psalmos davidicos*, 36.11, 70; 40.21; 43.23, 33, 36, 44, 67, 79 (CSEL 64.77–78, 129; 242–243; 279–280, 285–286, 288, 293, 309, 318). Sometimes he quotes one version, as in *Expositio in Psalmum cxviii*, 9.20; 17.18; 22.36 (CSEL 62.201–202; 386–387; 505–506) and *Enarrationes in xii psalmos davidicos*, 1.29, 31, 39–43, 44; 35.18; 37.33; 38.21; 43.54, 64, 73, 94 (CSEL 64.23–25, 26–27; 34–37; 61–63; 161–162; 225–227; 298–299; 302, 313–314; 328). Ambrose refers to the version of Theodotion only in ibid., 43.4, 33, 35, 36 (CSEL 64.260, 285–286, 287–288). He appears to have had access to Origen's *Hexapla*, where these texts are arranged in parallel columns; see *Epistola* 18 (Maur. 70).14 (CSEL 82/1.135); cf. *Expositio in Psalmum cxviii*, 4.16 (CSEL 62.75–76). Ambrose, along with Augustine, also used a Latin version of the Old Testament made from the Septuagint, including the Apocrypha, that was translated in Africa and in use there at the end of the second century. In interpreting the New Testament, though Ambrose used a pre-Vulgate Latin text, he frequently appeals to the original Greek. See *De incarnationis dominicae sacramento*, 82 (CSEL 79.265); *De Spiritu Sancto*, 2.46 (CSEL 79.103–104). See H. De Romenstin, *St. Ambrose, Select Works and Letters*, A Select Library of Nicene and Post-Nicene Fathers of the Christian Church, 2nd series, vol. 10 (Grand Rapids: Eerdmans Publishing Co., 1978) xiv; Homes Dudden, *The Life and Times of St. Ambrose*, 2:456; T. Thompson, *On the Sacraments and On the Mysteries*, rev. ed. (London: S.P.C.K., 1950) 9–10.

[209] See, e.g., *Expositio in Psalmum cxviii*, 4.15, 16; 10.44; 12.7; 14.29; 15.23; 17.35; 20.10 (CSEL 62.75–76; 229–230; 254–255; 318; 342; 394–395; 449–450); *Enarrationes in xii psalmos davidicos*, 1.43, 58; 36.39; 37.58; 40.11, 12; 47.4 (CSEL 64.36–37, 48; 101; 182; 235–236; 348–349); *De interpellatione Iob et David*, 4.7 (CSEL 32/2.272–273). See Homes Dudden, *The Life and Times of St. Ambrose*, 2:456.

variation[210] and indicating the reading which he preferred."[211] Ambrose did not read Hebrew.[212] When he ventured an explanation of Hebrew letters, words, or names, he was either following Philo or drawing on some source or sources now unknown. "If the verse were taken from a Gospel, he would, when necessary, compare, almost in the manner of a modern critic, the sentence on which he was commenting with the parallels in other Gospels.[213] He then explained the verse, often at considerable length, stating alternative views in cases where the interpretation was doubtful."[214]

R. H. Connolly's exhaustive study of the biblical quotations in *De sacramentis*[215] reveals quotations that agree with the Septuagint,[216] quotations found in pre-Vulgate (Old Latin) texts,[217] and quotations from a text that corresponds to the Vulgate.[218] We find illustrations of Ambrose using textual variants in order to interpret a text in both *De sacramentis* and *De mysteriis*, where Ambrose uses the phrases "the Greek has" *(Graecus habet)* or "the Latin said" *(Latinus dixit)*, and "what the Latin and the Greek said" *(quod Latinus dixit et quod Graecus)* to introduce a biblical quotation.[219] When it is a matter of interpretation, however, we find "in the Greek it is called" *(Graece dicitur)*,[220] where the reference is

---

[210] See, e.g., *Expositio in Psalmum cxviii*, 4.15; 5.26; 17.35; 22.14, 27 (CSEL 62.75; 95–96; 394–395; 495, 502). See Homes Dudden, *The Life and Times of St. Ambrose*, 2:456.

[211] See, e.g., *Expositio in Psalmum cxviii*, 9.13; 22.27 (CSEL 62.196–197, 502). See Homes Dudden, *The Life and Times of St. Ambrose*, 2:456.

[212] See *Enarrationes in xii psalmos davidicos*, 40.36 (CSEL 64.253–254). See Homes Dudden, *The Life and Times of St. Ambrose*, 2:456.

[213] See, e.g., *Expositio evangelii secundum Lucam*, 5.30, 31; 6.14, 44; 7.149ff.; 8.80; 10.129 (CCSL 146–147; 179–180; 189–190; 266ff.; 329; 382–383).

[214] Homes Dudden, *The Life and Times of St. Ambrose*, 2:456.

[215] R. H. Connolly, *The De Sacramentis a Work of Ambrose* (Oxford: Downside Abbey, 1942). For a summary of Connolly's findings, see Thompson, *On the Sacraments and On the Mysteries*, 10–13.

[216] See, for example, *De sacramentis*, 2.2.4; 4.2.5; 5.3.15 (SC 25bis.74–75; 104; 126).

[217] See, for example, ibid., 2.2.7; 2.7.20; 3.1.6; 4.3.10 (SC 25bis.78; 84; 94; 106).

[218] See, for example, ibid., 5.1.3; 5.3.13 (SC 25bis.120–122; 124–128); *De mysteriis*, 9.55 (SC 25bis.188).

[219] Ibid., 5.2.11; 5.4.24 (SC 25bis.124, 132). The masculine ending is puzzling to translate, though with *habet* the word *codex* (or "text") might be applied.

[220] Ibid., 5.4.24 (SC 25bis.132).

to the words "daily bread" in the Lord's Prayer, or "according to the Greeks" (*cum secundum Graecos*),[221] where Ambrose is referring to the Spirit descending in John 1:32. Ambrose uses this variety of texts and textual variants not to narrow and clarify the meaning of a passage but to deepen and expand it.

Direct and Uncritical Transfer of the Text. Finally, Ambrose quotes passages of Scripture and then treats them as if they had been written with his audience in mind.[222] The most obvious example of Ambrose's direct and uncritical transfer of Scripture is his application of Scripture as the "heavenly words" by which Christ establishes the Church's sacraments. Since Christ established baptism in Matthew 28:19, the bishop uses this passage to invoke the presence of the Trinity on the water.[223] In this same way, Ambrose uses a conflation of Matthew 26:26f., Mark 14:22f., Luke 22:19f., and 1 Corinthians 11:23f. with the addition of the phrase "looked up to heaven" from Mark 6:42 as the "heavenly words" with which the bread and wine of the Eucharist are consecrated.[224]

In other instances Ambrose simply quotes a passage of Scripture in order to explain the effect of a rite. In his explanation of the *ephphatha*, for example, Ambrose answers the question of why the bishop touched the candidate's nostrils in part by quoting 2 Corinthians 2:15: "so that you may say, as the holy apostle said, 'We are the aroma of Christ to God.'"[225] Similarly, in order to explain the innocence that results from baptism, Ambrose applies Canticles 8:5 to the angels watching the newly baptized approach the altar.[226]

Ambrose also puts the words of Scripture in the mouths of the neophytes in order to describe their response. In his discussion of their approaching the altar, Ambrose quotes Psalm 43:4 and tells the neophytes, "Your soul says, 'Then I will go to the altar of my God, to God who gives joy to my youth.'"[227] Whether quoting Scripture to show how the sacraments were established, to explain their effect, or to help his hearers find the words with which to respond to them,

---

[221] *De mysteriis*, 4.25 (SC 25bis.168).
[222] Craddock, *Preaching*, 138.
[223] *De sacramentis*, 2.4.10; 2.5.14 (SC 25bis.78; 80–82).
[224] Ibid., 4.5.21–23 (SC 25bis.114).
[225] Ibid., 1.1.3 (SC 25bis.60–62).
[226] Ibid., 4.2.5 (SC 25bis.104).
[227] Ibid., 4.2.7 (SC 25bis.62).

Ambrose uses Scripture in a direct and uncritical way, as if it was written with his audience in mind.

Means of Incorporation

We have previously suggested that Scripture was integral to Ambrose's mystagogy not only because he used it in order to interpret the meaning of the rites but also because these sermons overflow with scriptural references, allusions, images, and quotations. As we have said, a distinctive feature of Ambrose's preaching was his ability to "sound like the Bible."[228] In this section we will explore five ways that Ambrose incorporated Scripture into the content of his mystagogy. The methods that Ambrose used include (1) quotation, (2) narration, (3) summary, (4) allusion, and (5) speaking the Bible.

Quotation. In his mystagogical works, as in his other sermons and treatises, Ambrose makes extensive use of scriptural quotations. As we have said, Connolly has shown that the biblical quotations in *De sacramentis* and *De mysteriis* agree with the Septuagint and pre-Vulgate (Old Latin) texts.[229] Additionally, we find divergences from the Septuagint, which frequently parallel Scripture quotations in Ambrose's other, undisputed works, that are due either to loose quotations from memory or to paraphrases in a form in which the bishop of Milan has become accustomed to quoting the particular text.[230] One would expect to find this type of quotation in the transcript of preached sermons. These free quotations become obvious if one compares *De sacramentis* with parallel passages from *De mysteriis*, where Ambrose has corrected himself.[231]

We have discussed Ambrose's use of scriptural quotations as the "heavenly words" by which the sacraments are established, to explain the meaning of a rite, and to tell the neophytes how they are to respond.[232]

---

[228] Above, 92–93.

[229] See above, 240.

[230] See, e.g., *De sacramentis*, 1.3.10; 2.4.10; 2.5.15; 2.7.22, 23; 3.1.1; 3.1.3; 4.4.16, 17 (SC 25bis.64–66; 78–80; 82; 86–88; 90–92; 110).

[231] For example, cf. ibid., 1.3.10 (SC 25bis.64–66) and *De mysteriis*, 3.8 (SC 25bis.158–160); *De sacramentis*, 1.6.21 (SC 25bis.70–72) and *De mysteriis*, 3.12 (SC 25bis.162); *De sacramentis*, 4.2.5 (SC 25bis.104) and *De mysteriis*, 4.19 (SC 25bis.164).

[232] For our discussion of these three uses of scriptural quotations in *De sacramentis*, see above, 241.

Additionally, the bishop of Milan uses quotations from Scripture as the links with which he constructs intricate chains of reasoning in order to argue his point.[233] As part of these chains of reasoning, he cites scriptural quotations as biblical precedents in order to prove the validity of his assertions. For example, Ambrose quotes Acts 2:2-3 to prove the descent of the Spirit in baptism, Hebrews 7:3, 17 to prove that Melchizedek is a figure of Christ, and Psalm 33:9 to prove the effectiveness of the word of Christ.[234]

Narration. In addition to quoting Scripture texts, Ambrose also tells Bible stories. In his telling, Ambrose frames the stories in a way that makes them useful as examples of the sacraments or explanations of their meaning. Thus, by recounting how Moses purified the spring of Marah,[235] Ambrose demonstrates that "once [water] has received the cross of Christ, the heavenly sacrament, it begins to be sweet and agreeable to the taste. And it is right that it should be sweet, this water in which our guilt is canceled."[236] Ambrose tells the story this way: "Moses came into the desert, and the people were thirsty. They came to the spring of Marah and would have drunk. But when the water was first drawn, it was found to have a bitter taste; it was impossible to drink it. Then Moses put the wood in the spring, and the water which before was bitter now began to taste sweet."[237] By emphasizing the wood, Ambrose demonstrates the importance of the cross.

Similarly, in telling of Jesus washing the feet of his disciples,[238] the bishop of Milan expands the biblical account[239] and incorporates other passages of Scripture in order to show how the Milanese practice of washing the feet of the newly baptized is a sacrament and not merely an act of humility. In order to expound upon the salvific nature of this rite, Ambrose expands the dialogue between Jesus and Peter and includes the exchange between Jesus and John the Baptist where John says, "I need to be baptized by you, and do you come to me?"[240] In so

---

[233] *De sacramentis,* 1.2.7; 1.4.12; 3.1.1–3; 4.4.16, 17; 5.3.17 (SC 25bis.64; 66; 90–92; 110; 128). See above, 234–238.
[234] *De sacramentis,* 2.5.15; 4.3.12; 4.4.16 (SC 25bis.82; 108; 110).
[235] Exodus 15:23f.
[236] *De sacramentis,* 2.4.13 (SC 25bis.80).
[237] Ibid., 2.4.12 (SC 25bis.80).
[238] Ibid., 3.1.4–7 (SC 25bis.92–96).
[239] John 13:6-10.
[240] Matthew 3:14.

doing, Ambrose not only defends the Milanese practice of foot-washing; he elevates it to the level of a sacrament.

Summary. A third way that Ambrose incorporates Scripture into his mystagogy is by summarizing biblical events and passages of Scripture. These summaries include phrases and verses quoted from Scripture and serve to explain both theological concepts and liturgical actions. Thus, in justifying his practice of delaying instruction on the sacraments until after the neophytes have participated in the rites, Ambrose offers his understanding of the relationship between faith and understanding—namely, that for the Christian, faith comes first—by summarizing Romans 4:2, 3, 9: "To have given a reasoned account of [the sacraments] earlier would not have been right; for in a Christian faith is first. Therefore, at Rome the title of 'faithful' is given to those who have been baptized; and also our father Abraham was justified by faith, not by works. So you received baptism; you believed."[241] In order to teach that not all water heals, but only that water which has the grace of Christ, Ambrose gives as proof a summary of the story of the healing of Naaman the leper (2 Kings 1:5f.).[242] Ambrose also summarizes biblical stories—the crossing of the Red Sea, the spring at Marah, and Elisha's floating axe head—as examples of the power of God's word.[243]

Turning to liturgical actions, in explaining the meaning of the *ephphatha* the bishop of Milan asks, "Which mysteries of 'opening' were performed when the priest touched your ears and nostrils?" As an answer to this question, Ambrose summarizes the account of Jesus healing the deaf man who had an impediment in his speech (Mark 7:21f.).[244] As part of his explanation of the triple confession of faith in baptism,[245] Ambrose summarizes the account of Jesus' post-resurrection appearance in which he asks Peter three times if Peter loves him (John 21:15f.).[246] Finally, Ambrose gives a summary of the account of the soldiers piercing the side of the crucified Jesus as one reason why wine and water are poured into the eucharistic cup.[247]

---

[241] *De sacramentis*, 1.1.1 (SC 25bis.60).

[242] Ibid., 1.5.13–15 (SC 25bis.66–68). See above, 133–134.

[243] *De sacramentis*, 4.4.18 (SC 25bis.112). See Exodus 14; 15:23-25; 2 Kings 6:5-6.

[244] *De sacramentis*, 1.1.2 (SC 25bis.60).

[245] See above, 166–169.

[246] *De sacramentis*, 2.7.21 (SC 25bis.86).

[247] Ibid., 5.1.4 (SC 25bis.122). See John 19:31-34.

Allusion. A fourth way that Ambrose incorporates Scripture into his mystagogy is by using two or three words to allude to biblical events and images as part of his explanation of the sacraments. Ambrose refers to the flood to show that the Christian mysteries are more ancient than those of the Jews.[248] He refers to the biblical images of the flood, the Red Sea, and the pool of Beth-zatha in order to show the presence of the Trinity in baptism.[249] Adam and the serpent explain foot-washing;[250] creation demonstrates the power of the word of Christ.[251] Ambrose even alludes to the conclusion of the Gospel of John (21:25) in order to express his difficulty in keeping track of the deeds of Christ.[252]

Speaking the Bible. Nauroy calls Ambrose's style "speaking the Bible" and describes it as "the ultimate stage of incorporation of Scripture."[253] In addition to his extensive use of scriptural quotations, allusions, summaries, and images, Ambrose speaks the Bible by using scriptural language—words and phrases—to express his ideas. He uses 2 Corinthians 4:16 to express his belief that invisible things are greater than visible things.[254] In explaining the one name of the Triune God, Ambrose uses phrases from Acts 4:12 and 1 Peter 3:7: "This is the name of which it was said, 'In this must all find salvation.' It is in this name that you have all been saved, that you have been restored to 'the grace of life.'"[255]

More than this, Ambrose employs a synthetic speech that is allusive, even mysterious, like the biblical word itself.[256] He reduces verses of Scripture and concentrates biblical events to one or two words. He considers these words themselves to be autonomous entities, saturated with meaning and able to provide a direction for interpretation. The words of Scripture are for Ambrose the heart of a diffuse and complex symbolic system that is in part obvious and in part hidden and enigmatic.[257] Each word conceals within it a plurality of interpretations and

---

[248] *De sacramentis*, 1.16.23; 2.1.1 (SC 25bis.72, 74).
[249] Ibid., 2.3.9 (SC 25bis.78).
[250] Ibid., 3.1.7 (SC 25bis.94–96).
[251] Ibid., 4.4.15 (SC 25bis.110).
[252] Ibid., 2.4.12 (SC 25bis.108).
[253] Nauroy, "L'Ecriture dans la Pastorale d'Ambroise de Milan," 404.
[254] *De sacramentis*, 1.3.10 (SC 25bis.64–66).
[255] Ibid., 2.7.22 (SC 25bis.86).
[256] See above, 92–93.
[257] Nauroy, "L'Ecriture dans la Pastorale d'Ambroise de Milan," 405.

fits in chains of connotations infinitely exceeding the precise meaning that the word has in its context. In this way each word of Scripture contains a particular history. Although the words of Scripture perform a function in the sentence in which they are found, they also have meaning beyond the sentence that is revealed when the words are removed from the constraints of the place and time.

For Ambrose, "speaking the Bible" has only one purpose: to proclaim the person of the Christ, toward whom all Scripture converges and in whom all Scripture is explained. Thus the phrase "as a dove"[258] points to both the descent of the Holy Spirit at Jesus' baptism and the descent of the Holy Spirit in Christian baptism. As we might expect, Ambrose uses the meaning-laden phrases "buried with Christ"[259] and "death of Jesus"[260] to explain baptism. In explaining the healing of the paralytic at the pool of Beth-zatha,[261] Ambrose finds in the "mystical sense" of the paralytic's answer to Jesus, "I have no man [to carry me into the pool],"[262] the death of Christ.[263]

One cannot convey the power and beauty of Ambrose "speaking the Bible" through isolated examples. In order to fully appreciate this style, one should read through the sermons contained in *De sacramentis*. In so doing, one can best understand how Ambrose uses scriptural words and phrases to express his ideas and, in so doing, speaks the Bible.

REFLECTION: THE PNEUMATIC DIMENSION OF SCRIPTURE AS INTERPRETER OF THE RITES

The key to Ambrose's understanding of the Holy Spirit's role in using Scripture to interpret the rites is his view that Scripture is a mystery. Ambrose believed that Scripture is inspired by the Holy Spirit and, therefore, has a deeper meaning than what appears on the surface. With the eyes of faith Christians can see this mystical meaning of Scripture and its application to faith and life. The Christian pastor

---

[258] *De sacramentis*, 1.5.17 (SC 25bis.68): *quasi columba*.

[259] Ibid., 2.7.20 (SC 25bis.84–86): *Ideo et Christo es consepultus*. Cf. Romans 6:4; Colossians 2:12.

[260] *De sacramentis*, 2.7.23 (SC 25bis.86–88): *morte Iesu*. Cf. Romans 6:3.

[261] John 5:1-9.

[262] John 5:7.

[263] *De sacramentis*, 2.2.6–7 (SC 25bis.76–78). Cf. 1 Corinthians 15:21; 1 Timothy 2:5; Isaiah 19:20.

can find in the mystical interpretation of Scripture both the authority and the response to every situation and responsibility, including explaining the sacraments. This approach is neither "fundamentalism" nor "eisogesis" but a methodology based on the conviction that God's truth is contained in the Scriptures, which not only provide the message but the means of interpreting it. Thus Ambrose looks to the Bible in order to discover both the meaning of the rites and the language and images that he uses to explain them.

For Ambrose, the mystical meaning of Scripture is contained in the language of symbols. Its interpretation therefore requires a gift of divine grace. Yet, while today we generally attribute God's inspiration and aid in interpreting Scripture to the Holy Spirit, for the bishop of Milan the interpreter of Scripture cannot comprehend the deeper, mystical meaning without the illumination of Christ. For Ambrose, as for the entire exegetical tradition to which he belongs, the life of Christ is the truth that clarifies the various meanings of Scripture. Christ unites the disparity of the books of Scripture and provides the point of intersection and junction of all the verses of the word of God. Thus Christ is the true interpreter of the word of Scripture. The task of the Christian exegete is to expose, to show, to proclaim the truth that Christ reveals. This view of scriptural interpretation is in keeping with Ambrose's understanding of the sacraments as the means by which God gives the faithful the "eyes of faith," which enable them to see beyond the temporal to the eternal, beyond the surface to a deeper, mystical meaning.

Yet, in discovering the mystical meaning of Scripture, the Christian exegete relies on rules of interpretation. The conviction that Christ reveals the truth of Scripture rests on a complex hermeneutic science, which is indebted to both the exegetical tradition of the Church, the ancient exegesis of Homer, and the rabbinical exegesis of the books of the Pentateuch, particularly that of Philo of Alexandria. In employing this hermeneutic, Ambrose uses many methods of interpretation in order to bring the truth of God's word revealed in Christ into direct dialogue with the Christian people. Yet his ministry of the Word requires both science and meditation, diligence and humility, because in the final analysis Ambrose understands his role as interpreter of Scripture to be that of mediating between Christ and the Church.

In addition to discovering the truth of Scripture, for Ambrose, proclaiming that truth also requires the ability to use Scripture as the mode of expression. Thus the bishop of Milan intentionally incorporates Scripture into the content of his preaching to the degree that he "speaks the Bible." Ambrose's goal in this style of discourse is that in certain privileged moments his speech and the biblical style are so integrated that, in the words of the bishop, the voice of Christ is heard. In the next chapter we will explore how Ambrose crafted his sermons in order to make that happen.

Chapter 7

"Milky speech":
The Shape of Mystagogy

We recall from our discussion of Ambrose's views on preaching in Chapter 3 that the bishop of Milan distinguished three types of sermons: the sweet, the stinging, and the milky.[1] These distinctions are not based on the message or content of the sermon but are three ways of getting the message heard. Each type of sermon is an attempt to take seriously the point of contact where the message meets the listener. As such, they are distinct forms or structures for crafting a sermon. Milky sermons are designed for listeners like the newly baptized, who, in Ambrose's words, "cannot eat strong food but develop from infancy by drinking a natural milk."[2]

By distinguishing different sermon structures, Ambrose reminds us that "the form of a sermon is active, contributing to what the speaker wishes to say and do, sometimes no less persuasive than the content itself."[3] In this chapter we will therefore examine the shape of Ambrose's preaching on the sacraments to infants in the faith. In the first section of this chapter, we will determine the form (or forms) of Ambrose's mystagogical sermons. In the second section of this chapter, we will analyze *De sacramentis* to determine how these forms function to facilitate the listeners' apprehension of the message. To conduct this analysis, we will use what Craddock calls "qualities to be sought in preaching."[4] In the third and final section of this chapter, we will

---

[1] Above, 95. *Epistola* 36 (Maur. 2).5–6 (CSEL 82/2.5–6).
[2] Ibid.
[3] Fred B. Craddock, *Preaching* (Nashville: Abingdon Press, 1985) 172.
[4] Ibid., 153.

reflect upon the role of the Spirit in shaping mystagogical preaching. Like the process of crafting a sermon, which brings together insights and information from a variety of sources, this chapter will integrate many of the discoveries and insights made in previous chapters.

THE SHAPE OF *DE SACRAMENTIS*

In this section we will attempt to discover the structure or skeleton or shape of *De sacramentis*. Our approach will be to begin with the work as a whole and then focus on smaller and smaller areas of the text. Our examination of the overall plan of *De sacramentis* will reveal how Ambrose crafts his "course" on the sacraments. We will then look at individual sermons in order to determine what forms Ambrose uses to construct the units in which he treats individual rites and parts of rites. Finally, we will explore the ways that Ambrose "enriches the form,"[5] that is, his use of language, method of description, selection and use of illustrations, and development of the tone of these sermons.

Overall Structure

While there is no one canonical form for sermons, the design selected or created must be congenial not only to the Gospel but also to the ways human beings order, understand, and appropriate reality.[6] Undoubtedly that is why Ambrose uses the "text" on which his mystagogy is based—the neophytes' experience of the rites of initiation—to determine the shape of the sermons contained in *De sacramentis*. Although *De sacramentis* is a series of six sermons, these sermons are, in fact, episodes of the unfolding drama or chapters of the single story of Christian initiation in Milan. The sermons are organized as a journey through the rites of initiation, from entering the baptistry through the font to arrival at the altar for the celebration of the Easter Eucharist to the life of faith grounded in prayer. The liturgical rites determine the sequence of topics. Thus, sermons 1–3 are devoted to the baptismal liturgy, sermons 4–5 to the eucharistic liturgy, and the sixth to an instruction on individual prayer. Introductions and conclusions serve to connect each sermon to the whole by reviewing what has been said in the previous sermon and previewing what is to be covered in the sermon to follow.[7] Viewed

---

[5] Ibid., 194.
[6] Ibid., 171.
[7] *De sacramentis*, 1.6.24; 3.1.1; 3.2.15; 4.6.29 (SC 25bis.72; 90; 100; 118). See above, 135–136.

in their entirety, the overall structure reflects the rites of initiation from which the message of these sermons is drawn.

Harmless correctly observes that

"Cyril, Theodore, and Ambrose used their respective baptismal and Eucharistic liturgies as their outline, but differed from one another in emphasis: Cyril stressing how the liturgical present imaged the scriptural past; Theodore stressing how the liturgical present foreshadowed the eschatological future; and Ambrose stressing how visible rites pointed to invisible realities."[8]

Using the rites of initiation as the outline of his mystagogy helps Ambrose move his hearers from not seeing to seeing because the movement of this instruction is the same as that of the process of initiation. "It begins with the right knowledge of self and of self-limitedness, and ends with the greater self, the self which has been placed under the aegis of grace and whose knowledge is in prayer."[9] Peter Cramer sees a note of repose at the end of Ambrose's sermons, a satisfaction of the desire for God found in prayer; that is, the radical transition to grace that occurs within liturgical symbols. "Being inextricably bound up with the sensual attributes of symbol, with the concrete sign, conversion to 'seeing-in-faith' is itself never dissociated from sense, and therefore from a kind of aesthetics."[10] Between seeing with the eyes of the body, which for Ambrose is no more than a kind of blindness, and seeing with the eyes of faith, which is absolute vision, there is the impulsion of desire, which leads from one to the other.[11] Retracing the journey of initiation as the movement of his mystagogy allows Ambrose to capitalize on this desire.

In concluding our discussion of the shape of *De sacramentis* as a whole, we note that while the process of Christian initiation provides the overall movement of Ambrose's mystagogy, he does not follow this process exactly. As we said at the outset of Chapter 5,[12] because

---

[8] William Harmless, *Augustine and the Catechumenate* (Collegeville: The Liturgical Press, 1995) 364.

[9] Peter Cramer, *Baptism and Change in the Early Middle Ages, c. 200–c. 1150* (New York: Cambridge University Press, 1993) 65.

[10] *De sacramentis*, 1.6.24; 3.1.1; 3.2.15; 4.6.29 (SC 25bis.72; 90; 100; 118).

[11] Ibid. Cf. *De sacramentis*, 3.2.15; 4.2.7 (SC 24bis.100; 104).

[12] Above, 146–147.

Ambrose's audience was already familiar with the rites that he is explaining, the bishop of Milan sometimes alludes to one rite while explaining another and sometimes introduces rites out of the order in which they actually occurred.[13] Furthermore, rather than following neatly one after another, the rites are regularly interrupted by digressions,[14] parenthetic discussions,[15] and expositions of passages of scripture.[16] We will discuss these aspects of the arrangement of materials in *De sacramentis* in Chapter 8, when we consider Ambrose's mystagogy as proclamation event and show that these divergences are, in fact, indications that Ambrose's method of delivery was to preach without having prepared a manuscript.[17] In our next section we will outline the tools that Ambrose uses to create the units that treat the individual rites.

The Structure of the Sermons

Turning from *De sacramentis* as a whole to the sermons contained therein, we find that these sermons are composed of units that treat specific rites or parts of rites. For example, the first sermon includes units on the *ephphatha*,[18] prebaptismal anointing,[19] renunciation,[20] and consecration of the water.[21] In creating these units, Ambrose uses a number of simple techniques that, from our vantage point, have demonstrated for centuries that they can carry the burden of truth with clarity, thoughtfulness, and interest.[22] These tools include (1) using inductive reasoning, (2) providing definition, (3) moving from problem to solution, (4) progressing from the lesser to the greater, and (5) flashing back from the present to the past and then returning to the present. In selecting what tool to use to explain a

---

[13] For example, in *De sacramentis*, 4.2.5–6 and 5.3.14 (SC 25bis.104; 126), Ambrose alludes to the neophytes' vesting with white robes while discussing their approach to the altar. The neophytes' vesting with white robes is not mentioned where it actually occurred, between the footwashing and the spiritual seal. See above, 174.

[14] *De sacramentis*, 1.4.11–12 (SC 25bis.66).

[15] Ibid., 1.6.21 (SC 25bis.70–72).

[16] Ibid., 2.2.3–7 (SC 25bis.74–78).

[17] See below, 293.

[18] *De sacramentis*, 1.1.2–3 (SC 25bis.60–62).

[19] Ibid., 1.2.4–8 (SC 25bis.62–64).

[20] Ibid.

[21] Ibid., 1.3.9–10 (SC 25bis.64–66).

[22] Craddock, *Preaching*, 176.

specific rite, Ambrose first discerns what that rite is meant to achieve and then selects a technique with that end in mind. In this section we will describe each of these ways of presenting material and provide examples of how Ambrose uses them to illuminate the meaning of the rites.

Using Inductive Reasoning. Inductive reasoning moves from the particular to the general. In explaining the rites of initiation, Ambrose moves from the particular experience of his hearers to the significance of that experience for Christian faith and its implications for Christian life. The steps that Ambrose takes are (1) to remind the neophytes of their experience, (2) to explain that experience using what Ambrose considers to be the rite's biblical institution, and (3) to apply that meaning of the rite to the lives of the newly baptized. For example, in his treatment of the washing of the neophytes' feet,[23] Ambrose places his hearers where they were in the process—coming out of the font— and asks them what happened next. He then reminds them that they listened to the reading of the biblical account of Jesus' washing the disciples' feet.[24] He further reminds them that the bishop then put on an apron and, together with the presbyters, began this liturgy.

Ambrose then asks, "What does this mystery mean?" In answering this question, the bishop of Milan retells the biblical account of Jesus washing the feet of the disciples. In order to explain the meaning of the liturgical action, Ambrose expands the conversation between Jesus and Peter: "[Jesus] came to Peter, and Peter said to him: 'Do you wash my feet?'[25] That is to say: Do you, the master, wash the feet of the servant? Do you, the spotless one, wash my feet? Do you, the creator of the heavens, wash my feet?"[26] Ambrose then turns to and expands upon the similar conversation between Jesus and John the Baptist: "I need to be baptized by you, and do you come to me?"[27] He instructs his hearers to see the righteousness, grace, humility, and holiness in Jesus' action.[28] The implication is that the same righteousness, grace, humility, and holiness were present when the feet of the newly

[23] *De sacramentis*, 3.1.4–7 (SC 25bis.92–96).
[24] John 13:6ff.
[25] Ibid.
[26] *De sacramentis*, 3.1.4 (SC 25bis.92).
[27] Matthew 3:14.
[28] *De sacramentis*, 3.1.4 (SC 25bis.92).

baptized were washed. Continuing his explanation, Ambrose uses Jesus' words, "If I do not wash your feet, you have no part in me,"[29] to defend both continuing a practice different from that of Rome and regarding this rite as a mystery, that is, conducting it as part of the baptismal rite and not merely as an act of humility. Ambrose insists that this washing is a mystery and sanctification.[30] In order to justify these differences, Ambrose appeals to Peter as his witness.[31]

Ambrose then explains the difference that this sanctification makes in the neophytes' lives.[32] He uses Jesus' answer to Peter, that those who have bathed do not need to wash again except for their feet,[33] to show that this rite gives special help of sanctification on the place where Adam was tripped up and infected by the devil's poison, so that the devil cannot trip up the newly baptized.[34] The neophytes have their feet washed to wash away the serpent's poison. In this way foot-washing protects them from committing postbaptismal sin. Other examples of Ambrose's use of an inductive movement from the neophytes' experience of the rite to the rite's biblical explanation to the implications of the rite for the life of faith include the unit on the *ephphatha* and one of the units on baptism.[35]

Providing Definition. A second tool that Ambrose uses to illuminate the meaning of the rites is first to name and then to define them. Yet one distinctive feature of these definitions is that they take seriously the truth about mystery. As Harmless suggests, "a mystery can be

---

[29] John 13:8.
[30] *De sacramentis*, 3.1.5 (SC 25bis.94).
[31] Ibid., 3.1.6 (SC 25bis.94).
[32] Ibid., 3.1.7 (SC 25bis.94).
[33] Cf. John 13:10.
[34] Ambrose's association of the heel with the innate tendency to sin that is a consequence of the fall is derived from two Old Testament texts: (1) God's curse of the serpent in Genesis 3:15: "I will put enmity between you and the woman, and between your offspring and hers; he will strike your head, and you will strike his heel"; (2) Psalm 48:6, which in the Septuagint reads: "The iniquity of my heel will surround me." Ambrose explains his thought more fully in *Enarrationes in xii psalmos davidicos*, 48.8-9 (CSEL 64.365–366). In *De interpellatione Iob et David*, 2.2.4 (CSEL 32/2.235), Christ is the stag whose heel is invulnerable to the snakebite. Ambrose is perhaps also alluding to the myth of Achilles' vulnerable heel.
[35] *De sacramentis*, 1.1.2–3; 2.2.3–7 (SC 25bis.60–62; 74–78).

pointed to, hinted at, even glimpsed, but it cannot be defined or exhausted."[36] Thus, Ambrose piles up meanings rather than seeking clear definitions. Baptism is tomb[37] and womb,[38] death[39] and resurrection,[40] absolution,[41] and new birth.[42] Baptism heals, cleanses, washes away sins, sanctifies, cancels guilt, and makes members of the Church. In Ambrose's mystagogy, definitions are "both/and" rather than "either/or." His "logic is more associative than discursive, more poetic than philosophical."[43] These "both/and" definitions serve to broaden the hearers' horizons and open them to many possibilities.

A second distinctive feature of these definitions is that they are composed of images rather than syllogisms. Again, these images take seriously the truth about mystery, namely, that no one image can hold and contain the full meaning of a rite. Thus, rather than selecting a single image that best sums up the essence of a rite, Ambrose unravels image after image in order to lift up different aspects and dimensions of the rite, thereby plumbing the depth of its meaning. In order to fully understand baptism, one must appreciate the baptismal significance of creation,[44] the flood,[45] Israel's passing through the Red Sea,[46] the spring of Marah,[47] the cleansing of Naaman the leper,[48] Elisha's floating axe-head,[49] the second tabernacle in the Temple,[50] Jesus'

---

[36] Harmless, *Augustine and the Catechumenate*, 367.
[37] *De sacramentis*, 3.1.1 (SC 25bis.90).
[38] *De mysteriis*, 9.59 (SC 25bis.190–192).
[39] *De sacramentis*, 2.6.19; 7.20, 23 (SC 25bis.84, 86–88).
[40] Ibid., 3.1.1 (SC 25bis.90).
[41] Ibid., 3.1.2 (SC 25bis.90).
[42] Ibid.
[43] Harmless, *Augustine and the Catechumenate*, 367.
[44] *De sacramentis*, 3.1.3 (SC 25bis.90–92); *De mysteriis*, 3.9 (SC 25bis.160).
[45] *De sacramentis*, 1.6.23; 2.1.1 (SC 25bis.72; 74); *De mysteriis*, 3.10–11 (SC 25bis.160).
[46] *De sacramentis*, 1.4.12, 6.20–22 (SC 25bis.66; 70–72); *De mysteriis*, 3.12–13 (SC 25bis.162).
[47] *De sacramentis*, 2.4.12–5.13 (SC 25bis.66–68); *De mysteriis*, 3.14–15 (SC 25bis.162).
[48] *De sacramentis*, 1.5.13–15; 2.3.8 (SC 25bis.66–68; 78); *De mysteriis*, 3.16–18 (SC 25bis.164).
[49] *De sacramentis*, 2.4.11 (SC 25bis.78–80).
[50] Ibid., 4.1.1–4 (SC 25bis.102).

baptism in the Jordan,[51] and his healing of both the paralytic at the pool of Beth-zatha[52] and the man born blind,[53] as well as death and burial,[54] resurrection and birth.[55] In allowing these images and echoes to pile up, their "meanings cluster and set off vibrations among themselves. . . . [This] piling up evokes experience—an experience that presses the hearer beyond the words themselves."[56]

Moving from Problem to Solution. In order to express our need for baptism, the method that Ambrose selects is first to outline humanity's problem and then to describe God's solution to that problem.[57] The problem that Ambrose raises, simply stated, is the Fall and its consequences.[58] Quoting Genesis 1:1 and 2:17, Ambrose asserts that in the beginning God created humanity so that we would never die as long as we never tasted sin. The problem is that humanity sinned, became subject to death, and was driven out of Paradise. The Lord, desiring God's gifts to last forever and in order to destroy all the wiles of the serpent and to cancel out all the harm it had done, sentenced humanity to death.[59] This solution created another problem: death is a divine sentence that cannot be remitted by humankind. God's solution to this problem was to transform the divine sentence of death into a divine gift by making humanity die and rise again. Ambrose views death as a gift because when it comes, death puts an end to sin; when we die we do, in fact, stop sinning.[60] But in order that God's gift might continue forever, Christ invented the resurrection, which restores the heavenly gift that was lost through the deceit of the serpent. Thus both death and resurrection are solutions to the problem of sin; death is the end of sin, and resurrection is the reformation of our nature.

Building upon the previous problem and solution, Ambrose then asserts that baptism was invented as God's solution to two problems:

---

[51] Ibid., 1.5.15–19 (SC 25bis.68–70); *De mysteriis*, 4.24–25 (SC 25bis.168–170).
[52] *De sacramentis*, 2.2.3–7 (SC 25bis.74–76); *De mysteriis*, 4.19 (SC 25bis.164).
[53] *De sacramentis*, 3.2.11–15 (SC 25bis.106–110).
[54] Ibid., 2.6.19, 7.20, 23 (SC 25bis.84–88).
[55] Ibid., 3.2.11 (SC 25bis.98).
[56] Harmless, *Augustine and the Catechumenate*, 367.
[57] *De sacramentis*, 2.6.16–19 (SC 25bis.82–84).
[58] Ibid., 2.6.17 (SC 25bis.82–84).
[59] Genesis 3:19.
[60] Cf. Romans 6:7.

(1) the deceits and tricks of the devil prevailing in this world and (2) the impossibility for human beings buried in the earth to rise again.[61] To break the hold of the devil in this world, a means was found to make living men and women, that is, women and men who are physically alive, die and rise again.[62] That means is baptism. Ambrose argues that in baptism human beings are buried in the font without the loss of life. He then declares that since water, like dirt, is from the earth, the heavenly sentence: "You are dust and to dust you will return" is still served. Thus by being immersed in the waters of baptism, human beings return to the earth without physically dying. Once the divine sentence is served, there is room for God's gift and remedy, namely, resurrection. In this way baptism solves the problem of the Fall and its consequences.

Progressing from the Lesser to the Greater. In order to prove the greatness of the Christian sacraments, the technique that Ambrose employs is to move his hearers from the lesser to the greater or, more accurately, from the great to the greater. He begins by asserting the greatness of the Jewish sacraments, namely, that we marvel at the Jewish mysteries because they are preeminent for their antiquity and their holiness. He then promises that the Christian sacraments are older and more godly than the Jewish mysteries.[63]

In considering baptism, Ambrose begins with the extraordinary event of Israel's passing through the Red Sea and shows how Christian baptism is even greater.[64] Whereas all the people that made that passage died in the desert, those who pass through the font do not die but rise again. Furthermore, since the flood is a figure of baptism and occurred earlier than the Jewish mysteries, the Christian sacraments are greater because they are older.[65]

Ambrose makes the same assertion that the Christian sacraments are older and more divine than those of the Jews in his treatment of

---

[61] *De sacramentis*, 2.6.18 (SC 25bis.64).

[62] Ibid., 2.6.19 (SC 25bis.64).

[63] Ibid., 1.4.11 (SC 25bis.66). Harmless is correct that, to a conservative society like the Romans, the novelty of Christianity made it suspect. Thus Christian apologists felt compelled to create for it a more ancient lineage. Harmless, *Augustine and the Catechumenate*, 102.

[64] *De sacramentis*, 1.4.12 (SC 25bis.66).

[65] Ibid., 1.6.23 (SC 25bis.72).

the Eucharist. Once again he uses the movement from lesser to greater to prove his case. That the Eucharist is older than the manna in the wilderness is evident from the sacrifice of the bread and wine of Melchizedek, who lived at the time of Abraham and is the figure of Christ.[66] In showing that the Eucharist is holier, Ambrose again begins by asserting the greatness of the manna from heaven.[67] But the Eucharist is even more godly because it was established by Christ in person during his lifetime.[68] Furthermore, those who ate the manna died; those who eat the body of Christ have their sins forgiven and will never die.[69]

A second way that Ambrose moves from the lesser to the greater in order to show the greatness of the Christian sacraments is by moving from sign to fulfillment, from figure to reality. He understands the crossing the Red Sea to be but the figure of God's grace while baptism is the reality.[70] The descent of the Spirit as a dove at Christ's baptism and in the sound of wind at Pentecost were both signs given so that unbelievers might be called to faith.[71] "But now in our case the privilege of faith is offered. In the beginning there were signs for the sake of unbelievers; but for us who live in the time of the Church's full growth the truth is to be grasped, not by signs, but by faith."[72] In this same way, Ambrose compares the Eucharist with the sacrifice of Melchizedek and concludes that the figure is not greater than the reality.[73]

Flashback. In order to make visible what is invisible, in order to help the newly baptized see what is unseen, a fourth tool that Ambrose uses is what we might call a biblical "flashback." He places the newly baptized in the rites of initiation and identifies their experience with that of a biblical character. Ambrose then flashes back to the biblical character's story, retelling it in such a way that the character's experience becomes the neophytes' experience. For example, Ambrose uses the person of Naaman the leper to help his hearers see that there was

---

[66] Ibid., 4.3.10–12 (SC 25bis.106–108).
[67] Ibid., 4.4.13 (SC 25bis.108).
[68] Ibid., 4.4.14–15 (SC 25bis.108–110).
[69] Ibid., 4.5.24 (SC 25bis.116).
[70] Ibid., 1.6.20 (SC 25bis.70).
[71] Ibid., 2.5.14, 15 (SC 25bis.80–82).
[72] Ibid., 2.5.15 (SC 25bis.82).
[73] Ibid., 5.1.1 (SC 25bis.120).

more going on in baptism than what appeared to the human eye.[74] He places his hearers as they are drawing near the font and seeing both the font itself and the bishop consecrating the water. Ambrose then connects the neophytes' reaction to the font—"Is that all?"—with that of Naaman the Syrian, who, although he was ultimately cleansed, began by doubting.[75] After asserting that there was invisible activity going on in baptism and that what is unseen is greater than what is seen, Ambrose tells the story of Naaman's cleansing, of how Elisha told him to go and bathe in the Jordan to be cleansed.[76] Naaman reflected that there were better rivers in his country; however, he went to the Jordan, bathed, and was cleansed.[77] Ambrose then returns to the present, to the baptismal font, in order to make the point that the power to cleanse is not in what is seen (the water) but in the (invisible) grace of Christ.[78]

Ambrose uses this same approach to help the newly baptized understand how they come to see with the eyes of faith.[79] He asks the neophytes, "What happened after this?" and places them in that moment when they approached the altar. They can see what they could not see before. Ambrose then asks, "What is this mystery?" Namely, how is it that after baptism the neophytes can see with the eyes of faith what they were blind to before? In answering this question, the bishop of Milan identifies their experience with that of the man born blind who is brought to Jesus to be cured.[80] Ambrose then flashes back to the biblical account of Jesus healing this man, retelling the story in order to emphasize Jesus' anointing the man's eyes with clay and telling him to go and wash in the pool of Siloam. "Rising, he went and washed and came back seeing."[81]

Once again the biblical character's experience becomes the neophytes' experience. Ambrose returns to the present and tells his hearers to

---

[74] Ibid., 1.3.9–10 and 1.5.13–14 (SC 25bis.64–68).

[75] Ibid., 1.3.9–10 (SC 25bis.64–66).

[76] This transition is interrupted by a digression to a tangential topic, i.e., Ambrose's declaration of the superiority of the Christian sacraments over those of the Jews. Ibid., 1.3.11–12 (SC 25bis.66).

[77] Ibid., 1.5.15 (SC 25bis.68).

[78] Ibid.

[79] Ibid., 3.2.11–15 (SC 25bis.98–100).

[80] John 9:6f.

[81] John 9:6-7.

think about the eyes of their heart.[82] They were able to see bodily things with their bodily eyes, but they were not able to see sacramental things with the eyes of their heart.[83] So when they put in their names for baptism, Christ put mud on their eyes—reverence, prudence, and the awareness of their frailty—and sent them to the font where Christ's cross is preached and in which all their errors are redeemed.[84] They went to the font, washed, came to the altar, and began to see[85] what they had not seen before. Ambrose tells the newly baptized that "through the font of the Lord and the preaching of the Lord's passion, at that moment your eyes were opened. Before you seemed to be blind of heart, but now you began to perceive the light of the sacraments."[86]

This "before/after" pattern impresses upon the hearers that conversion is the normative model for becoming a believer. The "conversion" is not just on the moral level or a change of ways of living; it is an intellectual and even an aesthetic "conversion." Faith leads Christians to learn to think differently, to accept something besides ordinary experience as fundamentally real, and to "see," "hear," and "experience" this new reality. Here Ambrose is telling the neophytes what he is attempting to accomplish in his mystagogy: he is offering them new, scripturally based patterns of perceiving the ordinary.[87]

Enriching the Structure

Thus far in our examination of the shape of Ambrose's mystagogy, we have examined the overall structure of *De sacramentis* and forms used to create units that treat individual rites. We now turn to elements that serve to "enrich the form."[88] The challenge of this section is to bear in mind that our goal is to develop a method of mystagogical preaching for the contemporary Church. Therefore, while a detailed

---

[82] *De sacramentis*, 3.2.12 (SC 25bis.98–100).

[83] Ibid.

[84] Ibid., 3.2.12, 14 (SC 25bis.100).

[85] Cf. John 9:7.

[86] *De sacramentis*, 3.2.15 (SC 25bis.100).

[87] "Seeing with the eyes of faith" is typically Origenistic; at the end of *On First Principles* (4.4), Origen speaks of the need to develop "spiritual senses" if we are to read the Scriptures correctly. See Karl Rahner, "The 'Spiritual Senses' According to Origen," *Theological Investigations* 16, trans. David Morland, O.S.B. (New York: The Seabury Press, 1979) 81–103.

[88] Craddock, *Preaching*, 194.

analysis of the verb forms, sentence structure, and word choices of the Latin text of *De sacramentis* would prove most interesting, that kind of detailed textual analysis is not particularly germane to our purpose. Consequently, we will limit our discussion of the means employed to enrich the form of *De sacramentis* to four general areas: (1) use of language, (2) method of description in terms of both the kinds of images employed and the ways that they are described, (3) selection and use of illustrations, and (4) the tone of these sermons.

Language. In preaching, there are two types of language: *informational language* and *experiential language.*[89] Informational language is designed to convey information. In *De sacramentis* there are several types of informational language. First, there is factual information about Christian practice. Ambrose tells the newly baptized that at Rome those who have been baptized are called *fideles,* or "faithful,"[90] and footwashing is not practiced as part of the baptismal rite.[91] He informs them of aspects of the liturgy that they may have missed, such as the fact that as soon as he enters the baptistry, the bishop first performs an exorcism on the water and then invokes and prays that the water be sanctified and the Trinity dwell there.[92] Likewise, Ambrose provides his hearers with both the "sacramental words" of the Eucharist[93] and the words of the Lord's Prayer.[94]

A second type of informational language found in *De sacramentis* is the meaning of unfamiliar words. *Ephphatha,* for example, is a Hebrew

---

[89] Philip Wheelwright distinguishes between *steno-meanings* or "meanings that can be shared in exactly the same way by a very large number of persons" and "open language." *Steno-meanings* "are not limited to objects. . . . They include shareable abstractions too." These "common meanings can be made and kept exact by digital method—by pointing to examples." "Open language" is "language employed for the purpose of either emoting or persuading." Open language seeks to express "a greater fullness of knowledge, a yearning of the mind toward what lies beyond the reach of words as already used or as prescriptively defined." Philip Wheelwright, *Metaphor and Reality* (Bloomington, Ind.: University of Indiana Press, 1962) 33, 35, 38, 39–40.

[90] *De sacramentis,* 1.1.1 (SC 25bis.60).
[91] Ibid., 3.1.5 (SC 25bis.94).
[92] Ibid., 1.5.18 (SC 25bis.70).
[93] Ibid., 4.5.21–23, 6.27 (SC 25bis.114, 116).
[94] Ibid., 5.4.18 (SC 25bis.128).

word which in Latin means *adaperire*.[95] *Siloam* means "sent,"[96] and *paraclete*, according to Ambrose, means "consoler."[97]

Finally, as we saw throughout Chapter 6, a third kind of informational language found in *De sacramentis* is the content of Bible stories. In all these instances the language used to convey information is characterized by simplicity, accuracy, and straightforwardness.

The second kind of language used in preaching is designed to generate experience, feelings, and memory. We discovered several of the types of experiential language found in *De sacramentis* in Chapter 4 as part of our study of the neophytes as participants in mystagogy.[98] These include calls for the newly baptized to remember what they experienced,[99] emphasizing the neophytes' active involvement in the mysteries,[100] and appeals to their senses and emotions as well as to their minds.[101] This language is specific and concrete. For example, rather than being told to remember their entrance into the baptistry, the neophytes are told to recall whom they saw and what they said.[102] Experiential language is active, with emphasis placed on the verb.[103] It appeals directly to all of the senses—seeing, hearing, touching, smelling, tasting[104]—and has an emotional content, such as anxiety, disappointment, wonder, joy, curiosity, and doubt.[105] Finally, as we have seen in our discussion of the rites in Chapter 5 and Scripture in Chapter 6, and shall see in the remainder of our discussion of the structure of *De sacramentis*,[106] Ambrose's experiential language employs images rather than propositions.

Distinguishing these two types of language enables us to see two essential characteristics of the shape of *De sacramentis*. First, the amount

---

[95] Ibid., 1.1.2 (SC 25bis.60).
[96] Ibid., 3.2.14 (SC 25bis.100).
[97] Ibid., 6.2.10 (SC 25bis.142).
[98] Above, 137–141.
[99] Above, 137–138.
[100] Above, 137–138.
[101] Above, 137, 139–140.
[102] *De sacramentis*, 1.2.4 (SC 25bis.62).
[103] See, for example, ibid., 1.2.4, 3.9, 10; 5.1.3, 3.14 (SC 25bis.62, 64; 122, 126). See above, 138–139.
[104] See, for example, ibid., 1.3.9–10; 1.1.2–4; 3.1.1; 5.3.17 (SC 25bis.64; 60–62; 91; 1.2.8).
[105] See, for example, ibid., 1.3.9–10; 3.2.15; 4.3.8 (SC 25bis.64; 101; 107).
[106] See above, 197, 210–211; below, 264.

of experiential language far surpasses the amount of informational language. Second, informational language is used in service to the experiential. While experience is generally evoked in order to assist hearers in understanding an idea, a theory, or a concept, the opposite is true in Ambrose's mystagogy. Informational language is provided to assist the newly baptized in exploring, clarifying, understanding, and appreciating their experience of Christian initiation. Although these conclusions are difficult to codify, they become obvious when one reads *De sacramentis*.

Description. The goal of description is to create in one's hearers the experience of the subject matter. This purpose is grounded in the conviction that a sermon is not only to say something but to do something.[107] Description takes seriously the power of images. Drawing on the observations of contemporary homiliticians, James Wallace reflects on the power of images to effect deep change in people, lift them into truth, and move them beyond themselves.[108] Elizabeth Achtemeier writes that "if we want to change someone's life from non-Christian to Christian, from dying to living, from despairing to hoping, from anxious to certain, from corrupted to whole, we must change the images, the imaginations of the heart."[109] Craddock observes that in order to create new attitudes and behavior, images must be replaced, and this comes only gradually, by other images. Images are therefore necessary for removing from the mind inadequate, erroneous, and distorted attitudes and behavior.[110] Here we are speaking of the power of images, in Wallace's words, "to effect the deepest change possible, a change in life orientation, the theological journey of conversion."[111] Thomas Troeger writes of preachers building their sermons so that "listeners can step securely from image to image, from story to story, and thus climb up into the truth of their lives."[112] For Troeger, the preacher's use of images

---

[107] Craddock, *Preaching*, 200.

[108] James A. Wallace, *Imaginal Preaching: An Archetypal Perspective* (New York: Paulist Press, 1995) 17–18.

[109] Elizabeth Achtemeier, *Creative Preaching* (Nashville: Abingdon Press, 1981) 24.

[110] Craddock, *Preaching*, 201.

[111] Wallace, *Imaginal Preaching: An Archetypal Perspective*, 17.

[112] Thomas Troeger, *Creating Fresh Images for Preaching* (Valley Forge: Judson, 1982) 30.

makes possible a communal ascent into union with Truth. Walter Brueggemann reminds us of the power of images to move us outward by embodying an alternative vision of reality and giving us another world to enter.[113] Recognizing the power of images, *Fulfilled in Your Hearing* declares, "The more we turn to the picture language of the poet and the storyteller, the more that we will be able to preach in a way that invites people to respond from their heart as well as from their head."[114]

As we saw in our chapter on Scripture, Ambrose explains the meaning of the rites by drawing on biblical themes and imagery. As an example, we recall that Ambrose interpreted the Milanese rite of post-baptismal footwashing not only as an imitation of the humility Jesus demonstrated at the Last Supper but also as a way of cleaning out the venom left by Satan, that serpent whose bite had caused Adam to trip and fall.[115] Ambrose also drew heavily on traditional biblical types in order to make baptism understood for all that it is: salvation, cure, purification, new creation, new birth, transformation, incorporation, and illumination. Thus *De sacramentis* overflows with images that complete one another: the Spirit hovering over the waters at creation; the flood at the time of Noah; the Red Sea; Moses sweetening the desert spring; the cure of Naaman the Syrian.

As Botte has noted, the pedagogical effect Ambrose achieved was "not so much a harmonious synthesis as a series of tableaux . . . to be engraved on the memory of the neophytes."[116] By mutually completing each other, the interplay of images gives the neophytes "a rich, living idea of baptism"[117] more vital than abstract theories. Thus the first point to note about the method of description found in *De sacramentis* is that the ordering or organization of images is not as important as their abundance. Mystagogy is not linear, narrative sequential thinking. Especially in Ambrose's enthusiastic hands, it is more like a collage or a quilt; large, brightly colored images are stuck next to or on top of each other to create a general impression of abundance.

---

[113] Walter Brueggemann, *Finally Comes the Poet* (Philadelphia: Fortress Press, 1989) esp. 79–110.

[114] National Conference of Catholic Bishops, *Fulfilled in Your Hearing: The Homily in the Sunday Assembly* (Washington: United States Catholic Conference, 1982) 25.

[115] *De sacramentis*, 3.1.4–7 (SC 25bis.92–96).

[116] Botte, *Des Sacrements; Des Mystères*, 36.

[117] Ibid.

In this section we want to make two additional points about Ambrose's method of description. First, characters, actions, and settings all receive attention. For example, in illuminating the meaning of the renunciation,[118] Ambrose not only describes the actions of asking and answering questions, but he also tells the neophytes to think about the place where they made their promise and those to whom they made it. In describing the actions, Ambrose repeats the actual questions and answers in dialogue form.[119] Both the ministers and baptistry are described in terms of their functions. The levite (or deacon) ministers at the altar of Christ; the dignity of the bishop comes from his office and not from his person. The baptistry is the place where the neophytes received the sacraments.[120]

Again, in his treatment of baptism, characters, setting, and actions are all described. Ambrose first describes the characters in terms of their location; the bishop is already at the font and the deacons and priest are already in it when the neophytes come down into the water.[121] The action of baptism is next described. The neophytes are three times asked if they believe; they answer and are immersed.[122] Finally, the place, the font, is described as tomblike in shape.[123] In this same way Ambrose describes the sacredness of the altar, the ordinariness of the bread and wine, and the words of consecration in his first sermon on the Eucharist.[124] Once more, characters, actions, and setting all receive attention.

The third point to note about the method of description used in *De sacramentis* is one that we made previously in other contexts, namely, that descriptions are made with an economy of words and are therefore incomplete. In the introduction to our discussion of initiation in Milan in Chapter 5 and again in our discussion of the overall structure of *De sacramentis* in this chapter, we noted that since his hearers were already familiar with the rites to which he was alluding, Ambrose is not always very explicit about the precise details of these rites.[125] For

---

[118] *De sacramentis*, 1.2.5–8 (SC 25bis.62–64).
[119] Ibid., 1.2.5 (SC 25bis.62).
[120] Ibid., 1.2.6 (SC 25bis.62–64).
[121] Ibid., 2.4.16 (SC 25bis.82).
[122] Ibid., 2.6.20–21 (SC 25bis.86).
[123] Ibid., 3.1.1 (SC 25bis.90).
[124] Ibid., 4.2.7; 3.8; 4.14; 5.21 (SC 25bis.104; 106; 108–110; 114).
[125] Above, 146, 252.

example, we find neither the words and actions associated with the spiritual seal nor any mention of the newly baptized dressing in white robes.[126] While this economy of words may be a frustrating hindrance to liturgical scholars, it helped Ambrose's original hearers in two ways. First, alluding to the rites of initiation rather than describing them in full helped the neophytes to participate in mystagogy as they complete the picture. Second, describing the rites in vivid and complete detail would tend to dictate to the newly baptized how they should understand and respond to initiation rather than allowing them to enter more fully into their experience and discover its meaning for themselves.

In this section we noted three characteristics of the method of description found in *De sacramentis*. First, the organization of images is not as important as their abundance. Second, characters, actions, and settings are all described, and, third, descriptions are made with an economy of words. We turn now to the illustrative material contained in *De sacramentis*.

Illustration. In preaching, illustrations are stories, images, and anecdotes that are used to carry the message of the sermon. Specifically, illustrations are the means by which the preacher uses the familiar to introduce or explain the unfamiliar.[127] In this section, we want to make two points about the illustrations in *De sacramentis*. First, in his mystagogical works, Ambrose uses three kinds of illustrations to illuminate the mysteries: biblical illustrations, cultural illustrations, and natural illustrations. Second, the point of analogy between the thought and the image is clear.[128] Inasmuch as we devoted Chapter 6 to the use of Scripture and scriptural images, in this section we will limit our discussion to examples of the use of cultural and natural illustrative material in *De sacramentis*.

The most striking natural images used in *De sacramentis* are those of the sea and the fish. In order to move his hearers from the baptismal rite to the appropriate style of life that follows from baptism, Ambrose uses the natural images of the Christian as a fish and the world as a raging sea. Ambrose says:

---

[126] See above, 174–176.
[127] Craddock, *Preaching*, 204.
[128] Ibid., 204–205.

"Imitate the fish. . . . On the sea the tempest rages, storms shriek; but the fish swims on. It does not drown because it is used to swimming. In the same way, this world is the sea for you. It has diverse currents, huge waves, fierce storms. You too must be a fish, so that the waves of this world do not drown you."[129]

Describing the world or this life as a sea and a human being as tossed by the waves of sin is a favorite illustration of Saint Ambrose and is found throughout his works.[130] Using this illustration, Ambrose tells his hearers what it means to be in the world but not of the world.[131]

Turning to cultural images, in speaking of the prebaptismal anointing, Ambrose uses the image of the athlete to explain the significance of the rite. He says, "You are anointed as an athlete of Christ, as one slated to compete in the bout that is this world."[132] He compares the anointing before baptism with the preparation of the athlete for his contest. As such, the baptistry becomes the arena and the renunciation the conflict in which the devil and the world are defeated.[133] There is a similar passage in *De Helia et ieiunio* in which Ambrose asserts that we contend in a kind of spiritual arena. He says that the athlete is exercised and anointed daily.[134] The image of the athlete in the arena, naked, rubbed down with oil, is charged to express the noble combat of the Christian against the world.[135]

---

[129] *De sacramentis*, 3.1.3 (SC 25bis.90–92).

[130] Cf. *De Iacob et vita beata*, 8.35 (CSEL 32/2.52–53); *De patriarchis*, 5.26–27 (CSEL 32/2.139–140); *De interpellatione Iob et David*, 1.7.23; 1.9.30; 2.5.19; 4.9.34 (CSEL 32/2.225–226; 230–231; 244–245; 294).

[131] Cf. John 17:15-16.

[132] *De sacramentis*, 1.2.4 (SC 25bis.62).

[133] See above, 161–162.

[134] *De Helia et ieiunio*, 21.79 (CSEL 32/2.460–461). Cf. *De obitu Theodosii*, 24 (CSEL 73.383); *Epistola* 20 (Maur. 77).10 (CSEL 82/3.113). See above, 151–152.

[135] Cf. *De fuga saeculi*, 5.28 (CSEL 32/2.186–187). In other works Ambrose uses the image of the athlete to describe the effort required to comprehend Scriptures, the spirit against the passions, and the fights of martyrs against their persecutor. See, for example, *Expositio evangelii secundum Lucam* Prologue 6 (CCSL 14.5); *Hexaemeron*, 8.50 (CSEL 32/1.241–242); *De paradiso*, 12.55 (CSEL 32/1.212–213); *De Iacob et vita beata*, 1.8.36 (CSEL 32/2.26–27); *Contra Auxentium*, 6 (CSEL 82/3.85).

Ambrose also uses monetary images.[136] He compares the renunciation to a down payment on a loan and warns of the perils of defaulting. He also declares that faith in Christ is more precious than money because faith is an eternal rather than a temporal possession.[137] In order to convince the newly baptized that Christian sacraments are older and more godly than Jewish mysteries, a claim he will not prove until later in the sermon, Ambrose calls his words a promissory note and instructs his hearers to demand full payment.[138] As a final example, in his exposition of the Lord's Prayer, Ambrose uses monetary images to explain the petition "Forgive us our debts."[139] Comparing sin to money, he explains that though we were born rich, being made in the image and likeness of God, we lost the money we had when out of pride we became indebted to the devil.

Lastly, Ambrose uses one of his favorite images, the marriage feast,[140] to illustrate the relationship between Christ and the Church in the Eucharist. Ambrose describes marriage using lush sensual images drawn from the Canticle of Canticles.[141] He calls both Christ's judgment that the neophytes are clean and worthy and Christ's invitation to the sacraments as "kisses."[142] He describes the sacraments as "breasts . . . better than wine," because in them there is also a spiritual joy.[143] In order to tell the newly baptized that they cannot follow Christ unless he draws them to himself, Ambrose imagines the Church saying to Christ, "Draw us, so that we follow the scent of your perfumes."[144] He describes the King as drawing them into his "bedchamber," which is "a pantry" or "a cellar," full of "the best vintages, the best perfumes, the sweetest honey, the choicest fruits and dainties."[145] In treating the festal imagery, Ambrose shows the ways the spiritual world paradoxically inverts everyday life: "You are inebriated in

---

[136] Cf. *De Ioseph*, 11.63–66 (CSEL 32/2.112–113).

[137] *De sacramentis*, 1.2.8 (SC 25bis.64).

[138] Ibid., 1.4.11 (SC 25bis.66).

[139] Ibid., 5.4.27 (SC 25bis.134).

[140] See *De Isaac vel anima*, 5.46 (CSEL 32/1.670–671); *De patriarchis*, 4.22 (CSEL 23/2.136–137).

[141] *De sacramentis*, 5.2.5–11 (SC 25bis.122–124). On Ambrose's use of Canticles, see above, 220.

[142] Ibid., 5.2.5–7 (SC 25bis.122).

[143] Ibid., 5.2.8 (SC 25bis.124).

[144] Ibid., 5.2.9 (SC 25bis.124).

[145] Ibid., 5.2.11 (SC 25bis.124).

spirit. . . . For the one who is inebriated with wine totters and sways; the one who is inebriated with the Holy Spirit is rooted in Christ. And so, glorious is the inebriation which effects sobriety of mind."[146] The illustration of the marriage feast creates a much more vivid understanding of the relationship that Christ establishes with his people in the Eucharist than does a word such as "communion."

In this section we showed that the illustrative material in *De sacramentis* is of three types—biblical, natural, and cultural. Our examples demonstrate that the connection between the point being made and the material used to illustrate that point is clear. By using what is familiar, Ambrose helps his hearers to comprehend what is unfamiliar; using images from this life, Ambrose helps his hearers to comprehend the new life in baptism.

Tone. The final component that we want to examine in order to establish the rhetorical character of *De sacramentis* is the tone of these sermons. Tone is especially important in overcoming the burdens of communication, those things that the listeners bring to the message in terms of knowledge, attitude, feeling, and prior experience.[147] In order to examine the tone of *De sacramentis,* we therefore begin by exploring the neophytes' anticipated response to Ambrose's illumination of the sacraments. We will then attempt to discover how Ambrose shapes these sermons to meet the challenge of that response.

We outlined one aspect of the newly baptized's anticipated response in Chapter 4 as part of our discussion of their *ability to listen*.[148] The neophytes of Milan were active and involved listeners generally because of the prominent place of rhetoric in the culture; they were particularly interested in Ambrose's message on the sacraments because of their experience of the long, demanding, and mysterious process of Christian initiation. The burden of communication, then, was not to gain the neophytes' attention and to interest them in the message but to avoid disappointing their expectations and to maximize their already favorable interest.

A second burden of communication was that the newly baptized were uninformed about the meaning of the sacraments. The sermons contained in *De sacramentis* were their first instruction on the rites of

---

[146] Ibid., 5.3.17 (SC 25bis.128).
[147] Craddock, *Preaching*, 182.
[148] See above, 126–127.

initiation. The task, then, was to educate, to provide information, but not so much information that the newly baptized felt overloaded, overwhelmed, confused, and depressed.

A third burden of communication was the need to meet, overcome, and convert skepticism. In the movement from unseeing to seeing, from the visible to the invisible, some of the claims that Ambrose makes about the Christian sacraments are certainly unreasonable and perhaps even unbelievable; they were, therefore, met with a level of skepticism that needed to be addressed.

As we saw in Chapter 4, Ambrose's "catechetical style" includes a higher degree of intimate contact between the preacher and the listeners and a clearer and simpler form than what we find in his regular preaching. In order to create a spontaneous, improvisational, free style, Ambrose employs direct address, repetition, loose syntax, and dialogue.[149] Thus the tone of these sermons is familiar and paternal.[150] His method and mood of sharing information are supportive of his hearers' experience. He reminds them of what they have said, seen, heard, and done and then builds upon what they already know.[151] Ambrose makes information easy to remember through the use of repetition, alliteration, and sharp contrasts. He brightens information with analogies and concrete examples. Ambrose addresses his hearers' skepticism with openness and candor. He literally gives voice to his hearers' questions, doubts, disappointments, and objections to his explanations.[152] In this regard he does not feel the need to protect either his hearers, the rites, or God from what may at first seem unreasonable. Instead, Ambrose acknowledges his hearers' objections and doubts, responds to them, and then demands from his hearers a high level of participation that will lead them to move beyond reason to faith and to do so in an informed and serious way.

Summary

In the first half of this chapter we uncovered the shape or structure of *De sacramentis*. We found that the order of the rites of initiation provides the organization and movement of this series of six sermons. In this way the shape of Ambrose's mystagogy reflects the "text" from

---

[149] See above, 127.
[150] See above, 128.
[151] See above, 137–138.
[152] See above, 141–142.

which the message of these sermons is drawn. Individual sermons are composed of units devoted to specific rites. The rhetorical style and form of these units are drawn from a number of simple but time-honored ways of organizing material, selected according to the meaning of a given rite. In enriching these forms, experiential language, the amount of which far surpasses that of informational language, is given priority and emphasis; pure information is provided solely to assist the hearers in exploring and clarifying their experience. Similarly, actions, characters, and settings are all described rather than defined; the rites are described using an economy of words but an abundance of images.

In these ways the method of description aids the listeners in participating in the message. Familiar illustrations drawn from biblical, natural, and cultural sources are used to introduce and explain the unfamiliar sacraments. Finally, the tone of these sermons is direct and supportive, paternal and familiar, open and candid. Having established the shape of *De sacramentis*, we now turn to an analysis of how form and style function to facilitate the listeners' apprehension of the message.

STRUCTURE AND MYSTAGOGY

In this section we will ask how the shape of *De sacramentis* contributes to the hearing of Ambrose's message on the sacraments by the newly baptized, that is, how, if at all, the structure of *De sacramentis* assists the newly baptized to move from seeing with the eyes of the body to seeing with the eyes of faith. This section rests on the conviction that the shape of the sermon serves to arrest, accent, focus, and aid the listener's apprehension of the message.[153] While there is enough truth in the "twin convictions that a message of burning significance will, without art or skill, cut its own path to the hearer's heart, and that the Holy Spirit, without human contrivance, opens the listener's ear"[154] to "give pause and correction to any who become enamored with their own artistry,"[155] trusting in the power of God does not relieve preachers of the burden of the disciplines that prepare them to preach with the power of God. Discerning the message, crafting the sermon, and preparing to preach it all assist the Spirit in opening the listener to the power of the Gospel message.

---

[153] Craddock, *Preaching*, 172.
[154] Ibid., 154.
[155] Ibid.

Recognizing that our goal is to develop a method of mystagogical preaching for the contemporary Church, our method of analyzing the contribution that the shape of *De sacramentis* makes to mystagogy is contemporary. We will use as the lenses through which we will assess the structure of Ambrose's preaching on the sacraments what Craddock calls qualities commonly held to be desirable in sermons. These qualities to be sought in preaching are "comprehensive terms, few in number but specific enough to release and govern our creativity."[156] They are characteristics of a message "congenial to the gospel, to the listeners, to the context, and to sound principles of communication"[157] and include (1) unity, (2) ecclesial consciousness, (3) recognition, (4) identification, (5) anticipation, and (6) intimacy.

Unity

Unity leads us to look for a simple, affirmative statement that serves as a unifying theme or governing idea and provides the direction of the sermon. Ambrose himself tells us that "the sacraments which you have received are the theme of my sermon."[158] However, Ambrose's announcement provides neither a governing idea nor a direction for his preaching on the sacraments. In Chapter 4 we argued that the goal of Ambrose's mystagogy is to lead the newly baptized to enter more fully and deeply into their encounter with Christ in the rites of initiation, so that they move beyond worldly perception and see with the eyes of faith, which they received at baptism.[159] Ambrose states this theme explicitly in *De sacramentis*, 3.2.15:

"You went there [to the font], you washed, you came to the altar, you began to see what you had not seen before; that is to say, through the font of the Lord and the preaching of the Lord's passion, at that moment your eyes were opened. Before, you seemed to be blind of heart; but now you began to perceive the light of the sacraments."[160]

---

[156] Ibid.

[157] Ibid.

[158] *De sacramentis*, 1.1.1 (SC 25bis.60).

[159] Above, 125, 136–137, 259–260.

[160] *Isti, lavisti, venisti ad altare, videre coepisti quae ante non videras, hoc est: per fontem domini et praedicationem dominicae passionis tunc aperti sunt oculi tui; qui ante corde videbaris esse caecatus, coepisti lumen sacramentorum videre.* SC 25bis.100.

As we have said,[161] Ambrose assumes that in the rite of baptism God confers faith on the person baptized. In baptism God gives the person the new ability to see and understand the invisible, yet fundamentally real, mystery of salvation that he or she is entering. The mystagogical catecheses are attempting to get the person to "exercise" this new set of senses; however, the ability to do so, which the newly baptized did not have prior to baptism regardless of how much they desired it, is now there, waiting to be cultivated.

Ambrose repeats and restates this theme throughout *De sacramentis*. He tells the newly baptized that when they approached the font, they saw all they could see with the eyes of the body, all that is open to human sight, but they did not see what is done, the invisible action of God, which is far greater than what they saw.[162] Ambrose reminds his hearers that they saw bodily things with their bodily eyes, but they were not yet able to see sacramental things with the eyes of their heart; therefore, when they put in their names for baptism, Christ spread mud on their eyes and sent them to the font, where Christ's cross is preached.[163] He also tells his hearers to look beyond the literal meaning and see the mystery in Scripture.[164] Finally, Ambrose blesses the neophytes, asking that God may deign to illuminate more fully the eyes God has opened through Christ.[165] Beyond these obvious references, the movement from the visible to the invisible, from seeing with the eyes of the body to seeing with the eyes of faith, is the operating principle of much of Ambrose's exposition of the sacraments and interpretation of Scripture. Thus we can conclude that "see with the eyes of faith" is the theme that unites and provides direction for the sermons contained in *De sacramentis*.

Ecclesial Consciousness

The second quality to be sought in preaching is *ecclesial consciousness*. To understand a sermon's ecclesial consciousness is to examine the ways that the sermon is set within the tradition of the believing community. *Tradition* includes all those factors that shape the continuing life of the people of God, and the *believing community* includes not

---

[161] Above, 187–188.
[162] *De sacramentis*, 1.3.10 (SC 25bis.64–66).
[163] Ibid., 3.3.12 (SC 25bis.98–100).
[164] Ibid., 2.2.6 (SC 25bis.76).
[165] Ibid., 4.6.29 (SC 25bis.118).

only the congregation but the life of the universal Church, past, present, and future. These sermons are, of course, "traditional" because they treat the meaning of the Church's sacraments. More than this, we can identify four ways that these sermons are set within the tradition of the believing community. The most obvious aspect of these sermons' ecclesial consciousness is the integration of the Church's liturgy and Scripture into the content of *De sacramentis*. As we have seen,[166] not only are both liturgical and scriptural texts quoted and alluded to, words, phrases, and ideas from the liturgy and Scriptures are used to "season" these sermons.

A second aspect of the ecclesial consciousness of *De sacramentis* is Ambrose's acknowledgment of the Church beyond his congregation in his articulation of the relationship between the church of Milan and the church of Rome. In his exposition of footwashing, the bishop of Milan both declares his desire to follow the practices of the church of Rome in all things and defends his right to maintain practices different from that of Rome.[167]

Third, Ambrose discusses the theological issues that the Church is facing, namely, Arianism, and addresses what he perceives to be the Church's hostile relationship with the culture.[168]

Fourth, *De sacramentis* speaks for the Church, giving voice to both its response to the sacraments and joy and exultation in receiving the neophytes.[169]

Recognition

Recognition, the third quality to be sought in sermons, explores the ways that Ambrose structures his sermons to enable his hearers to recognize in his preaching their own experience, their own confession of sin and repentance, their own affirmation of faith, their own vision and hope, and their own burst of praise. Recognition is a hallmark of Ambrose's mystagogy, which, as we have seen, is grounded in particular people's experience of specific rites of initiation.[170] The tools

---

[166] See above, 200–204, 242–246.

[167] *De sacramentis*, 3.1.5–6 (SC 25bis.94).

[168] See, for example, ibid., 1.2.4, 5, 8, 4.11–12, 5.17–19; 2.1.2, 7.24; 3.1.3; 4.2.7, 3.9–12, 5.23; 6.2.10 (SC 25bis.62, 64, 66, 68–70; 74, 88; 100; 104, 106–108; 116; 142). See above, 194–195.

[169] *De sacramentis*, 5.2.7, 3.14 (SC 25bis.122, 126).

[170] Above, 190.

used to create recognition in his commentary on the rites include (1) conveying information, (2) giving a different perspective on the familiar, (3) including rather than omitting details, and (4) presenting the familiar with interest and enthusiasm.

Earlier in this chapter we discussed the purpose of informational language in *De sacramentis:* information is provided in order to assist the hearers in exploring, clarifying, understanding, and appreciating their experience of Christian initiation.[171] In using information to help the neophytes recognize the meaning and significance of their experience, Ambrose's pedagogical method is to give his hearers a different perspective on the familiar. For example, the baptistry is heaven, and ordinary bread and wine are the body and blood of Christ.[172] In this way he enables the newly baptized to see with the eyes of faith.

The descriptions of the rites in *De sacramentis,* though incomplete, are nevertheless most detailed, particularly concerning the involvement of the neophytes. We have seen that in addition to describing rites that are unique to initiation in Milan,[173] Ambrose reminds the newly baptized of where they were and who they were with, as well as what they saw, did, and said. Finally, Ambrose's claims of the greatness of the sacraments are an indication of his interest and enthusiasm.[174] Thus, recognition assumes that the listeners will know much of the material presented; sermons are structured to enable the hearers to identify and build upon what they already know.

A second way that the newly baptized recognize themselves in the sermons contained in *De sacramentis* is that these sermons give the neophytes a voice and engage them in dialogue. In Chapter 4 we discussed the ways that Ambrose speaks for the newly baptized as well as to them.[175] He includes in these sermons what the newly baptized want to say—their faith and their doubt, their joy and their disappointment. The techniques that Ambrose uses include asking the neophytes questions, putting their likely reactions to the rites into words, and raising their objections to his explanation of the mysteries.

---

[171] Above, 261–262.

[172] *De sacramentis,* 1.2.6; 4.4.14, 20 (SC 25bis.62–64; 108–110, 112).

[173] For example, ibid., 2.7.20; 3.1.4–7 (SC 25bis.84; 92–96). For our discussion of these unique features, see above, 191.

[174] We will have much more to say about Ambrose's attitude toward his subject matter in Chapter 8. See below, 285.

[175] See above, 141–142.

Through these methods the newly baptized are partners in a dialogue and therefore participants in mystagogy.

Identification

Identification is Craddock's fourth quality to be sought in a sermon. Kenneth Burke describes *identification* as "courtship, however roundabout," reminding us that the "act of persuasion may be for the purpose of causing the audience to identify itself with the speaker's interests; and the speaker draws on identification of interests to establish rapport between himself and his audience."[176] Craddock asks, "How do we draw and hold the listeners in the bond of identification so that the message may do its work on mind and heart?"[177] The answer is once again found in the fact that mystagogy is grounded in experience. Ambrose's primary concern is not that his hearers identify with him personally, though his catechetical style is intended to create such a bond;[178] he is concerned that the newly baptized identify with the rites of initiation so that the material presented in *De sacramentis* is re-experienced as it is related.

Ambrose uses several tools to create this identification. We have seen that, both in content and in structure, these sermons are a journey through the rites of initiation.[179] Ambrose places both himself and his hearers in the rites of initiation, and together preacher and listeners move from not seeing to seeing. The bishop serves as the neophytes' guide on this journey, pointing out the spiritual significance of physical settings, elements, and actions so that the newly baptized can discover the depth of the sacraments. In order to facilitate his hearers' re-experiencing the rites with new insight rather than simply receiving information about them, we have seen that Ambrose gives primary attention to the specific and particular rather than the general. He describes initiation as it was practiced in Milan and brings the rites to bear on the lives of the particular people with whom he is speaking.[180] Throughout *De sacramentis*, the event of initiation is presented from

---

[176] Kenneth Burke, *A Grammar of Motives, and a Rhetoric of Motives* (Cleveland: World Publishing, 1962) 647, 570.
[177] Craddock, *Preaching*, 163.
[178] See above, 136; 270.
[179] See above, 195; 250.
[180] See above, 148ff.

the perspective of the newly baptized,[181] and narration and description are used with emotional restraint and economy of words, all of which allow the newly baptized to identify with their experience of initiation and thereby discover the depth of the sacraments for themselves rather than being told what the sacraments mean.

Anticipation

Craddock's fifth quality is *anticipation*. Anticipation involves the tools used by the preacher to shape a sermon that creates and sustains expectation so that the message is not only presented but heard. Creating anticipation is the primary burden of movement in the sermon. In order to create anticipation, the preacher must know the end toward which the sermon will move and take great care in crafting the journey to get the listeners to that end.[182] We have previously discussed the fact that the newly baptized undoubtedly came to these sermons with a high level of anticipation because of the experience that led them to be baptized, the long and arduous process of initiation in which they had participated, the fact that they had received no previous explanation of the rites, and their expectations of the preacher.[183] Nevertheless, Ambrose structures his sermons so that they move in a way that creates and sustains expectation.

The movement of the overall structure of *De sacramentis* builds upon this anticipation as Ambrose leads his hearers from outside the baptistry into the "sanctuary of rebirth"[184] and from there to the altar, to the place that they had not been before, where they saw the things they had not seen before.[185] The movement is from a contest with the devil[186] to the joyous praise of the angels.[187] Thus the movement is deeper and deeper into mystery where the newly baptized encounter greater and greater holiness. As we saw earlier in this chapter, the individual sermons in *De sacramentis* effectively use a variety of movements to maintain the listeners' anticipation.[188] These tools include the

---

[181] See above, 136–141.
[182] Craddock, *Preaching*, 167.
[183] Above, 126–127.
[184] *De mysteriis*, 2.5 (SC 25bis.158).
[185] *De sacramentis*, 3.2.11 (SC 25bis.98).
[186] Ibid., 1.2.4–5 (SC 25bis.62).
[187] Ibid., 4.2.5 (SC 25bis.104).
[188] Above, 251ff.

movements from the specific to the general, the physical to the spiritual, the great to the greater, and the present to the biblical.

Intimacy

Our sixth and final quality is *intimacy*. Intimacy involves the tools that the preacher uses to establish and maintain a personal relationship with the hearers. We have already discussed some of the tools that the bishop of Milan uses to create and maintain an intimate relationship with the newly baptized. First, intimacy is maintained by the ongoing relationship between the preacher and hearers.[189] Ambrose was the neophytes' spiritual leader. His ministry to his people was grounded in worship. A gifted preacher, he made the ministry of the Word, particularly instructing candidates for baptism, his top priority.

The Christian community in Milan also knew their bishop as an important public figure who wielded both sacred and secular authority. In his preaching on the sacraments, Ambrose also used a catechetical style to maintain an intimate relationship with the newly baptized.[190] He uses direct address, questions, and a familiar tone to engage his hearers in an intimate dialogue. Other tools used to create and maintain intimacy include attitude, eye contact, and an oral style. We will discuss these aspects of Ambrose's preaching to the newly baptized in the next chapter.

REFLECTION: THE PNEUMATIC DIMENSION OF THE SHAPE OF MYSTAGOGY

The Holy Spirit does not act to give faith by convincing, through argument, or by articulating a systematic theology; rather, the Holy Spirit is experienced in events. Jesus experienced the Holy Spirit at his baptism, and the disciples experienced the Holy Spirit at Pentecost. The Church experiences the Holy Spirit in Word and Sacrament. For this reason *De sacramentis* is crafted to create an event in which the Spirit acts. The characteristics of this event include experience, relationship, continuity, vision, and mission. These characteristics are manifested in the movement of these sermons. As we reflect upon the Spirit's role in the shape of mystagogy, we will describe each of these characteristics, retrace the movements in which they are manifested, and speculate on how they provide an opportunity for the Spirit to act.

---

[189] See above, 88.
[190] See above, 126–128.

De sacramentis is crafted so that the neophytes will experience God in their instruction on the meaning of the sacraments. These sermons do not merely convey information about God; they give the newly baptized an experience or, better still, a deeper experience of the rites of initiation in which God is active. We have seen that the overall shape and movement of *De sacramentis* is a journey through the mysteries. These sermons place the hearers within the rites of initiation. Their experience is reinforced by the use of images, which provide an experience of the breadth and depth of the rites, rather than syllogisms, which reduce the rites to premise or definition. Information is provided only to help the newly baptized bring order to and find meaning in their experience. In this deeper experience of the rites, Ambrose believes the Spirit acts to enable the newly baptized to see using the vision of faith.

Second, the tone of these sermons is intended to create an intimate relationship between preacher and listeners. Familiar and dialogical, this tone both validates the neophytes' experience of the rites and invites them into a mutual exploration of that experience. This affirmation and invitation is reinforced by the several ways in which *De sacramentis* gives voice to the neophytes' reactions, questions, and objections. Thus the preacher functions not as the definitive source of information but as a spiritual guide who points out the significance of the liturgy but allows the newly baptized to plumb the depths of the mysteries for themselves. When people feel safe and valued, they are more open to the Spirit.

Third, Ambrose's extensive use of biblical material in these sermons signals to his hearers that there is a continuity between God's activity in the Old and New Testament and the Spirit's activity in the sacraments. Ambrose uses Scripture to open up the manifold, multi-imaged world of meaning that the mysteries are waiting to release, letting their pent-up power of signification burst forth. By grounding his explanations of the rites in biblical narratives and images and then building upon them, the bishop of Milan's underlying message to the newly baptized is that God is acting in the rites as God has acted in the history of salvation recorded in Scripture. Thus these sermons move from sign to fulfillment, from figure to reality, from God's activity then to God's same activity now. The drama of salvation is being played out to the full right here. Believing that the Spirit is active, the newly baptized are more open to the Spirit's activity.

Fourth, Ambrose's mystagogy is structured to facilitate the Spirit's giving the neophytes the vision to see beyond the physical. The movement of these sermons is from earthly to heavenly, from the temporal to the eternal. Inductive movement, which begins with physical actions and settings, is used to enable the newly baptized to see the significance of the physical. Biblical images are sewn together to assist the newly baptized to glimpse the Spirit acting in the sacraments.

A final characteristic of the way *De sacramentis* is structured to facilitate the Spirit's activity is its emphasis on mission. Explanations of the rites are followed by their implications for daily life. Thus the movement is from participation to comprehension to action. For example, the newly baptized receive a special sanctification on their feet so that they are not tripped up by the devil; the implication is that they are to be sure-footed in avoiding sin. Along with the mission, Ambrose conveys that, through the rites, the Spirit gives the ability to carry it out.

To summarize, *De sacramentis* is crafted to create neither a convincing argument nor a systematic theology but an experience, an event in which the Holy Spirit actively participates. In our next chapter we will therefore attempt to lift Ambrose's mystagogy off the pages of *De sacramentis* in order to glimpse and reflect upon what that proclamation event may have been like.

Chapter 8

"But now my voice grows weak and time is running out": Mystagogy as Proclamation Event: Delivery

"But now my voice grows weak and time is running out."[1] So Ambrose brings to a close his first sermon to the newly baptized. This simple remark shows that Ambrose was not only concerned about the content of his message; he was also concerned about the quality of his delivery. That Ambrose recognized the importance of sermon delivery to effective preaching is not at all surprising. As we have said, the bishop of Milan, who was trained in and fond of rhetoric, preached in the cathedral of Milan, seat of the empire and often the voice of the Western Church, where how one said something was as important as what one said. Thus Ambrose instructed his presbyters to pay attention to their delivery by taking pains to speak vigorously and distinctly.[2]

In his mystagogical preaching, attending to the realities of sermon delivery was especially important as Ambrose sought to engage his hearers in a dialogue in order to bring them to a deeper experience and understanding of the mysteries. More than conveying information, Ambrose re-created the neophytes' experience, instilled a perspective on that experience, and called for a committed response to it. Words alone were not enough. The bishop of Milan needed to address the neophytes' hearts as well as their minds. As important as *what* he said was *how* he said it.

In this chapter we underscore the importance of sermon delivery as we explore mystagogy as proclamation. We acknowledged in Chapter 1

---

[1] *De sacramentis*, 1.6.24 (SC 25bis.72). On Ambrose's concern about the constraints imposed by time, see also ibid., 3.2.15 (SC 25bis.100).

[2] Above, 96.

that we are at an obvious disadvantage in making any conclusions about Ambrose's delivery because we cannot gather with the neophytes and listen as he preaches.[3] Still, the evidence that we do possess, particularly *De sacramentis*, reveals very helpful insights into how these sermons were preached. Before turning to Ambrose's mystagogy, we begin this chapter by reviewing two reasons why delivery is as important to mystagogical (and all other) preaching as the message itself. In the second section of this chapter, we discuss eight contributing factors to effective sermon delivery and their implications for Ambrose's mystagogy. Finally, in the third part of this chapter, we reflect upon the Spirit's role in delivery by imagining *De sacramentis* as an event.

WHY DELIVERY IS ESSENTIAL TO EFFECTIVE PREACHING

In his book *From Text to Sermon: Responsible Use of the New Testament in Preaching*, Ernst Best states that he is least of all concerned to talk about the way the sermon material ought to be presented, summing up "the nuts and bolts of sermon construction" as "an introduction, three points, and a conclusion," and sermon delivery as "avoid words derived from Latin and Germanically turned phrases."[4] Best is convinced of the power of the Gospel to make itself heard.[5] Reminding preachers that trusting in the power of God does not relieve us of the burden of preaching with the power of God,[6] Paul Harms compares sermon delivery to "the foetus become child" and asserts that "it is possible for the child to be stillborn."[7] While contemporary preachers and assemblies may not be as impassioned about sermon delivery as Harms, today we overwhelmingly agree that sermon delivery is a vital part of preaching. This conviction rests on two conclusions.

First, studies show that what we say is but a small part of effective communication.[8] Words by themselves do not automatically have

---

[3] Above, 18.

[4] Ernst Best, *From Text to Sermon: Responsible Use of the New Testament in Preaching* (Atlanta: John Knox Press, 1978) 7.

[5] See above, 271.

[6] Ibid.

[7] Paul Harms, *Power from the Pulpit: Delivering the Good News*, The Preacher's Workshop Series (St. Louis: Concordia Publishing House, 1977) 28.

[8] For example, according to Bergan Evans of Northwestern University, we speak about 20,000 words a day. However, the speaking of those 20,000 words

meaning for the hearer, or at least not the meaning that the speaker intends. Meanings get assigned to words and phrases, very largely, by the nonverbal response of communicators to their own words. Accuracy of meaning for hearers grows to the degree that they perceive a consistency of the speaker and the speaker's message. Meaning for hearers grows to the degree to which they see speakers incarnate their message.[9]

Furthermore, words alone do not move listeners to change or to act. While the message communicates, the manner inspires. Delivery calls the passions to the aid of words.[10] Thus Augustine reports that Ambrose's sermons contained both solid instruction and the power of convincing those who heard them.[11] Inasmuch as the goal of Ambrose's mystagogy is not merely to provide information about the sacraments but to form the neophytes into Christians—that is, his task is to inspire and not merely to inform—*how* Ambrose speaks about the mysteries is as important as *what* he says.

Second and more important, God knows that how one communicates is as important as what one says. Thus God shows great care in how God communicates with us. The word of God is living and active. Neither God nor God's word can be packaged but must be experienced. In the fullness of time, God came in the person of the Son.[12] Today God's Spirit comes to us in word and sacrament. Sermons, then, are not mere words. They are events, moments when God's presence, grace, and power are experienced.[13] This is particularly true of preaching on the mysteries, which are the means by which God's transforming

---

only takes about 25 minutes. "All the rest of the time he [the speaker] spends communicating with others is done by nonverbal means. It is also true that the eye is at times more efficient than the ear in terms of the amount and specificity of the information it can collect." Robert L. Benedetti, *The Actor at Work* (Englewood Cliffs: Prentice-Hall, Inc., 1970) 19.

[9] Cf. Rob Anderson and Veronica Ross, *Questions of Communication: A Practical Introduction to Theory*, 2nd ed. (New York: St. Martin's Press, 1998), chap. 2, esp. 63–67; chap. 4, esp. 171–176; Zeno Vender, "Meaning," in *International Encyclopedia of Communications*, Erik Barnouw, ed. (New York: Oxford University Press, 1989) 3:1–5; Harms, *Power from the Pulpit*, 28.

[10] Cf. Harms, *Power from the Pulpit*, 31.

[11] Above, 89.

[12] Cf. Galatians 4:4.

[13] Mary Catherine Hilkert, *Naming Grace: Preaching and the Sacramental Imagination* (New York: Continuum, 1997) 46ff.

presence, grace, and power bring new life. Therefore, in addition to words, mystagogical preaching involves the whole person both of the preacher and the listeners, the liturgical context, and the physical space. To neglect these elements is to reduce mystagogical preaching to a text and in so doing to present an incomplete picture. Therefore, despite the fact that we are at an obvious disadvantage, we include in our study a discussion of the essential components of effective sermon delivery as they apply to Ambrose's mystagogy.

ESSENTIAL COMPONENTS OF EFFECTIVE SERMON DELIVERY

In this section we explore essential components of effective sermon delivery and their implications for Ambrose's mystagogical preaching. While contemporary books on preaching method agree on the importance of sermon delivery, the move from manuscript to proclamation is given little attention in comparison to those stages of the process that result in the creation of the manuscript. In defining the topics to be discussed in this section, we have therefore drawn upon a variety of resources. Inasmuch as we discussed the listeners' *ability to listen* in Chapter 4,[14] we group the remaining topics under three headings: (1) the preacher, (2) the liturgical context, and (3) the architectural setting.

The Preacher

The preacher is the incarnation of the message as well as the bearer of it. In this section we explore the contribution that Ambrose as the preacher made to mystagogy as proclamation. The factors that contributed to Ambrose's incarnation of his message include his attitude, character, habits of sermon preparation, style and method of delivery, voice, and use of nonverbal communication.

Attitude. When it comes to sermon delivery, preachers' inner attitude, how they see themselves and what they are about, is all-important.[15] Preachers' attitudes about both their role and the message they proclaim affects essential ingredients of effective sermon delivery such as tone, posture, energy level, and enthusiasm. Craddock is correct that "the absence of faith is almost impossible to disguise for any period of

---

[14] Above, 126–127.
[15] Walter Burghardt, *Preaching: The Art and the Craft* (New York: Paulist Press, 1987) 116.

time" and that passion makes the preacher persuasive.[16] We have previously discussed Ambrose's attitude toward preaching, the rites of initiation, and the newly baptized. He regarded preaching as the foremost responsibility of a bishop;[17] the Eucharist was so important to Ambrose that he celebrated it daily and encouraged the neophytes to receive it every day.[18]

Ambrose felt that the transformation from unseeing to seeing, from things temporal to things eternal, from life in this world to divine life was promised to all Christians in the waters of baptism. This conviction formed the heart and was the goal of his preaching in Milan.[19] He calls baptism the passage from earthly to heavenly, from sin to life, from guilt to grace, from vileness to holiness, from death to resurrection.[20] Holding baptism in such high regard, the instruction of those who were to be baptized was especially important to Ambrose.[21] His high regard for the newly baptized is evident in the fact that he addresses them as holy people,[22] dear brothers,[23] and the sweet fragrance of Christ,[24] and speaks of the Church's joy at their redemption.[25]

From these references we can safely conclude that Ambrose's concern for the neophytes extended to their instruction during the week after their baptism. No longer preparing the neophytes for baptism, Ambrose's task was to lead them to experience and comprehend the mysteries in all their depth, "to the end that [they] may have the grace of the Father, Son, and Holy Spirit."[26] If Ambrose's attitude was reflected in his delivery, we can expect a caring tone, an inviting posture, a high level of energy, and a sincere enthusiasm for his task.

Character of the Preacher. The second contributing factor to effective sermon delivery is the character of the preacher. We recall here

---

[16] Fred B. Craddock, *Preaching* (Nashville: Abingdon Press, 1985) 24.

[17] For preaching as a principal duty of a bishop, see Second Vatican Council, *Christus Dominus* (Rome, 1965) no. 12.

[19] Above, 94–95.

[20] *De sacramentis*, 1.4.12; 1.5.15 (SC 25bis.66; 68). See above, 53–54.

[21] Paulinus, *Vita Ambrosii*, 38 (Navoni, 116). See above, 101.

[22] *De sacramentis*, 1.6.24; 6.5.26 (SC 25bis.72; 154).

[23] Ibid., 3.2.15 (SC 25bis.100).

[24] Ibid., 4.1.4 (SC 25bis.102).

[25] Ibid., 5.3.14 (SC 25bis.126).

[26] Ibid., 1.6.24 (SC 25bis.72).

Cassiodorus's comment that Ambrose's teaching was not inferior to his life.[27] From his instructions to his presbyters,[28] we can conclude that Ambrose would agree with William Willimon that the preacher's chief homiletical-moral task is to be yoked so securely and joyously to the word that in the process of the proclamation of the word, we become the word, and it dwells in us richly.[29] Ambrose believed that in order to teach people virtue, bishops should surpass all others in the practice of Christian values, and that in order to counsel others in Christian virtue, priests ought to practice that virtue themselves.[30] Ambrose's lifestyle, built on poverty, concern for the poor, prayer, and fasting, reflects his convictions. Thus there was consistency between the messenger and his message.

Walter Burghardt claims that preachers are most strongly yoked to the word and therefore preach best when they are suffering servants.[31] Burghardt says that somehow

"suffering charges our words with fresh power because we are uncommonly aware that of ourselves we can do nothing, that if these words are to strike fire, it is the Lord who must light the flame. It is then that we are doing what is perhaps the most difficult thing Christ asks of us: we are entrusting our whole self to the Lord who alone can change hearts through our tongues. We come through more effectively, more passionately because we are sharing more intimately in the passion of our Lord and of our sisters and brothers."[32]

Ambrose's ministry of forging the Church's place of prominence over paganism, Judaism, Arianism, and the empire made him a powerful but often suffering servant. If Burghardt is correct, Ambrose's delivery surely exhibited the power of an urgent message and the conviction that God alone creates faith and new life.

---

[27] Above, 89.
[28] Above, 77–78.
[29] William H. Willimon, "The Preacher as an Extension of the Preaching Moment," in *Preaching on the Brink: The Future of Homiletics*, ed. Martha J. Simmons (Nashville: Abingdon Press, 1997) 170.
[30] Above, 77.
[31] Burghardt, *Preaching: The Art and the Craft*, 117.
[32] Ibid.

Habits. More obvious than the effect that the quality of the preacher's life has on sermon delivery is the influence exerted by the quality of the preacher's habits of sermon preparation. Craddock says that "the minister is prepared [to preach] by the study and reflection that [have] gone into the sermon and by the prayer in which the sermon has been bathed."[33] In Chapter 5 we discussed how Ambrose went about "gathering from the holy Scriptures."[34] As we have seen, he was convinced that the Bible's mode of expression was the most appropriate for pastoral speech. Therefore, in his preaching Ambrose both incorporated biblical quotations and paraphrases and reproduced the texture and rhythm of Scripture to such a degree that message and messenger became one.[35] This was possible because Ambrose devoted himself to a life of disciplined study. For Ambrose this discipline included silently reading and reflecting upon Scripture,[36] studying (and borrowing from) Greek sources,[37] and, in the case of mystagogy, contemplating the rites.

Yet, Burghardt is correct that "sheer study is not enough."[38] Preachers must know God, God's people, and the world as well. This is particularly true of mystagogy, which involves more than formulating sacramental theology. Mystagogy is the challenging task of prayerfully reflecting upon the meaning and implications that the Christian mysteries specifically celebrated have for real people and discovering how to communicate that message in ways they will understand.

In addition to his disciplined study, Ambrose met this challenge by grounding himself in his daily ministry of celebrating the Eucharist and his ceaseless devotion to prayer. He was involved in the lives of his people as their pastor, judge, confessor, counselor, and, for the neophytes, as the one who had initiated them into the mysteries. Ambrose was active in the corporate life of the community as he represented the Church to the empire. The one place that Ambrose's preparation for mystagogical preaching might be lacking is the preparation of sermon manuscripts.

---

[33] Craddock, *Preaching*, 212.
[34] *De sacramentis*, 1.6.24 (SC 25bis.72).
[35] Above, 92; 242.
[36] Above, 104.
[37] Above, 99–100.
[38] Burghardt, *Preaching: The Art and the Craft*, 59.

Style and Method of Delivery. Preachers must decide whether they will deliver their sermons extemporaneously, from memory, or from a manuscript. We have previously argued that Ambrose's general method of sermon delivery was to preach from memory.[39] He was not concerned that his mystagogical sermons be oratorical masterpieces, in part because of his confidence as a speaker, undoubtedly because he was a tired, overworked bishop preaching every day during the week following Easter, but also because his aim was to engage the neophytes in a dialogue. These were conversations between the bishop and his newest children. Christine Mohrmann has demonstrated that in comparing *De sacramentis* and *De mysteriis*, we find that the genre of *De sacramentis* is the spoken language; that is, it is of an "oral style." In addition to the catechetical style that we discussed in Chapter 4,[40] the characteristics of this oral style include sentence structure, the arrangement of materials, and the "tics"—certain idiosyncracies—of Ambrose the speaker.

The sentence structure of *De sacramentis* reflects an oral style in three ways. First, sentences are limited to those elements that are strictly necessary and very concrete.[41] For example, the verb is highlighted when the intent is to express an action and eliminated when a general idea is being presented. In our discussion of the methods employed by Ambrose to lead the neophytes to re-experience the rites of initiation, we showed how he places the verb at the beginning of sentences to express action.[42] Examples of eliminating the verb to present an idea include: *ubi certamen, ibi corona,*[43] *vere totum ubi tota innocentia, tota pietas, tota gratia, tota sanctificatio,*[44] *omnes quidem sancti evangelistae,*

---

[39] Above, 105.

[40] Above, 127–136.

[41] Christine Mohrmann, "Le style oral du *De sacramentis* de saint Ambroise," *Vigiliae Christianae* 6 (1952) 175; G. Lazzati, "L'autenticità del De sacramentis e la valutazione letteraria delle opera di S. Ambrogio," *Aevum* 29 (1955) 28; Steven Oberhelman, *Rhetoric and Homiletics in Fourth Century Christian Literature: Prose, Rhythm, Oratorical Style, and Preaching in the Works of Ambrose, Jerome, and Augustine* (Atlanta: Scholars Press, 1991) 103.

[42] Above, 138–139.

[43] *De sacramentis* 1.2.4 (SC 25bis.62). "where the contest, there the crown."

[44] Ibid., 1.3.10 (SC 25bis.66). "(There) truly (is) all where (there is) all innocence, all godliness, all grace, all sanctification."

omnes apostoli praeter proditorem omnes sancti,[45] *Bonae aquilae circa altare: ubi enim corpus ibi et aquilae*,[46] and *bona praesumptio sed moderata.*[47]

Second, in limiting his statements to the essential elements, Ambrose's syntax becomes very rudimentary and, in fact, disappears. Thus the essential elements of sentences are strung together without conjunction or subordination.[48] In *De sacramentis* we find, for example, *Deinde accessisti proprius, vidisti fontem, vidisti sacerdotem . . . ingressus es, vidisti aquam, vidisti sacerdotem, vidisti levitam*,[49] *isti, lavisti, venisti ad altare, videre coepisti*,[50] and *Iussit dominus factum est caelum, iussit dominus facta est terra, iussit dominus sunt maria, iussit dominus omnis creatura generata est.*[51] From these examples, we see that the unity of the sentence is not maintained by syntactic elements but by intonation and diction.

A third way the sentence structure of *De sacramentis* reflects spoken language is the pure and simple juxtaposition of the elements of a statement without subordination.[52] We find, for example, *Venit dominus noster Iesus Christus ad piscinam, multi aegri iacebant. Et facile ibi multi aegri iacebant ubi unus tantummodo curabatur. Deinde ait ad illum, paralyticum: descende. Ait ille: hominem non habeo.*[53] Once again, this

---

[45] Ibid., 3.2.11 (SC 25bis.98). "Indeed, all (are) holy evangelists, all apostles except the traitor, all holy."

[46] Ibid., 4.2.7 (SC 25bis.104). "Good eagles (are) about the altar: for where the body, there also the eagles."

[47] Ibid., 5.4.19 (SC 25bis.130). "A good boldness, but a modest one."

[48] Mohrmann, "Le style oral du De Sacramentis de saint Ambroise," 174; Lazzati, "L'autenticità del De sacramentis e la valutazione letteraria delle opera di S. Ambrogio," 27; Oberhelman, *Rhetoric and Homiletics in Fourth Century Christian Literature*, 102. Cf. Walter J. Ong, *Orality and Literacy: The Technologizing of the Word* (New York: Methuen, 1982) 36f.

[49] *De sacramentis*, 1.3.9, 10 (SC 25bis.64). "Then you drew near, you saw the font, you saw the bishop. . . . You entered, you saw the water, you saw the bishop, you saw the levite."

[50] Ibid., 3.2.15 (SC 25bis.100). "You went, you washed, you came to the altar, you began to see."

[51] Ibid., 4.4.15 (SC 25bis.110). "The Lord commanded, the heaven was made, the Lord commanded, the earth was made, the Lord commanded, the seas were made, the Lord commanded, every creature was produced."

[52] Mohrmann, "Le style oral du De Sacramentis de saint Ambroise," 174–175.

[53] *De sacramentis*, 2.2.6 (SC 25bis.76.) "Our Lord Jesus Christ came to the pool, many sick were lying there. And, naturally, there many sick were lying

juxtaposition without syntactical subordination requires that the intonation of the speaker provides subordination.

A second indication of the oral style of *De sacramentis* is the arrangement of materials. First, we find parenthetic phrases that shatter the syntactic unity of a sentence.[54] For example, we read, *Caeterum qui per hunc fontem transit, hoc est a terrenis ad caelestia—hic est enim transitus, ideo pascha, hoc est transitus eius, transitus a peccato ad vitam, a culpa ad gratiam, ab inquinamento ad sanctificationem—qui per hunc fontem transit, non moritur resurgit.*[55] Here Ambrose interrupts his comparison of the biblical account of passing through the Red Sea with Christians passing through the font in order to explain how baptism is a *passover*. Again, in his commentary on footwashing, Ambrose asserts that the bishop carried out this ministry and then interrupts himself to account for the fact that some of the neophytes' feet were washed by presbyters: *Succinctus sacerdos—licet enim et presbyteri fecerint, tamen exordium ministerii a summo est sacerdote—succinctus, inquam, summus sacerdos pedes tibi lavit.*[56]

The second way that the arrangement of materials in *De sacramentis* reflects an oral style is that Ambrose moves from topic to topic and adduces arguments as they must have occurred to him as he preached. The first sermons in *De sacramentis* give the impression that the bishop of Milan was fatigued and hardly able to concentrate. He even muddles examples drawn from the liturgical readings.[57] This is the case with Ambrose's commentary on the story of Naaman found in 2 Kings 5:1-14, which, according to the *Missale Ambrosianum*, was the first reading for the *missa pro baptizatis* on Tuesday of Easter week.[58] Ambrose refers to this pericope in *De sacramentis* 1.3.9,[59] following a

---

where only one was healed. Then he said to the paralytic: Descend. He said: I have no man." See also ibid., 4.3.11, 4.16 (SC 25bis.106, 110).

[54] Mohrmann, "Le style oral du De Sacramentis de saint Ambroise," 175; Lazzati, "L'autenticità del De sacramentis e la valutazione letteraria delle opera di S. Ambrogio," 28; Oberhelman, *Rhetoric and Homiletics in Fourth Century Christian Literature*, 102–103.

[55] *De sacramentis*, 1.4.12 (SC 25bis.66).

[56] Ibid., 3.1.4 (SC 25bis.92).

[57] Christine Mohrmann, "Observations sur le *De sacramentis* et le *De mysteriis* de Saint Ambroise," *Ambrosius Episcopus* (Milan: Università Cattolica del Sacro Cuore, 1978) 111.

[58] Above, 212–213.

[59] SC 25bis.64.

passage on the Old Testament typology of the crossing of the Red Sea. Then, in 1.5.13,[60] he returns to Naaman, with a certain spontaneity. The account that follows is somewhat disordered. Ambrose returns to Naaman again in 2.3.8, where the young slave girl is presented as a prefiguration of the Church.[61] In *De mysteriis,* on the other hand, Ambrose has taken pains to give coherence and continuity to his arguments. In *De mysteriis,* 3.16–17,[62] Ambrose refers to the account of Naaman as coming from the assigned reading and then presents its meaning in a clear and well-ordered way. His typological exegesis of the young slave girl as a prefiguration of the Church follows immediately in *De mysteriis,* 3.18.[63] Similarly, the various baptismal images, which were scattered throughout *De sacramentis,* are gathered together and listed in historically chronological order in *De mysteriis*: creation, the flood, crossing the Red Sea, the episode of Naaman, and the pool at Beth-zatha.[64]

Finally, comparing *De sacramentis* and *De mysteriis* reveals that *De sacramentis* contains elements of syntax and style that are so unique that they must constitute the "true tics" of Ambrose the preacher. Mohrmann defines these "tics" as those small idiosyncracies of improvised speech of which one is hardly aware and therefore does not write down, even in hasty notes.[65] These "tics" become obvious when one compares Ambrose's mystagogical works because they seem to have been consciously eliminated or avoided in *De mysteriis.* For Ambrose these "tics" include cultivated speech, the high frequency of questions, and the use of *ergo* to mark the progression of his thought.

Mohrmann argues that an examination of the vocabulary of *De sacramentis* reveals that it is not written using popular language but is an example of cultivated speech.[66] Though the language is simple, we do not find examples of popular idiom. For example, the expression *hoc est,* which belongs to cultivated and literary language, occurs twenty-eight times in *De sacramentis,* while the phrase *id est,* an

---

[60] Ibid., 66.
[61] SC 25bis.78.
[62] Ibid., 164.
[63] Ibid.
[64] *De mysteriis,* 3.9–4.25 (SC 25bis.160–170).
[65] Mohrmann, "Observations sur le *De sacramentis* et le *De mysteriis* de Saint Ambroise," 116–117.
[66] Mohrmann, "Le style oral du De Sacramentis de saint Ambroise," 170.

example of popular speech, appears only twice.[67] As a second example, in his use of conjunctions, Ambrose employs *quod* twenty-five times, *quia* twenty-two times, *ut* twice, and *quoniam* once.[68] *Quoniam*, which is both common and biblical, is only used by Ambrose once, before a biblical quotation. *Quia* was more popular than *quod* and very typical of Christian Latin. *Quia* was the conjunction favored by Augustine in his sermons. *Quod* was the most distinguished conjunction and the conjunction most often used by Ambrose. In both cases we see Ambrose, the distinguished aristocrat, remaining faithful to his cultivated speech.

We have previously addressed Ambrose's use of didactic questions to involve the neophytes in his mystagogy.[69] Here we discuss the short questions consisting of one, two, or three words. As we said in Chapter 1, the monotonous repetition of this second type of question in *De sacramentis* was frequently regarded as a feature not in keeping with the style of Ambrose's authentic works and therefore was one of the principal arguments against attributing the authorship of this work to Saint Ambrose. As evidence of this second type of question, we find in *De sacramentis*, 49 instances of *quid significat nisi, quid est nisi, quid significat, quid est, quare,* and *quomodo,* none of which occur in *De mysteriis*.[70] Faller showed that Ambrose had a predilection for asking questions.[71] Mohrmann correctly concludes that it is inconceivable that Ambrose, writing quickly, had formulated all these questions in advance of preaching. Rather, these questions reflect Ambrose's extemporaneous speech. While they are a natural part of oral communication, they are not something that Ambrose would write down as part of his preparation.[72]

Finally, Ambrose frequently uses the word *ergo* not to show a causal relationship but simply to mark the progression of his thought.[73] This

---

[67] Ibid., 171.

[68] Ibid., 174.

[69] Above, 147–149.

[70] Mohrmann, "Observations sur le *De sacramentis* et le *De mysteriis* de Saint Ambroise," 118.

[71] Otto Faller, "Ambrosius, der Verfasser von *De sacramentis*. Die innere Echtheitsgrunde. *Zeitschrift für katholische Theologie* 64 (1940) 83–85.

[72] Mohrmann, "Le style oral du *De sacramentis* de saint Ambroise," 172.

[73] Mohrmann, "Observations sur le *De sacramentis* et le *De mysteriis* de Saint Ambroise," 118.

ergo is sometimes placed before and sometimes after a verb at the beginning of a sentence. One does not find in Ambrose's use of *ergo* evidence of his concern for style; rather, *ergo* appears where Ambrose would have said it spontaneously and perhaps unconsciously. Examples include: *ergo didicisti; didicisti ergo; ergo venisti;* and *venisti ergo*.[74] Ambrose seems to have avoided using *ergo* in this way in *De mysteriis*.

From the sentence structure, arrangement of material, and true "tics" of the preacher contained in *De sacramentis*, we conclude that the genre of these sermons is spoken language or oral style. Mohrmann logically asserts that a preacher who writes quickly what he intends to say could not, even if he wanted to, so perfectly imitate the oral style that we find in *De sacramentis*.[75] Thus, not only did Ambrose preach without a manuscript, he did not even prepare one.

Voice. While we cannot hear the responsiveness, clarity, and variety[76] of his voice, we do know that Ambrose instructed his presbyters that the voice must remain true to the inner meaning of the words it utters by being plain, clear, distinct in pronunciation, full of life, and natural, that is, free of both a rough twang and a dramatic accent.[77] As we have seen, an analysis of the text of *De sacramentis* reveals the essential role that Ambrose's voice played in his mystagogical preaching. Our preacher used intonation and diction to convey both the unity of thoughts and ideas and subordination when he made comparisons. This suggests that Ambrose used a wide range of vocal variety in order to speak with an inflectional pattern that assisted the newly baptized in hearing, comprehending, and reacting to his instructions.

Ambrose's desire to establish a dialogue with the neophytes suggests that his voice was responsive to both his message—including the emotions, motivations, and demands that lie behind the words—and his hearers' reaction, and clear in terms of precise articulation in order to be understood. The presence of the "tics" of Ambrose's speech suggests that his voice was natural and conversational and not rehearsed. Finally, we must remember that ancient basilicas did not have sound amplification systems; preachers had to project, even shout. Thus

[74] *De sacramentis*, 4.3.9; 4.4.20; 5.3.12; 5.3.14 (SC 25bis.106; 112; 124; 126).

[75] Mohrmann, "Le style oral du *De sacramentis* de saint Ambroise," 171.

[76] Charles L. Bartow, *The Preaching Moment: A Guide to Sermon Delivery* (Nashville: Abingdon Press, 1980) 69–90.

[77] Above, 96.

Ambrose's awareness of and concern for the importance of the voice is evident in the fact that he stopped preaching when his voice grew weak.[78]

Nonverbal Communication. "Words expect both vocal response and physical action."[79] The preacher therefore needs to respond to the demands of the preaching moment with body as well as with mind and voice. If preachers do not, they can be assured that what the body is saying—or failing to say, through noninvolvement—is what will be "heard."[80] The task of the preachers is to say something with their bodies appropriate to the words they are speaking and to their purpose in speaking them. Visual aspects of nonverbal communication include the preacher's overall appearance, posture, gestures, facial expression, and eye contact.[81]

We have previously discussed Ambrose's physical appearance as it is presented in the fifth-century mosaic in the Basilica di Sant'Ambrogio in Milan.[82] Based on this portrait, Frederick Homes Dudden offers the following description of the bishop of Milan:

"According to this representation, Ambrose was of short stature and rather delicate appearance. His face was elongated, his forehead high, his nose long and straight, his lips thick; his eyes were large, and one of the eyebrows was perceptibly higher than the other. He had short hair and beard—perhaps light brown in colour—and wore a drooping mustache. His general expression was grave and even a little melancholy."[83]

Embodied in Ambrose's short, frail person were the authority of his episcopal office and the awe undoubtedly associated with his role as steward of the mysteries of God.[84] "The bishop, clad in the garments

---

[78] Above, 89, n. 6; 281.

[79] Bartow, *The Preaching Moment*, 37.

[80] See Julius Fast, *Body Language* (New York: M. Evans and Co., 1970) 5, 18, 173. Although this is a popular work, it offers helpful insights into the important role that body language plays in preaching.

[81] Bartow, *The Preaching Moment*, 92–99.

[82] Above, 78–79. See Figure 2, above, 79.

[83] Frederick Homes Dudden, *The Life and Times of St. Ambrose* (Oxford: Clarendon Press, 1935) 1:114.

[84] Cf. 1 Corinthians 4:1.

of a high magistrate, entered the church in solemn procession, preceded by the insignia of his official rank, candles and book. Flanked by his presbyters, he was seated on a throne, the *sella curulis* of a Roman official."[85]

While we cannot know the specific gestures that Ambrose used in his preaching on the mysteries, we do know that he recognized that "the condition of the mind is often seen in the attitudes of the body" and "the movement of the body is a sort of voice of the soul."[86] He deplored uncouth gestures and affected mannerisms.[87] As for facial expression and eye contact, we can only assume that a bishop trained in rhetoric who addressed the newly baptized directly with a familiar, paternal tone in order to engage them in a dialogue and lead them into the mysteries also looked at his hearers directly and allowed the transforming power of the mysteries to be seen on his face as well as heard in his words.

The Liturgical Context

That the liturgical context is vital to preaching is most obvious in the way the sermon is defined and its limits set by the liturgy.[88] The language of prayer and Scripture, ritual action, physical environment, and structures of the ministry all cooperate to form a specific style that influences both the style and content of the homily. John Allyn Melloh writes that preaching learns from the liturgy.[89] The shape of the liturgy suggests constraints on the form of preaching. Perhaps even more important, the liturgy itself teaches the preacher how to image theological concepts such as praise, salvation, grace, sin, and repentance. The liturgical texts and ritual actions themselves teach the attentive preacher how to shape an image-laden homily consonant with the tradition of worship. Geoffrey Wainwright asserts that the constant features and qualitative wholeness of the liturgy also provide preaching with a certain freedom.[90]

---

[85] Richard Krautheimer, *Early Christian and Byzantine Architecture*, 4th ed., rev. Richard Krautheimer and Slobodan Čurčić (New Haven, Conn.: Yale University Press, 1986) 40.

[86] *De officiis ministrorum*, 1.18.71 (PL 16.44).

[87] Ibid., 1.18.72–74 (PL 16.44-45).

[88] Craddock, *Preaching*, 42.

[89] John Allyn Melloh, "Preaching and Liturgy," *Worship* 65 (1991) 415f.

[90] Geoffrey Wainwright, "The Sermon and the Liturgy," *Greek Orthodox Theological Review* 28 (Winter 1983) 346. See also Craddock, *Preaching*, 42.

Surrounded as it is by the stable and well-tried elements of Scripture readings, Creed, and anaphora, the unrepeatable sermon can afford a certain boldness of mind and heart as it seeks to bring home the Christian message imaginatively and penetratingly to a particular group of people at this time and in this place. As long as the traditional actions of the liturgy keep the classical expression of the faith before the people, the preacher is free to attempt both the translations and transposition of the Gospel that changes in culture demand and the prophetic "reading" of personal, local, national, or worldwide situations in the light of the Gospel. Thus the style of the liturgy provides a stable point of reference within which to encounter the contemporaneity of faith.

In terms of the preaching event itself, every Christian assembly, but especially a gathering of the newly baptized, needs to be founded upon the word of God. The Liturgy of the Word provides the opportunity for every member of the congregation to hear the voice of Christ and to renew the response of faith by which he or she is joined to Christ's body. When the Scriptures are read and when they are proclaimed, God speaks to his people.[91] Through his ministers Christ himself proclaims his Gospel to a particular gathering on a particular day and seeks from them the response of faith. In the case of mystagogical preaching, the desired response is a fuller and deeper participation in the mysteries that leads the newly baptized to accept God's gift of faith with praise and thanksgiving, acknowledge their need for God, and declare their willingness to live out the Gospel in ordinary life. The Liturgy of the Word readies the community to outwardly express this response in hymns and psalms, in prayer—both petitions and the great prayer of thanksgiving said by one on behalf of all, and in the reception of the sacrament. Ambrose writes:

"'Even though you are weak, still Christ cares for you. He says to his disciples, "You give them something to eat."[92] You have the apostolic food'—that is, the lessons from Scripture read during the first part of the service—'eat that, and you will not faint. Eat that first, that afterward you may come to the food of Christ, to the food of the Lord's body, to the feast of the sacrament, to that cup with which the souls of the faithful are inebriated.'"[93]

[91] Second Vatican Council, *Dei Verbum* (Rome, 1965) nos. 21, 24, 25.
[92] Matthew 14:16.
[93] *Expositio in Psalmum cxviii*, 15.28 (CSEL 62.344). As cited in Homes Dudden, *The Life and Times of Saint Ambrose*, 2:457.

In this way preaching constitutes the bridge between God's call and our response and makes the act of worship a reality in the lives of the worshipers here and now. Thus the liturgy has an impact on sermon delivery by preparing the preacher to preach and the congregation to listen, by setting the context in which the preaching event takes place, and by offering the first opportunity for the community to respond in prayer, praise, action, and mission.

That Ambrose's mystagogical preaching took place within a liturgical context is evident from his references to the lessons from Scripture read when the sermons contained in *De sacramentis* were preached.[94] As we have seen, there were three readings—a reading from the Old Testament, the Epistle, and the Gospel.[95] Between the lessons responsorial psalms were intoned and the *Alleluia* was sung.[96] *De sacramentis* also contains numerous references to time that indicate that these services were held daily during the week following Easter. These references include: "Let us content ourselves today. . . . Tomorrow I will declare";[97] "Yesterday, the subject of our instruction was";[98] "Tomorrow, we will treat";[99] and "Tomorrow and on Saturday we will speak."[100] From these references we conclude that the six sermons

---

[94] *De sacramentis*, 2.2.3, 7.23; 3.2.8; 6.2.9 (SC 25bis.74; 86; 141).

[95] Above, 105, n. 84; 211–213.

[96] On the intoning of psalms between the lessons, see *Epistola* 77 (Maur. 22).4, 7 (CSEL 82/3.129, 130). On the *Alleluia*, see *Apologia Prophetae David*, 42 (CSEL 32/2.324–325).

[97] *De sacramentis*, 1.6.24 (SC 25bis.72).

[98] Ibid., 3.1.1 (SC 25bis.90).

[99] Ibid., 3.2.15 (SC 25bis.100).

[100] Ibid., 4.6.29 (SC 25bis.118). The text of this reference is suspect. I am here following the emendation advocated by Hervé Petit and adopted by Botte in his critical edition: *crastina die et sabbato [et] dominica de oration < e et de oration > is ordine dicemus*. Faller's edition reads, *crastina die et sabbato et dominica de orationis ordine dicemus*, which is translated "tomorrow, Saturday, and on Sunday." Faller did not punctuate this text, leaving open the question of whether Ambrose is speaking of two days (*crastina die = sabbato, et dominica*) or, equally possible, three days (*crastina die, sabbato et dominica*). The best manuscript evidence has *crastina die et sabbato et dominica*. In addition, the mention of Sunday poses literary and liturgical problems. Seven sermons would be necessary, and there are only six in *De sacramentis*. It also seems strange that the instruction of the newly baptized continues until the following Sunday. Thus the text is translated "tomorrow and on Saturday" rather than "Tomorrow, Saturday,

contained in *De sacramentis* were preached from Monday through Saturday of the week following Easter.[101]

Beyond these references to lessons and time, *De sacramentis* and *De mysteriis* shed no light on the character of these liturgies. The later Ambrosian *Manuale* mentions a special Mass for the newly baptized. As late as the time of Beroldus (twelfth century), a rubric directs that Mass be said *pro baptizatis* on Holy Saturday and during Easter week.[102] Based on the available evidence, we can neither confirm nor deny that Ambrose knew of the practice of holding two daily Masses during the week after Easter. Nevertheless, conducting mystagogical catechesis within the context of the eucharistic liturgy is in keeping with the spirit of *De sacramentis*. Ambrose presents approaching the altar, seeing what the newly baptized had not seen before, and receiving the bread and wine of the Eucharist as the climax of initiation and the privilege of the baptized,[103] and encourages the neophytes to receive the sacrament daily.[104] These instructions, as well as Ambrose's overall purpose of leading the neophytes to enter more fully and deeply into the mysteries, are enhanced when the newly baptized are given the opportunity to participate in the mystery and receive the sacrament daily as part of their postbaptismal catechesis. We described the order of the celebration of the Eucharist in Chapter 5.[105]

The most spectacular rite of the paschal week was that the newly baptized dressed in the white robes they received at baptism, distin-

---

and on Sunday." For a full discussion of these arguments, see Hervé Petit, "Sur les catéchèses postbaptismals de S. Ambroise," *Revue bénédictine* 68 (1958) 256–264; Bernard Botte, *Ambroise de Milan: Des Sacrements; Des Mystères: Explication du Symbole*, SC 25bis (Paris: Les Éditions du Cerf, 1980) 210–211.

[101] See Petit, "Sur les catéchèses postbaptismals de S. Ambroise," 264. Homes Dudden says that these sermons were preached from Tuesday through Sunday. Homes Dudden, *The Life and Times of St. Ambrose*, 1:342. Finn asserts that these homilies were preached on Monday, Tuesday, Wednesday, Friday, and Saturday. Thomas M. Finn, *From Death to Rebirth: Ritual and Conversion in Antiquity* (New York: Paulist Press, 1992) 228.

[102] Archdale A. King, *Liturgies of the Primatial Sees* (London: Longmans, Green and Co., 1957) 319–320; Petit, "Sur les catéchèses postbaptismals de S. Ambroise," 261–265.

[103] Cf. *De sacramentis*, 3.2.11, 15 (SC 25bis.98, 100).

[104] Ibid., 5.4.25–26; 6.5.24 (SC 25bis.132, 152).

[105] Above, 180–185.

guishing them from the rest of the faithful. Ambrose is one of the first to formally attest to this practice in the West,[106] and this custom is the origin of the designations that the days of this week received. In the oldest Milanese documents these days are known as *in albis, in albas,* and *de albis:* the week is designated *sabbato albis depositis* and *sabbato albas depositas;* and by extension the following day is called *dominica albis depositis, dominica in albis depositis, dominica albas depositas,* and *dominica post albas.*[107]

The Architectural Setting

The space in which preaching occurs has the power to either enhance or detract from effective sermon delivery.[108] Most obviously, the worship space impacts the preaching event by its acoustics.[109] The atmosphere or ambiance created by the worship space, along with the feelings and memories that the faith community associates with it, also affect preaching by the influence they exert on both the listeners and the preacher. In this section we will discuss the architectural setting of Ambrose's mystagogy. First, we will propose the cathedral as the place where Ambrose preached his mystagogical homilies. Second, we will describe that space using the data available to us. Finally, we will discuss the memories and emotions that the newly baptized associated with it.

Though Ambrose nowhere indicates where his instructions to the newly baptized during the week after Easter took place, it is logical to assume that he delivered his mystagogical sermons in the cathedral for three reasons. First, the liturgical context of mystagogy, particularly if the Eucharist was celebrated, makes the cathedral the appropriate setting. Second, the cathedral—specifically, the altar—is the place to which the journey of initiation had brought the neophytes. Holding these instructions in the cathedral highlights and celebrates their new status as full members of the Church. Third, the cathedral of Milan, called by Ambrose *Basilica nova quae major est* and later known

---

[106] *Expositio evangelii secundum Lucam,* 5.25 (CCSL 14.144); *De sacramentis,* 4.2.5–6; 5.2.14 (SC 25bis.104; 126); *De mysteriis,* 7.34 (SC 25bis.174).

[107] Petit, "Sur les catéchèses postbaptismals de S. Ambroise," 262.

[108] See James F. White and Susan J. White, *Church Architecture: Building and Renovating for Christian Worship* (Akron: OSL Publications, 1998) 26–28.

[109] See Craig A. Satterlee, "Preaching and Acoustics," *Environment and Art Letter* 12 no. 3 (May 1999) 30–33.

as *basilica aestiva* and Santa Tecla,[110] was itself overwhelming and would have had a powerful impact on the neophytes.

Built apparently around the middle of the fourth century after Constantine[111] and situated in the center of the ancient city on a northwest/southeast axis in relation to the current Duomo, the remains of the cathedral were first encountered by chance in 1943 under wartime conditions.[112] The site was explored a second time in 1960 to 1962, when the subway station was built in Piazza Duomo. On this occasion large tracts of the foundation and, against an apse, the low parts of walls were uncovered. This was enough to outline the entire structure (see Figure 5). The cathedral was approximately 223 feet long and 150 feet wide (c. 67.6 meters by more than 45 meters), making it not much smaller than Saint John Lateran in Rome.[113] The nave was flanked by two side aisles on either side. The roof was supported by outer and inner colonnades, presumably arcaded. The nave continued as a chancel to the semicircular apse. Behind the apse stood the octagonal

---

[110] *Epistola* 76 (Maur. 20).1 (82/3.108). For a summary of the arguments in favor of assigning these references to Santa Tecla, see Ada Grossi, *Santa Tecla nel Tardo Medioevo: La Grande Basilica Milanese, il Paradisus, i Mercati* (Milan: Edizioni Et, 1997) 21.

[111] The only documentary evidence that we possess concerning the date of construction is that the synod of 355 was apparently convened in the cathedral and that in 386 the cathedral now excavated was still known as the new cathedral, as opposed to the old, or small, cathedral, the *basilica vetus* or *minor*; then still extant and in use. The size of the synod of 355, attended by more than three hundred bishops, not counting their clergy, the emperor, his suite and the congregation, suggests that it met in the large new cathedral. Thus a date of construction prior to 355 is indicated. Concomitantly, its designation thirty years later as still the new cathedral suggests that it had been built within living memory, especially inasmuch as the old cathedral most certainly could not have predated the Edict of Milan of 313. Thus a date around 350 seems reasonable for the new cathedral. Richard Krautheimer, *Three Christian Capitals* (Berkeley: University of California Press, 1983) 76–77.

[112] The discovery and subsequent first excavation of Santa Tecla was due to the devoted energy of A. De Capitani d'Arzago. The results were published posthumously: A. de Capitani d'Arzago, *La "Chiesa maggiore" di Milano* (Milan, 1952). The results of the second excavation, directed by M. Mirabella Roberti, and the reconstruction of the plan, were published by him first in *Arte Lombarda* 8 (1963) 77ff., and more recently, with some revision of his original proposals, in *Atti del Congresso sul Duomo di Milano* (Milan, 1969) 31f.

[113] Krautheimer, *Early Christian and Byzantine Architecture*, 84.

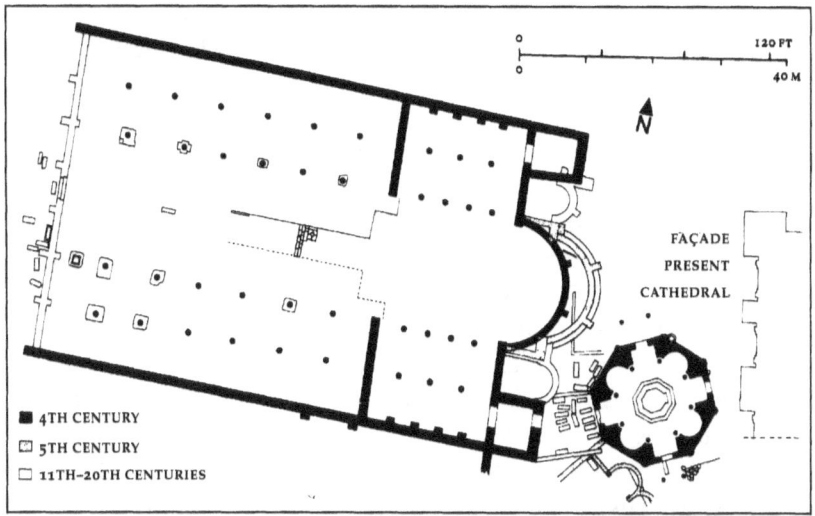

Figure 5 Reconstruction of the Basilica di Santa Tecla and baptistry, Milan. Plan adapted from Richard Krautheimer, *Early Christian and Byzantine Architecture* (New Haven, Conn. Yale University Press, 1986) 84. Reprinted with permission.

baptistry.[114] An altar enclosure or *bema* slightly raised above nave-level filled the area of the chancel. There was a raised pathway rising in the middle of the nave and connected to the presbytery. This *solea* was used for the bishop's solemn entry and linked the chancel to the *ambo*, which was far forward in the nave.[115] Two deep wings extended sideways, each divided into two aisles and communicating with the chancel area through a quintuple arcade. Small side chambers projected east from the outer aisles in the wings. In neither the chancel area nor in the nave did the number of outer and inner supports coincide. Although the function of the chancel wings can only be conjectured, it is presumed that they served the offertory rite.[116] The quality of this cathedral's construction, together with the lavish materials used, set it apart from anything else known in northern Italy at this time.

Thirty years prior to the discovery of the remains of the cathedral, Richard Krautheimer proposed that the double cathedral typical of

---

[114] See above, 196–197.
[115] See Krautheimer, *Three Christian Capitals*, 74, idem, *Early Christian and Byzantine Architecture*, 102.
[116] Ibid., 84.

early Christian construction of Byzantine influence was found throughout Lombardy (Milan, Pavia, Bergamo, Brescia, Verona).[117] Based on this study, scholars concluded that the cathedral of Milan was a "dual cathedral," having not one but two basilicas. Ambrose himself mentions two basilicas: *Basilica nova, hoc est intramurana quae major est* and *Basilica vetus, ecclesia basilica minor*.[118] This hypothesis led scholars to theorize that the Basilica di Santa Maria Maggiore, originally thought to have been consecrated in 836,[119] in fact existed since the early centuries of Christianity and constituted the cathedral of Milan's second seat during the time of Saint Ambrose. The consecration of this basilica in the eighth century did not mark its construction but rather a radical renovation of the existing church, called the *vetus* at the time of Saint Ambrose.[120]

Several hypotheses based on the concrete needs of the time have been offered to explain the use of two basilicas. One hypothesis, based on climatic concerns, proposes that the Basilica di Santa Maria Maggiore was known as the *Basilica iemalis* (Winter Basilica), because it was smaller and better protected from the winter cold than Santa Tecla, which was a large, well-lit building, more appropriate for summer.[121] Supporting this theory, the liturgical manuscripts of the Ambrosian Rite testify to the congregation's moving from Santa Tecla to Santa Maria Maggiore on the anniversary of the dedication of that church on the third Sunday in October and returning to Santa Tecla on Easter Eve.[122]

---

[117] Richard Krautheimer, "Die Doppelkathedrale in Pavia," in Richard Salomon, ed., *Opicinus de Canistris Weltbild und Bekenntnisse eines avignonesischen Klerikers des 14. Jahrhunderts* (London: Warburg Institute, 1936) 323–337.

[118] *Epistola* 76 (Maur. 20).1, 10 (CSEL 82/3.108, 113).

[119] See Oswaldus Holder-Egger, *Gesta Federici I imperatoris in Lombardia auct. cive mediolanensi: Annales mediolanenses maiores* (Hannover: Impensis Bibliopolii Hahniani, 1892) for "836 aedificata east ecclesia Sanctae Mariae Maioris Mediolani." See Grossi, *Santa Tecla nel Tardo Medioevo: La Grande Basilica Milanese, il Paradisus, i Mercati*, 22.

[120] Grossi, *Santa Tecla nel Tardo Medioevo*, 22. Although modern scholars tend to think that this hypothesis is most probable, it remains a theory. The archeological excavations under the present Duomo reveal nothing decisive about the relationships between the church renewed or rebuilt in 836 and the buildings that preceded it.

[121] Ibid.

[122] Ibid.

A second theory attributes the use of the double cathedral to liturgical motivations tied to symbolic meaning. According to this hypothesis, we find in the use of two cathedrals the images of the visible and invisible Church: the Church on earth and the Church in heaven, and the persecuted Church and the Church triumphant. In the liturgical movement from Santa Maria Maggiore to Santa Tecla on Easter Eve, the congregation participates in the passage from seen to unseen, earth to heaven, persecution to victory, death to resurrection. Ada Grossi rightly argues that there is no conflict between this liturgical hypothesis and the references to the two basilicas as *aestiva* and *iemalis*, summer and winter. However, these titles do not have climatic connotations but refer to the two periods delineated from the liturgical migrations.[123] The "summer" period runs from Easter Eve to the dedication of Santa Maria Maggiore and "winter" from Advent to Good Friday. The references to the basilicas as *aestiva* and *iemalis* are therefore terms of common use derived from the fact that the celebrations tied to Santa Tecla were carried out mostly in spring and summer, while those that occurred in Santa Maria Maggiore fell in autumn and winter.

In addition to being the setting of the congregation's liturgical movement from death to new life, the *basilica nova* was also the place of the celebration of the mystery of the Eucharist, from which the neophytes had once been excluded. After being dismissed for so long, on Easter they finally entered the crowded basilica and were embraced by the Christian community as fellow members of the body of Christ. Through baptism they came to the place that they had not come to before, where they saw the things that they had not seen before.[124] Seeing the holy altar all arranged, Ambrose says, quoting Psalm 23, the neophytes cried, "You have prepared a table before me."[125] While he is certainly not speaking literally, Ambrose's description indicates that he is aware of the profound impact that entering the cathedral and coming to the altar had on his hearers. By preaching his mystagogical homilies in the cathedral, Ambrose uses the physical space to aid the neophytes in re-experiencing their initiation and participating in the instructions.

---

[123] Ibid.
[124] *De sacramentis*, 3.2.11 (SC 25bis.98).
[125] *De mysteriis*, 8.43 (SC 25bis.129).

It is difficult to say anything conclusive about this basilica as the setting for preaching. We know nothing of the acoustics of the space except that Augustine's description of both Ambrose's preaching and the congregation's singing suggests that they were very good. Even if we could describe the basilica acoustically, this knowledge is not particularly helpful to our purpose because every space is acoustically unique.[126] More important than knowing the acoustical realities of the basilica of Milan is becoming familiar with and accounting for the acoustics of the space in which one preaches. As for the exact location within the basilica where these sermons were preached, during the time of Saint Ambrose the bishop most often spoke while sitting on his throne in the apse.[127] This arrangement simultaneously enhanced Ambrose's authority and made it more difficult to establish an intimate link with his hearers and to engage them in dialogue.

REFLECTION:
THE PNEUMATIC DIMENSION OF SERMON DELIVERY

In this chapter we recalled that God comes to us through experience and that, more than words, preaching is an event in which we experience God's presence, grace, and power. In preaching, Christ himself proclaims his Gospel to particular people and seeks from them the response of faith. In reflecting upon the Spirit's role in delivery, it is helpful to consider *De sacramentis* as preached sermons. Rather than analyzing *De sacramentis* as an ancient text, we can contemplate Ambrose's mystagogical homilies by imagining how one of the neophytes of Milan might report his or her experience of mystagogy:

"Still wearing the white robes that we received when we were baptized, we make our way to the *basilica nova*. We feel both excited and exhausted—so much has happened to us! I am overwhelmed by the images that float in my mind—oil and water, lots of water, bread and wine, baptistry and altar. The words that I spoke and the promises that I made echo in my head. For every image there is a question.

---

[126] Satterlee, "Preaching and Acoustics," 30.

[127] Yngve Brilioth, *A Brief History of Preaching*, trans. Karl E. Mattson (Philadelphia: Fortress Press, 1965) 26. Presbyters, to whom the bishop could delegate the responsibility of preaching, customarily made use of the ambo, from which the texts were read.

There are so many pieces of this puzzle and I am just beginning to think about how they all fit together.

"At last we come to the basilica. I am surprised to feel my heart pounding as I enter. I have seen the basilica before but somehow today it looks different. It looks magnificent. For so long we have been welcome guests here, belonging but not completely, sent away before the congregation moved to the altar. But now this is *our* house. On Easter we were embraced as members of the family. Nothing is kept from us now. Today we will go to the altar once more and see the mystery of the bread and cup, which, we are told as we receive them, are somehow the body and blood of Christ.

"The room quiets a bit as the bishop enters. Preceded by candles and book and flanked by his presbyters, he processes to the apse and ascends the steps of his throne. Ambrose looks tired and serious today. But in those great eyes I can see the sparkle of whatever it is that dares him to go toe to toe with the emperor. All throughout Lent we have listened to this man tell us stories of faith and explain how we are to live. On the night of our baptism, his was the face in the darkness asking us questions: 'Do you renounce? Do you believe?'[128] His were the hands that touched our ears and washed our feet. Now he is going to tell us what it all means.

"When the bishop is seated, the deacon calls for silence. Then the lessons are read. One of them is about Jesus healing the paralytic by the pool.[129] Between the lessons there is singing, beautiful singing; it is the song of angels. The room is quiet now. We are of one mind, one heart. Ambrose begins to speak.

"'I shall begin now to speak of the sacraments,' he says. 'What did we do on Saturday?'[130] As the bishop answers his own question and describes what we did, my mind drifts back to the baptistry and I find myself going through the ceremonies all over again. The images continue to float in my mind—the font, a levite, and a presbyter—but in flashes they are beginning to come together. 'You were rubbed down like an athlete, Christ's athlete,' Ambrose is saying, 'in preparation for an earthly wrestling match. . . . Keep what you said in mind. The words of the guarantee you gave must never fade from your memory.'[131]

---

[128] *De sacramentis*, 1.2.5; 2.7.20 (SC 25bis.62; 84).
[129] John 5:1-9.
[130] *De sacramentis*, 1.1.1 (SC 25bis.60).
[131] Ibid., 1.2.4, 5 (SC 25bis.62).

I remember; I can still hear the words. Baptism, it seems, means turning your back on the world.

"Now Ambrose is pulling from the Scriptures things we had never heard before—about Naaman the Syrian, the Jewish people passing through the sea, back to Naaman, then Christ going down into the water, back to the Red Sea, now the flood—and joining them to the rites.[132] These are not instructions on how we are to live but insights into what God is doing both in history and in the font. Ambrose says that what happened in the Bible prefigures what really happened to us in baptism;[133] these events reveal God's liberating presence determining the history recorded in the Bible and our history determined in the font. He says, 'Greater than the Jewish people passing through the sea, in the waters of baptism you passed from sin to grace, from vileness to holiness, from death to life.'[134]

"In explaining how this happens, Ambrose distinguishes between what is seen and what is done, between earthly things and heavenly things,[135] between the matter and its consecration, the action and its effect.[136] He tells us that through baptism God gives us the faith to glimpse the mystery, to see with the eyes of faith, and he calls upon us to use those eyes to view both our lives and the world.[137] And I am beginning to see, at least a little.

"Ambrose takes great pains to speak gently; he uses his voice to bring us along. He asks us questions. Some of those questions prod my thinking; others are the questions that I would ask myself. By what he says and how he says it, it feels as though the bishop is speaking directly to me. 'Be on the alert. Keep faith with Christ, guard that faith, which is far more precious than money.'[138] Ambrose tells us, and from somewhere deep inside me, something tells me I can keep faith with Christ. Something tells me I will. 'But now my voice is getting tired and time is running out,' the bishop says, 'so that's enough for today.'[139] He tells us that our ears must be attentive and our hearts

---

[132] Ibid., 1.3.9–6.23 (SC 25bis.62–72).
[133] Ibid., 1.5.19 (SC 25bis.70).
[134] Ibid., 1.4.12 (SC 25bis.66).
[135] Ibid., 1.3.10 (SC 25bis.64).
[136] Ibid., 1.5.15 (SC 25bis.68).
[137] Ibid., 3.3.12, 15 (SC 25bis.100). Cf. ibid., 1.3.10 (SC 25bis.64).
[138] Ibid., 1.2.8 (SC 25bis.64).
[139] Ibid., 1.6.24 (SC 25bis.72).

properly disposed, so that we retain the things he tells us and have the grace of God.[140] With a blessing he is finished."[141]

Christ is not explained, Christ is experienced. Like the mysteries, the instruction that followed was an opportunity for the newly baptized to encounter and experience Christ. Throughout this study we have explored the many ways that Ambrose attempted to create a dialogue. This dialogue was not between the bishop and the neophytes but between God and God's people. Through Ambrose's preaching and the people's listening, embedded in liturgy and supported by a great basilica, the Spirit spoke and the neophytes heard. Faith began to take hold; the world began to look different. The newly baptized began to respond, and Christians began to be formed.

Today the Spirit of God revealed in Christ continues to speak and act in water and word, in bread and cup, and even in sermons first preached in the basilica of Milan during the week after Easter some sixteen hundred years ago. Through *De sacramentis*, both as text and as event, the Spirit continues to invite us to dialogue about the mysteries and come to see through the eyes of faith. Our responsibility as mystagogues is to preach on the mysteries in a way that enhances the Spirit's invitation to our people. In the next chapter we will formulate a method for carrying out this responsibility.

[140] Ibid.
[141] This fictional narrative, written by the author, is based on *De sacramentis,* 1, and draws upon insights articulated in this and earlier chapters.

Chapter 9

"We too are not without discernment": Discerning a Method of Mystagogical Preaching

We come at last to the task of proposing a method of mystagogical preaching for the contemporary Church. Ambrose himself offers a clue as to how we might proceed. In explaining why the church of Milan washes the feet of those being baptized even though the Roman Church does not, the bishop of Milan asserts that "we, too, are not without discernment; and what other places have done well to retain, we, too, do well to maintain."[1] Following Ambrose's lead, we might look upon our task in this chapter as *discerning* from the practice of others, namely, Ambrose and the church of Milan, what it is well for our Church to maintain or, more accurately, what it is well for our Church to regain.

The legitimate question arises as to whether we can, in fact, propose a *method* of mystagogical preaching. Is there a method underlying the sermons contained in *De sacramentis*, and assuming there is, can we appropriate that method for ourselves? The National Conference of Catholic Bishops correctly observes that "every art is based on a theory and a method, and preaching is no exception."[2] Preachers can learn from preachers, such as Saint Ambrose, "through whose words they have heard the Word of God."[3] Nevertheless, "ultimately, individual preachers will have to develop their own method."[4] For the

---

[1] *De sacramentis*, 3.1.5 (SC 25bis.94).
[2] National Conference of Catholic Bishops, *Fulfilled in Your Hearing: The Homily in the Sunday Assembly* (Washington: United States Catholic Conference, 1982) 29.
[3] Ibid.
[4] Ibid.

methods "that most of us use are ultimately and wondrously quite personal, a combination of learnings from a variety of sources that we have found valuable."[5]

Discerning a method of mystagogy from Ambrose's preaching on the sacraments is therefore the appropriate way to proceed because it allows us to glean, evaluate, and incorporate insights from the bishop of Milan into our own method of preaching. This is especially important for mystagogy, which, as we have asserted from the outset of our study, is individual and unique, because its goal is to help particular neophytes discover the meaning of the specific rites of Christian initiation in which they have participated.[6] Thus the method of preaching proposed in this chapter is *a* method of mystagogy rather than *the* method of mystagogy.[7] Like the approach to preaching provided in *Fulfilled in Your Hearing*, the method of mystagogy outlined in the following pages "is not intended as—nor could it possibly be—a foolproof system for producing outstanding homilies."[8] Rather, we will offer "detailed yet flexible guidelines"[9] for incorporating every component of mystagogical preaching—preacher, listeners, rites, Scripture, form, delivery, and the work of the Spirit—recognizing that "the value of any method for preaching is that it does not demand conformity but discloses opportunity."[10]

This chapter is divided into six sections. The first four sections correspond to the four steps in the method of mystagogical preaching that we discern from Saint Ambrose: (1) question Ambrose's assumptions, (2) arrive at the message, (3) craft the homily, and (4) retrace the journey. In section five we will concretize our method by providing a

---

[5] Paul Scott Wilson, *Imagination of the Heart: New Understandings in Preaching* (Nashville: Abingdon Press, 1988) 13.

[6] Above, 8, 290–291.

[7] Even a cursory comparison of the methods of preaching underlying the mystagogical catecheses of Ambrose of Milan, Cyril of Jerusalem, John Chrysostom, and Theodore of Mopsuestia reveals that, although there are similarities, each method is unique. While we will highlight certain similarities and differences between Ambrose's method and the methods of these other fourth-century mystagogues in the course of the following discussion, a systematic comparison is beyond the scope of this study. For an example of these differences, see above, 251.

[8] National Conference of Catholic Bishops, *Fulfilled in Your Hearing*, 29.

[9] Wilson, *Imagination of the Heart*, 13.

[10] Ibid.

specific "how to" example of mystagogical preaching. In the sixth section of this chapter, we once again conclude with a "pneumatic reflection," this time on the role of the Spirit in the method that we are proposing.

QUESTION AMBROSE'S ASSUMPTIONS

Inasmuch as we are attempting to discern from Ambrose's mystagogy a way of preaching for the contemporary Church, the first step in our method is to ask whether the assumptions underlying Ambrose's mystagogy are applicable to, and have value for, the Church's ministry today. Five issues are particularly deserving of consideration: (1) God's presence and activity in the rites, (2) the relationship between Church and culture, (3) the connection between explanation of, and participation in, the sacraments, (4) the role of the preacher, and (5) the patristic approach to Scripture.

God's Presence and Activity in the Rites

For Ambrose, there is more going on in the rites of initiation than what is perceivable by human sight. Ambrose was convinced that the Triune God is present in the rites of initiation to both give the neophytes faith and to enable them to see the mysteries, themselves, and the world through the eyes of faith that they received. Ambrose summarizes the effect of God's activity in the rites, saying:

"You went there [to the font], you washed, you came to the altar, you began to see. That is to say, through the font of the Lord and the preaching of the Lord's passion, at that moment your eyes were opened. Before, you seemed to be blind of heart. But now you began to perceive the light of the sacraments."[11]

In his mystagogy, Ambrose stresses the inner dynamic of the sacraments—the invisible activity of God. The rites are the continuing drama of salvation.[12] For Ambrose, the economy of salvation continues in our midst in our liturgical celebrations, where by faith we recognize and celebrate God's saving activity continuing in our daily lives. Ambrose finds in the process of Christian initiation an obvious sense of drama in which we ritually re-enact the dynamic passage into a

[11] *De sacramentis* 3.2.15 (SC 25bis.100).
[12] Above, 195–196.

new world of consciousness, the world of salvation history, and our turning toward and incorporation into God's saving activity in Christ.

Ambrose also believes that, through mystagogical preaching, God leads the newly baptized to see their lives and the world through the eyes of faith that they received at baptism, that is, to see beyond the temporal to the eternal, beyond the realities of this world to the reality of God's kingdom. Mystagogy demands that we trust in the unseen activity of God at work in the sacraments and understand faith not as intellectual assent but as choosing a way of life.

Church and Culture

The second issue that a contemporary mystagogue must consider is whether we live in a world in which mystagogy—sustained reflection on the Church's rites of initiation—has value and meaning for faith and life. In order to answer this question, the contemporary mystagogue must come to some conclusion about the relationship between faith and culture, Church and world. Specifically, the mystagogue must determine whether the culture reinforces the Christian faith. If, in fact, the world in which we live can be counted on to teach and support the Christian faith and way of life, mystagogy is unnecessary. We can assume that the sacraments are ends in themselves, things that Christians want to participate in because that is what Christians do. We can assume that the meaning of the sacraments is something Christians feel they need to know, not because it relates to their everyday lives but so they have a correct understanding of Christian doctrine. If the world in which we live can be counted on to teach and support the Christian faith and way of life, we can assume that Christians will embrace and understand instruction on baptism and the Eucharist that is academic, speculative in its theology, and propositional, because such instruction is so highly valued. In such a world, mystagogy like that of Saint Ambrose is not necessary. However, we do not live in such a world.

Our historical narrative, which in Chapter 2 set the stage for our analysis of Ambrose's mystagogy, reveals that Ambrose's preaching on the sacraments is a response to culture and that the fourth-century culture from which mystagogy emerged, with its diverse forms of religion, competing value systems, and nominal Christianity, is very similar to our own.[13] By the second half of the fourth century, late Roman

---

[13] As we discussed in Chapter 1, the liturgists who created the R.C.I.A. looked to the mystagogical catecheses of the fourth century, and this is what

society had become friendly toward, and even supportive of, Christian worship and institutions, with the exception of the brief reign of Julian (361–363). By the time of Theodosius, Roman society had become nominally Christian, to the point that legal measures were undertaken to repress the traditional pagan cults. Nevertheless, a large element of paganism still remained, even among Christians, and the old nobility, especially in Italy, often refused on traditional grounds to adopt Christianity even in name. Despite the fact that society publicly supported Christianity, the Church could not look to the culture to support and sustain the formation of Christians and, in fact, had to be culturally critical and continue to preach against forms of idolatry.

The bishop of Milan's understanding of faith as choosing a way of life is a consequence of his view that the world is hostile to Christianity. Ambrose felt it his duty to call his congregation from the excesses of Milanese society to the higher ideal of the Christian life.[14] His

---

contemporary commentators on the rite do as well. Above, 8. A main reason that the contemporary Church draws upon the fourth and fifth centuries as a source for liturgical renewal is that they seem to have been the time when the Eastern and Western liturgies, as we know them, were formed. Much of what we know about liturgy prior to this time is speculation.

Providing an important cautionary note against viewing the period of the early Church (or any period of Church history for that matter) as a perfect age and attempting to re-create it in our own time, Paul Bradshaw argues that the period of the fourth and fifth centuries is a surprising choice as a model for the worship of our day. Bradshaw contends that Christian worship of the fourth and fifth centuries does not represent the most primitive form of Christian worship but is a liturgy in transition as the Church struggled to respond to the union of Church and state brought about by the Peace of Constantine.[1] Bradshaw argues further that our congregations are more pre-Constantinian in size, and the Church is emerging from our identification with a nominally Christian society. Yet, while the Church of the fourth century was moving toward greater identification with the culture and the contemporary Church is moving away from it, both that period and our own are "in-between times" when the relationship between Church and world is being redefined. The transitory nature of both periods makes the fourth century a useful model. Paul F. Bradshaw, "The Liturgical Use and Abuse of Patristics," *Liturgy Reshaped*, ed. Kenneth Stevenson (London: SPCK, 1982) 134–145.

[1] Ibid., 134.

[14] Above, 72ff.; 122–123.

mystagogical works reflect his hostility toward the world.[15] Our discussions of Ambrose and the empire and Ambrose as moral leader help us to understand the reasons for this antagonism.[16] In the ancient world the problem of idolatry was a fact of virtually every sphere of public life. This idolatry threatened to relegate the Church to a separate enclave within the culture. Ralph Keifer is correct that both the Church's refusal to compromise with the idolatry of the state and its immense concern for direct care of the poor make clear that the Church's understanding of evangelization had nothing in common with a gospel of personal salvation that elicits no concern for justice and gladly joins in "contemporary forms of emperor worship."[17] As we reflect upon the historical context of Ambrose's mystagogy, it becomes apparent that the fourth-century culture from which mystagogy emerged is similar to our own.

The core similarity between the fourth century and the twenty-first is that the Church could not then and cannot now look to the culture for the formation of Christians. In the twenty-first century, the Christian direction of culture is highly ambiguous at best. Although we live in a culture that, in the minds of a majority of its citizens, is Christian, it is in many respects polytheistic and pagan. There are several reasons why this is so. First, the Church no longer stands securely at the center of society. The waves of immigration, which provided the Church with a steady source of new members, are effectively two generations behind us, and the ethnic neighborhoods, which afforded the Church a secure place in society, have been eroded in the aftermath of World War II. Rather than being a Christian society, contemporary culture is characterized by a variety of moralities that include historic religions, new forms of religious life, and secular alternatives to religion.[18] For many today, Christianity is reminiscent of the nominal life of faith practiced by the vast majority of fourth-century catechumens, who viewed baptism as an eschatological act meant to prepare one for the life to come, participated in the Church's rites when it was socially

---

[15] Above, 192–195.

[16] Above, 51–60; 72–77.

[17] Ralph Keifer, "Christian Initiation: The State of the Question," *Worship* 48, no. 7 (August–September 1974) 397–398.

[18] James F. Gustafson, "The Sectarian Temptation: Reflections on Theology, the Church, and the University," *CTSA Proceedings* 40 (1985) 83.

appropriate, and appeared irregularly, if at all, in church.[19] In his much publicized book, *The Naked Public Square: Religion and Democracy in America*, Richard John Neuhaus argues that we are facing a crisis in our society because faith has become so privatized that religious discourse has been increasingly excluded from our public life.[20]

Second, in the absence of commonly held religious values, the discipline that binds society together is being supplied by the marketplace. Faith has become so privatized, individualized, and dematerialized that society's need for public discipline, once met by religion, is now provided by the values of advanced global capitalization.[21] Contentment and gratitude are replaced by desire and want. Faithfulness is measured by success. Character is reduced to image. Even congregations of the Church program their ministry and mission in response to a consumer mentality. In the wake of the Second Vatican Council, the Flemish Dominican theologian Edward Schillebeeckx observed that the "world of efficiency" he experienced in the United States, marked by what is known as "American pragmatism," stands in stark contrast to the anti-pragmatic world of *spiritualité*.[22]

Third, more and more, people are concluding that the Church's traditional language and understanding of God, salvation, and revelation are not relevant to their lives. Schillebeeckx explains that one's understanding of the world, God, and oneself are all interrelated.[23] When one of these components shifts, the others necessarily shift as well. In the case of our secularized, pluralistic society, the relationship between humanity and the world changed, rendering the Church's traditional understanding and articulation of the relationship between God and humanity, formulated as it was in response to a previous worldview, irrelevant. Thus Schillebeeckx finds himself "profoundly unsettled by

---

[19] Cf. above, 34–35; 120–121.

[20] Richard John Neuhaus, *The Naked Public Square: Religion and Democracy in America* (Grand Rapids: William B. Eerdmans Publishing Co., 1984).

[21] Roger Clapp, "At the Intersection of Eucharist and Capital: On the Future of Liturgical Worship," 2000 Annual Meeting of the North American Academy of Liturgy, January 4, 2000, Tampa, Florida.

[22] Edward Schillebeeckx, "Epilogue: The New Image of God, Secularization and Man's Future on Earth," *God the Future of Man*, trans. N. D. Smith (New York: Sheed & Ward, 1968) 170. My articulation of the theology of Edward Schillebeeckx is indebted to Diane Steele, S.C.L.

[23] Ibid., 44–65.

what he interpreted as a pervasive crisis of faith undergone among people living in secularized pluralistic societies such as the United States."[24]

Fourth, in responding to this crisis of faith and the need to reinterpret the faith for a secularized, pluralistic world, the contemporary Church increasingly articulates the relationship between God and humanity in terms of personal salvation and privatized faith. In so doing, contemporary forms of evangelization replace a Christianity that stands in contrast to the "world of efficiency" with a Christianity that has no concern for justice and is very comfortable with participation in profit, greed, instant gratification, and material success. Neil Postman illustrates this point using televangelism. Postman argues convincingly that attempts to make religion more entertaining have stripped away "everything that makes religion an historic, profound and sacred human activity. . . . [T]here is no tradition, no theology, and, above all, no sense of spiritual transcendence."[25] Postman sums up the credo of this kind of religion as "offering people what they want" and notes that no great religious leader, from the Buddha to Moses to Jesus to Mohammed to Luther, offered people what they want, only what they need.[26]

If the contemporary mystagogue concludes that we do not live in a Christian culture, the first step in a method of mystagogical preaching is to let go of the assumption that Christians will automatically be formed in the faith. As in the fourth century, we can no longer assume that religious identity and meaning will largely be forged by a culture that is assumed to be fundamentally Christian. A consequence of this new reality is that, as in the fourth century, the Church in some quarters is coming to expect more of its members than a conventional religiosity that manifests itself in compliance with certain minimal regulations. The Church is instead coming to expect of its members the capacity to undergo radical and lasting transformation. Mystagogues expect, even demand, transformation.

As we have seen, radical transformation—moving from not seeing to seeing—is the goal of Ambrose's mystagogy. We have previously

---

[24] Philip Kennedy, O.P., *Schillebeeckx*, Outstanding Christian Thinkers Series, ed. Brian Davies, O.P. (Collegeville: The Liturgical Press, 1993) 43.

[25] Neil Postman, *Amusing Ourselves to Death: Public Discourse in the Age of Show Business* (New York: Penguin Books, 1985) 116–117.

[26] Ibid., 121.

argued that mystagogical preaching offers great promise for enlivening and enlarging the faith community's liturgical and sacramental life and the identity and mission that flow from it.[27] This potential for transformation, together with the obvious need for developing the period of mystagogical catechesis within the catechumenate,[28] make learning to preach mystagogically essential to the life of the Church.

Explanation and Participation

It is important for mystagogues to make a decision about the relationship between participation in the rites and receiving an explanation of them. Will sacramental catechesis proceed or follow participation in the rites? Or, more accurately, what kind of sacramental catechesis is prerequisite for participation in the rites? Ambrose's approach is to withhold instruction on the sacraments until after participation in the rites. Like Cyril of Jerusalem, Ambrose gives no instruction on baptism, the Eucharist, and the Lord's Prayer until *after* his hearers have experienced these rites for the first time during their initiation at the Easter Vigil.[29] Then his method of instruction is to draw upon his hearers' own experience. His sermons are organized as a journey through the rites of initiation, from entering the baptistry through the font to arrival at the altar for the celebration of the Easter Eucharist. Along the way Ambrose asks, "What did we do?" "What did you see?" "What did you say?" In answering these questions, Ambrose moves his hearers from images, words, and actions to the significance of these images, words, and actions for Christian faith and their implications for Christian life.

This pedagogical approach found expression in the *disciplina arcani*.[30] Ambrose gave two reasons for the "discipline of secrecy": the desire to show reverence for the sacraments and the sound educational principle that truth must be conveyed gradually and adapted to the circumstances and apprehensions of the hearers.[31] Ambrose believed in a

[27] Above, 7–8.

[28] Ibid.

[29] Above, 186–188. Theodore of Mopsuestia teaches the catechumens the mysteries of baptism in the days before they are baptized but withholds instruction on the Eucharist until after the Easter Vigil. John Chrysostom explains baptism in advance of the Easter Vigil and does not include a systematic treatment of the Eucharist in his mystagogical sermons.

[30] Above, 155–156.

[31] Above, 156.

pedagogy of recognition; one learns better if one has seen and experienced before being instructed.[32] Ambrose also trusted in the power of God active in the sacraments. He asserts that it is better for the light of the sacraments to be inculcated in the candidates as a surprise.[33] Ambrose believed that the rites themselves have an inherent pedagogy in terms of the inner light that infuses itself in the unsuspecting. The mysteries were not intended to be readily understood but to have a deep emotional impact and to leave a lasting impression on those being initiated.[34]

For Ambrose, baptism and the Eucharist are an encounter with God, and an encounter with God comes as a surprise awareness of a new meaning of life. Furthermore, faith is needed to understand the sacraments, and faith is given at baptism.[35] Thus, to explain the sacraments to the uninitiated would betray rather than portray them. Mystagogy, then, is the neophytes' opportunity to see the mysteries through the eyes of faith they received at baptism by retracing their journey of initiation. Thus the goal of Ambrose's mystagogy is not that the newly baptized merely understand the meaning of the rites but that they enter more fully into them in faith.

That explanation followed participation in the rites does not imply that there was no preparation or formation prior to participation. In fourth-century Milan preparation for baptism included daily instruction in both the biblical stories of faith and the morality of the Christian life, fasting, scrutinies, and learning the Creed.[36] The distinctiveness of this preparation is its emphasis on doing rather than understanding, formation rather than comprehension. In a most convincing study, Alan Kreider argues, "the records of the early Christians [show] . . . that conversion involved change not just of belief but also of belonging and behavior."[37] Conversion to Christianity included changes in ethics and solidarity, as well as understanding, all within an experience of God. Therefore, rather than a classroom, candidates experienced Lent as a kind of "boot camp," an intense time that

[32] See above, 16.
[33] Above, 187.
[34] Above, 188.
[35] Above, 187.
[36] Above, 149ff.
[37] Alan Kreider, *The Change of Conversion and the Origin of Christendom* (Harrisburg, Pa.: Trinity Press International, 1999) xv.

produced both anxiety and anticipation, a time in which they get in shape to receive the sacraments. Ambrose's instruction of candidates for baptism prior to their participation in the rites was not on the meaning of the sacraments but involved learning the biblical narratives, the stories of faith. Through these narratives candidates were taught the manner of life that befits the baptized and were provided with models to imitate and principles to follow.[38]

Fasting separated the candidates from, and set them in stark contrast to, the excesses and self-gratification of Milanese society, not only by removing them from the culture but by teaching them that as Christians they have obligations to the poor and the needy. For Ambrose, true fasting is inseparable from the work of justice.[39] In the scrutinies, candidates' readiness to receive the mysteries was not evaluated according to their comprehension of the meaning of the sacraments but by whether they were being sanctified.[40] Furthermore, in his instruction on the Creed, Ambrose did not emphasize that the candidates need to correctly understand the Creed but that they recite it daily in order to enjoy its power to ward off shocks to mind and body and to shield them from temptation.[41] In all these ways, the purpose of preparation for participation in the rites was not to ensure that candidates for baptism correctly comprehended the meaning of the sacraments but to make certain that, like athletes, they follow a rigorous discipline of daily training in order to be in shape to participate in both the rites and the new life that flows from them.[42]

Ambrose's practice of delaying explanation of the sacraments until after candidates had participated in the rites suggests the value of what Harmless calls "the pedagogy of silence."[43] Ambrose recognized that silence can teach, that the rites themselves teach, and that the rites and not the mystagogue should have the first word.[44] Ambrose believed that the inner light of the mysteries infused itself better on the unsuspecting. Of course, he could assume that the symbolism of the

[38] Above, 150–151.
[39] Above, 151.
[40] Above, 152–153.
[41] Above, 153–155.
[42] Above, 151–152.
[43] William Harmless, *Augustine and the Catechumenate* (New York: Pueblo Publishing Co., 1995) 362ff.
[44] Ibid.

rites would speak for itself, for the rites were large, dramatic, and overwhelming.

Explaining the sacraments after participation in the rites transcends the question of whether there was, in fact, an authentic *disciplina arcani* in the early Church and whether the Church today can and should maintain such a discipline of secrecy. We may dismiss the *disciplina arcani*; we may observe that whereas the early Church practiced a discipline of secrecy, the Church today practices a secrecy of neglect when it comes to sacramental catechesis. After preparing candidates for participation in the rites by preprogramming their experience, sacramental catechesis stops; the unspoken assumption seems to be that the Church has said everything it has to say about baptism before candidates reach the font and the Eucharist before they ever receive the bread or drink from the cup.[45] A pedagogy of explanation after experience of the rites implies a change in the emphasis of preparation for participation.

The Church needs to alert candidates to the worth of the sacraments and that participation in the sacraments means committing oneself to Christ. Certainly the Church will tell candidates the biblical stories of faith, that baptism is the forgiveness of sin and the beginning of new life, and that Christ is truly present in the Eucharist. More important, preparing candidates for baptism involves training them to live the baptismal life, readying them to experience Christ's presence in the Eucharist, and recognizing that preparation is no substitute for sacramental experience.

The Preacher: Steward of the Mysteries and Spiritual Guide

In his first letter to the church at Corinth, Saint Paul writes, "Think of us in this way, as servants of Christ and stewards of God's mysteries."[46] Ambrose regarded himself as a steward of the mysteries. Worship was the heart of Ambrose's pastoral ministry; he looked upon baptism and the Eucharist as central to the life of both the Christian and the Church. The bishop of Milan taught and exhorted his

---

[45] Since the Middle Ages the Western Church has prized cognitive understanding as requisite for participation in the sacraments. For example, since the Fourth Lateran Council in 1215, confession and absolution have been required in order to participate in the Eucharist and, since the Lutheran Reformation, it has been expected that participation in the Lord's Supper will be preceded by catechetical instruction or even the rite of confirmation.

[46] 1 Corinthians 4:1.

priests that preaching, presiding at the Eucharist, and the instruction of those preparing for baptism are special priorities of pastoral ministry.[47] Ambrose's people knew their bishop best as a liturgical presence, preaching and presiding at the celebration of the Eucharist, often every day.[48] Ambrose's example calls the Church to recognize that if the sacraments are to be a transforming force, baptism and Eucharist must be central to our ministry.

Second, the preacher's role in mystagogy is that of a spiritual guide. Although the bond between the preacher and the listeners is an important part of mystagogy, as it is in all preaching, in mystagogy the primary connection is between the listeners and their experience of the rites.[49] From the structure and content of *De sacramentis*, we can conclude that in his instruction of the newly baptized, Ambrose saw his role as that of the neophytes' spiritual guide.[50] A guide is one who shows the way by leading, directing, or advising, usually by reason of his or her greater experience with the course to be pursued.

Ambrose's guidance through the journey of Christian initiation is grounded in both the history, structure, and theology of the rites and his experience of God, the rites, the neophytes, and the world. More than being the source of information and knowledge about the sacraments, mystagogues are, in the words of Mark Searle, "tour guides of the Kingdom." Mystagogues help Christians find their way through their experience of the rites in order to discover the meaning and significance for faith and conversion contained therein.

As spiritual guides, preachers will take seriously that mystagogy is reflection on the listeners' experience of the rites of initiation. Unlocking a given faith community's experience involves seriously listening to the members of that community. Ambrose did not know the neophytes intimately and individually. Rather than participating in special interactions aimed at acquainting the bishop with the newly baptized, Ambrose came to know them in the course of his ministry, particularly through the process of Christian initiation.[51] The reason that someone chose to be baptized was particularly significant because, rather than being a common practice, baptism at the time of

---

[47] Above, 93.
[48] Above, 67.
[49] Above, 276–277.
[50] Above, 276; 279.
[51] Above, 112ff.

Saint Ambrose stood at the threshold of becoming a purely eschatological and individualistic act best postponed until one's involvement with the world was over.[52]

Ambrose's example teaches that, rather than undertaking a "listening tour," listening to the faith community can be the way pastors carry out their ministry, occurring in the course of the calling to pastor, counsel, teach, and serve. By keeping their eyes open to the realities of their people's lives and their ears attuned to their people's questions and reactions to issues of faith, worship, and sacrament, mystagogues continuously listen to their people in order to inform and shape their understanding of the sacraments. Thus, listening in order to guide need not be a cumbersome burden or even an additional task.

Ambrose's example also invites ministers to consider the governing model of their ministry. Are they chiefly administrators, evangelists, counselors, community activists, or stewards of the mysteries and tour guides of God's kingdom? In answering this question, ministers might reflect upon the amount of time and energy they spend preaching and presiding. Ministers might contemplate whether the people of God think of them and know them best as a liturgical presence. Ministers might ask themselves how important is it to help their people grow in their experience, understanding, and appreciation of the Church's worship and its implications for faith and life? Are we as concerned with forming people in faith as we are with bringing people to faith? Should the Church's pedagogical approach be to provide information about God or to help people encounter and experience God? Mystagogy calls the Church and its leaders to re-examine and perhaps to reprioritize pastoral ministry.

The Patristic Approach to Scripture

Mystagogy calls us to rediscover and appreciate what Pamela Jackson describes as "the Patristic understanding and use of the Word proclaimed in the worshiping assembly as catalyst for conversion."[53] Ambrose, like all the Fathers, perceived the Church "as living in the world of the Bible in the sense that the Church understands itself in Biblical terms and sees itself as a continuation of God's saving work recorded in the Bible; initiation into such a community therefore in-

---

[52] Above, 120–121.

[53] Pamela Jackson, *Journeybread for the Shadowlands: The Readings for the Rites of the Catechumenate, RCIA* (Collegeville: The Liturgical Press, 1993) 1.

cludes drawing converts into the Biblical world."⁵⁴ The rites are understood to be a reenactment of salvation history; the realities of the Old Testament are figures of both Jesus' actions in the New Testament and the sacraments of the Church. Ambrose therefore interprets the rites of initiation almost exclusively in terms of scriptural stories, images, admonitions, and segments of psalms. Profoundly versed in Scripture, Ambrose not only looked to the Bible for the meaning of the sacraments, he found it natural to express his ideas in biblical language.⁵⁵

Ambrose viewed Scripture as a mystery. For Ambrose, understanding the mystical sense of Scripture means seeing that the facts of the Old Testament are, in relation to the New Testament, type, figure, and shadow.⁵⁶ For Ambrose, understanding Scripture as a mystery means that a given passage cannot be reduced to a single meaning. He therefore adopts a kind of "explanatory pluralism," which allows both the bishop and his hearers to select from among a number of alternative interpretations or even to maintain more than one.⁵⁷

The notions that Scripture is a mystery, that the Old Testament is interpreted by means of the New and the New Testament interpreted by means of the Old, and that a given passage of Scripture has more than one meaning are completely foreign to our approach to Scripture, having been replaced by a historical-critical method of biblical exegesis. The historical-critical method has made a point of criticizing the exegetical method of the Fathers by emphasizing their lack of scientific rigor and analytical precision, their lack of any truly historical perspective, and their lack of critical distance from the text of Scripture.⁵⁸ In so doing, the historical-critical method has reduced the exegetical method of the Fathers to a strictly historical source of information that is useful for illuminating the thought of the Fathers but is of no use in our own exegesis of the same text of Scripture. The historical-critical method had so convinced us of its superior way of uncovering the meaning of a biblical text that any other method was ruled "uncritical" and therefore simply passé to the Church.⁵⁹

---

⁵⁴ Ibid., 5.

⁵⁵ Above, 210.

⁵⁶ Above, 223.

⁵⁷ Above, 221–222.

⁵⁸ Frances M. Young, *Biblical Exegesis and the Formation of Christian Culture* (Cambridge–New York: Cambridge University Press, 1997) 3.

⁵⁹ Mark Chapman, "Early Christian Mystagogy and the Formation of Modern Christians," *Currents in Theology and Mission* 21 (August 1994) 291.

While the historical-critical method once enjoyed the same nearly universal application in the Church today that the patristic method of exegesis did in the fourth century, recent developments have challenged the once predominant historical-critical approach to exegesis. Canon criticism, structuralism, and literary-critical studies have produced new perspectives and methods. Hermeneutical discussions and liberation theologies questioned the basis and value of what are increasingly, but erroneously, regarded as the 'traditional' methods.[60] While the patristic approach to Scripture provided a sort of conceptual unity to the Church even while allowing for significant differences, the historical-critical method has produced fragmentation, rendering Scripture unintelligible to anyone except trained experts in the history, language, culture, and beliefs of the centuries and peoples spanned by the Bible, thereby distancing the Church from its Scriptures.

Furthermore, the historical-critical approach discovers the "true meaning" of Scripture by disassembling and atomizing the text of Scripture in order to uncover its authenticity, authorial intent, philosophical and cultural influences, and the writer's own religious experience. The untrained reader of the Bible is warned against the oversimplification of reading for the plain sense of the text and left with bits and fragments of the text so scrutinized and analyzed that their original coherence is lost amid all the pieces of the puzzle.[61] Thus Frances Young argues that the Fathers would condemn much modern exegesis for its exclusive focus on the "earthly" and its lack of concern with the "heavenly" dimension of the text.[62] This criticism in no way negates the fact that we have benefited inestimably in our knowledge and insight from the critical work done in textual, historical, linguistic, and cultural studies of Scripture. Our understanding of the Bible and of the faith is richer and better for it. The problem is not that the historical-critical method is in use; the problem arises when it displaces all other methods and comes to be seen as an end in itself, the final step in the process of interpreting Scripture. In the words of

---

[60] Young, *Biblical Exegesis and the Formation of Christian Culture*, 2. Cf. idem, *The Art of Performance: Towards a Theology of Holy Scripture* (London: Darton, Longman & Todd, 1990).

[61] Chapman, "Early Christian Mystagogy and the Formation of Modern Christians," 292.

[62] Young, *Biblical Exegesis and the Formation of Christian Culture*, 3.

Walter Brueggemann, the historical-critical method is "essential but not sufficient."[63]

The Church is increasingly recognizing that preaching and teaching cannot end here. All preaching and teaching is compelled to go beyond historical criticism, to return the coherence and wholeness to the text, and to bring Scripture to bear on the lives of Christians. Unfortunately, the historical-critical method provides no guidance for reassembling the unity of Scripture; in fact, the historical-critical method is opposed to the idea of the unity of Scripture. And so the preacher and teacher must invent or intuit his or her own way of finding the unity of Scripture after historical criticism has laid the pieces at her or his feet. Too often the content of preaching becomes either an examination of form-critical fragments, which reduces the sermon to an exegetical lecture, or the preacher's personal or political agenda rather than the grace and redemption of the Bible.[64] Thus Walter Wink declares, "Historical biblical criticism is bankrupt."[65] He uses "bankrupt" in the "exact sense of the term." Businesses that go bankrupt are not valueless, not incapable of producing useful products. "The one thing wrong—and the only thing—is that it is no longer able to accomplish its avowed purpose for existence: to make money."[66] Biblical criticism "is bankrupt solely because it is incapable of achieving what most of its practitioners considered its purpose to be: to interpret the Scriptures so that the past becomes alive and illumines our present with new possibilities for personal and social transformation."[67]

Young argues that a reassessment of the Fathers' assumption that the Bible has a "spiritual" meaning is necessary today, as is a review of the procedures whereby they unraveled the symbols discerned in the text.[68] It is as a method of finding the coherence of Scripture as a whole in order to address Christians today that patristic exegesis becomes instructive. The Fathers interpreted Scripture by its application to

---

[63] Walter Brueggemann, "The Faithfulness of Otherwise," University of Notre Dame, February 4, 2000.

[64] Chapman, "Early Christian Mystagogy and the Formation of Modern Christians," 292.

[65] Walter Wink, *The Bible in Human Transformation. Toward a New Paradigm for Biblical Study* (Philadelphia: Fortress Press, 1973) 1.

[66] Ibid.

[67] Ibid., 2.

[68] Young, *Biblical Exegesis and the Formation of Christian Culture*, 3.

Christian life and interpreted the life of the Christian by its correspondence to Scripture. In this way the Fathers sought a dynamic whole not only in Scripture but also between Scripture and the Christian life.

Scripture and Church are united by the Church's experience of Christ's presence in baptism and Eucharist. Baptism changes who Christians are and Scripture provides the language, description, and images that illuminate what that change looks like in the lives of believers. Receiving the Eucharist makes the neophytes different; Scripture gives the framework for how to live with this difference. At the same time, the life and experience of the Church determine what the Scriptures mean. The sacraments are at the heart of the Church's life and experience; therefore, baptism and Eucharist provide the context for interpreting Scripture. From this convergence of liturgy and Bible, of Scripture and sacrament, the Fathers derived their images and metaphors and language for describing and encouraging the Christian life.

Mystagogy invites us to retrieve this convergence and union of Scripture and liturgy, not by abandoning historical criticism, but by assigning the historical-critical method its proper place as an intermediate step in the process from the first reading of Scripture to announcing the Good News. For while the results of historical-critical research are not what we preach, they do provide valuable perspectives on the Bible that the early Church never had. Nevertheless, it is by recovering the unity of Scripture and Church, of God's saving activity in the Bible and God's saving activity in the sacraments, that Scripture will remain relevant to the formation of Christians as its formative principles, its world of meaning, its cultural system, and as the structure of language that sets the Christian life apart from life in a post-Christian world in which we cannot take for granted that the culture will be shaped by Christian values. As Mark Chapman observes, "Such was also the world as the ancient Fathers would have described it, so perhaps it is time that we listen again to them for how to live in it."[69] While this patristic approach to Scripture is alien to us, it offers the contemporary Church valuable insights and perspectives on how to understand and proclaim the sacraments as the continuing activity of God addressed to us here and now.

---

[69] Chapman, "Early Christian Mystagogy and the Formation of Modern Christians," 293.

Summary

In this section we examined five assumptions underlying Ambrose's mystagogy and argued in favor of their relevance to and value for the contemporary Church. We called for trust that God is present and active in the sacraments to give faith and in mystagogy to enable the Christian to see through the eyes of faith. We showed that, as in the fourth century, the Church cannot look to the culture for the formation of Christians; consequently, faith should be understood as the choice to live as a Christian in a post-Christian culture rather than as intellectual assent. We invited preachers to see themselves as stewards of the mysteries and spiritual guides and advocated both a pedagogy of silence and a preparatory catechesis aimed at training candidates to live the Christian life. Finally, we showed that the patristic approach to Scripture can assist the Church in interpreting the Bible today. In all these ways mystagogy is relevant to, and has value for, the contemporary Church. We therefore now turn to a method for the creation of a mystagogical homily.

ARRIVE AT THE MESSAGE

In this section we will explore how one arrives at the message or determines the content of mystagogy. The mystagogue arrives at a message by moving through a four-step process: (1) establish the "text," (2) evaluate the rites, (3) interpret the meaning of the rites, and (4) spell out the implications of participation for daily life. This process takes seriously that liturgy is the "text" on which mystagogy is based, that Scripture provides the means for interpreting this "text," and that the experience of both the preacher and the listeners are the best source for determining how the sacraments are applicable to the faith community's everyday life in the world.

Establish the "Text"

Inasmuch as the sacraments are God's means of giving faith and new life, the rites are the starting point for understanding God's saving activity in our lives. The truly distinctive feature of mystagogical preaching is that the "text" on which these sermons are based is not a passage of Scripture but the rites of initiation in which the listeners have participated.[70] Although the rites are inseparable from

---

[70] Above, 145.

Scripture,[71] the goal of mystagogy is to draw the hearers more deeply into sacramental acts and not scriptural texts. By sacramental acts we mean a living experience that encompasses words, actions, objects, place, and time. Thus, when we say that the rites provide the "text" of mystagogy, we are speaking of more than a liturgical document.

The first step in preparing a mystagogical homily, then, is to establish the "text" on which the sermon will be based by reconstructing the rites as they were celebrated. Christian initiation both in fourth-century Milan and as it is prescribed in ministries of Christian formation such as the R.C.I.A. is an intense and complex process. For example, in Milan baptism included *ephphatha*, entering the baptistry, prebaptismal anointing, renunciation, exorcism and consecration of the water, immersion, postbaptismal anointing, footwashing, vesting in white robes, spiritual seal, and procession to the altar.[72] In addition to words, the rites involve movement and setting, separation and touch, light and darkness, clothing and nudity, secrecy and revelation, water—a lot of water—and oil, bread, and wine. In his reconstruction of the "text," Ambrose describes the rites as they were celebrated in Milan.[73]

In reconstructing a celebration of the rites, the liturgy provided in a worship book and Sunday bulletin is the appropriate place to begin; however, it is essential to pay attention to the complexity of the rites by including in the reconstruction not only words but also how the words were spoken, actions and movement, objects and participants, place and time. Break the rites down into their component parts or units and give attention to each. Include the details of how the listeners participated, what they saw, said, heard, did, and what was said and done to them. Include inconsistencies and questionable or objectionable practices; do not gloss over them. Do not idealize the rites; describe them as they were actually celebrated and not according to a liturgist's vision.

Evaluate the Rites

Establishing the liturgical "text" on which mystagogy is based naturally leads one to assess and evaluate the rites as they were celebrated. Making judgments on liturgical celebrations is going to happen. It is

[71] Above, 185–186; 210.
[72] Above, 156ff.
[73] Above, 191ff.

therefore best to incorporate evaluation into a method of mystagogical preaching. For Ambrose, the rites are the ongoing drama of salvation, God's saving activity continuing in our midst. The liturgy's setting, words, objects, images, and gestures were generous, even lavish. There was much going on in terms of the liturgy's symbolism and even more in terms of God's unseen activity. In order to speak for themselves, our rites need dramatic elements—pilgrimage, place, time, characters, dialogue, objects and actions—so that they are a faith event. The Church today needs rites that are worthy of celebrating the paschal mystery, and we need to celebrate them worthily. While we cannot readily measure God's unseen activity in our liturgical celebrations, we can assess their quality as the continuing drama of salvation.

It is important to note that we do not evaluate the rites so that we can somehow "correct" past celebrations in our mystagogical reflection. Mystagogy is based on the hearers' actual experience of the rites and not on some ideal. Rather than providing grounds for an apologetic, evaluating the rites serves two purposes. First, evaluation cautions us about what it may or may not be appropriate to assert about the mysteries in mystagogical reflection. Simply put, it is unconvincing and perhaps even inappropriate to speak of baptism as a "saving flood" when it is administered by sprinkling droplets from a finger bowl or to assert that our celebration of the Eucharist makes us one body when it is administered using individual wafers and glasses of wine. Second, evaluating the rites invites us to contemplate how we might celebrate the mysteries in the future in order to better convey and communicate God's unseen saving activity and the new life of faith that flows from it. For, in many instances, embracing mystagogy necessitates and leads to liturgical renewal.

Interpret the Rites

In this section we will provide a step-by-step process for moving from the liturgical "text" to the meaning of the rite. We (1) begin with the rites themselves, (2) turn to Scripture, (3) use several tools of interpretation, (4) pile up meanings, and (5) rely on the Church's tradition.

Begin with the Rites Themselves. The place to begin to interpret the meaning of the rites is with the rites themselves. Do not start with a theological concept and use the rites to illustrate that point. Rather, begin with a unit or component of a rite or with a word, action, or object and ask what we did and why we did it. Consider how the hearers reacted to the rite. Be sensitive to what they might want to say about the sacraments as well as to what they need to hear about them. Ambrose includes in his mystagogy expressions of his hearers' faith, doubt, anger, love, joy, gratitude, questions, and disappointment.[74] Determining what the hearers want to say about a rite will help mystagogues determine what they can assume about the listeners' initial understanding of the meaning of the sacraments.

Beginning with the rites also means ensuring that interpretation is in keeping with the history, structure, and theology of the rites.[75] Ambrose's mystagogy is not original thought but is based on a solid understanding of what the Church has determined worship and sacrament mean. His interpretation of individual rites is in keeping with his understanding of the overall meaning of the sacrament.[76] Ambrose finds this history, structure, and theology in the Bible and as the Bible is interpreted in the tradition of the Church. For him, the history of the Christian sacraments is found in the Old Testament, where the sacraments are prefigured. For example, Ambrose sees Jesus giving the structure of the *ephphatha* in his healing of the man who was deaf and dumb, the structure of Christian baptism in his own baptism in the Jordan, and the structure of postbaptismal footwashing in his washing of the disciples' feet. Ambrose also found his sacramental theology in Scripture; the presence of the Triune God added to ordinary elements brings about sacramental effect. Ambrose also continually studied and drew upon the theology of the Greek Fathers.[77] Yet he did not parade his knowledge and learning. Theology was used to help the newly baptized discover the meaning of their experience.[78] Nevertheless, it is always present, running in the background, underpinning everything that Ambrose says.

Ambrose's example reminds mystagogues to read sacramental theology, not as a specific part of preparing a mystagogical homily, but more generally as part of continuing education so that they can make contemporary theology accessible to their people. While sacramental theology does not provide the substance or content of mystagogy, mystagogy is based on a solid understanding of the history, structure,

---

[74] Above, 141–142.
[75] Above, 198–199.
[76] Above, 199.
[77] Above, 84; 100.
[78] Above, 261–263.

and theology of worship and sacrament, which is found in Scripture and the theology of the Church. As we shall see, our method of interpreting the sacraments begins with the rites and moves to the Scriptures. In this movement, sacramental theology and the Church's tradition provide an appropriate check of our interpretation of the rites.

Turn to Scripture. Mystagogy is inseparable from Scripture.[79] While the sacraments provide the "text" on which mystagogy is based, Scripture is the means by which this "text" is both interpreted and illustrated. Ambrose looks to the Scriptures for both the meaning of the sacraments and the images that he uses to explain them. So extensive is the wealth of biblical material in Ambrose's preaching on the sacraments that the bishop of Milan intertwines passages from Scripture with the step-by-step flow of sacramental actions in such a way that the two become a single reality.

In mystagogy the meaning of the rites will not be found logically or systematically but through their biblical symbolism. Ambrose interprets the meaning of the rites of initiation in terms of scriptural images, stories, admonitions, and portions of psalms. Harmless says that in mystagogy one "free associates for scriptural stories,"[80] and it does in fact seem as though some of the sermons contained in *De sacramentis* are the free associations of a fatigued bishop preaching in the week after Easter.[81] Yet, to describe mystagogy in this way is too simplistic. Rather than "free association," Ambrose's preaching on the sacraments suggests that mystagogy is "informed association." Ambrose's familiarity with Scripture is so vast that he can "free associate" biblical and sacramental connections and associations.

The example of Saint Ambrose reminds mystagogues to make the effort to read Scripture and think biblically.[82] Reading Scripture in preparation for mystagogy involves seeing the big picture. Rather than dissecting an individual pericope, mystagogy calls for seeing the whole of Scripture and the ways that biblical themes, images, and stories connect, intersect, and reflect one another. A second way to read Scripture in preparation for mystagogy is as part of a deliberate effort to cultivate scriptural images and express oneself using biblical

---

[79] Above, 185–186; 210–211.
[80] Harmless, *Augustine and the Catechumenate*, 364.
[81] Above, 288.
[82] Above, 98.

language. A third way to read Scripture in preparation for mystagogy is in order to learn—and to learn to tell—the foundational or archetypal biblical stories that comprise salvation history. Simply stated, mystagogues take seriously Ambrose's instruction to read so that, reading and understanding much, we have much with which to nourish others.[83]

The first place to look for Scripture with which to plumb the depths of the mysteries is to examine the biblical images and symbols contained in the rite. Ambrose also selected the scriptural texts he used to interpret the sacraments from the lessons assigned to the liturgies for the newly baptized during the week following Easter and from a well-established tradition of using Scripture to explain the rites.[84] This tradition, which began in the New Testament, suggests and even imposes both what texts one uses to explain the sacraments and how those texts are to be interpreted. Contemporary mystagogues should consult these same resources when using Scripture to interpret the rites.

Use Several Tools of Interpretation. With the liturgical "text" in one hand and the text of Scripture in the other, we now consider how to bring the two into relationship in order to uncover the meaning of the rites. The simple answer is, rather than relying on a single approach, use several tools of interpretation. In his mystagogical works Ambrose uses six methods to uncover the mystical sense of Scripture and the meaning of the rites: (1) typology, (2) allegory, (3) chains of reasoning, (4) interpreting the intent of the text, (5) translation, and (6) direct and uncritical application of the text.[85] In the following paragraphs we will describe how contemporary mystagogues can use each of these tools to interpret both the liturgical "text" and the text of Scripture.

Typology. Ambrose uses biblical figures or types to explain the sacraments both ritually and theologically. His presuppositions are that the rites are a reenactment of salvation history, and the realities of the Old Testament are figures of both Jesus' actions in the New Testament and the sacraments of the Church. Typology is entirely biblical;[86] it is

---

[83] Above, 104.
[84] Above, 211–214; 217–219.
[85] For a full description of these methods, as well as Ambrose's application of them, see above, 200–203; 225–242.
[86] Above, 225–230.

first used in the Old Testament and is also used in the New Testament to show that God's promises are fulfilled in the person of Jesus of Nazareth. The apostles used typology in their preaching.

The difference between typology and contemporary methods of interpretation is that typology, understanding Scripture as the work of God, approaches the Bible as a whole, expecting one event or image to give meaning to another.[87] Typological interpretation assumes that there is an objective correspondence between the eras of salvation history recorded in Scripture; the events of Scripture are not unrelated or related only in a single-direction, straightforward flow of time but rather are eras and events that reflect upon and correspond to one another objectively, in the creating and redeeming purpose of the will of God.[88] God stands above history and at its center, creating all history from the center outward in both directions in such a way that the two directions parallel and mirror one another as type and fulfillment.[89] The word "type" may be used for any "model" or "pattern" or "parable" foreshadowing its fulfillment, whether an event or an oft-repeated ritual. It is not its character as historical event that makes a type; what matters is its integrity; its "reality," whether as event or simply as narrative or character or act; its autonomy and yet its capacity significantly, often prophetically, to mirror another event or narrative or character or act.[90]

Typology sees the sacraments as the expression of constant modes of divine action. The form of the sacrament provides the key to the biblical types by which the meaning of the divine action is to be understood. By studying the types one can discover the pattern of how God acts and see that the sacraments fit this pattern. In this way

---

[87] It is a necessary presupposition of modern historical methods that both God and the supernatural or transcendent realm be excluded from all talk and reasoning. God is not part of the "historical" world; God is accessible to "private" experience, but not to "scientific" knowledge. Modern historical exegesis, then, is methodologically atheistic. Ancient exegesis—pagan or Christian or Jewish—is explicitly theistic; it assumes that Scripture is the work of God, acting in and through human authors and events, and that is precisely the source of its meaning.

[88] Enrico Mazza, *Mystagogy: A Theology of Liturgy in the Patristic Age*, trans. Matthew J. O'Connell (New York: Pueblo Publishing Co., 1989) 10–11.

[89] Chapman, "Early Christian Mystagogy and the Formation of Modern Christians," 284.

[90] Young, *Biblical Exegesis and the Formation of Christian Culture*, 154.

typology reveals, first, that, as God acted in the past, so God is acting now and will act in the future and, second, that the event of Christ's death and resurrection is contained in the sacraments of the Church. In order to establish a type, Ambrose lifts up a characteristic of a rite's objects, actions, or participants—the bishop touching candidates' ears, the font's tomblike shape, or passage through the water—and shows that it is identical to the characteristic of a biblical event.

Allegory. An allegory is a series of metaphors that cuts a text loose from its moorings of time, place, and historical circumstance and gives it a timeless, spiritual meaning. Using allegory enables Ambrose to discover the essential agreement of Old Testament, New Testament, and the sacraments by allowing him to see through the opacity of the text of Scripture to its underlying truth. For example, Ambrose asserts that the promises the candidates made during the renunciation are kept in heaven and not on earth by using a series of liturgical allegories to prove that the bishop and priests are angels. For the bishop of Milan, to think allegorically is part of what it means to see with the eyes of faith. Ambrose's use of this method demonstrates that allegory can be thoroughly christological and rooted in history as the bishop of Milan directs his hearers back to the change wrought in history by the life, death, and resurrection of Christ.[91]

In the patristic period, to interpret something allegorically often meant simply to recognize metaphor rather than taking something very woodenly according to the letter.[92] All language was understood to be symbolic, that is, words were not a self-contained system but pointed to something beyond themselves. There was a necessary connection between the words and the idea they expressed, even if the idea in some sense transcended the words with which it was enunciated. The critical question was what is symbolized or referred to.[93] Allegory lies on a spectrum and cannot be sharply differentiated from other figures of speech.

But there is allegory and allegory.[94] Today debate is needed about potential criteria for distinguishing justifiable and unjustifiable "allegory."[95] While we must guard against imposing a foreign, subjective

---

[91] Above, 232.
[92] Young, *Biblical Exegesis and the Formation of Christian Culture*, 154.
[93] Ibid., 120.
[94] Ibid., 190.
[95] Ibid., 3.

meaning on a text that bears no relation to the text's original meaning, without a form of allegory that allows at least for analogy, the biblical text can only be an object of archeological interest.[96] All reading of texts that involves entering the text-world, appropriating the perspective of the text, or reading ourselves into the text is in some sense allegorical.[97]

Chains of Reasoning. Ambrose strings biblical images together as the components in the construction of intricate chains of reasoning. His purpose is not so much to clearly explain the meaning of the sacraments to his hearers as it is to overwhelm them with the depth of the mysteries. Thus Ambrose is not content to use a single image but instead spins out image upon image so that the listeners get caught up in layers of meaning. For example, Ambrose overwhelms his hearers with a string of scriptural snapshots in order to convince them of the greatness of the sacraments.[98] First he asserts the greatness of the sacraments. Next he explains them by drawing so heavily on God's mighty acts recorded in the Old Testament that his hearers are led to compare the sacraments with those wonders. Ambrose then asserts that the greatness of the sacraments lies in God's invisible saving activity at work in them and shows how this invisible activity is greater than God's actions in the Old Testament. Finally Ambrose brings the sacramental act and the biblical images together by declaring that the same divine activity is occurring in both.

Ambrose's construction of chains of reasoning reminds us that explaining and comprehending the sacraments have as much to do with standing in awe as they do with intellectual clarity. While our critical sophistication may render the comparison of Old and New Testament wonders ineffective, mystagogues can overwhelm their hearers with the magnitude of the rites by using multiple images in rapid succession and by comparing not the miracles but their intent. Israel's freedom gained by their passage through the sea is an indication of the freedom we receive by our passage through the font. Abraham and Sarah's joy at the birth of Isaac pales in comparison to God's joy at our new birth in baptism. The same Spirit that stirred Peter to speak on Pentecost was poured into us at baptism, emboldening us to share

[96] Ibid., 120.
[97] Ibid., 191.
[98] Above, 234–236.

the Good News. A leper made clean points to the cleansing and new life that we receive by water and the Spirit. How great is God's gift in baptism!

Intent of the Text. This interpretive method seeks to show that the intent of a rite is in keeping with biblical themes. Ambrose's argument for retaining footwashing as a part of baptism rests on the fact that his understanding of the intent of the rite is sanctification. He makes his point by arguing that the biblical account of Jesus washing the disciples' feet shows that those whose feet are washed will be sanctified.

Translation. In using translation to interpret the liturgical "text," Ambrose seeks to remove the barriers to comprehension that are due to difficulties with language so that the liturgy will speak for itself. Thus Ambrose explains that *ephphatha* means *adaperire* or "be opened." Ambrose's use of translation to interpret Scripture differs from that of modern scholars in that, rather than seeking an original text by setting aside inaccurate versions and incorrect variants, Ambrose uses multiple versions and variants of a text in order to add to, enrich, and thicken a text's meaning. He carefully notes variations in the Greek and Latin versions or compares the sentence on which he is commenting with the parallels in other Gospels; however, rather than declaring which is the original text to be followed, Ambrose states alternative views. Through his use of a variety of texts and textual variants, he reminds us that in mystagogy the goal of interpretation is not to narrow and clarify meaning but to deepen and expand it.

Direct and Uncritical Transfer of the Text. Finally, Ambrose quotes passages of both the liturgy and Scripture and then treats them as if they had been written with his audience in mind. He uses this method of interpretation to show that Christ establishes the Church's sacraments, to explain the effect of a rite, and to express the neophytes' response to the mysteries. In this way Ambrose strengthens the link between the rites of initiation and the biblical history of salvation.

Pile Up Meanings. Using numerous methods of interpretation will result in a host of meanings, which is good. The purpose of mystagogy is to open up and expand the baptized's experience, understanding, and appreciation of the rites of Christian initiation. The task of mystagogy is to help the faithful explore and plumb the depth of the mysteries. In interpreting the rites, mystagogues therefore pile up meanings rather than reduce the sacraments to syllogisms. Meaning is presented in terms of "both/and" rather than "either/or." Ambrose understands that the rites do not speak logically or systematically but through their symbolism.[99] Their logic is more associative than discursive, more poetic than philosophical.

Ambrose, therefore, piles up meanings rather than seeking clear definitions. For him, baptism is tomb and womb, death and resurrection, absolution and new birth. Baptism heals, cleanses, washes away sins, cancels guilt, and incorporates one into community. Similarly, the white robe that the neophytes wear evokes the shining garments worn by the resurrected Christ, the bridal garment, apple blossoms, snow, and clean clothes. Through this symbolism baptismal transformation is explained as participation in Christ's resurrection and ascension, intimacy with Christ, the blossoming of grace, forgiveness of sins, cleansing of the soul, return of innocence, and a reflection of the life to be lived in partnership with Christ. By piling up meanings, Ambrose takes seriously the truth about mystery; mystery can be pointed to, hinted at, and even glimpsed, but it cannot be defined or exhausted.

Rely on the Church's Tradition. Mystagogy is not original work. Ambrose did not worry about having something novel or even original to say about the sacraments.[100] Rather than innovative works, Ambrose's mystagogy reflects a well-established tradition of using Scripture to explain the meaning of the sacraments. We have observed the similarities between *De sacramentis* and *De mysteriis* and the *Mystagogical Catecheses* of Cyril of Jerusalem.[101] Ambrose's originality and creativity are found in what he chose to emphasize from the tradition he had received, filtering it through his own experience.[102] For example, Ambrose's teaching that the words of Christ convert the bread and wine of the Eucharist into the body and blood of Christ was probably derived from Greek sources.[103] His contribution lay in making both the neophytes' experience of the rites and the Church's theology of the sacraments accessible to his people.[104]

[99] Above, 197.
[100] Above, 99.
[101] Above, 322, n. 53.
[102] Above, 100–101.
[103] Above, 184.
[104] Above, 84.

Ambrose's mystagogical works reflect a well-established tradition.[105] Rather than searching for cutting-edge language and images with which to explain the sacraments, contemporary mystagogues should learn this tradition, both so that they can share this treasure with their people and so that their mystagogy is in keeping with it.[106] The fact that the Church's tradition has been both said and heard before only adds to its value, particularly inasmuch as the contemporary Church does not know this tradition. Yet, rather than borrowing directly, the bishop of Milan, like all the Fathers, filtered this tradition through his own experience, exercising originality and creativity in what he chose to emphasize to his people.[107] This is also the challenge to the contemporary mystagogue. In this way the Church's tradition informs the faith community's experience, and the faith community's experience informs the Church's tradition.

Spell Out the Implications of Participating in the Rites

Finally, mystagogues must address the question of how participating in the mysteries is relevant to everyday life. Mystagogy understands the sacraments not as ends in themselves but as means to new life. Consequently, Christian initiation has implications for how one lives in the world. Ambrose draws from the rites appropriate lessons for Christian living; he spells out the implications of the mysteries for his hearers' real lives, most notably a Church confronted by Arianism and a culture that was largely pagan.[108] Ambrose does this by describing the new life that flows from the sacraments and the ways that this style of life is different from that endorsed by the world. He tells the newly baptized that to choose eternal life rather than life in this world involves making hard choices in everyday life. However, in the sacraments they receive the faith and strength necessary to make these choices and live the new life.[109]

---

[105] Above, 214–215.

[106] In addition to the explanation and illustrations provided in this study, helpful resources include the mystagogical catecheses of the Fathers, available in Edward Yarnold, S.J., *The Awe-Inspiring Rites of Initiation: The Origins of the R.C.I.A.*, 2nd ed. (Collegeville: The Liturgical Press, 1994) 67–250, and a volume such as Jean Daniélou, *The Bible and the Liturgy* (Ann Arbor: Servant Books, 1979) or Jackson, *Journeybread for the Shadowlands*.

[107] Above, 100–101; 216–217.

[108] Above, 195–196.

[109] Above, 192–193.

Ambrose's example suggests that mystagogues articulate the implications of participating in the rites for everyday life in specific and concrete ways. Stated simply, we cannot declare that baptism is salvific if we cannot tell particular people what they need to be saved from. At the same time, mystagogues assure that in the sacraments the faithful receive from God everything they need to live as God's people.

The keys to describing with specificity both the responsibilities of baptism and the Eucharist and the blessing God gives are not found in theology or perhaps even in Scripture. In order to describe the implications of participation in the rites and the faith, vision, strength, and commitment that God gives specifically and concretely, mystagogues need to look to their prayer and reflection on the difference baptism and the Eucharist have made in their own lives and listen for the differences the mysteries make in the lives of God's people.

Ambrose's experience of baptism had an extraordinary impact on his life.[110] He understood that by being baptized he was making his home not in Roman society but in the kingdom of God.[111] Thus he describes baptism as the passage from earth to heaven, from sin to life, from guilt to grace, from vileness to holiness, from death to resurrection.[112] Baptized only after he came to accept his election as bishop as a divine call, Ambrose looked upon the decision to be baptized as a response to the call of God that leads Christians to enter into, and emerge from, the font to live according to Christ's pattern.[113] The transformation promised to all people in baptism was the goal of all of Ambrose's preaching in Milan.[114]

Ambrose's example suggests that mystagogues must know more than what the Church and its theologians teach about the sacraments. As spiritual guides, mystagogues must know their own experience. They need to make available to their people what they themselves believe about the sacraments. In so doing, mystagogues will have something real and important to say about the difference the sacraments make in their lives and in the lives of their people, and they will be able to say it concretely.

---

[110] Above, 48–50.
[111] Above, 107.
[112] *De sacramentis*, 1.4.12 (SC 25bis.66). See above, 53, 54.
[113] *De sacramentis*, 1.1.1; 6.2.7; 6.5.26 (SC 25bis.6; 140; 154). See above, 53.
[114] Above, 94.

In order to make sacramental experience available to mystagogy, regularly meditate on and pray about the sacraments, not as vague concepts or in some idealized way, but as they are actually celebrated in your faith community. Use objects. Think of the chalice, used week in and week out for over thirty years. Reflect upon actual experiences: the couple, married for over sixty years, who support and steady one another as they teeter forward to receive Communion or the small hand of the child, trembling as it reaches to receive the bread. What do these things say about the Eucharist? Use words and actions. What does the way the water is administered tell us about baptism? What is the tone when the congregation prays the Lord's Prayer or recites the Creed? What does this tone tell us about God? Think of what it means to you to be baptized and to receive the Eucharist. How does it make you feel? What difference does it make in your life, in who you are, and in the way you live? Answer these questions specifically, concretely, and in terms of today. Finally, reflect on the ways that participating in the mysteries gives you and the people you serve the faith and strength necessary to live this new life.

Summary

In this section we have presented a strategy for arriving at the message of a mystagogical homily. The approach that we have outlined is to establish the liturgical "text" on which the homily is based and then to use biblical associations and connections to interpret that "text." We emphasized that the message does not need to be novel or original but should reflect the heritage out of which the Church has traditionally interpreted and understood the sacraments. We also asserted that in order to give the faithful an experience of the breadth and depth of the sacraments, mystagogy piles up meanings rather than selecting one of many interpretations. Finally, although the message does not need to be original, an essential part of articulating the meaning of the sacraments is spelling out in specific ways the implications of participating in the rites for daily life in the world. Having arrived at a message, we now turn to the question of how one crafts a mystagogical homily.

CRAFT THE HOMILY

In Chapter 7 we affirmed that the form of a sermon contributes to what the preacher wants to say and do, at times being no less persuasive than the content itself, and described the shape of Ambrose's mystagogy as, in the words of the bishop himself, "milky speech."[115] As sermons intended for infants in the faith, the form of mystagogy is simple, and the style of mystagogy is conversational. Mystagogy is not the occasion to parade theological sophistication or display rhetorical brilliance. Yet, just as sound theology undergirds mystagogy's content, so rhetorical expertise is required to shape mystagogy. While these sermons are not rhetorical masterpieces in terms of their oratorical sophistication, speaking about subjects as complex as baptism and the Eucharist in a clear, plain, and straightforward manner requires the planning and skill that comes from practice.

Harmless is correct in calling catechesis a "theater of the Word." Its drama is salvation history, its script is the Scriptures, and its actors include everyone.[116] This is particularly true of mystagogy. Our study of *De sacramentis* shows that Ambrose's mystagogy is characterized by spontaneity, direct address, familiar tone, the inclusion of questions, narratives and quotations from both liturgical and scriptural texts, and techniques aimed at recreating the listeners' experience. While Ambrose recognized the danger of the pretentious use of rhetoric for the purpose of self-advertisement,[117] mystagogy requires the cultivation of rhetorical skill in order for its spontaneous character to become natural to the preacher and effective for the hearers.[118]

The Structure of Mystagogy

The structure of mystagogy is determined by two factors: the shape of the rites and the goal of mystagogy. The structure of Ambrose's mystagogy reflects the "text" of the neophytes' experience of initiation from which the message of these sermons is drawn.[119] As we have seen, the order of the rites of initiation provides the shape of *De sacramentis*.[120] Ambrose's example suggests that the structure of the mystagogical sermon should follow the order of the unfolding drama of the rites of initiation. The liturgical rites determine the sequence of topics. In addition to gaining the listeners' attention, introductions and conclusions, both for sermons and for topics within sermons, should

---

[115] Above, 249.
[116] Harmless, *Augustine and the Catechumenate*, 349.
[117] Above, 97–98.
[118] Above, 95ff.
[119] Above, 145–146.
[120] Above, 250–251.

reinforce that a rite is part of a greater whole by placing it in context. In this way mystagogy becomes a journey through the rites of initiation.

Inasmuch as the shape of the sermon serves to arrest, accent, focus, and aid the listeners' comprehension of the message,[121] the form of mystagogy should facilitate the message. There should be a unifying theme or governing idea that provides direction for the sermon. As we have said, Ambrose called the newly baptized to fully participate in mystagogy, that is, to enter so fully and deeply into their experience of the mysteries that they came to understand and appreciate their initiation as an encounter with Christ and, as a result, allow this encounter with Christ to become the guiding force of their lives. For Ambrose, this happens when the newly baptized see using the eyes of faith that they received at baptism.[122] Employing the order of the rites as the structure of his mystagogy helped him to accomplish this goal and to move his hearers from not seeing to seeing because the movement of these sermons is the same as the process of initiation.

The mystagogue should determine the goal of mystagogy in terms of what the listeners will think, feel, decide, and do with their experience of the rites, and structure the sermons to reinforce that goal. Reflect upon the reason for deepening and expanding the meaning and significance of the experience of baptism and the Eucharist. Ambrose's involvement in the lives of his people led him to regard mystagogy as the opportunity for his hearers to learn how they would engage in and carry out their struggle against the hostile world.[123] In this same way, the insights gained from listening to the listeners and reflecting on both the rites and the world will help contemporary mystagogues determine in what direction and in what ways deepening and expanding experience of the rites is possible and beneficial. For example, contemporary Christians might be helped to experience the sacraments as more than personal encounters in which an individual receives forgiveness. They might be helped to contemplate and respond to the implications of participation in the sacraments for the way they lead their everyday lives in the world. When crafting the mystagogical homily, the preacher should state the goal expressly at some point and repeat and restate it throughout.[124]

---

[121] Above, 271.
[122] Above, 125; 136–137; 259–260.
[123] Above, 126.
[124] Above, 273.

Individual sermons do not treat entire sacraments, such as baptism and Eucharist, but are composed of units devoted to specific rites, such as renunciation and immersion. Ambrose breaks the rites down into their component parts and treats each specifically.[125] In creating and explaining these units, he draws from five simple but time-honored rhetorical devices for organizing material: (1) using inductive reasoning, (2) providing definition, (3) moving from problem to solution, (4) progressing from the lesser to the greater, and (5) flashing back from the present to the past and then returning to the present. In determining what structure to use to explain a specific rite, Ambrose first discerns what that rite is meant to achieve and then selects a form that helps to achieve that end.[126]

The movement from the specific to the general is a three-step process: (1) remind the neophytes of their experience, (2) explain that experience using the rite's biblical institution, and (3) apply that meaning of the rite to the lives of the newly baptized.[127] This inductive movement helps expand simple objects and actions to their spiritual meaning and implications for faith and life.

In providing definitions, first name and then illuminate the rite by using images, which evoke experience, rather than syllogisms, which reduce it. Recognize that no single image can contain the full meaning of a rite. Therefore, use many images to plumb the depth of a rite's meaning by lifting up its different aspects and dimensions. When creating the sermon, allow these images to echo and pile up so that their meanings cluster and reverberate and, in so doing, evoke experience that pushes the hearers beyond the images themselves. Use "both/and" definitions to deepen the hearers' comprehension, thicken the rite's meaning, and open the community to new possibilities.[128]

In order to employ the movement from problem to solution, contemporary mystagogues will need to reconsider humanity's "problem" and God's "solution." For Ambrose the problem was death and the solution is baptism, which is death without dying.[129] Contemporary mystagogues may, for example, prefer to speak of the ways we are less than fully human and that in baptism God restores us to what we were intended to be in creation.

[125] Above, 252.
[126] Above, 252ff.
[127] Above, 253.
[128] Above, 255.
[129] Above, 256–257.

In progressing from the lesser to the greater,[130] Ambrose moves in two ways. First, he begins with the greatness of Old Testament wonders and then asserts that the Christian sacraments are even greater. Second, he moves from sign to fulfillment, showing how the Old Testament events are figures and the sacraments the fulfillment of the single reality of God's saving activity in Christ. In employing this structure today, emphasize the faith dimension of the biblical event rather than its historical accuracy. The question is not whether Israel really crossed the Red Sea but the significance of this passage for God's people then and now. This structure assumes a level of faith on the part of the hearers. To those who argue that we are using biblical events and images for our own purpose and not in keeping with the author's original intent, Gerard Sloyan responds that "while the biblical authors had no idea that their writings would be used to proclaim God's redeemer, they would not be at all surprised that they are."[131]

By biblical "flashback"[132] we mean identifying sacramental experience or experience of the rites with the experience of a biblical character and then asserting that the biblical character's experience provides insights into the meaning of the sacramental experience. Just as Naaman's reaction to the Jordan—"Is that all?"—is our reaction to the font, so we were cleansed from sin when we emerged from the font in the same way that Naaman was cleansed from leprosy when he emerged from the river. This device builds on the hearers' own experience and serves to insert that experience into the history of salvation recorded in Scripture.

Enriching the Structure

As we did in Chapter 7, we will confine our discussion of the means employed to enrich the form of mystagogy to five areas: (1) use of language, (2) method of description in terms of both the kinds of images employed and the ways that they are described, (3) selection and use of illustrations, (4) incorporation of liturgical and scriptural texts, and (5) the tone of these sermons.

Language. Both informational and experiential language are used in mystagogy; however, experiential language, the amount of which far

[130] Above, 257–258.
[131] Gerard Sloyan, "Preaching the Easter Season," University of Notre Dame, January 21, 1999.
[132] Above, 258–260.

surpasses that of informational language, is given priority and emphasis.[133] In fact, informational language is used in service to experiential language. Pure information is only provided to assist the hearers in exploring, clarifying, understanding, and appreciating their experience of Christian initiation. Thus, mystagogy employs a pedagogy of recognition; sharing information in support of experience reminds the listeners of, and helps them to recognize, their own experience, feelings, and response and then builds on what they already know.[134]

In order to ensure that experiential language is specific, concrete, and active, ground mystagogy in a particular celebration of specific rites. Emphasize the verb in order to highlight the listeners' participation.[135] Appeal directly to all the senses by describing the rites in terms of where they took place, who was there, and what the participants saw, heard, did, and said.[136] Lace language with an emotional content such as anxiety, disappointment, wonder, joy, curiosity, or doubt in order to present the rites with interest and enthusiasm.[137] As is true of so much in mystagogy, experiential language should employ images rather than propositions.

In order to enhance the effect of experiential language, appeal to the listeners to enter more fully and deeply into their experience of initiation.[138] Call upon them to see beyond what they saw, to look beyond the physical in order to comprehend its spiritual significance. Tell the listeners to remember their experience. Spell out the implications of participating in the rites.[139]

Description. Description plays a very important role in mystagogy because mystagogy uses the power of images to affect deep change, unite with truth, and invite into a new reality.[140] As we have said, the meaning of the rites is both determined and explained by drawing upon biblical types and images. The rites are described using an economy of words but an abundance of images. The pedagogical intent is not to teach the faithful a systematic theology of the sacraments

---

[133] Above, 261–263.
[134] Above, 274–275.
[135] Above, 138–139.
[136] Above, 139–140.
[137] Above, 141–142.
[138] Above, 136–141.
[139] Above, 143.
[140] Above, 263–266.

but to engrave a series of tableaux on their memory.[141] Thus mystagogy understands that rather than drilling the doctrine of the Real Presence into people's heads, we tell them the stories of Jesus feeding the five thousand, eating with outcasts and sinners, the Last Supper, and the road to Emmaus. When we search for an image to explain baptism, crossing the Red Sea is a better pick than making it to the Final Four.[142] Multiple images are used to point to, and connect with, one another in order to express the full meaning of a rite. Thus the organization of images is not as important as their abundance.

In illuminating the rites, actions, characters, and settings, all receive attention and are described rather than defined. Descriptions are not explicit about precise details, because describing the rites in vivid and complete detail tends to dictate to the hearers how they should understand and respond to initiation rather than allowing them to enter more fully into the experience. Describing the rites by limiting details aids the listeners in participating in mystagogy as they fill in the missing pieces in order to complete the picture.

Illustration. In mystagogy, illustrations are familiar stories, images, and anecdotes drawn from biblical, natural, and cultural sources and used to introduce and explain the unfamiliar sacraments.[143] Cultural and natural images, taken from this life, help the hearers comprehend the meaning of the new life in baptism. Nevertheless, the primary illustrations used to depict the meaning of the rites are biblical. Harmless suggests that mystagogues free associate to gather biblical, natural, and cultural images and then probe each image in terms of the rite to see how it emerges as a type or an antitype.[144] For cultural and natural images, this is as good a method as any. However illustrative material is selected, it is essential that the analogy between the thought and the illustration of the thought be clear, even obvious.

Incorporate the Texts of Liturgy and Scripture. A fourth way that the structure of mystagogy is enriched is that the text of both liturgy and

---

[141] Above, 264.

[142] While enticing, the Easter Vigil sermon in which the congregation was told that, in baptism, God makes us bigger champions than the Duke basketball team was but a quick dip into the depths of the sacrament's meaning.

[143] Above, 266–269.

[144] Harmless, *Augustine and the Catechumenate*, 365–366.

Scripture is integrated into these sermons. By incorporating liturgical and scriptural texts, mystagogy acknowledges the Church beyond the congregation and articulates that the rites fit into that tradition. In this way mystagogy contains *ecclesial consciousness*; that is, the continuing life of both the congregation and the Church are addressed in these sermons.[145]

One way to incorporate liturgy and Scripture is to quote texts as if they had been written with this audience in mind. This is obviously true for the text of the liturgy and can also be true for Scripture. A second method is to allude to specific rites or parts of rites or to biblical stories or images. A third method is to incorporate words, phrases, and ideas from liturgy and Scripture to "season" these sermons. Finally, express ideas and reactions using liturgical and scriptural language.

Tone. Tone helps to overcome the burdens of communication.[146] The first factor that determines tone is the hearers' anticipated response to the message. Ambrose's task of leading the newly baptized to participate in mystagogy was made easier by the fact that he could assume them to be active, attentive, interested, and involved listeners.[147] Nevertheless, he structured his mystagogy to foster his listeners' participation by using a catechetical style, re-creating his listeners' experience of the rites, and giving them a voice in mystagogy.[148]

In order to determine the hearers' anticipated response, mystagogues can conduct a mental "audience analysis" by spending time filtering through all that they see and hear in the course of ministry. Among the issues to be considered are the relationship of the congregation and the community, the reasons the listeners participate in the rites, and the listeners' experience of worship. In considering the relationship of the congregation and the community, reflect on how influential the Church is in the community. Think about what roles the listeners play in the community—their jobs, their activities, and their lifestyles—and the ways these roles both reinforce and challenge their faith. What societal attitudes and activities strengthen their faith? What temptations and complacencies conflict with and even

---

[145] Above, 273–274.
[146] Above, 269–270.
[147] Above, 126–127.
[148] Above, 127ff.

threaten their faith? What are the listeners' fears, hopes, challenges, and joys?

In thinking about why the listeners participate in the rites, reflect on why the listeners seek to be baptized or to have their children baptized and why they come to the Lord's table. We might be tempted to respond that contemporary Christians received baptism as infants as a matter of course and therefore cannot answer the question as to why they were baptized. This response reminds us that mystagogy implies an accompanying renewal of sacramental practice. Aidan Kavanagh argues that the R.C.I.A. provides "a solid counterbalance against infant baptism's becoming a malign abnormality due to pastoral malfeasance, theological obsession, or the decline of faith among Christian parents into some degree of merely social conformity."[149] Kavanagh observes that according to the Second Vatican Council, the norm for baptism is

"solemn sacramental initiation done especially at the paschal vigil and preceded by a catechumenate of serious content and considerable duration. This implies strongly, even if it does not require, that the initiate be an adult or at least a child well advanced in years.[150] The conciliar emphasis is clearly on the adult nature of the norm of Christian initiation, deriving as it does from the New Testament doctrine of conversion[151] . . . [T]he baptism of adults as the norm throws infant baptism into perspective as a benign abnormality as long as it is practiced with prudence as an unavoidable pastoral necessity—in situations such as the frail health of the infant, or in response to the earnest desire of Christian parents whose faith is vigorous and whose way of life gives clear promise that their child will develop in the faith of the Church."[152]

---

[149] Aidan Kavanagh, *The Shape of Baptism: The Rite of Christian Initiation* (New York: Pueblo Publishing Co., 1978) 110.

[150] Second Vatican Council, Constitution on the Sacred Liturgy (1963), nos. 64–68; Constitution on the Church (1964), no. 14; Decree on the Church's Missionary Activity (1965), nos. 13–14, concerning catechumens and the catechumenate. See also the Decree on the Pastoral Office of Bishops in the Church (1965), no. 14, and the Decree on the Ministry and Life of Priests (1965), no. 6.

[151] On Christian initiation's derivation from the New Testament doctrine of conversion see, for example, Decree on the Church's Missionary Activity, no. 13.

[152] Kavanagh, *The Shape of Baptism*, 109.

Kavanagh's insights into the rites, coupled with the post-Christian culture in which we live, make clear that if pastors are not asking why people seek baptism or come to the table, they need to be. An important implication of considering why people seek to participate in the sacraments is that the contemporary Church will need to come to terms with its own practice. For example, why does the contemporary Church often engage in the indiscriminate baptism of infants and then exclude baptized children from the Lord's table? In addition to reflecting on why the listeners participate in worship, contemplate what these listeners' experience of worship was like. What united the worshiping community in this celebration of the rites? What did the assembly truly share in common? Was the listeners' faith fortified or discouraged by the worshiping community?

The second factor that determines the tone of these sermons is the desire to guide the hearers into a fuller experience and deeper understanding and appreciation of the sacraments. Mystagogy makes use of a "catechetical style," a style whose purpose is not merely conveying information but the formation of Christians.[153] The aim of this style is to engage the listeners in a dialogue so that they do not remain passive. It is characterized by a higher degree of intimate contact between the preacher and listeners, a clearer and simpler form, and a spontaneous, improvisational manner, which includes direct address, repetition, loose syntax, and dialogue.

In order to create a bond of intimacy and facilitate participation, use the word *you* when speaking to or of the listeners and the word *we* to express connection with them. Use simple sentences and conversational (though not vulgar or slang) grammar and vocabulary. Ask questions to move the sermon along, to hold the listeners' attention, and to prompt and involve them. Employ repetition, alliteration, and sharp contrasts to make information easier to remember. Finally, make information accessible, clear, and concrete by telling (biblical) stories and examples that include direct discourse and dialogue. Provide information, but not so much information that it overloads or overwhelms.

Use tone to make the hearers comfortable raising, addressing, and overcoming their skepticism. Be direct and supportive, paternal and familiar, open and candid. Give voice to the hearers' questions, doubts, disappointments, and objections to explanations.[154] Ask questions, put

---

[153] Above, 127ff.; 270.
[154] Above, 142; 270.

the hearers' likely reactions into words, raise their objections to what seems unreasonable. Do not protect either the listeners, the rites, Scripture, or God.

Finally, although the tone of these sermons is intended to create intimacy and facilitate participation, mystagogues must be clear about their role. The listeners are to identify primarily with their experience of the rites, not with the preacher.[155] The preacher's role as spiritual guide is to help the listeners reexperience the rites. Spiritual guides point out the spiritual significance of the physical settings, elements, and actions but do not draw attention to themselves.

Summary

Facilitating the listeners' identification with, and participation in, the rites is the reason that mystagogy is structured as a journey through the rites of initiation. The listeners are placed within the context of the rites, and particular rites are described specifically from the perspective of the participants. Providing a sacramental experience that the people of God can enter deeply into, and identify with, is a reason that we need rites that create anticipation and excitement, and need to build upon that anticipation through a pedagogy of silence. Whereas the journey of initiation creates anticipation, retracing that journey in mystagogy moves the hearers deeper and deeper into mystery, where they encounter greater and greater holiness. Having planned the trip, we now turn to the subject of sermon delivery and how we retrace the journey.

RETRACE THE JOURNEY

We speak of delivering the mystagogical homily as "retracing the journey" in order to re-enforce our conviction that mystagogy is an event in which God is active and the entire faith community participates. Ambrose knew that how one says something is as important as what one says. This is particularly true in mystagogy for three reasons. First, the preacher is attempting to engage the listeners in a dialogue and re-create their experience of initiation. Second, while words alone can convey information, words alone are not enough to evoke a perspective on the listeners' journey of initiation and to elicit a committed response from them. Third, and most important, God is not encountered in words alone but in the Word experienced, incarnated, and proclaimed.

[155] Above, 276.

In Chapter 8 we discussed eight contributing factors to effective sermon delivery and their implications for Ambrose's mystagogy.[156] Recognizing that all eight of those components should be considered in order to ensure effective sermon delivery, in this section we will concentrate on those components that seem to have unique implications for mystagogy. As we did in Chapter 8, we will begin with the preacher, move to the liturgical context, and conclude with the architectural setting.

The Preacher

In this section we will reflect on the implications that the preacher's attitude, character, habits, and method and style of delivery have for mystagogical preaching. Recognizing the impact that the preacher's attitude has on the proclamation event,[157] preachers should hold the same convictions about the sacraments that they want to instill in their hearers. If mystagogues want the sacraments to be a transforming power in the lives of their people, mystagogues need to trust in the power of the sacraments to transform their own lives. The event of mystagogy will also be shaped by how the preacher views his or her role. The mystagogy of a "distiller of truth" will be very different from the mystagogy of a "steward of the mysteries." For this reason we have advocated for mystagogues understanding their role as that of spiritual guide.[158]

The character of the preacher can greatly affect how the message will be received by the hearers.[159] Therefore, if mystagogues are going to spell out the implications for participating in the sacraments and call their hearers to live differently in the world, mystagogues themselves need to strive to live this new life in ways that differentiate them from the world. Mystagogues take the implications of baptism and the Eucharist for their own lives most seriously. In so doing, they both inform, nuance, and add credibility to the message and assure the hearers that they have firsthand knowledge of the struggles and challenges that come from taking the implications of being baptized and receiving the Eucharist seriously.

Turning to the preacher's habits, while on the surface mystagogy may look like conversational reflection between pastor and people,

---

[156] Above, 284–304.
[157] Above, 284–285.
[158] Above, 321–322; 339.
[159] Above, 285–286.

this effect requires careful preparation. The method that we are proposing calls for disciplined study of Scripture and the Church's teaching on liturgy and sacrament, conscious listening to and involvement in the daily lives of the faithful, contemplation of the rites as mysteries, personal prayer and reflection, and the cultivation of rhetorical skills. Mystagogy's spontaneous and improvisational style should not lull the preacher into thinking that off-the-cuff remarks will pass for sustained reflection on the sacraments.

As for the delivery itself, while there is no single method or style of sermon delivery,[160] the mystagogical tasks of establishing intimacy, engaging in dialogue, and leading into experience are all made more difficult when the preacher reads from a manuscript or is chained to notes and is therefore rendered incapable of addressing the assembly directly. A tour conducted by a guide who reads from a travelogue pales in comparison to a tour conducted by a guide who knows the terrain. Mystagogy is intended to engage the faithful in conversation; the spontaneity, direct address, and improvisation of a "catechetical style"[161] are facilitated by freedom from a manuscript. This style is also enhanced by the considered use of voice, gestures, body language, and eye contact.

The Liturgical Context

The R.C.I.A. specifies that "since the distinctive spirit and power of the period of postbaptismal catechesis or mystagogy derive from the new, personal experience of the sacraments and of the community, its main setting" is a liturgical context, namely, the Sunday celebration of the Eucharist during the Easter season.[162] Mystagogy is founded on the experience of the mysteries and the word of God. The Sunday Mass provides every member of the assembly the opportunity to hear the voice of Christ and to renew the response of faith by which he or she is joined to Christ's body.[163]

The Sunday celebration of the Eucharist during the Easter season includes readings from the Lectionary that are particularly appropriate for mystagogy. The readings assigned for Year A are especially rich in

---

[160] Above, 288.

[161] Above, 127–135; 270.

[162] International Commission on English in the Liturgy, *Rite of Christian Initiation of Adults* (Collegeville: The Liturgical Press, 1988) 247.

[163] Above, 296.

images for mystagogy: the road to Emmaus;[164] baptism prefigured in the flood;[165] the newly baptized devoting themselves to the apostles' teaching and to fellowship, to the breaking of bread and the prayers;[166] new birth through the living and enduring word of God;[167] Paul's call to "set your minds on things that are above, not on things that are on earth, for you have died and your life is hidden with Christ in God";[168] and "a chosen race, a royal priesthood, a holy nation, God's own people."[169] The homily and the general intercessions should take into account the presence and needs of the newly baptized.[170] The experience of entering more deeply into the mysteries is enhanced when the assembly is given the opportunity to participate in the mysteries and receive the sacrament as part of mystagogy.[171]

In Milan the most dramatic feature of the liturgies for the newly baptized was that the neophytes wore the white robes they received at baptism throughout the octave of Easter. The R.C.I.A. directs that special places in the congregation are to be reserved for the newly baptized and their godparents.[172] Creative thought should be given to discover ways to highlight and celebrate the special status of the newly baptized even as they are being assimilated into the community of faith.

The Architectural Setting

The liturgical context of mystagogy—the Sunday Eucharist—makes the worship space and not a classroom the appropriate place for mystagogy. Furthermore, the worship space is where Christian initiation is celebrated, and arriving at the altar is the climax of the journey of initiation. Holding mystagogy in the worship space also highlights and celebrates the neophytes' new status as full members of the Church.

[164] Luke 24:13-35.
[165] 1 Peter 3:13-22.
[166] Acts 2:42.
[167] 1 Peter 1:23.
[168] Colossians 3:2-3.
[169] 1 Peter 2:9.
[170] International Commission on English in the Liturgy, *Rite of Christian Initiation of Adults*, 248.
[171] Above, 298.
[172] International Commission on English in the Liturgy, *Rite of Christian Initiation of Adults*, 248.

The space in which preaching occurs has the power to either enhance or detract from effective sermon delivery.[173] Ambrose's cathedral enhanced his mystagogy.[174] The *basilica nova* was large and lavish. In addition to being the setting of both the congregation's liturgical movement from death to new life and the celebration of the mystery of the Eucharist, from which the neophytes had once been excluded, the *basilica nova* itself was overwhelming and undoubtedly had a powerful impact on the neophytes.

Consider how the worship space can help the neophytes to more fully experience the rites when they are initiated, participate in mystagogy, and re-experience their initiation as the rites are illuminated. The Church needs a place to *celebrate* the mysteries, "a building that will point to a reality beyond itself, [that will] remind us that we're sojourners on this earth with a destination—the city of New Jerusalem—that we glimpse (however imperfectly) from this place where we enact our holy rites."[175] In terms of mystagogical preaching, become familiar with and account for the acoustics of the space in order to enhance an intimate, conversational atmosphere. Consider the location within the worship space where these sermons will be preached and the arrangement of the assembly for their impact on both the perception of the preacher's authority and the establishment of intimacy and dialogue.

APPLYING OUR METHOD

In the four previous sections we laid out the steps in a method of mystagogical preaching—question Ambrose's assumptions, arrive at the message, craft the homily, and retrace the journey. Though as a theoretical model mystagogical preaching may seem complicated and overwhelming, in practice it is a simple, straightforward process. Harmless is correct that "in practice, the art of mystagogy is a good deal simpler than one might think."[176] In this section we will therefore move from theory to practice and, hopefully, from complexity to clarity as we provide an example by using our method to create a

---

[173] Above, 299. See James White and Susan J. White, *Church Architecture: Building and Renovating for Christian Worship* (Akron: OSL Publications, 1998) 26–28.

[174] Above, 299–304.

[175] David Philippart, "Like Living Stones," *Environment and Art Letter* 12, no. 3 (May 1999) 34.

[176] Harmless, *Augustine and the Catechumenate*, 365.

simple mystagogical homily. Our approach in this section is to provide a running commentary as we work through the process.

Question Ambrose's Assumptions

Inasmuch as we already argued in favor of the relevance of the assumptions underlying Ambrose's mystagogy to the contemporary Church,[177] here we will offer some limited observations on how these premises are manifested in the faith community for which this mystagogy is intended, Saint Timothy Lutheran Church, where I serve as pastor. Both pastor and people have experienced and are convinced of the unseen activity of God at work in liturgy, Word and Sacrament. This is a congregation of less than twenty people who, when questioned about why they work so hard to keep their congregation going, often speak of encountering Christ in weekly worship. While the members of this congregation would not say that the community in which they live is a post-Christian culture, they would say that they struggle with the erosion of the family, lack of commitment to the Church, and that when measured by ecclesiastical and cultural yardsticks, their church is dying. The friction between faith and culture becomes most clear when this faith community contemplates its future. While some members argue that the congregation must become "bigger and more successful," the majority have come to believe that faithfulness to the Gospel calls them to embrace their congregation's inevitable death and celebrate a resurrection by dedicating their remaining resources to the start of a new mission in some other location.

Saint Timothy has adopted a mystagogical approach to sacramental catechesis, that is, instruction follows participation in the rites. This is true for both traditional times of instruction on the meaning of the sacraments, such as first communion instruction, and when introducing new liturgical practices, such as the weekly celebration of the Eucharist and footwashing on Maundy Thursday. Prior to participation, people are given cues on the mechanics of the liturgy, that is, how one participates. After participating in the rite, instruction on its meaning takes the form of shared reflection on the experience. The result has been an eagerness on the part of the community to experience God in worship rather than to understand "why" we do this and what the rites are supposed to "do."

[177] Above, 311–326.

We have been able to use this approach in part because the part-time nature of my pastoral ministry, focused as it is on Sunday worship, makes me chiefly a liturgical presence and steward of the mysteries rather than an administrator, community leader, or even counselor. While a few members of the congregation find insights gained from historical-critical exegesis "interesting," the majority find this approach "academic" (code for boring) and unrelated to their lives. My preaching in this context has become simpler, less crafted and more conversational, concrete, and limited to a single, explicitly stated insight.

Arrive at the Message

The "text" on which this mystagogy is based is the celebration of baptism at the congregation's Easter Eucharist. The bulletin insert in which this liturgy is printed in full provides our starting point as we establish the text. The candidate is the fourteen-year-old foster child of members of the congregation. It is generally known that he has been in trouble with the law. The order for baptism is that found in the *Lutheran Book of Worship*;[178] however, it has been modified to incorporate an explicit reference to baptism as participation in Christ's death and resurrection, the Easter renewal of baptismal promises by the entire community, and an invitation to the entire congregation to come to the font and be marked with the sign of the cross in remembrance and renewal of their own baptism. The minister marked the sign of the cross on each person's head with baptismal water and said, "You are a baptized child of God." In the insert the rite is broken down into the following units: presentation, prayers, thanksgiving over the water, renunciation and profession, baptism, laying on of hands, signing with the cross, giving the light, welcome, and sharing the peace. Inasmuch as this is intended to be an example of mystagogy, we will limit our discussion to the unit entitled baptism rather than explaining the entire rite.

For this celebration the font, a finger bowl in a wooden stand tucked away in the corner of the chancel, was replaced by a large antique bowl and pitcher (which were used on Maundy Thursday for footwashing) placed on a small table midway down the center aisle. The candidate

---

[178] Lutheran Church in America, The American Lutheran Church, The Evangelical Lutheran Church of Canada, The Lutheran Church—Missouri Synod, *Lutheran Book of Worship* (Minneapolis: Augsburg Publishing House, 1978) 121–125.

was baptized "in the name of the Father, and of the Son, and of the Holy Spirit" as water was poured over his head three times. The pastor was generous in his use of water; the candidate, who was initially nervous and stood with his head bowed, was amused by the mess the pastor made. The congregation was excited about the baptism and participated enthusiastically. The people seemed eager when it was time for them to come forward to receive the water and blessing. The intention in using a large bowl and pitcher, placing them in the center of the congregation, baptizing with generous amounts of water, and inviting the entire congregation to come to the font was to make baptism more prominent and increase the drama of the celebration. In talking to people after the service, it occurred to me that although we were not immersing in a baptismal pool, to these people the celebration seemed lavish, a different perspective than my own.

Turning to Scripture in order to interpret the meaning of this celebration of baptism, we find that the liturgy is packed with biblical images and stories. For example, the prayer said over the font rehearses God's use of water in the biblical narrative of salvation history: creation, flood, Israel's passage through the sea, Jesus' baptism in the Jordan. In the renunciation and profession, there is explicit reference to Paul's teaching that in baptism we are buried with Christ and lay dead in order that as Christ was raised from the dead by the splendor of the Father, we too might walk in newness of life. There are also references to the light of Christ shining within us and to baptism as cleansing and rebirth. The congregation coming forward to the place of baptism and their reaction to the size of the bowl and the amount of water used suggests to me Naaman coming to the Jordan and the paralyzed man at the pool of Beth-zatha. Finally, the second reading for the Sunday on which this sermon will be preached, the Second Sunday of Easter, blesses God who has "given us a new birth in a living hope through the resurrection of Jesus Christ from the dead, and into an inheritance that is imperishable, undefiled, and unfading."[179] Finally, this being the Easter season, the account of Christ's resurrection that was read last Sunday is undoubtedly running through people's heads. We will use these biblical images to both explain and illustrate baptism.

As I reflect upon these images, the tools that I should use to interpret them become apparent. The biblical accounts of God using water to create, drown evil, set free from slavery, cleanse, heal, and give new

---

[179] 1 Peter 1:3-4.

life are all *types* of baptism. The Easter context, the candidate's desire to be baptized as part of beginning anew and changing the direction of his life, and the congregation coming to the water in the same way that Naaman, the paralytic, and Jesus came to the water provide appropriate entrees into these types.

We are, of course, speaking metaphorically *(allegorically)* in saying, for example, that the baptismal bowl is a river or pool, that walking down the aisle to the bowl is a journey or pilgrimage, and that water poured over someone's head and spilling out of the bowl onto the floor of the nave constitutes a flood. We can link these images and metaphors using *chains of reasoning* in order to express their common reality; Naaman's journey to the Jordan, the women's journey to the empty tomb, and this faith community's journey to the font are all about God healing and giving new life. By piling up meanings, using all these images and meanings rather than selecting one, the faith community receives a powerful sense of what happened in the candidate's baptism and their own. Of course, we want to check these interpretations to ensure that they are in keeping with the Church's tradition and theology.

Finally, we must address the question of what difference participating in this rite makes in these people's real lives. Though the candidate is not familiar with the term "conversion," both he and the congregation are aware that his decision to be baptized involves choosing a way of life different from the way he had lived. Using larger symbols and positioning the place of baptism front and center hopefully communicated that their baptism, like Jesus' resurrection, is not an event that happened long ago, which should be tucked away in a corner, but is the power of God at work in our lives today. To take baptism seriously is to share in Christ's death and resurrection, to live in a way that proclaims that in death there is new life. For this assembly, the calling to die and rise with Christ has important implications for whether the congregation should continue to struggle to survive.

Craft the Homily

Creating the homily is perhaps the heart of mystagogy. Begin by determining the theme or focus statement for the homily, what the listeners will think, feel, decide, and do. For this homily the focus statement is: "In baptism, we shared in Christ's death and resurrection. Remembering that we are baptized, we experience Christ's new life so that we can live that new life today." Next, use the shape of the rite to create the structure of the sermon. In this case the structure might be: the candidate is baptized; the people come to the baptismal bowl; they are signed with the cross in baptismal water and are told that they are children of God; they celebrate the Eucharist. Next set the rite in context and use multiple images to explain its meaning. Finally, enrich the sermon through the use of language, description, illustration, incorporation of liturgy and Scripture, and tone. Perhaps the best way to illustrate this process is to provide an example of a portion of a homily with commentary in explanatory footnotes.

"Do you remember what we did last Sunday?[180] On that great Easter Day, after hearing about the women making their way to the empty tomb, we made our own Easter journey.[181] We brought Dillon to the bowl, to the font, to the baptismal pool, and we came here ourselves.[182] What were you thinking when I poured the water on Dillon's head, 'in the name of the Father, and of the Son, and of the Holy Spirit'?[183] Did it occur to you that Dillon was sharing in Christ's death and resurrection, or were you just worried that I was spilling water on the floor?[184] What would you say if I told you that I made a mess on purpose? I wanted you to see how big and powerful baptism is. It's not just a sprinkle; it's a bath.[185] When we come to the waters of baptism, we bathe in Christ's death and resurrection; we bathe in God's gift of new life.[186]

"Now the Bible tells us what happens when we bathe in God's gift of new life.[187] Naaman was a Syrian general. Naaman was a powerful

---

[180] The assembly is directly addressed and called upon to remember what we did last Sunday.

[181] The rite is placed in its liturgical context.

[182] Here I am summarizing the rite that I am going to describe. The phrase "the bowl, the font, the baptismal pool" is intended to enlarge this body of water in the minds of the hearers.

[183] I am here quoting the baptismal formula.

[184] The questions are intended to help the listeners reflect upon their experience. The question about spilling anticipates some people's likely reaction. The last question contains a statement of the theme "sharing in Christ's death and resurrection."

[185] Use of natural images.

[186] Statement of the theme.

[187] In these paragraphs I use a series of biblical images to lift up different dimensions of baptism. I retell biblical stories in narrative form. The movement is from the lesser to the greater.

man. Naaman had troops and chariots at his disposal; he also had leprosy. One day his servant said to Mrs. Naaman, 'If Naaman wants to be cured, he should go to Israel, and they will make him well.' Now Mrs. Naaman told Naaman, and Naaman told the king of Syria, and the king sent him to the king of Israel with VIP credentials. When the king of Israel was told that a man had been sent to him to have his leprosy cured, he tore his clothes, which is a biblical way of saying that he had no idea of what to do. But the prophet Elisha knew what to do. He told the king to send the man to him, and when Naaman showed up, Elisha told him, 'Go down and bathe in the Jordan and you will be cured.' Now I've seen the Jordan and, let me tell you, it's no Colorado River; it's a backyard creek. And it left Naaman mightily unimpressed. Naaman thought to himself, 'He wants me to wash in this?' But his servants said to him, 'Why not give it a try?' Then he went into the Jordan, bathed there, and came out cured. So too we come to a bowl of water.[188] But it's not just any water; it's water mixed with God's Word. We are bathed in it 'in the name of the Father, and of the Son, and of the Holy Spirit.' Our lives are cleansed of everything that would destroy us, and we are made clean, new, soft as a baby's bottom.

"John's Gospel tells us about a pool called Beth-zatha, where sick people hung out. When the pool bubbled like a hot tub,[189] God was said to be touching the water, and the first one in was cured. Baptism is better than that pool. You see, in baptism God touches the water and everyone is cured. In baptism God touches the water and everyone is first.[190] When we come to the waters of baptism, God does for us what he did for Jesus when Jesus came to the Jordan. God calls us God's beloved and pours out the Holy Spirit upon us.

"How does this happen? In today's reading from First Peter, we heard that God has 'given us a new birth into a living hope through the resurrection of Jesus Christ from the dead.'[191] This new birth is baptism. For, as Saint Paul tells us, in baptism we are buried with Christ and lay dead so that, as Christ was raised from the dead by the glory of the Father, we too might walk in newness of life.[192] In baptism

---

[188] Here I move from the biblical narrative to its application to baptism.
[189] Use of a cultural image.
[190] Repetition is used to reinforce God's presence in baptism.
[191] 1 Peter 1:3-4.
[192] Incorporation of biblical text cited in liturgy.

God is present in the water to join us to Christ. In baptism we share in Christ's death and resurrection. In baptism Easter happens for us.[193]

"And so you came down the aisle to the font. After church last Sunday, some of you told me you didn't like that bowl of water smack dab in the center of the aisle. You said you almost knocked it over or fell over it yourself.[194] And what did I say to you? 'Exactly! That's the point!' Baptism is central to our life and not something that happened long ago, something that we tuck away in the corner of our lives like we tuck our baptismal font away in the corner of the chancel. You came down the aisle to the font. You saw the water.[195] I dipped my hand into it and touched your forehead. I touched you with Christ's cross, as was done at your baptism, as we do on Ash Wednesday. This time I made the cross with baptismal water. You were touched with the water that was touched by God. And you heard the words, 'You are a baptized child of God.'[196] Easter happened for you.

"When you think about it, our Easter journey is better than the women's. For while they found only an empty tomb, in baptism we encounter the risen Christ. Encountering Christ changes people.[197] We see the change Dillon is making in his life. Dillon, we're proud of you, and we will help you in every way we can. But making the Easter journey of baptism also changes and challenges this church. The question we are empowered to ask is how we as a congregation can take Easter most seriously. Knowing that God in Christ has brought us from death to new life, we can wrestle with the question of what is the best way that Saint Timothy can witness to the world that God brings new life out of death. We can dare to ask, Could it be that our congregation's best witness to Christ is to face death in order to live anew?

"As we did last Sunday, as we do every Sunday, we continue our Easter journey by moving from the font to the table, where we encounter the risen Christ and are joined to him in bread and cup.[198] That Christ is present in the supper to strengthen us for our journey is something we will talk about. For now it is enough to receive him

---

[193] Statement and restatement of the theme.

[194] Here I am voicing the hearers' objections.

[195] Direct address and appeal to the senses.

[196] Quotation from the liturgy.

[197] Here I move into the implications of participating in this rite.

[198] I am attempting to place both the rite and this sermon in their liturgical context.

with joy, knowing that in baptism he brought you safely from death to new life."

Retrace the Journey

Sermon delivery is a most personal matter, and so the best I can offer are my own observations. As I contemplate preaching this sermon, it occurs to me that the baptismal bowl and pitcher should be exactly where they were when this baptism was celebrated and that I should preach from the aisle and the font rather than from the ambo. It also occurs to me to use gestures to reenact the rite: pouring water, blessing the font when I talk about God's presence in the water, and marking a cross on an imaginary forehead. I want to be familiar enough with the text so that I can give the illusion of extemporaneous speech. I also want to use eye contact to enhance direct address. Finally, while the implications for daily life are most real and serious, I do not want my tone to allow them to overwhelm the good news of this message.

REFLECTION: THE PNEUMATIC DIMENSION OF A METHOD OF MYSTAGOGICAL PREACHING

At this writing the method of mystagogy proposed in this chapter remains largely a blueprint. We have yet to put this method into practice and discover the fruits of our labor. Consequently, just as we could not point to evidence of the Spirit's activity in Ambrose's mystagogy, neither can we offer proof that the Spirit will be active in mystagogy based on this method. The "next steps" in this investigation would therefore be, first, to "field test" this method by teaching it to pastors and subsequently interviewing both them and their congregations about its effectiveness and, second, to explore whether the language of symbol, image, and experience speaks to our culture. Even a cursory review of the recent presidential campaign, with its emphasis on providing experience and creating meaning through layers of images, suggests that the language of symbolism does speak to our culture.

In the absence of concrete data that verifies the Spirit's involvement in our approach to mystagogy, we will devote this reflection to reviewing five convictions about the Spirit underlying or, better yet, springing from the method proposed in this chapter. First, Ambrose's example suggests that in preaching, the Spirit is encountered through discipline and not by some miraculous, extraordinary means. Ambrose's preaching on the sacraments resulted from liturgical participation, involvement in the lives of his people, study, and prayer. From Ambrose we learn that the Holy Spirit speaks and acts through a method of mystagogical preaching and is not constrained by it.

Second, the preacher is a vessel through whom the hearers might encounter and receive the Holy Spirit. Preachers are the voice of the Spirit and do not speak for themselves or by their own authority. Consequently, we have suggested that the role of the mystagogue is that of steward of the mysteries and spiritual guide.

Third, mystagogy takes seriously that Christ calls people to himself through the Spirit in personal encounters in order to give them new life and transform their way of living in the world. In fact, the Spirit of Christ not only gives new life and transformation, the Spirit also sustains this transformation and brings it to completion. Both the Christian mysteries and mystagogy are encounters in which the Spirit of Christ gives and sustains new life and transformation. The rites of initiation are God's means of making us participants in the mystery of salvation. Through baptism Christians enter into the saving activity of Christ, hoped for in the Old Testament, accomplished once and for all in Jesus' suffering, death, and resurrection, and awaiting complete fulfillment in Christ's return. The sacraments are the means by which we participate in Christ's saving activity in the time between his resurrection and his return. Through baptism and the Eucharist we receive faith and vision as God brings us "from earthly things to heavenly things, from sin to life, from guilt to grace, from vileness to holiness."[199] In our encounter with Christ in baptism, we share in Christ's death and, more than being brought back to life, we receive new life. In the Eucharist we receive spiritual food by which Christ is sealed within us. Mystagogy is an opportunity to experience God's grace, Christ's presence, and the Spirit's power in such a way that we open ourselves to God, cling to Christ, view our lives and the world through the eyes of faith, which we received at baptism, and are equipped to live according to this vision. To see with the eyes of faith is to perceive the invisible activity of God by experiencing the spiritual realities behind sensible appearances. The task of mystagogy, then, is to reveal the pneumatic dimension of the rites of initiation, that is, to help the faithful discover how God's saving activity in Christ is contained in the liturgical action. Mystagogy accomplishes this task by providing a

---

[199] *De sacramentis*, 1.3.12 (SC 25bis.66).

fuller, deeper experience of the mysteries and by engaging in a dialogue about them not only between the preacher and the congregation but, through that conversation, also between heaven and earth, between Christ and his Church.

Fourth, mystagogy views Scripture as a mystery inspired by the Holy Spirit that provides the key to understanding how God's saving activity in Christ is contained in the sacraments. Inspired by the Spirit, mystagogues can find in Scripture both the meaning of the rites and the language and images used to explain them. Both Scripture and the rites speak in the language of symbols. The life of Christ is the lens through which this language of symbols is understood.

Fifth, our method assumes that mystagogy is an event in which the Spirit will act; therefore, these sermons are crafted in such a way that the hearers will best experience God in their instruction on the sacraments. In order to create this event, the hearers are addressed directly, engaged in dialogue, and invited into a deeper experience rather than given information. Mystagogy is structured to show the continuity of God's saving activity in the Old and New Testaments and God's activity in the sacraments. Through this continuity the faith community comes to experience and understand that God is acting in the rites as God has acted in the history of salvation recorded in Scripture. The tone of these sermons is intended to create an intimate relationship of trust so that the community will be open to the Spirit. Finally, these sermons include an emphasis on mission.

CONCLUSION

God comes to us through experience. Participating in the mysteries and reflecting on them in mystagogy are both events in which we experience God's presence, grace, and power. Christ himself proclaims his Gospel to particular people and seeks from them the response of faith. Ambrose says:

"You went there [to the font], you washed, you came to the altar, you began to see what you had not seen before; that is to say, through the font of the Lord and the preaching of the Lord's passion, at that moment your eyes were opened. Before, you seemed to be blind of heart; but now you began to perceive the light of the sacraments."[200]

---

[200] Ibid., 3.2.15 (SC 25bis.100).

In the rites of initiation God gave faith and opened the neophytes' eyes to see with the eyes of faith; however, the newly baptized came to understand and appreciate what happened to them in the rites only when Ambrose invited them into the mysteries and led them deeper and deeper into holiness. God is still opening the eyes of faith in baptism and the Eucharist. Inviting the faithful into the mysteries, leading them deeper and deeper into holiness, helping them to understand and appreciate what happens to them in the sacraments is the privilege and calling that a fourth-century bishop extends to a twenty-first-century Church. We pray that this study will in some way equip the Church to respond to Ambrose's call and accept his invitation.

Bibliography

SELECT WORKS OF SAINT AMBROSE

Beyenka, Mary Melchior, O.P. *Saint Ambrose: Letters.* The Fathers of the Church, Vol. 26. New York: Fathers of the Church, Inc., 1954.

Botte, Bernard. *Ambroise de Milan: Des Sacrements; Des Mystères; Explication du Symbole.* Sources Chrétiennes 25bis. Paris: Les Éditions du Cerf, 1980.

Callam, Daniel, O.S.B. *On Virginity by Ambrose, Bishop of Milan.* Toronto: Peregrina Publishing Co., 1980.

Cazzaniga, Egnatius. *S. Ambrosii Mediolanensis Episcopi: De virginibus, Libri tres.* Turin: G. B. Paravia and Co., 1948.

Chadwick, Henry. *Saint Ambrose: On the Sacraments.* Chicago: Loyola University Press, 1960.

Corpus Christianorum. Series Latina, Vol. 14. Turnhout, 1953ff.

Corpus Scriptorum Ecclesiasticorum Latinorum, Vols. 73, 79, 82. Vienna, 1866ff.

Deferrari, Roy J. *Saint Ambrose: Theological and Dogmatic Works.* The Fathers of the Church, Vol. 44. Washington, D.C.: Catholic University of America Press, 1963.

DeRomestin, H. *Saint Ambrose: Select Works and Letters.* A Select Library of Nicene and Post-Nicene Fathers of the Christian Church, Second Series, Vol. 10. Grand Rapids: Eerdmans Publishing Co., 1978.

Gori, Franco. *Sant'Ambrogio: Abramo: Opere esegetiche II/II.* Milan: Bibliotheca Ambrosiana; Roma: Città nuova, 1984.

Gryson, Roger. *Ambroise de Milan: La Pénitence.* Sources Chrétiennes 179. Paris: Les Éditions du Cerf, 1971.

McCauley, Leo P., et al. *Funeral Orations by Saint Gregory Nazainzen and Saint Ambrose*. The Fathers of the Church, Vol. 22. New York: The Fathers of the Church, Inc., 1953.

McHugh, Michael P. *Saint Ambrose: Seven Exegetical Works*. The Fathers of the Church, Vol. 65. Washington, D.C.: Catholic University of America Press, 1982.

Migne, J.-P. *Patrologia cursus completus. Series Latina*, Vols. 14–16. Paris, 1841ff.

Ramsey, Boniface. *Ambrose*. New York: Routledge, 1997.

Savage, John J. *Saint Ambrose: Hexameron, Paradise, and Cain and Abel*. The Fathers of the Church, Vol. 42. New York: Fathers of the Church, 1961.

Schmitz, Josef. *Ambrosius: De Sacramentis = Über Die Sakramente. De Mysteriis = Über Die Mysterien*. Fontes Christiani 3. Freiburg im Breisgau; New York: Herder, 1990.

Thompson, T., and J. H. Srawley. *St. Ambrose: "On the Mysteries," and the Treatise "On the Sacraments," by an Unknown Author*. New York: The Macmillan Company, 1919.

———. *On the Sacraments and On the Mysteries*. Rev. ed. London: S.P.C.K., 1950.

Tomkinson, Theodosia, trans. *On Abraham by Saint Ambrose of Milan*. Etna, Calif.: Center for Traditionalist Orthodox Studies, 2000.

OTHER ANCIENT AUTHORS

Aristotle. *On Rhetoric: A Theory of Civic Discourse*. Trans. George A. Kennedy. New York: Oxford University Press, 1991.

———. *Rhetoric*. Trans. W. Rhys Roberts; *Poetics*. Trans. Ingram Bywater. New York: Modern Library, 1984.

Augustine, Bishop of Hippo. *The Works of Saint Augustine: A Translation for the 21st Century*. Pt. 1, Vol. 1. Trans. Maria Boulding, O.S.B., and ed. John E. Rotelle, O.S.A. Hyde Park, N.Y.: New City Press, 1997.

———. *On Christian Teaching*. Trans. R.P.H. Green. New York: Oxford University Press, 1997.

Cicero, Marcus Tullius. *De oratore*. Cambridge, Mass.: Harvard University Press, 1988.

Corpus Christianorum. Series Latina, Vol. 27. Turnhout, 1953ff.

Cuming, Geoffrey J. *Hippolytus: A Text for Students.* Bramcote, Notts.: Grove Books, 1976.

Hippolytus. *La tradition apostolique de Saint Hippolyte.* Liturgiewissenschaftliche Quellen und Forschungen 39. Trans. Bernard Botte. Münster, Westfalen: Aschendorff, 1963.

Migne, J.-P. *Patrologiae cursus completus. Series Graeca,* Vol. 32. Paris, 1864–1891.

Nicetas of Remesiana. His Life and Works. Ed. A. E. Burn. Cambridge: University Press, 1905.

Origen. *On First Principles.* Trans. G. W. Butterworth. London: S.P.C.K., 1936.

Paulinus of Milan. *Vita di Sant'Ambrogio: la prima biografia del patrono di Milano.* Ed. Marco Navoni. Fonti, Vol. 6, Cinisello Balsamo: San Paolo, 1996.

Quintilian. *Institution oratoire.* Trans. Jean Cousin. Paris: Société d'édition les Belles Lettres, 1975–1980.

TEXTS AND STUDIES OF THE MYSTAGOGICAL WORKS OF AMBROSE OF MILAN

Atchley, C. "The Date of *De sacramentis.*" *Journal of Theological Studies* 30 (1929) 281–86.

Botte, Bernard. *Bulletin de théologies ancienne et médiévale* 6 (1950).

Ceillier, Remi. *Histoire générale des auteurs sacrés et ecclésiastiques.* Vol. 5. Paris: L. Vivès, 1858–1863.

Connolly, R. H. The De Sacramentis a Work of Ambrose. Two Papers. Oxford: Downside Abbey, 1942.

Faller, Otto. "Was sagen die Handschriften sur Echtheit der sechs Predigten S. Ambrosii de Sacramentis?" *Zeitschrift für katholische Theologie* 53 (1929) 49–52.

———. "Ambrosius, der Verfasser von *De sacramentis.* Die innere Echtheitsgrunde." *Zeitschrift für katholische Theologie* 64 (1940) 1–14, 81–101.

Gamber, Klaus. *Die Autorschaft von De Sacramentis.* Regensburg: Pustet, 1967.

———. "Nochmals zur Frage der Autorschaft von De Sacramentis," *Zeitschrift für katholische Theologie* 91 (1969) 587–589.

Hitchcock, F.R.M. "Venerius, Bishop of Milan, Probably Author of the *De sacramentis, Hermathena* 70 (1947) 22–38; ibid., 71 (1948) 19–35.

Lazzati, G. "L'autenticità del De sacramentis e la valutazione letteraria delle opera di S. Ambrogio." *Aevum* 29 (1955) 17–48.

Ledwich, William. "Baptism, Sacrament of the Cross: Looking Behind St. Ambrose." *The Sacrifice of Praise: Studies on the Themes of Thanksgiving and Redemption in the Central Prayers of the Eucharistic and Baptismal Liturgies: In Honour of Arthur Herbert Couratin.* Ed. Bryan Spinks. Rome: C.L.V. Edizioni Liturgiche, 1981.

Mohrmann, Christine. "Le style oral du *De sacramentis* de saint Ambrose." *Vigiliae Christianae* 6 (1952) 168–177.

_____. "Observations sur le *De sacramentis* et le *De mysteriis* de Saint Ambroise." In *Ambrosius Episcopus*. Milan: Università Cattolica del Sacro Cuore, 1978.

Morin, G. "Pour l'authenticité du *De sacramentis*." *Jahrbuch fur Liturgiewissenschaft* 8 (1928) 86–106.

Parodi, Bonaventura. *La catechesi di Sant'Ambrogio, Studio di pedagogia pastorale.* Genoa, 1957.

Petit, Hervé. "Sur les catéchèses postbaptismals de S. Ambroise." *Revue bénédictine* 68 (1958) 256–264.

Satterlee, Craig A. "The Process of Christian Initiation Described by Ambrose of Milan." Ph.D. Candidacy Research Essay, University of Notre Dame, March 6, 1998.

Schermann, T. "Die pseudo ambrosianische Schrift De sacramentis." *Römische Quartalschrift* 17 (1903) 36–53.

Schmitz, Josef. "Zum Autor der Schrift 'De Sacramentis.'" *Zeitschrift für katholische Theologie* 91 (1969) 58–69.

Tillemont, Lenain de. *Memoires pour servir à l'histoire ecclésiastique des six premiers siècles*, Vol. 10. Paris, 1705.

Yarnold, Edward. "Did St. Ambrose Know the Mystagogic Catecheses of St. Cyril of Jerusalem?" *Studia Patristica* 12, Pt. 1. Ed. E. Livingstone. Louvain: Peeters, 1975.

_____. "The Ceremonies of Initiation in the *De Sacramentis* and *De mysteriis* of St. Ambrose." *Studia Patristica* 10. Ed. F. L. Cross. Berlin: Akademie-Verlag, 1970.

WORKS ON SAINT AMBROSE

Biermann, Martin. *Die Leichenreden des Ambrosius von Mailand: Rhetorik, Predigt, Politik.* Stuttgart: F. Steiner, 1995.

Campbell, Robert Stanislaus. "The Explanatio Symboli ad Initiandos of St. Ambrose of Milan: A Comparative Study." Thesis, University of Notre Dame, 1974.

Campenhausen, Hans Freiherr von. "Ambrosius." *Latienische Kirchenväter.* 2nd rev. ed. Stuttgart: W. Kohlhammer, 1965.

_____. *Ambrosius von Miland als Kirchenpolitker.* Berlin and Leipzig: W. de Gruyter, 1929.

_____. *Men Who Shaped the Western Church.* Trans. Manfred Hoffmann. New York: Harper and Row, 1964.

Caprioli, Adriano. "Battesimo di Agostino, Imagine di Chiesa e Figura di Christiano." *Agostino a Milano: Il Battesimo: Agostino Nelle Terre di Ambrogio.* Ed. M. Sordi. Palermo: Edizioni Augustinus, 1988.

Courcelle, Pierre Paul. "Anti-Christian Arguments and Christian Platonism from Arnobius to Ambrose." *The Conflict Between Paganism and Christianity in the Fourth Century.* Ed. Arnoldo Momigliano, 151–192. Oxford: Clarendon Press, 1963.

_____. "Plotin et saint Ambroise." *Revue de Philologie* 76 (1950) 29–56.

_____. *Recherches sur Saint Ambroise: "Vies" Anciennes, Culture, Iconographie.* Paris: Études Augustiniennes, 1973.

Duval, Yves-Marie. "Ambroise, de son élection à sa consécration." *Ambrosius Episcopus: atti del Congresso internazionale di studi ambrosiani nel XVI centenario della elevazione di sant'Ambrogio alla cattedra episcopale, Milano, 2–7 dicembre 1974.* Ed. G. Lazzati, 2:243–283. Milan: Vita e pensiero, 1976.

_____. "L'originalité du 'De virginibus' dans le mouvement ascetique occidental: Ambroise, Cyprien, Athanase." *Ambroise de Milan: XVIe centenaire de son élection épiscopale: dix études.* Ed. Yves-Marie Duval, 9–66. Paris: Études Augustiniennes, 1974.

Faller, Otto. "Ambrosius, der Verfasser von *De sacramentis.* Die inneren Echtheitsgründe."*Zeitschrift für katholische Theologie* 64 (1940) 1–14, 81–101.

_____. "La date della consacrazione vescovile de sant'Ambrogio." *Ambrosiana: scritti di storia, archeologia ed arte pubblicati nel XVI centenario della nascita di sant'Ambrogio, CCCXL–MCMXL.* Ed. Arturo Faccioli. Milan: Biblioteca Ambrosiana, 1942.

Fontaine, Jacques. *Naissance de la poésie dans l'occident chrétien*. Paris: Études Augustiniennes, 1981.

———. "Prose et poésie: L'interférence des genres et styles dans la création litéraire d'Ambroise de Milan." *Ambrosius Episcopus*. Ed. Giuseppe Lazzati, 1:124–170. Milan: Università Cattolica del Sacro Cuore, 1976.

Francesconi, Giampietro. *Storia e Simbolo: "Mysterium in Figura": La Simbolica Storico-Sacramentale nel Linguaggio e nella Teologia di Ambrogio di Milano*. Brescia: Morcelliana, 1981.

Ganshof, F. L. "Note sur l'élection de évêques dans l'empire romain au IVe et pendant le première moitié du Vme siècle." *Revue internationale des droits de l'Antiquité* 4 (*Mélanges Vissher* 3, 1950) 467–498.

Grace, Madeline. "Lest We Forget." *Emmanuel* 100 (September 1994) 409–413.

Gryson, Roger. "Les élections épiscopales en Occident au IVe siècle," *Revue d'Histoire Ecclésiastique* 75 (1980) 257–283.

Haeringen, J. H. van. "De Valentinian II et Ambrosio: illustrantur et digeruntur res anno 386 gestae." *Mnemosynae*, 3rd series, 5 (1937).

Homes Dudden, Frederick. *The Life and Times of St. Ambrose*. 2 vols. Oxford: Clarendon Press, 1935.

Jacob, Christoph. *"Arkandisziplin," Allegorese, Mystagogie: Ein Neuer Zugang zur Theologie des Ambrosius von Mailand*. Theophaneia 32. Frankfurt am Main: Anton Hain, 1990.

Lamirande, Emilien. *Paulin de Milan et la "Vita Ambrosii": Aspects la religion sous le Bas-Empire*. Paris and Montreal: Desclée/Bellarmin, 1983.

Lenox-Conyngham, Andrew. "A Topography of the Basilica Conflict of A.D. 385/6 in Milan." *Historia* 31 (1982) 353–363.

———. "Ambrose and Philosophy." *Christian Faith and Greek Philosophy in Late Antiquity: Essays in Tribute to George Christopher Stead*, 112–128. Leiden: Brill, 1993.

———. "The Judgement of Ambrose the Bishop on Ambrose the Roman Governor." *Studia Patristica* 17, Pt. 1. Ed. E. Livingstone, 62–65. Oxford: Pergamon Press, 1983.

———. "Juristic and Religious Aspects of the Basilica Conflict of A.D. 386." *Studia Patristica* 18 (1985) 55–58.

Lizzi, Rita. "Ambrose's Contemporaries and the Christianization of Northern Italy." *Journal of Roman Studies* 80 (1990) 164–165.

Madec, Goulven. *Saint Ambroise et la philosophie*. Paris: Études Augustiennes, 1974.

Mara, Maria Grazia. "Ambrose of Milan." *Patrology*, Vol. 4. Ed. Angelo di Bernardino. Trans. Placid Solari. Westminster, Md.: Christian Classics, 1994.

McLynn, Neil B. *Ambrose of Milan: Church and Court in a Christian Capital*, Berkeley and Los Angeles: University of California Press, 1994.

Monachino, Vincenzo. *S. Ambrogio e la cura pastorale a Milano nel secolo. IV.* Milan: Centro Ambrosiano di Documentazione e Studi Religiosi, 1973.

Moohead, John. *Ambrose: Church and Society in the Late Roman World*. London; New York: Longman, 1999.

Palanque, Jean Remy. *Saint Ambroise et l'Empire romain*. Paris: E. de Boccard, 1933.

Paredi, Angelo. *Saint Ambrose: His Life and Times*. Trans. M. Joseph Costelloe. Notre Dame: University of Notre Dame Press, 1964.

Ratti, A. "Il più antico ritratto di S. Ambrogio." *Ambrosiana: Scritti vari pubblicati ne XV centenario dalla morte di sant'Ambrogio*, 5–74. Milan, 1897.

Rosso, G. "La 'lettera alle vergini': Atanasio e Ambrogio." *Augustinianum* 23 (1983) 421–452.

Saint-Laurent, George E. "Augustine's Hero–Sage–Holy Man: Ambrose of Milan." *Word and Spirit* 9. Ed. V. Capanaga, J. Leclercq, et al., 22–34. Petersham, Mass.: St. Bede's Publications, 1987.

Taylor, H. Granger. "The Two Dalmatics of Saint Ambrose." *Bulletin de Liaison, Centre International d'Étude des Textiles Anciens* 57–58 (1983) 127–173.

Tonzig, Luisa Teresa Coraluppi. "The Teaching of St. Ambrose on Real Presence, Its Misunderstanding in Later Tradition, and the Significance of Its Recovery for Contemporary Eucharistic Theology." Ph.D. dissertation, Duquesne University, 1988.

Toscani, Giuesseppe. *Teologia della chiesa in sant'Ambrio*. Milan: Università Cattolica del Sacro Cuore, 1974.

Williams, Daniel H. *Ambrose of Milan and the End of the Nicene-Arian Conflicts*. Oxford: Clarendon Press, 1995.

WORKS ON MYSTAGOGY AND THE ANCIENT AND MODERN CATECHUMENATE

Ancilli, E. *Mistagogia e direzione spirituale*. Milan, 1985.

Beckmann, J. "L'Initiation et la célébration baptismale dans les missions, du XVI siècle à nos jours." *La Maison-Dieu* 58 (1959) 48–70.

Cramer, Peter. *Baptism and Change in the Early Middle Ages, c. 200–c. 1150*. New York: Cambridge University Press, 1993.

Dujarier, Michel. *A History of the Catechumenate: The First Six Centuries*. Trans. Edward J. Haasl. New York: William H. Sadlier, 1979.

⸺. *The Rites of Christian Initiation: Historical and Pastoral Reflections*. Trans. and ed. Kevin Hart. New York: William H. Sadlier, 1979.

Evangelical Lutheran Church in America. *Welcome to Christ*. Minneapolis: Augsburg Fortress, 1997.

Evangelical Lutheran Church in Canada. *Living Witnesses: The Adult Catechumenate*. Canada: ELCIC, 1992.

Finn, Thomas M. *Early Christian Baptism and the Catechumenate*. Vol. 1: *East and West Syria*. Message of the Fathers of the Church 6. Collegeville, Minn.: The Liturgical Press, 1992.

Fischer, Balthasar. *Signs, Words and Gestures: Short Homilies on the Liturgy*. New York: Pueblo Publishing Co., 1981.

⸺. *Early Christian Baptism and the Catechumenate*. Vol. 2: *Italy, North Africa, and Egypt*. Message of the Fathers of the Church 6. Collegeville, Minn.: The Liturgical Press, 1992.

⸺. *From Death to Rebirth: Ritual and Conversion in Antiquity*. New York: Paulist Press, 1997.

Grey, Mary C. *The Candles Are Still Burning: Directions in Sacrament and Spirituality*. Collegeville, Minn.: The Liturgical Press, 1995.

Guardini, Romano. *Sacred Signs*. St. Louis: Pio Decimo Press, 1956.

⸺. "La prédication mystagogique." *La Maison Dieu* 158 (1984) 137–147.

Harmless, William. *Augustine and the Catechumenate*. New York: Pueblo Publishing Co., 1995.

Huck, Gabe. *Preaching About the Mass*. Chicago: Liturgy Training Publications, 1992.

Hughes, Kathleen. *Saying Amen: A Mystagogy of the Sacraments*. Chicago: Liturgy Training Publications, 1998.

International Commission on English in the Liturgy. *The Rite of Christian Initiation of Adults*. Rev. ed. Collegeville, Minn.: The Liturgical Press, 1988.

Jackson, Pamela E. J. *Journeybread for the Shadowlands: The Readings for the Rites of the Catechumenate, RCIA*. Collegeville, Minn.: The Liturgical Press, 1993.

_____. "The Meaning of 'Spiritale Signaculum' in the Mystagogy of Ambrose of Milan." *Ecclesia Orans* 7, no. 1 (Rome, 1990) 77–94.

Johnson, Maxwell E. "The Postchrismational Structure of Apostolic Tradition 21, the Witness of Ambrose of Milan, and a Tentative Hypothesis Regarding the Current Reform of Confirmation in the Roman Rite." *Worship* 70 (January, 1996) 16–34.

_____. *The Rites of Christian Initiation: Their Evolution and Interpretation*. Collegeville, Minn.: The Liturgical Press, A Pueblo Book, 1999.

Joncas, Jan Michael. *Preaching the Rites of Christian Initiation*. Chicago: Liturgy Training Publications in cooperation with the North American Forum on the Catechumenate, 1994.

Kavanagh, Aidan. *Confirmation: Origins and Reform*. New York: Pueblo Publishing Co., 1988.

_____. *The Shape of Baptism: The Rite of Christian Initiation*. New York: Pueblo Publishing Co., 1978.

Keifer, Ralph. "Christian Initiation: The State of the Question." *Worship* 48, no. 7 (August–September, 1974) 392–404.

Kemp, Raymond. "The Rite of Christian Initiation of Adults at Ten Years." *Worship* 56, no. 4 (July, 1982) 309–326.

Kreider, Alan. *The Change of Conversion and the Origin of Christendom*. Harrisburg, Pa.: Trinity Press International, 1999.

Mazza, Enrico. *Mystagogy: A Theology of Liturgy in the Patristic Age*. Trans. Matthew J. O'Connell. New York: Pueblo Publishing Co., 1989.

McDonald, William. "Paideia and Gnosis: Foundations of the Catechumenate in Five Church Fathers," Ph.D. Dissertation, Vanderbilt University, 1998.

McDonnell, Kilian, and George T. Montague. *Christian Initiation and Baptism in the Holy Spirit: Evidence from the First Eight Centuries.* Collegeville, Minn.: The Liturgical Press, 1991.

Philippart, David. *Saving Signs, Wondrous Words.* Chicago: Liturgy Training Publications, 1996.

Regan, David. *Experience the Mystery: Pastoral Possibilities for Christian Mystagogy.* Collegeville, Minn.: The Liturgical Press, 1994.

Riley, Hugh M. *Christian Initiation: A Comparative Study of the Interpretation of the Baptismal Liturgy in the Mystagogical Writings of Cyril of Jerusalem, John Chrysostom, Theodore of Mopsuestia, and Ambrose of Milan.* Washington, D.C.: Catholic University of America Press, 1974.

Satore, D. "La mistagogia, modello e sorgente di spiritualita cristiana." *Rivista Liturgica* 73 (1986) 508–521.

Whitaker, E. C. *Documents of the Baptismal Liturgy.* Rev. ed. London: S.P.C.K., 1970.

Wilde, James A. *Before and After Baptism: The Work of Teachers and Catechists.* Chicago: Liturgy Training Publications, 1988.

Yarnold, Edward. *The Awe-Inspiring Rites of Initiation: The Origins of the R.C.I.A.* 2nd ed. Collegeville, Minn.: The Liturgical Press, 1994.

_____. "Baptism and the Pagan Mysteries in the Fourth Century." *Heythrop Journal* 13 (1972) 247–267.

_____. "Initiation: The Fourth and Fifth Centuries." *The Study of Liturgy.* Rev. ed. Ed. Cheslyn Jones, Geoffrey Wainwright, Edward Yarnold, S.J., and Paul Bradshaw, 130–31. New York: Oxford University Press, 1992.

_____. "The Authorship of the Mystagogical Catecheses Attributed to Cyril of Jerusalem." *Heythrop Journal* 19 (1978) 143–161.

WORKS ON PREACHING AND RHETORIC

Achtemeier, Elizabeth. *Creative Preaching.* Nashville: Abingdon Press, 1981.

Anderson, Rob, and Veronica Ross. *Questions of Communication: A Practical Introduction to Theory.* 2nd ed. New York: St. Martin's Press, 1998.

Baker, Sheridan. *The Complete Stylist and Handbook.* 3rd ed. New York: Harper and Row, 1984.

Barnouw, Erik. *International Encyclopedia of Communications.* New York: Oxford University Press, 1989.

Bartow, Charles L. *The Preaching Moment: A Guide to Sermon Delivery*. Nashville: Abingdon Press, 1980.

Benedetti, Robert L. *The Actor at Work*. Englewood Cliffs, N.J.: Prentice-Hall, 1970.

Best, Ernst. *From Text to Sermon: Responsible Use of the New Testament in Preaching*. Atlanta: John Knox Press, 1978.

Bohren, Rudolf. *Predigtlehre*. Munich: Chr. Kaiser Verlag, 1971.

Brilioth, Yngve. *Landmarks in the History of Preaching*. London: S.P.C.K., 1950.

———. *A Brief History of Preaching*. Trans. Karl E. Mattson. Philadelphia: Fortress Press, 1965.

Brueggemann, Walter. *Finally Comes the Poet*. Philadelphia: Fortress Press, 1989.

———. "The Faithfulness of Otherwise," University of Notre Dame, February 4, 2000.

Burghardt, Walter. *Preaching: The Art and the Craft*. New York: Paulist Press, 1987.

Burke, Kenneth. *A Grammar of Motives, and A Rhetoric of Motives*. Cleveland: World Publishing Company, 1962.

Buttrick, David. *Homiletic: Moves and Structures*. Philadelphia: Fortress Press, 1987.

Cameron, Averil. *Christianity and the Rhetoric of Empire: The Development of Christian Discourse*. Berkeley: University of California Press, 1991.

Carroll, Thomas K. *Preaching the Word*. Message of the Fathers of the Church 11. Wilmington, Del.: Michael Glazier, 1984.

Craddock, Fred B. *Preaching*. Nashville: Abingdon Press, 1985.

Deferrari, Roy J. "St. Augustine's Method of Composing and Delivering Sermons." *American Journal of Philology* 43 (1922) 97–123.

Evangelical Lutheran Church in America. *The Use of the Means of Grace: A Statement on the Practice of Word and Sacrament*. Minneapolis: Augsburg Fortress, 1997.

Fast, Julius. *Body Language*. New York: M. Evans and Co., 1970.

Harms, Paul. *Power from the Pulpit: Delivering the Good News*. St. Louis: Concordia Publishing House, 1977.

Hilkert, Mary Catherine. *Naming Grace: Preaching and the Sacramental Imagination*. New York: Continuum, 1997.

Long, Thomas G. *The Witness of Preaching*. Louisville: Westminster/John Knox Press, 1989.

MacMullen, Ramsey. "The Preacher's Audience." *The Journal of Theological Studies* 40 (1989) 503–511.

Melloh, John Allyn. "Preaching and Liturgy." *Worship* 65 (1991) 409–420.

National Conference of Catholic Bishops. *Fulfilled in Your Hearing: The Homily in the Sunday Assembly*. Washington, D.C.: United States Catholic Conference, 1982.

Oberhelman, Steven M. *Rhetoric and Homiletics in Fourth Century Christian Literature: Prose, Rhythm, Oratorical Style, and Preaching in the Works of Ambrose, Jerome, and Augustine*. Atlanta: Scholars Press, 1991.

Old, Hughes Oliphant. *The Reading and Preaching of the Scriptures in the Worship of the Christian Church*. Vol. 2, Grand Rapids: William B. Eerdmans Publishing Co., 1998.

Ong, Walter J. *Orality and Literacy: The Technologizing of the Word*. New York: Methuen, 1982.

Satterlee, Craig A. "Preaching and Acoustics." *Environment and Art Letter* 12, no. 3 (May, 1999) 30–33.

Second Vatican Council. *Christus Dominus* (Rome, 1965).

———. *Dei Verbum* (Rome, 1965).

Troeger, Thomas. *Creating Fresh Images for Preaching*. Valley Forge: Judson, 1982.

Wainwright, Geoffrey. "The Sermon and the Liturgy." *Greek Orthodox Theological Review* 28 (Winter, 1983) 337–349.

Wallace, James A. *Imaginal Preaching: An Archetypal Perspective*. New York: Paulist Press, 1995.

Wheelwright, Philip. *Metaphor and Reality*. Bloomington, Ind.: University of Indiana Press, 1962.

Willimon, William H. "The Preacher as an Extension of the Preaching Moment." *Preaching on the Brink: The Future of Homiletics*. Ed. Martha J. Simmons. Nashville: Abingdon Press, 1997.

Wilson, Paul Scott. *Imagination of the Heart: New Understandings in Preaching*. Nashville: Abingdon Press, 1988.

WORKS ON EARLY AND MODERN LITURGY

Alzati, Cesare. *Ambrosianum Mysterium: The Church of Milan and its Liturgical Tradition*. Trans. George Guiver, C.R. Cambridge: Grove Books, 1999.

Botte, Bernard. *Le canon de la messe romaine*. Louvain: Abbaye du Mont César, 1935.

Bradshaw, Paul F. "The Liturgical Use and Abuse of Patristics." *Liturgy Reshaped*. Ed. Kenneth Stevenson, 134–45. London: S.P.C.K., 1982.

_____. *The Search for the Origins of Christian Worship*. London: Oxford University Press, 1992.

Burreson, Kent J. "The Anaphora of the Mystagogical Catecheses of Cyril of Jerusalem." *Essays on Early Eastern Eucharistic Prayers*. Ed. Paul F. Bradshaw, 131–133. Collegeville, Minn.: The Liturgical Press, 1997.

Connell, Martin F. "*Nisi Pedes*, Except for the Feet: Footwashing in the Community of John's Gospel." *Worship* 70, no. 4 (1996) 20–30.

Die Liturgie des vierten Jahrhunderts. Münster, 1893.

Férotin, M. *Liber ordinum en usage dans l'église wisigothique et mozarabe d'Espagne du V au XI siècle*. Monumenta Ecclesiae Liturgica 5. Paris, 1904.

Jasper, R.C.D., and G. J. Cumming. *Prayers of the Eucharist: Early and Reformed*. 3rd ed. Collegeville, Minn.: The Liturgical Press, 1975.

Jungmann, Joseph A., S.J. *The Mass of the Roman Rite*. Westminster, Md.: Christian Classics, 1986.

King, Archdale A. *Liturgies of the Primatial Sees*. London: Longmans, Green and Co., 1957.

Klauser, Theodore. *A Short History of the Western Liturgy: An Account and Some Reflections*. 2nd ed. Trans. John Halliburton. New York: Oxford University Press, 1979.

Lowe, E. A. *Inquisitio de lege ad missam celebrare*. Henry Bradshaw Society 58. London, 1920.

Lutheran Church in America, The American Lutheran Church, The Evangelical Lutheran Church of Canada, The Lutheran Church–Missouri Synod. *Lutheran Book of Worship*. Minneapolis: Augsburg Publishing House, 1978.

Magistretti, Marcus. *Monumenta veteris Liturgiae Ambrosianae*. Milan: Apud U. Hoepli, 1897–1904.

Mazza, Enrico. *The Eucharistic Prayers of the Roman Rite.* Trans. Matthew J. O'Connell. Collegeville, Minn.: The Liturgical Press, 1986.

_____. *The Origins of the Eucharistic Prayer.* Trans. Ronald E. Lane. Collegeville, Minn.: The Liturgical Press, 1995.

Mitchell, Leonel. "Ambrosian Baptismal Rites." *Studia Liturgica* 1 (1962) 241–254.

Morin, G. "Depuis quand und canon fixe à Milan? Restes de ce qu'il remplacé." *Revue bénédictine* 51 (1939) 101–108.

Nelson, Paul R. Unpublished presentation given to the Lutheran caucus of the North American Academy of Liturgy, January 4, 1997, Chicago, Illinois.

Philippart, David. "Like Living Stones." *Environment and Art Letter* 12, no. 3 (May, 1999) 34–39.

Rerum liturgicarum libri II. Vol. 1. Augustae Taurinorum, 1757.

Righetti, Mario, *Manuale di Storia Liturgica.* 2nd ed. Milan: Ancora, 1959.

Stevenson, Kenneth W. *Eucharist and Offering.* New York: Pueblo Publishing Co., 1986.

Tally, Thomas J. *The Origins of the Liturgical Year.* 2nd ed. Collegeville, Minn.: The Liturgical Press, 1991.

van der Horst, Pieter W. "Silent Prayer in Antiquity." *Numen* 41 (1994) 1–25.

White, James F., and Susan J. White. *Church Architecture: Building and Renovating for Christian Worship.* Akron: OSL Publications, 1998.

Wilson, H. *A Classified Index to the Leonine, Gelasian, and Gregorian Sacramentaries.* Cambridge, 1892.

Winkler, Gabriele. "Confirmation or Chrismation? A Study in Comparative Liturgy." *Living Water, Saving Spirit: Readings on Christian Initiation.* Ed. Maxwell E. Johnson, 202–219. Collegeville, Minn.: The Liturgical Press, 1995.

WORKS ON FOURTH-CENTURY MILAN AND THE PATRISTIC PERIOD

Baehrens, G. *XII Panegyrici latini.* Leipzig, 1911.

Bonner, Stanley. *Education in Ancient Rome.* Berkeley: University of California Press, 1977.

Brivio, Ernesto. *A Guide to the Duomo of Milan*. 3rd ed. Trans. Liliana Zaccarelli Fumagalli. Milan: Veneranda Fabbrica del Duomo di Milano, 1997.

Brown, Peter. *Augustine of Hippo: A Biography*. Berkeley: University of California Press, 1967.

———. *The Body and Society: Men, Women and Sacred Renunciation in Early Christianity*. New York: Columbia University Press, 1988.

———. *The Cult of the Saints: Its Rise and Function in Latin Christianity*. Chicago: University of Chicago Press, 1981.

———. *Power and Persuasion in Late Antiquity: Toward a Christian Empire*. Madison, Wis.: University of Wisconsin Press, 1992.

Calderini, Aristide. *La "Forma urbis Mediolani" nell'anno bimillenario di Augusto*. Milan: Istituto di studi romani, 1937.

———. *L'Anfiteatro romano*. Milan: Ceschina, 1940.

Capitani d'Arzago, Alberto de. *Il Circo romano*. Milan: Ceschina, 1939.

———. *La "Chiesa maggiore" di Milano: Santa Tecla*. Milan, 1952.

Chadwick, Henry. *The Role of the Christian Bishop in Ancient Society*. Berkeley: Center for Hermeneutical Studies in Hellenistic and Modern Culture, 1979.

Courcelle, Pierre. "Quelques symboles funéraires du néoplatonisme latin." *Revue des Études Anciens* 46 (1944) 65–73.

Daley, Brian E., S.J. "Building a New City: The Cappadocian Fathers and the Rhetoric of Philanthropy." *Journal of Early Christian Studies* 7, no. 3 (Fall, 1999) 431–461.

De Marchi, A. *Antiche epigrafi di Milano*. Milan, 1917.

Diehl, Ernst. *Inscriptiones Latinae Christianae Veteres*. Berlin: Apud Weidmannos, 1961–1967.

Frend, W.H.C. *The Rise of Christianity*, Philadelphia: Fortress Press, 1984.

Grillmeier, Alois. *Christ in Christian Tradition*. 2 vols. Trans. John Bowden. Atlanta: John Knox Press, 1975.

Grossi, Ada. *Santa Tecla nel Tardo Medioevo: La Grande Basilica Milanese, il Paradisus, i Mercati*. Milan: Edizioni Et, 1997.

Holder-Egger, Oswaldus. *Gesta Federici I imperatoris in Lombardia auct. cive mediolanensi: Annales mediolanenses maiores*. Hannover: Impensis Bibliopolii Hahniani, 1892.

Jerf, Ernst. *Vir venerabilis: Untersuchungen zur Titulatur der Bischöfe in der ausserkirchlichen Texten der Spätantike.* Beiträge zur Theologie 26. Vienna: Herder, 1970.

Krautheimer, Richard. "Die Doppelkathdrale in Pavia." *Opicinus de Canistris Weltbild und Bekenntnisse eines avignonesischen Klerikers des 14. Jahrhunderts.* Ed. Richard Salomon, 323–337. London: Warburg Institute, 1936.

———. *Three Christian Capitals.* Berkeley: University of California Press, 1983.

———. *Early Christian and Byzantine Architecture.* 4th ed. Revised Richard Krautheimer and Slobodan Curcic. New Haven, Conn.: Yale University Press, 1986.

Lizzi, Rita. *Vescovi e strutture ecclesiastiche nella città tardoantica.* Como: New Press, 1989.

Marrou, Henri-Irénée. *A History of Education in Antiquity.* Trans. George Lamb. Madison, Wis.: University of Wisconsin Press, 1982.

McKinnon, James. *Music in Early Christian Literature.* Cambridge, N.Y.: Cambridge University Press, 1987.

Palastra, A. "I cimiteri paleocristiani Milanesi." *Archivio Ambrosiano* 28 (1975) 25–26.

Peiper. *Ordo urbium nobilium.* Leipzig, 1886.

Pellegrino, M. "Il primo bibliografo di S. Ambrogio: Paolino di Milano." *La Scuola Cattolica* 79 (1951) 151–162.

Pharr, C. "Roman Legal Education." *The Classical Journal* 34 (February 1939) 257–258.

Roberti, Mario Mirabella. *Arte Lombarda* 8 (1963).

———. *Atti del Congresso sul Duomo di Milano.* Milan, 1969.

Roberti, Mario Mirabella and Angelo Paredi. *Il Battistero Ambrosiano di San Giovanni alle Fonti.* Milan: Veneranda Fabbrica del Duomo di Milano, 1974.

Seeck, Otto. *Geschichte des Untergangs der antiken Welt.* Vol. 5. Stuttgart, 1923.

Sordi, Marta. "Milano al Tempo di Agostino." *Agostino a Milano: Il Battesimo: Agostino nelle Terre di Ambrogio.* Ed. M. Sordi. Palermo: Edizioni Augustinus, 1988.

Veyne, Paul. *A History of Private Life: From Pagan Rome to Byzantium.* Vol. 1. Trans. Arthur Goldhammer. Cambridge: Harvard University Press, 1987.

WORKS ON EARLY EXEGESIS AND THE USE OF SCRIPTURE

Barnard, Leslie W. "To Allegorize or Not to Allegorize." *Studia Theologica* 36, no. 1 (1982) 1–10.

Chapman, Mark E. "Early Christian Mystagogy and the Formation of Modern Christians." *Currents in Theology and Mission* 21 (August, 1994) 284–293.

Daniélou, Jean. *The Bible and the Liturgy.* Ann Arbor: Servant Books, 1979.

Dawson, David. *Allegorical Readers and Cultural Revision in Ancient Alexandria.* Berkeley: University of California Press, 1992.

De Lubac, Henri, S.J. *Medieval Exegesis: The Four Senses of Scripture.* Trans. Mark Sebanc. Grand Rapids: William B. Eerdmans Publishing Company, 1998.

Droge, Arthur J. *Homer or Moses? Early Christian Interpretation of the History of Culture.* Hermeneutische Untersuchungen zur Theologie 26. Tübingen: J.G.B. Mohr, 1989.

Duval, Yves-Marie. "L'Ecriture au Service de la Catechese." *Le Monde Latin Antique y La Bible.* Ed. J. Fontaine and C. Pietri. Paris: Beauchesne, 1985.

Ellebracht, Mary Pierre. "Today This Word Has Been Fulfilled in Your Midst." *Worship* 60, no. 4 (July, 1986) 347–361.

Froelich, Karifried. *Biblical Interpretation in the Early Church.* Philadelphia: Fortress Press, 1984.

Jackson, Pamela. "Ambrose of Milan as Mystagogue." *Augustinian Studies* 20 (1989) 93–107.

Jacob, Christoph. "Der Antitypos als Prinzip Ambrosianischer Allegorese: Zum Hermeneutischen Horizont der Typologie." *Studia Patristica* 25. Ed. E. Livingstone, 107–14. Louvain: Peeters, 1993.

Jilek, August. "Symbol und Symbolisches Handeln in Sakramentlicher Liturgie: Ein Beitrag an Hand der Mystagogischen Katechesen." *Liturgisches Jahrbuch* 42, no. 1 (1992) 25–62.

Ledwich, William. "Baptism, Sacrament of the Cross: Looking Behind St. Ambrose." *The Sacrifice of Praise: Studies on the Themes of Thanksgiving and Redemption in the Central Prayers of the Eucharistic and Baptismal Liturgies: In Honour of Arthur Herbert Couratin.* Ed. Bryan Spinks. Rome: C.L.V. Edizioni Liturgiche, 1981.

Lundberg, Per. *La typologie baptismale dans l'ancienne Eglise.* Uppsala: A.-B. Lundequistska, 1942.

Nauroy, Gerard. "L'Ecriture dans la Pastorale de Ambroise de Milan." *Le Monde Latin Antique et La Bible*. Ed. J. Fontaine and C. Pietri. Paris: Beauchesne, 1985.

Rahner, Karl. "The 'Spiritual Senses' According to Origen." *Theological Investigations* 16:81–103. Trans. David Morland, O.S.B. New York: The Seabury Press, 1979.

Ramos-Lisson, Domingo. "Tipologia de Jn 9:6-7 en el De sacramentis." *Ambrosius Episcopus: atti del Congresso internazionale di studi ambrosiani nel XVI centenario della elevazione di sant'Ambrogio alla cattedra episcopale, Milano, 2–7 dicembre 1974*. Vol. 2. Ed. G. Lazzati, 336–44. Milan: Vita e pensiero, 1976.

Ruina, David T. *Philo in Early Christian Literature: A Survey*. Minneapolis: Fortress Press, 1993.

Savon, Hervé. *Saint Ambrose devant l'exégèse de Philon le juif*. Paris: Études Augustiniennes, 1977.

———. "La Temps de l'exégèse allegorique dans la Catechese d'Ambroise de Milan." *La Temps Chrétien de la fin de l'Antiquité au Moyen Age: IIIe–XIIIe siècles: Actes du Colloque, 9–12 mars, 1984*, 345–361. Paris: Centre National de la Recherche Scientifique, 1984.

Scheit, H. *Die Taufwasserweihegebete*. Münster: Verlag der Aschendorffschen Verbuchhandlung, 1935.

Torjesen, Karen Jo. *Hermeneutical Practices and Theological Method in Origen's Exegesis*. Berlin and New York: Walter de Gruyter, 1986.

Torvend, Samuel Edward. *The Typology of the Basilica Conflict Between Ambrose of Milan and the Imperial Court: A Study in the Use of Biblical 'Exempla' in Ambrosian Sermons Preached Between 385–386*, Ph.D. Dissertation, Saint Louis University, 1990.

Trigg, Joseph W. *Biblical Interpretation*. Message of the Fathers 9, Wilmington, Del.: Michael Glazier, 1988.

Wink, Walter. *The Bible in Human Transformation. Toward a New Paradigm for Biblical Study*. Philadelphia: Fortress Press, 1973.

Young, Frances M. *Biblical Exegesis and the Formation of Christian Culture*. Cambridge; New York: Cambridge University Press, 1997.

———. *The Art of Performance: Towards a Theology of Holy Scripture*. London: Darton, Longman & Todd, 1990.

WORKS ON RELIGION AND CONTEMPORARY CULTURE

Clapp, Roger. "At the Intersection of Eucharist and Capital: On the Future of Liturgical Worship," 2000 Annual Meeting of the North American Academy of Liturgy, January 4, 2000, Tampa, Florida.

Gustafson, James F. "The Sectarian Temptation: Reflections on Theology, the Church, and the University." *CTSA Proceedings* 40 (1985) 83–94.

Kennedy, Philip, O.P. *Schillebeeckx*. Outstanding Christian Thinkers Series. Ed. Brian Davies, O.P. Collegeville, Minn.: The Liturgical Press, 1993.

Neuhaus, Richard John. *The Naked Public Square: Religion and Democracy in America*. Grand Rapids: William B. Eerdmans Publishing Co., 1984.

Postman, Neil. *Amusing Ourselves to Death: Public Discourse in the Age of Show Business*. New York: Penguin Books, 1985.

Schillebeeckx, Edward. "Epilogue: The New Image of God, Secularization and Man's Future on Earth," *God the Future of Man*. Trans. N. D. Smith. New York: Sheed & Ward, 1968.

Index

allegory, 200–201, 230–234, 334–335
allusion, 245
altar, procession to, 179–180
Altar of Victory, 51, 57
Ambrose of Milan
  appearance, 78–80, 294; baptism, 47, 49–52, 285; birth, 33; as bishop, 35–36, 101, 107, 108; and congregational song, 55, 67–68, 118–119; death, 84–85; education, 36–38; and emperors, 60–61; episcopal election, 36, 44–47; faith, 34–36, 80–83; family, 33–35; governor, 38, 43–44, 113; liturgical ministry, 67–68; metropolitan, 70; moral leader, 72–78; pastor, 68–70; personality, 80–81; on prayer, 81–83; Roman Empire and, 51–67; social background, 34–35, 62; theologian, 83–84; wealth and property, 63–65; worldview, 94
  preaching: assessment of, 89–91, 106–108; delivery, 18, 95–96, 105, 284–295; funeral, 96–97, 102–103; goal of, 94–95; Holy Spirit and, 89, 109–110; liturgy and, 105–106; originality of, 90–91, 99–102; preparation for, 104–105; rhetoric in, 95–98; Scripture and, 91–92, 98–100, 108, 207ff.; style, 102–103; teaching on, 93–98; tone, 129; types of, 95, 249
  works, 12 n 21; *Contra Auxentium*, 55, 97; *De Abraham*, 76, 103, 150; *De fide*, 52, 82; *De Helia et ieiunio*, 72–73, 81, 100 n. 56, 103, 151–152; *De mysteriis* (See *De mysteriis*); *De Nabuthae*, 63, 72-73, 100 n. 56, 103; *De officiis ministrorum*, 46, 63, 78, 84, 93, 95–96, 100 n. 56, 101; *De penitentia*, 69, 82; *De sacramentis* (See *De sacramentis*); *De Tobia*, 72-73, 100 n. 56; *De virginibus*, 83; *Epistola 77*, 56 n. 112; *Epistola extra coll 1*, 59; *Explanatio symboli ad initiandos*, 22, 153–155; *Expositio evangelii secundum Lucam*, 155
anaphora, 181–182
anointing(s), postbaptismal, 170–172; prebaptismal, 161–163
anticipation, 277–278
Arians, Arianism, 23, 35 n. 19, 36, 45, 51–57, 60, 67, 97, 193–195
Aristotle, 15, 16
asceticism, 34–35, 71, 79, 81
athlete, 94, 152, 162–163, 193, 267
Augustine of Hippo, 5, 7, 15, 16, 49, 55, 67, 68, 79, 84, 89, 91, 102, 113–114, 119–120, 283
Auxentius of Milan, 44, 45, 64, 84

baptism, adult, 348–349; biblical types of, 198–199, 214, 217, 224, 255–256; Christ and, 165; cross and, 165; decision for, 120–122; disappointment with, 142; death and resurrection, 51, 167–171, 256–257; Easter and, 3 n. 6, 156; effects of, 169; Epiphany and, 148; faith and, 136–137; forgiveness and, 168–169; in Milan, 166–170; new birth, 169–170; postponement of, 48, 120–121; Trinity and, 165 (See also *Rite of Christian Initiation of Adults*; rites of initiation)

baptistry, entrance into, 158, 161, 232–233; in Milan, 158–161, 166, 267

basilica conflict, 51, 52–55, 61, 68

Beth-zatha, 214, 224, 235–237

bishops, advocate for the poor, 63–64; as instrument of grace, 59; personal virtue of, 77–78; as official preacher, 3 n. 5; secular authority of, 62

Callinicum, 51, 58, 60, 66

catechesis, 115, 317, 341; moral, 150–151; postbaptismal (See mystagogy), sacramental and experience, 186–188, 317–320

catechetical style, 127–136, 270, 349

catechumen(s), 35, 46–47

catechumenate, ancient, 2 n. 3, 149–150; modern, 4

cathedral of Milan, 87–88, 116, 149–150, 299–304

Catholics, 35, 44–45, 47

chains of reasoning, 234–238, 335–336

Christ, baptism of, 166, 199, 258; and institution of baptism, 165, 238; and institution of the Eucharist, 183–185, 238; foreshadowed in OT, 227–238; as interpreter of Scripture, 222

Chrysostom, John, 3, 11, 21, 216, 317 n. 29

Church, and culture, 94, 312–317 (See also faith and culture), Empire and, 59–61, 123, 312–313; fourth century, 114–115; 312–313

Cicero, 15, 16, 37, 42, 97, 100

competentes, 113,149

Constantine, 57

Constantius, 47

Constantius II, 57

conversion, 260, 318

councils and synods, 3 n. 4, 24 n. 80, 36

Craddock, Fred, 16

creation, 214, 224

creed, 153–155, 223

Cross, sign of (see also baptism, cross and)

Cyril of Jerusalem, 3, 11, 150, 186, 214–216, 251, 317

De mysteriis, 11–13, 20, 31–32, 47, 83

De sacramentis, 11–14, 17, 20–29, 32; authorship, 24–26; date, 23–24; genre, 20, 26–27; history of, 20–23; oral style of, 27–28, 288–293; physical imagery, 139–140; relationship to *De mysteriis*, 12, 20, 27, 28–29, 291–293; structure, 250–260, 288

definition, 254–256, 343

delivery: attitude and, 284–285; character and, 285–287; habits and, 287–288; importance of, 282–284; method of, 288ff.; and mystagogy, 350–354; nonverbal communication and, 294–295; as retracing the journey of initiation, 350–354; voice and, 293–294

description, 263–266, 345–346

direct application of text, 200, 241–242, 336

disciplina arcani, 149, 155–156, 317, 320

Easter (see baptism, Easter and)

ecclesial consciousness, 273–274

Elisha, 183, 214, 224, 229, 232 (see also Naaman)
Enrollment, 148–149
Ephphatha, 157–158, 228, 241, 244, 252, 254, 261–262
Epiphany (see baptism, Epiphany and)
Eucharist, 54, 59, 67, 180–185; biblical types of, 198–199, 214, 217, 230, 237–238, 257–258
exorcism, 165 (also see scrutinies)

faith, culture and, 122–123, 312–317 (see also Church, culture and); eyes of, 137, 189–190, 224, 251, 259–260, 272–273, 311–312 (see also baptism, faith and; rites of initiation, faith and)
fasting, 151–152
flashback, 258–260, 344
flood, 198, 214, 224, 229, 257
font, 50; coming out of, 169; in Milan, 160–162, 166; as tomb, 167
footwashing, 172–173, 191, 243, 253–254

garment, baptismal (see white robe)
Gervasius, martyr, 55, 82, 84
Gratian, 52–53, 57, 61

Holy Spirit, and sermon delivery, 304–307; and the human heart, 115, 152; and the listeners, 142–144; and a method of mystagogy, 18–19, 362–364; and the rites of initiation, 204–205; and preaching, 18–19, 271; and the preacher, 108–110; and Scripture, 246–248; and the shape of mystagogy, 278–280

identification, 276–277
illustration, 266–269, 346
image, imagery, 139–140, 255, 263–264; biblical, 264–264; cultural, 267–268; natural, 266–267

immersion, 167–169
inductive reasoning, 253–254, 280, 343
intent, interpretation by, 201–202, 336
interpretation, methods of (see allegory; allusion; chains of reasoning; direct; intent; narration; speaking the Bible; summary; thematic; translation; typology)
intimacy, 127, 129, 174–175, 278, 349

Jerome, 99
Jews, Judaism, 57–59, 193–194
Justina, 52–53, 61

language, 261–263, 344–345
lectionary, 211; in Milan, 211–213, 294–295; and mystagogy, 352–353
lenten instruction, 149–151
lesser to greater, 257–258, 344
Lord's Prayer, 182

Marah, 165, 183, 214, 224, 229
Marcellina, 34–35, 56–60, 64, 82
marriage, 76–77
martyrs, martyrdom, 55–57, 82, 121–122
Milan,
  church of: composition, 116–118; spiritual hierarchy, 115 (See also cathedral, Ambrose and congregational song)
  city of, 38–42; society, 73–77
myron, 170–171
mystagogy, assumptions underlying, 311–327; Church's tradition and, 337–338; definition, 2; within the Eucharist, 298, 352–354; goal, 2, 4, 7, 125, 145, 190, 272–273, 336–337, 342; listeners' participation in, 111–112, 124–142, 347; liturgy and, 185–204, 327–340; method of, 8, 10, 14, 309ff.; in Milan, 297–304; need

389

for, 4-10; preacher's role in, 320–324, 350–352; as preaching, 2, 3–32; RCIA and, 5–7; Scripture and, 214ff., 331–337; structure of, 189–190, 250–260, 271–278, 341–350; symbolic logic of, 197, 251, 331; techniques, 115, 264, 317–320, 336–340 (see also catechetical style, definition, flashing back, inductive reasoning, lesser to greater, problem to solution, speaking the Bible)

Naaman, 198, 214, 224, 230, 258–259
narration, narrative, 133–135, 243–244
neophyte(s), 1, 31–32; of Milan, 116–123; ability to listen, 119–120, 126–127, 269–270; decision to be baptized, 120–122; and mystagogy; 2, 3, 6, 17, 124–142
Nicene Creed, 35, 36, 47–49

offering, 180–181
Origen of Alexandria, 83–84, 100ff., 230
orthodoxy, 36–37, 47, 52

pagans, paganism, 31, 51, 57, 77, 193–194
Paulinus of Milan, 33–34, 41, 46–47, 69, 80, 84, 90, 93
Peace of Constantine, 2 n. 3
Philo of Alexandria, 84, 100ff., 230
Plato, Platonism, 42, 84, 100, 230
poor, poverty, 63–65
preaching, architectural setting and, 253–254, 299; assembly's role in, 87 n. 3, 111–112, 122; as event, 2, 8; Holy Spirit and, 18–19, 271; liturgical context of, 295–297, 352–353; metatextual elements of, 18, 294; method of, 14, 309–310; preacher's role in, 87–88, 109–110; qualities of effective, 106–110; Scripture and, 209ff.; thematic vs. text-based, 209–211
problem to solution, 256–257, 343
profession of faith, 166–167
Protasius, martyr, 55, 82, 84

questions, 131–133, 142
Quintilian, 15, 16, 37
quotation, 242–243

recognition, 274–276
Red Sea, 183, 198, 214, 224, 229, 232, 257, 258
renunciation, 163–164, 196
repetition, 135
resurrection, 169–171 (see also baptism, death and resurrection)
rhetoric, cultivating listeners, 126; politics and, 43–44; training in, 36–37; bishops and, 95–97
Rite of Christian Initiation of Adults (RCIA), 4 n. 11, 5 n. 13, 10, 349–350
rites of initiation, and Christian living, 140–141, 191–195, 338–340; as drama of salvation, 195–197, 311–312; recreating experience of, 137–141; faith and, 136–137, 188–190, 244; God's presence in, 311–312; in Milan, 156–185, 190–191; incorporating into mystagogy, 200–204, 346–347; as mystery, 197–198; and Scripture, 185–186, 198–199, 210–211; as symbol, 197; as "text" for mystagogy, 145, 327–329; and the Trinity, 195, 199
Roman Empire: and Christianity, 34–35, 312–313; culture, 35, 43, 77–78; law, 37–38; world view, 94

sacraments, 32, 199, 257, 312, 326; centrality of, 320–321; prefigured in Old Testament, 214ff., 227, 235, 258

San'Ambrogio, Church of, altar, 87; mosaic of St. Ambrose, 78–79
Satyrus, 34–36, 38, 102, 122
Scripture: and Historical Critical Method, 322–326; incorporating into mystagogy, 242–246, 346–347; and mystagogy, 214ff.; as mystery, 220–225, 323; patristic approach to, 207ff., 322–326; rites of initiation and, 185–186, 199, 210–211; threefold meaning of, 222–224
scrutinies, 152–153
sea, 94, 193, 221, 266–267
sermon: delivery (see delivery), method of preparation, 14; qualities to be sought in, 272ff.; structure, 249, 250, 271
Simplicianus, 49, 114
sin, 168–169, 173, 256–257
Song of Songs, 83, 174–175
speaking the Bible, 92–93, 245–246
spiritual seal, 176–179
summary, 244
Symmachus, 58

thematic interpretation, 202–203
Theodore of Mopsuestia, 3, 11, 150, 251, 317 n. 29
Theodosius, 57–59, 60, 61, 65–67
Thesssalonika, 66
tone, 129–131, 269–270, 347–350
translation, interpretation by, 203, 238–241, 336
typology, 201, 217, 225–230, 332–334

unity, 272–273

Valentinian I, 46
Valentinian II, 47, 52
virginity, virgins, 34–35, 70–71, 78, 81, 83
Vita Ambrosii, 33 n. 6

water, consecration of, 165–166
white robe, 138, 174–176, 298–299, 353

www.ingramcontent.com/pod-product-compliance
Lightning Source LLC
Chambersburg PA
CBHW031229290426
44109CB00012B/211